CONSTITUTIONAL PRACTICE

Constitutional Practice

Rodney Brazier

CLARENDON PRESS ·OXFORD

Oxford University Press, Walton Street, Oxford OX2 6DP
Oxford New York Toronto
Delhi Bombay Calcutta Madras Karachi
Petaling Jaya Singapore Hong Kong Tokyo
Nairobi Dar es Salaam Cape Town
Melbourne Auckland
and associated companies in
Berlin Ibadan

Oxford is a trade mark of Oxford University Press

Published in the United States
by Oxford University Press, New York

First published 1988
Reprinted (new as paperback) 1990

British Library Cataloguing in Publication Data
Brazier, Rodney
Constitutional practice
1. Great Britain. Government
I. Title
354.41
ISBN 0-19-825596-9
ISBN 0-19-825681-7 (pbk.)

Library of Congress Cataloging in Publication Data
Brazier, Rodney.
Constitutional practice / Rodney Brazier.
Includes index.
1. Great Britain—Politics and government—1979-   I. Title.
JN231.B683 1988   320.44—dc19   88-10099
ISBN 0-19-825596-9
ISBN 0-19-825681-7 (pbk.)

Set by Colset Private Ltd, Singapore
Printed in Great Britain by
Courier International
Tiptree, Essex

For Margot and Vicky

ACKNOWLEDGEMENTS

Many people have helped me in writing this book. Several serving and retired civil servants and Ministers are acknowledged in footnotes: they gave me their time over even minor details, and I much appreciate it. The Public Information Office of the House of Commons has been, as always, a model of efficient and courteous public service, and the Public Record Office went beyond its duty in the assistance which it gave me. Mr. G. F. Lock, Assistant Librarian of the House of Commons Library, kindly read chapter 9 in draft and saved me from a number of errors, but any which remain there—or elsewhere—are my sole responsibility. The publishers of *Public Law* gave me permission to use two articles which originally appeared in that journal as the bases for chapters 2 and 3. My friends and colleagues in the Faculty of Law generously allowed me a term's study leave partly to finish the book.

I thank them all.

R. B.
University of Manchester
February 1988

CONTENTS

CONTENTS

TABLE OF STATUTES

1

Introductory

This book seeks to describe and analyse the current working of British central government. It is written from the perspective of a constitutional lawyer who believes that the opinions of Ministers, civil servants, politicians, historians, and other academic writers are as helpful in divining the meaning of the British constitution as the views of those who may be learned in the law. The emphasis is placed on the organization and powers of the government, although two chapters are devoted to Parliament entirely in its own right (rather than as just an adjunct through which governments achieve and retain their authority), and a final chapter considers the constitutional position of the judiciary. As the book is concerned with constitutional and political issues affecting central government, not with detailed administration, the organisation of the civil service is omitted. It is important to understand both how governments come to office and the nature of their powers, not least because the tradition of highly centralized administration in London is still very strong and has helped to endow any government with considerable authority over the nation's affairs. The task undertaken is, therefore, to identify the hands in which that power lies and to set forth the institutions and procedures through which it is exercised.

Wherever possible the approach is prescriptive. The aim is to explain in any particular situation what may and should appropriately be done. Where prescription is not possible, perhaps because there is a clear divergence of opinion between the political parties as to what the constitution ordains, the reasons behind those differences are explained and then ways forward are suggested which are in keeping with my perception of the spirit of the constitution. If such differences fall to be tested it will obviously be for those with the ability to practise the tenets of the constitution to decide which course to take, and what is suggested in these pages may be of some assistance. An example is provided by the clutch of problems which could arise on the election of a hung Parliament. Before each of the last three general elections the return of a House of Commons in which no party would have an absolute majority of seats was awaited with bated breath almost as much by certain commentators as by the Liberal and Social Democratic Parties. All were disappointed, and so two key questions did not need to be answered. One was whether the Labour Party was right to believe that the largest party in such a House is entitled to form a minority government, or whether the Alliance parties were nearer the mark in insisting that a coalition, or some parlimentary pact short of coalition, should be tried first. The other question was whether (as Labour thought) a Prime Minister at the head of a minority government is automatically entitled to a dissolution on request at any time of his choosing, or whether (as the Alliance parties believed) a dissolution might only be granted if no other government could be formed from the existing House. Now no one can know whether the Conservative and Labour Parties will remain as the only parties of government, the ins and the outs. The failure, however, of any other party or grouping to translate the multi-party politics which exist in the country (as demonstrated by the millions of non-Conservative and non-Labour votes cast in recent general elections) into a multi-party House of Commons seems to show that two-party parliamentary politics are as entrenched as at any time since the 1930s. But in case a hung Parliament is returned some day, answers to hung Parliament questions are offered here.[1] Speculation must not, however, be open-ended about other things that are most unlikely to happen in this country. The political parties in the main believe in basic fair play (although not to the extent of even trying to reach a consensus on the reform of the unfair electoral system);[2] they accept the fundamental principles of western liberal democracy; they usually follow a rough and ready collection of Queensberry rules. Accordingly, the unthinkable need not be thought, or at least not for too long.[3]

While the primary purpose is to expound, criticism is made where it seems justified and suggestions are offered as to how matters could be better ordered. One of the famous features of the constitution is that it is not static, and, although reform of it is not favoured by the present government, we must avoid being obsessed with the constitution as it is, and must not assume that that is as it always will be. At the same time, however, the entire reform agenda is not taken here. The selection of

---

[1] See chapter 3. At the time of writing the Liberal Party and the Social Democratic Party are being merged into the Social and Liberal Democratic Party. It is obviously much too soon to predict whether that development will hasten the actual posing of hung Parliament questions.

[2] This is considered at the end of chapter 9.

[3] Some such questions (such as what would happen if a government defeated on a vote of confidence refused either to recommend a general election or to resign) are considered in chapter 8.

topics in any work on the British constitution always allows a degree of idiosyncratic choice based on the writer's opinion of what is of importance and interest. So, for instance, devolution is important, but is uninteresting to me and is left out; whether a new Bill of Rights should be enacted is both important and interesting, but the question is so well considered by others that it is not treated here.

Overriding concern for the practical working of government is one reason for the unusual title of this book. Another is that the whole system of British central government is based on practice, not law. (There is, of course, a limited amount of statute law which must be and is taken into account.) The choice of title underlines the fundamental and these days uncontroversial point that an understanding of central government requires a detailed consideration of 'rules' which are not rules of law properly so called. Large tracts of the constitution are subject only to these 'rules', such as, for example, the powers of the Sovereign, the existence of and relationships between the Prime Minister and the Cabinet, the relationships between the government and Parliament, between the two Houses (and the internal working of each), and the appointment and disciplining of the judiciary. Whether to label these 'rules' as conventions, principles, doctrines, practices, understandings, maxims, or precepts; whether the courts recognize or declare them; which of them (if any) are binding (and if so why), and what consequence (if any) flows from the breach of any or all of them, are questions which are amply explored elsewhere. John Mackintosh thought that the difference between law and convention was unimportant, because in the development of the constitution both rested on the necessities of political life: laws could be repealed or conventions changed if that were found to be desirable.[4] But that difference is very important for those who are most intimately concerned in Westminster and Whitehall with the daily working of central government. For them, the possible solutions to any given problem require answers to severely practical questions. Does a particular solution require legislation, or could it be achieved by administrative or procedural means? If legislation would not be needed, then would that particular solution be in accordance with precedent and practice? If it would not be in such accordance, could its adoption be justified to Parliament and to the general public? Arcane examination of the nature of constitutional conventions is of very little use to these practitioners, and to that end it is eschewed here; but it is hoped that it is

---

[4] John Mackintosh, *The British Cabinet* (3rd edn., 1977), p. 12.

quite clear in this book whether any proposition is or is not one of law, so that the means of bringing about any alteration to it would be equally apparent.

Even by the time of the last edition of his still valuable work on Cabinet government, published in 1959, Sir Ivor Jennings remained convinced that it was necessary to keep in its pages Victorian constitutional precedents back as far as 1841, the year in which Sir Robert Peel became Prime Minister for the second time.[5] In the main he also kept to a minimum any consideration of recent events.[6] For the last edition of his book on the Cabinet before his untimely death, John Mackintosh felt justified in ignoring events before the Reform Act 1867, the statute which he felt established a broadly representative House of Commons and consequently representative government as we now know it.[7] On the other hand he was, unlike Jennings, completely ready to take advantage of the very latest noteworthy happenings which threw light on the Cabinet system, whether revealed through autobiographies, biographies, published diaries and letters, or leaks. We are now only a decade short of the twenty-first century. It seems somewhat odd to postulate the constitutional practice appropriate to that century by reference to what happened in the nineteenth and also by failing to give whatever proper consideration is possible to recent constitutional and political developments. An awful lot of water has flowed under Westminster Bridge since Queen Victoria died, and only information from this century, and ideally from after 1945, is deployed here. Even after the passage of the Representation of the People Act 1884, only a mere 60 per cent or so of the adult male population (or about twenty-eight per cent of the whole adult population) had the vote.[8] All adult men, and women over 30, had to wait until the Representation of the People Act 1918 for the franchise; not until the Representation of the People Act 1928 were women equated with men in being entitled to vote at 21.[9] So the principle of fully representative democracy was only enshrined in law some sixty years ago, and it is *that* democracy upon which modern British government is based.

Other important things, too, have occurred in recent decades and they must be fully taken into consideration if a realistic picture of the

---

[5] Sir Ivor Jennings, *Cabinet Government* (3rd edn., 1959).

[6] For his reasoning, see Jennings, op. cit., pp. 8–13.

[7] Mackintosh, op. cit., pp. 18–20.

[8] See Colin Turpin, *British Government and the Constitution : Text, Cases and Materials* (1985), p. 18.

[9] The voting age was lowered to 18 by the Representation of the People Act 1969.

contemporary constitution is to be drawn. Since 1945 the power of the Prime Minister in relation to the Cabinet has continued to grow, so that an incumbent may do more by virtue of personal authority, rather than as a result of collective ministerial decision, than was previously the case.[10] Again, it was not until 1965 that the Conservative Party fell into line with the Labour and Liberal Parties by adopting a formal and democratic procedure through which to elect its Leader, so that the need for the Queen to exercise her personal judgement in the choice of a new Prime Minister has been further reduced, although not completely removed.[11] That, and other developments, shows a desirable trend towards politicians taking primary responsibility for the resolution of political crises. Moreover, the formalization of the Shadow Cabinet system (in the Conservatives' case as late as 1964), and the reorganization of government departments (beginning in the same year) have greatly affected the composition and membership of any Cabinet.[12] What amounts to an adverse vote in the House of Commons requiring either a dissolution or the government's resignation has also altered in the last twenty years.[13] Ministerial responsibility, too, has been affected by a number of political developments, including the introduction of the departmental select committees in 1979[14] and the increased use of committees in the House of Lords since 1974,[15] which have both altered how each House elicits information from Ministers and civil servants. For all these, and other reasons, it is essential where it can be done to turn to the more recent pages of constitutional history for guidance as to the meaning of the British constitution as we approach the year 2000, rather than to the older, and in some cases inappropriate, volumes.

[10] This is described in chapters 5 and 6.
[11] See chapter 2.
[12] See the respective explanations given in chapters 4 and 7.
[13] See chapter 9.
[14] See chapter 9.
[15] See chapter 10.

2

Choosing a Prime Minister

The appointment by the Sovereign of a Prime Minister is an act done by virtue of the royal prerogative. In theory the Queen could commission anyone she pleased to form a government. But in practice such a notion is entirely removed from reality, because of course today the royal discretion is subject to several limiting factors, the most important of which is that in making an appointment she should commission that person who seems able to command a majority in the House of Commons. The other restraints are that the person chosen must be a Member of Parliament (or be about to occupy his seat as an MP after a general election), must not be a peer (unless he can disclaim his peerage under the Peerage Act 1963 and seek a seat in the House of Commons), and must usually be the elected Leader of his or her party. It is possible to go further than noting these limitations and to argue that, although the formal *appointment* of a Prime Minister is a prerogative act, the actual *choice* no longer normally lies with the Queen at all: in that sense the selection of a new Prime Minister does not depend upon any prerogative power. For, the argument runs, in most cases (say after a general election) the identity of the politician who is to remain or is to become the Prime Minister is obvious. Further, each of the political parties now has machinery for electing its Leader,[1] so that there should be no repetition of controversial events like those of 1957 and (particularly) of 1963, when the Queen had to become involved in the actual evolution of a new Prime Minister as distinct from his formal appointment to office.[2]

---

[1] For the current rules see Appendix B. Broadly, the Leader of the Conservative Party is elected by MPs taking the Conservative whip, in a system which allows for more than one ballot so that candidates may be eliminated to ensure that the victor receives an overall majority of the votes cast on the final ballot. Labour's electoral college system is examined below. The Social and Liberal Democratic Party will conduct a postal ballot of its members throughout the country.

[2] In 1957, when Sir Anthony Eden resigned, the Queen consulted Sir Winston Churchill (presumably as a former Conservative Prime Minister) and the Marquess of Salisbury (Lord President of the Council and Leader of the House of Lords in Eden's government). Both recommended Macmillan rather than the only other candidate, R. A. Butler. Lords Salisbury and Kilmuir had polled individual members of Eden's Cabinet. For published accounts, see, for example, Harold Macmillan, *Riding the Storm* (1971), pp. 180–5; Lord Butler, *The Art of the Possible* (1971), pp. 195–7; and Lord Kilmuir, *Memoirs: Political Adventure* (1961), p. 285. In the

Today, it might be said, the party election machinery would make the choice, in consequence of which the Queen would probably be insulated from the contenders and from having to prefer (or seem to prefer) one man or woman rather than any other. This restrictive view of the prerogative is generally correct, but the royal prerogative of choice, as distinct from that of appointment, of a new Prime Minister is not dead, but dormant. There could still be far from fanciful instances in which the Queen would have to act without the protection of any prior party election of a Leader. Suggestions will be made in this chapter, however, which might keep to a minimum the involvement of the Queen and her prerogative and which would make the maximum use of parliamentary democracy.

General election

There have been twenty-four changes this century of Prime Minister or of government or of both. Of those changes, nine involved a person becoming Prime Minister by being able to form a government after a general election, ousting a sitting government;[3] ten concerned succession to the office through the resignation of a member of the same party but not entailing the collective resignation of the government;[4] two involved a change of party government without a general election;[5]

---

ferocious 1963 battle, there were at various times a number of candidates to succeed Macmillan. He tried to ensure that (in his words) 'the customary processes of consultation' about the Leadership were carried out as widely as possible within the Conservative Party, but the controversy over the methods and the result remains. Lord Home 'emerged'. For published versions, see, for example, Randolph Church, *The Fight for the Tory Leadership* (1964), especially chapters 6–10; Lord Home, *The Way the Wind Blows* (1976), pp. 180–5; Harold Macmillan, *At the End of the Day* (1973), chapter 15; Lord Butler, op. cit., pp. 241–50; and Iain Macleod, 'The Tory Leadership', *The Spectator*, 17 January 1964. See also Geoffrey Marshall, *Constitutional Conventions* (1984), pp. 29–32.

[3] MacDonald (1924); Baldwin (1924); MacDonald (1929); Attlee (1945); Churchill (1951); Mr Wilson (1964); Mr Heath (1970); Mr Wilson (March 1974); and Mrs Thatcher (1979).

[4] Balfour (1902, succeeding his uncle Salisbury); Asquith (1908, in succession to the dying Campbell-Bannerman); Lloyd George (1916, taking over the war coalition from Asquith); Baldwin (1922, succeeding the dying Bonar Law); Baldwin (1935, replacing MacDonald as head of the 'National Government'); Chamberlain (1937, on Baldwin's retirement); Eden (1955, on Churchill's oft-delayed but encouraged retirement); Macmillan (1957, succeeding Eden on his illness); Sir Alec Douglas-Home (1963, succeeding Macmillan on *his* illness); and Mr Callaghan (1976, having been elected Leader of the Parliamentary Labour Party on Mr Wilson's retirement).

[5] When Campbell-Bannerman formed a Liberal government in 1905 after the resignation of Balfour, and when the Conservatives broke up Lloyd George's coalition in 1922 to install Bonar Law.

and on three occasions the resignation of the Prime Minister was a constitutional device to enable him to form a new government—on two occasions to form a coalition,[6] on the other to break up a coalition and to create a one-party government.[7]

It is trite to observe that there are only three possible results of a general election. The sitting government and Prime Minister may be sustained in office with an absolute majority in the House of Commons (as in 1906, 1918, 1922, 1931, 1935, 1950, 1955, 1959, 1966, October 1974, 1983 and 1987). Or the government party might lose the election, one other party being returned with an overall majority (as in 1924, 1945, 1951, 1964, 1970 and 1979). Last, the electoral system might produce a hung Parliament, that is, one in which no single party has an absolute majority in the House of Commons. This is rare: it happened at the two general elections in 1910, in 1923, in 1929, and then not again until February 1974.[8]

The constitutional consequence of the first result is that the Prime Minister continues in office, refreshed if the number of his party's seats has increased, relieved that even if his majority has been reduced he is at least left with a majority.[9] He does not need to see the Queen, for the use of the prerogative in relation to the Prime Ministership is not required. The practical effect of the second result is, of course, dramatic. The day after polling, when the result is clear,[10] the defeated Prime Minister will seek and obtain an audience of the Queen to offer his resignation and that of his government, and (perhaps) to give advice about his successor. A defeated Prime Minister need not offer advice about a successor when the Leader of the Opposition has been returned with a homogeneous majority Commons party behind him.[11] The Prime Minister will appreciate that he could not form a government from the new House and have its confidence; the victorious Leader obviously could, and no doubt the Queen will know the election results as quickly and in the same manner

[6] The 1915 coalition under Asquith in succession to his Liberal administration, and the 'National Government' in 1931, headed by MacDonald who had been Prime Minister of a minority government immediately before that.

[7] The 1945 caretaker Conservative government formed by Churchill after Labour had refused to continue the wartime coalition until the defeat of Japan, as Churchill would have preferred. See Sir Winston Churchill, *The Second World War*, vol. vi, *Triumph and Tragedy* (1985 Penguin edn.), chapter 35, especially pp. 508–19. A list of senior Ministers since 1945 is given in Appendix A.

[8] The details and the consequences are considered in the next chapter.

[9] As, for example, when Attlee's 1945 government, which had been returned with a majority of 146, found itself with a majority of only 8 after the 1950 general election.

[10] In 1979, Mr Callaghan resigned *before* the election returns had given the Conservative Party an absolute majority, but it was obvious from the trend of voting and computer forecasts that this was coming. In the event, the Conservatives secured a 43-seat absolute majority.

[11] A former Prime Minister has written that the outgoing Prime Minister need not give advice in such circumstances: Harold Wilson, *The Governance of Britain* (1976), p. 24.

as anyone else—by watching the television or listening to the radio. But the constitutional niceties may be maintained: even when the course of action is clear, as in 1979, when Mr Callaghan had to make way for Mrs Thatcher, it is preferable for the Queen to be advised whom to send for in order to preserve the comfortable notion that at the change of an administration, an event which must be inextricably linked with party politics, the Queen still acts only on ministerial advice. (An oddity can, however, be noted here. Unless the outgoing Prime Minister is scrupulous about the order in which he presents his remarks and resignation to the Queen at his farewell audience, the Queen might in fact not be acting on ministerial advice at all if the resignation precedes any recommendation. She would then merely be hearing advice from a former Prime Minister. But in the excitement of a government being turned out by the electorate, such minutiae are easily overlooked.) In neither of these results does the prerogative of choice of a new Prime Minister have any role. The third possible consequence of a general election, however—the return of no single party to the Commons with an absolute majority of seats—may lead to a change of Prime Minister and could involve that prerogative. The formation of a government from a hung Parliament involves so many questions that the whole of the next chapter is devoted to it.

Resignation through illness or old age

Since 1900 seven Prime Ministers have resigned their office while the government has remained otherwise intact, their departure being forced by ill health or old age or both. The men concerned were Salisbury (1902), Campbell-Bannerman (1908), Bonar Law (1923),[12] MacDonald (1935),[13] Churchill (1955),[14] Eden (1957)[15] and Macmillan

[12] Campbell-Bannerman resigned as Prime Minister on 6 April and died on 22 April 1908; Bonar Law resigned on 20 May 1923 and died the following October.

[13] MacDonald had been the titular head of the 'National Government' since its formation. His health declined through those years, and although he remained in that government as Lord President of the Council under Baldwin after his final resignation as Prime Minister in 1935, he resigned with Baldwin in 1937 and died later in that year.

[14] Churchill was extremely reluctant to leave office because he believed that he could promote peaceful coexistence between the Soviet Union and the West. He was finally convinced that he should go in April 1955 at the age of 80. For an account of the struggle to ease him from office, see Harold Macmillan, *The Tides of Fortune* (1969), pp. 533, 537, 539–41, and 544–5.

[15] Eden bore the British responsibility for the Suez invasion in 1956, but it was a recurrence of a debilitating illness which forced his resignation in January 1957. For his own account, see Sir Anthony Eden, *Full Circle* (1960), pp. 581–4; and see Robert Rhodes James, *Anthony Eden* (1986), chapter 14.

(1963).[16] The pressure of high office in modern Britain leading to, or exacerbating, an illness, or an impossible political situation for which an illness could provide the opportunity for an honourable exit, both mean that the constitutional process will continue to have to provide from time to time a new Prime Minister from an existing government, the intention being that the government, having the confidence of the House of Commons, should continue in office. How would that process work today?

The easiest answer would depend upon a happy combination of circumstances. If there were no urgency about the transfer of office, with no emergency actual or imminent, there would be, it is submitted, no need for an unseemly rush—and more importantly no need to involve the prerogative of choice. The ordinary party election machinery would be used to elect a new Leader of the party forming the existing government; the outgoing Prime Minister would wait for that election result, (perhaps) recommend his successor, and then resign. The new Leader would then be appointed. This certainly could be the procedure if the reason for the resignation were old age, as with Churchill, for an additional few weeks in office could scarcely make much difference. On the other hand, what might be termed the 'alarmist' view deserves to be examined. Party elections can be relatively slow affairs. The transfer of office from Mr Wilson to Mr Callaghan in 1976, for example—a case of voluntary retirement which will be considered below—took three ballots and three weeks to complete, and the election of Mrs Thatcher in 1975— the Conservatives being in opposition at the time—took two ballots and nearly two weeks.[17] The 'alarmist' might argue that such a period would be intolerable if the country faced any grave emergency; and moreover that, even when comparative calm reigns, there is an ever-present need for someone to hold the office of Prime Minister, blessed with the

[16] He had to resign quite suddenly in order to undergo surgery which would need prolonged recuperation, an event which he termed in his autobiography a 'stroke of fate': Harold Macmillan, *At the End of the Day*, chapter 15.

[17] The election of Mr Heath as Leader of the Conservative Party in July 1965, on the other hand, took only 6 days, thus showing that, depending on the circumstances, a party election can be concluded fairly speedily. Sir Alec Douglas-Home had announced his intention to resign the Leadership on 22 July at a meeting of the 1922 Committee; nominations were called for by 26 July, and although Mr Heath did not have the arithmetical lead for outright victory over his rivals Mr Maudling and Mr Powell when the result was announced on 27 July, they immediately withdrew, and Mr Heath's name alone was placed in nomination for the second ballot the following day and he was declared to be the winner. See George Hutchinson, *Edward Heath* (1970), pp. 138–44 and Appendix III to that book for the details and the then current election rules.

authority which that office brings. So, for example, on this view a latter-day stricken Eden could not and should not be expected to stay in office despite his illness until a successor were elected; or if some economic emergency gripped the nation and the Prime Minister's health collapsed, a replacement with the political and moral authority to govern would be needed much faster than any party's election system could supply one. At first sight this argument seems to render the use of the party election inappropriate and the employment of the royal prerogative of choice as in, say, 1963, the more attractive. But objections can be seen on a moment's reflection. If a Labour government were in office at the relevant time, it would be difficult to see how that Party would accept anyone other than an elected successor to be Prime Minister, particularly after the Party's statement in 1957 that it would not expect anyone to accept office as Prime Minister unless he had first been elected Leader of the Parliamentary Labour Party.[18] This attitude is perhaps reinforced both by the manner of the exit of Mr Wilson in 1976 (involving a voluntary and leisurely retirement from office), and by the Party's election rules introduced in 1981, which are underpinned by the desire for greater party participatory democracy. If a Conservative government were in power, such deeply rooted attachments to the concept of an elected Leader, as opposed to one who has 'emerged' and been appointed Prime Minister through the exercise of the royal prerogative, might not exist. But the prospect of another 'emergence' would remind the Party of the divisions on Eden's resignation and the open warfare which surrounded Macmillan's resignation: an election according to the Party's current procedure would almost certainly be more attractive to the Conservatives.

A solution is suggested which combines the requirements of always having someone, with next to no power vacuum, at the helm, together with what today may be taken as being the common preference in the political parties for the Leader (and hence Prime Minister) to be elected. Save for the case where a Prime Minister is to resign as the result of advanced years, and therefore where speed is not essential and an ordinary party election could take place, the following course of action is proposed to find a new Prime Minister for a continuing government. First, the outgoing Prime Minister would inform the Queen and his parliamentary party of his illness and desire to resign.[19] Secondly, the

---

[18] See Geoffrey Marshall and Graeme Moodie, *Some Problems of the Constitution* (5th edn., 1971), pp. 47–8.

[19] For the suggested procedure if the Prime Minister were to die suddenly, see note 23.

Queen would ask the Prime Minister's deputy (if there were one), or the number two in the order of precedence in the Cabinet list[20] (if there were no formal deputy), to take charge of the government, while retaining his portfolio, but *without* appointing him Prime Minister.[21] He would look after the government on as much of a care and maintenance basis as circumstances permitted, deciding only urgent matters and then only with Cabinet consent if this were possible.[22] Thirdly, the government party would proceed to an election as expeditiously as might be and, when a successful candidate was elected, the Prime Minister (if able, or the deputy or number two if not) would recommend him as successor, resign, and the new Leader would kiss hands on appointment as Prime Minister.[23] In such a way the democratic ideal would be preserved; at no time would the government be rudderless, and the Queen would remain isolated from party politics.

It might be objected that for a politician to act as a 'caretaker' might in itself enhance his chances in the subsequent Leadership election, simply by his being seen to fulfil the duties of the office of Prime Minister.[24] But it is equally possible that he could spoil any chances he might have had by making some political slip. And even if the 'caretaker' solution is still disliked, would not a strong argument in its favour be that the automatic selection of the 'caretaker' by virtue of his position

[20] The Cabinet 'pecking order' can be seen in the list of Ministers published periodically in *Hansard*. That order is taken to be the Prime Minister's. Labour's 1981 rules provide (S.O. 5(4)) that the elected Deputy Leader shall become Leader, if a vacancy occurs, until a new Leader is elected at a Party conference. Hence, he would be clearly marked out for this role, regardless of which ministerial portfolio he held.

[21] This could be seen to be analogous to two historical episodes. Eden asked Butler, the Lord Privy Seal, in 1956–7 'to preside at Cabinet meetings' during the Prime Minister's illness (see Sir Anthony Eden, op. cit., p. 569), and Macmillan asked Butler (then First Secretary of State) in 1963 'to take charge of the Government' during the former's illness (see Lord Butler, op. cit., p. 241). In both cases Butler retained his portfolio.

[22] Powers which are personal to the office of the Prime Minister could not be exercised until a new Leader was elected and Prime Minister was appointed. Although some of these powers are quite important, it is difficult to see why, if they should fall to be used in the interim, they could not wait. For a useful compilation of some of these powers, see E. C. S. Wade and A. W. Bradley, *Constitutional and Administrative Law* (10th edn., 1985 by A. W. Bradley), p. 259.

[23] If the Prime Minister were to die suddenly, I suggest that the procedure set out in the text should still be followed, omitting references to the outgoing Prime Minister. No Prime Minister has died in office this century, although there have been some near misses: see note 12. Had Mr Wilson died during his premiership Labour MPs would have been summoned to a meeting within 48 hours and an exhaustive ballot would have been held there and then. The new Leader would then have been appointed Prime Minister by the Queen, who had apparently approved the plan. See Tony Benn, *Out of the Wilderness: Diaries 1963–1967* (1987), p. 263.

[24] Thus, Butler might twice have thought that acting as head of the government, in 1956–7 and in 1963, might ultimately help his accession to the Conservative Leadership. In neither case, however, did it. Both episodes took place, of course, before the Conservative Party had Leadership election rules: the 1963 event encouraged the adoption of such machinery.

preordained either by the stricken Prime Minister or (in the case of a Labour government) by his position as Deputy Leader of the Labour Party[25] means that that selection would keep the Queen above the party infighting, and overall would ensure that the royal prerogative of choice of a new Prime Minister in this context would have no part to play?

As a matter of strict law, party elections can neither preclude nor pre-empt the prerogative of choice.[26] If a Prime Minister indicated that he wished to resign because he was ill, the Queen would indeed be acting in accordance with constitutional law if she were then and there to accept his resignation and appoint a successor after taking whatever soundings seemed appropriate. But that law has upon it a rich gloss of practice, realism, and political sophistication which, I suggest, would preclude a repeat of events such as those which occurred in 1963. This gloss was added when all the parties came to accept the desirability of Leadership elections—that is, after 1965.

Voluntary retirement

A Prime Minister might find himself in the still unusual but fortunate position of being able to decide for himself when to retire, with no pressure to do so from his party, still healthy, not too advanced in years, and with no wish to hold ministerial office again. In this century only two men have been in such a situation: Baldwin in 1937 and Mr Wilson in 1976.

Voluntary retirement provides the means for the simplest choice of a new Prime Minister save only for the outright victory of an opposition party at a general election. Provided that the outgoing politician considers that he is fully capable of carrying out the functions of his office until his successor is chosen,[27] all that he needs to do is to inform his Cabinet, party, and the public of his intention,[28] await the outcome of the ballot, go to the Queen to advise her of the circumstances and to resign.[29] Thus

[25] See note 20.

[26] This statement will be considered more fully below when the Labour Party's 1981 Leadership rules are considered.

[27] If he thinks that he is not so capable, then the procedure outlined above on the use of a caretaker could apply.

[28] Mr Wilson informed the Queen and the Speaker in 1975 of his intention of retiring, and he made his plans clear to the Cabinet and public on 16 March 1976. For Mr Callaghan's account of his succession as Prime Minister see James Callaghan, *Time and Chance* (1987), pp. 390–4.

[29] In *The Governance of Britain* (1976), p. 22, Harold Wilson states that the Prime Minister resigns *and then* informs the Queen of the result of the ballot. Strictly, the Queen would not be acting on ministerial advice once the Prime Minister had actually resigned.

the democratic process is seen to be carried out, crowned by the dignity of the Queen's appointment of a person to be Prime Minister who, through that process, is patently the choice of his party.

One potential danger to this dignity may be inherent in the election itself, which could provide yet another example of the modern weakness of the convention of collective Cabinet responsibility.[30] The candidates in the Leadership election might feel obliged to show their party colleagues why they should be preferred,[31] and this could lead to the espousal of policies alternative to those of the government and of the outgoing Prime Minister. In the 1976 changeover, for instance, Mr Benn produced a statement which was little short of an alternative manifesto.[32] This development should not, however, cause concern. It would be extremely odd if the various candidates did not have different policies, or different interpretations of policies, from which their party was to make a choice. If the party electorate is to make an informed choice, those differences should be made public. Our constitutional system is now mature enough to recognize this so as to eschew any idea of a need for anything like an 'agreement to differ' for the duration of the campaign.[33] It has to be accepted that, if a sitting government is to elect a new Leader, collective responsibility must at least be viewed very liberally throughout the election of the new Leader and Prime Minister.[34]

Emergency coalition

From the easiest way of identifying a new Prime Minister it is now necessary to examine a more difficult case: the need to form a coalition

[30] On ministerial responsibility, see chapter 7.

[31] Mr Wilson's successor in 1976, however, did not: he remained aloof, allowing his managers to gather the votes.

[32] But as Mr Benn said during the election to choose a successor to Mr Wilson as Leader of the Parliamentary Labour Party and thus as Prime Minister, 'If a man stands to be Prime Minister or Leader of a great party, the people are entitled to know the platform on which he stands.' In his campaign in 1981 for the Deputy Leadership of the Labour Party, which was in opposition at the time, Mr Benn was criticized for advocating some policies (such as on Northern Ireland) which were not in accordance with those of the Shadow Cabinet of which he was a member.

[33] This is not to say that in Parliament at least the Cabinet's policy must be advocated and defended.

[34] Another objection might be that, whatever other criticisms might be made of the prerogative of choice in (say) 1957 and 1963, it did at least produce a Prime Minister quickly, thus to a degree avoiding uncertainty which (it is always claimed) is bad for economic and industrial affairs. Against this perfectly legitimate point of view must be balanced the advantage of a democratic election producing a Leader who is unarguably the choice of his party.

government from an existing House of Commons as a result of an emergency of such a grave character that only a government composed of representatives of more than one party would have the political authority to take the measures necessary to meet it.[35] If it is agreed by the leading politicians of the main parties that the circumstances requiring an emergency coalition exist, and that a coalition could be formed which would have the confidence of the Commons, then the major question must be: who is to lead it? Three possibilities present themselves.

The sitting Prime Minister might be thought to be the most appropriate choice.[36] The events of August 1931 are so well known that only the salient features will be noted here.[37] Realizing that the minority Labour government which he had formed in 1929 could not—indeed, would not—take effective measures against the economic and financial storm which was battering Britain, MacDonald decided to resign. Urged on by George V, however,[38] he agreed to take office again as Prime Minister of a 'National Government', including the Conservative Party and the Samuelite Liberals, both of which groups readily fell in with the plan. MacDonald failed to convince all but an embarrassingly small number of his Labour colleagues to join him in the 'National Government', which was returned with an enormous Commons majority at the general election of 1931—in which the Labour Party was smashed.[39] To take another set of circumstances, there might (again) be an obvious choice of man or woman to head the new coalition who was not the Prime Minister. Thus, in the First World War, dissatisfaction with Asquith's leadership led to the emergence of Lloyd George as Prime Minister in 1916, and, in the Second, Churchill was chosen by general consent, even though he was not the first choice of (among others)

[35] This is not the same as the consequences of a newly elected Commons in which no party has an overall majority, which are discussed in the next chapter.

[36] As was MacDonald in 1931 (at least by George V and MacDonald himself), but as Chamberlain was not in 1940 (mainly because Labour refused to serve under him).

[37] For accounts of this episode, see Reginald Bassett, *1931: Political Crisis* (1958); David Marquand, *Ramsay MacDonald* (1977), pp. 604–70; and Sir Harold Nicolson, *King George V* (1952), chapters 26–7.

[38] 'The King impressed on the Prime Minister that he was the only man to lead the country through the crisis and hoped that he would reconsider the situation. His Majesty told him that the Conservatives and Liberals would support him in restoring the confidence of foreigners in the financial stability of the country': Sir Clive Wigram, Private Secretary to George V, quoted in Sir Harold Nicolson's *King George V*, p. 464. No one today considers that the King acted with anything other than total propriety throughout this crisis.

[39] The results were: Conservatives 471 seats, National Labour 13, Samuelite Liberals 33, Simonite Liberals 35, Lloyd George Liberals 4, Labour 46, Independent Labour Party 6.

George VI[40] to take over from Chamberlain. Baldwin succeeded MacDonald in 1935 in continuance of the 'National Government', and Chamberlain similarly followed Baldwin in 1937.[41] In only the Asquith–Lloyd George transfer was there real controversy over the transfer of power. But, thirdly, there could be the case of a coalition being essential, the sitting Prime Minister being unacceptable, and *no* clear successor being present. Indeed, the position could be more complicated if none of the party Leaders was acceptable, which could happen if, for example, not even the gravity of the emergency could override personal antagonisms. How in this situation—and indeed in the other two types of coalition crisis just outlined—could the royal prerogative be exercised in a manner which would protect the user from allegations of political partisanship? Is there any solution of a general character to the problems which could arise with a present-day creation of a coalition which might reconcile the desire of the political parties for a role in the choice of the new Prime Minister with what could be an unavoidable personal selection of a new Prime Minister made by the Queen? A tentative suggestion is offered here, in an attempt to keep the prerogative of choice out of the political fray. As will be seen, it could not work in all circumstances.

Clearly, if a broad consensus is desired rather than a royal selection based on limited soundings, some form of election will be necessary. Equally plainly, however, an individual party election carried out under the current party rules could be of little help: it would be confined to one party when the whole point of the exercise would be to identify a Member of Parliament who would have cross-party support in a coalition. In this unique (and infrequent) contingency, should not the House of Commons itself take up the task of choosing the new Prime Minister? The existing government would, if feasible, continue in office until he or she was appointed. Candidates would allow themselves to be nominated for the office, and as soon as possible a secret ballot would be held of all MPs under (say) the superintendence of the Speaker.[42] The first-past-the-

---

[40] As George VI recorded in his diary on 10 May 1940, Chamberlain and the King 'had an informal talk over his successor. I, of course, suggested Halifax, but he told me H. was not enthusiastic. . . . I was disappointed . . . as I thought H. was the obvious man . . .' (quoted by Sir John Wheeler-Bennett, *King George VI: His Life and Reign* (1958), pp. 443–4. The King was then easily persuaded to send for Churchill.

[41] The 'National Government' was really a Conservative government, with 471 Conservative MPs dominating it with the support of a small band of Liberals and an even smaller group of National Labour men.

[42] It is safe to assume that the successful candidate today would be an MP. He could be a peer only if he had made it clear that he intended to disclaim his peerage and seek a seat in the Commons, assuming that he came within the provisions of the Peerage Act 1963—broadly, that he had succeeded to the peerage within the previous 12 months (s. 1(2)) or that he had been an MP when he succeeded, and had disclaimed it or would disclaim it within one month (s. 2(1)).

post system would have to be used because presumably the emergency would not allow the time for any form of exhaustive election.[43] If Parliament stood adjourned—as it did in August 1931—the Speaker and the Lord Chancellor could recall it, acting on the existing Prime Minister's request.[44] The man or woman receiving the most votes would be recommended by the Prime Minister to the Queen to form a coalition government. The Queen would then receive the outgoing Prime Minister's resignation and exercise the prerogative to appoint the new one. Thus, even at a time of serious constitutional crisis, the ideal of election might work in harmony with the royal prerogative.

Of course, this scheme is tentative, and objections to it can easily be foreseen. Urgency of the hypothetical crisis might require a choice within hours, not days, in which case the former manner of use of the prerogative, advised as best as may be, would have to be relied upon. Moreover, if one party had a substantial Commons majority, its candidate might be assured of election, regardless of the views of the other parties. This would not, however, necessarily follow. MacDonald was accepted by the Conservative Party and the Samuelite Liberals in 1931 to head the 'National Government', even though Labour was in a minority in the Commons and MacDonald's new creation, the National Labour Party, was minuscule. Again, how could the suggested scheme operate at all if Parliament were not just adjourned but dissolved when the need for a coalition arose? It could not: the prerogative of choice would have to be activated. And after the Labour Party's adoption of a widely based electoral college to elect its Leader,[45] an election confined to MPs alone might be too narrowly based for its taste and thus be unacceptable to it.[46]

Loss of the party Leadership

No Prime Minister has enjoyed his tenure of office without criticism from his own parliamentary party from time to time; some have faced revolts within their own party on particular issues;[47] a few have, in effect, been forced from office by their own party.[48] Does the introduction

---

[43] The election would be organized 'through the usual channels'—the Leader of the House and his shadow, the Whips, and representatives from the minor parties.

[44] House of Commons Standing Order 12; sessional orders of the House of Lords.

[45] To be discussed shortly.

[46] But would it be preferable to a choice made from Buckingham Palace?

[47] It is impossible to think of a government, certainly since the Second World War, which has not faced such revolts, resulting in changes in policy or open defeat in the Commons.

[48] Examples may be seen in Churchill's reluctant retirement in 1955, and the rejection of Chamberlain in May 1940 when his majority of about 200 fell to 81 in the debate on the Norwegian campaign as a result of Conservative abstentions and votes against him.

in 1965 of formal rules governing the election of the Conservative Leader, so that all the main parties have Leadership election machinery, potentially affect the security of a Prime Minister? And how, if at all, do those rules affect the royal prerogative of choice of a new Prime Minister if one is, in effect, removed from office by his party? It is here that the Labour Party's arrangements call for special scrutiny.

Although at the time it was seen as no more than the correction of an anomaly, only at the Labour Party's annual conference in 1979 was the formal position of the Leader of the Parliamentary Labour Party brought into line with the *de facto* position by his being accorded the title of 'Leader of the Labour Party'.[49] The changes in the method of electing the Leader, introduced at the special conference at Wembley in January 1981, and the 1980 requirements about reselection of candidates have, however, possibly laid a constitutional minefield.

Broadly, the rules require that an electoral college choose the Leader.[50] A weighted voting system is used, giving seventy per cent of the votes to the Party outside Parliament—forty per cent to trade unions and other affiliated organizations, thirty per cent to the constituency Labour parties—leaving the previously autonomous Parliamentary Labour Party (PLP) with only thirty per cent. The system was first used in 1981 to elect the Deputy Leader.[51] In 1983, on the retirement of Mr Foot, Mr Kinnock was elected Leader by the electoral college and Mr Hattersley was elected Deputy Leader.[52] This system could present three separate constitutional problems. The first is centred on the attitude of the PLP. Now, the Leader of that parliamentary party with an overall majority is entitled to be asked to form a government. Under the old system, the Leader of the PLP would be seen to enjoy the confidence of that body because it had elected him through an exhaustive ballot.[53] The obvious danger under the 1981 arrangements is that, given the overwhelming percentage of votes from outside the Commons, a new Leader might

[49] *Constitution* (1981), cl. VI.

[50] *Constitution and Standing Orders* (1981), S.O. 5. See also Dawn Oliver, 'The Constitutional Implications of the Reforms of the Labour Party' [1981] *Public Law* 151.

[51] The incumbent, Mr Healey, narrowly retained the post on the second ballot with 50.426 per cent, beating Mr Benn (49.574 per cent). The revised 1981 constitution provides for the Deputy Leader to become Leader automatically if 'the Party Leader, for whatever reason, becomes permanently unavailable . . .' (S.O. 5(4)), until a new Leader is elected at a Party conference. The status of the Deputy Leader has thereby been enhanced.

[52] He obtained over 71 per cent of the electoral college votes to his nearest rival's 19 per cent. Mr Hattersley was elected Deputy Leader in a separate ballot, securing over 67 per cent of the votes.

[53] He could, of course, have lost that confidence, but it is noteworthy that since 1945 there have been only two contests for the Leadership otherwise than on the retirement (Attlee in 1955 and Wilson in 1976) or death (Gaitskell 1963) of the Leader. And a Labour Prime Minister, under the old system, could not be challenged: see the now superseded *Standing Orders for the Election of the Officers and Parliamentary Committee of the P L P in Opposition*, S.O. 9.

have little support in the PLP. Leaving aside for present purposes the polarizing of the different parts of the Party which would take place,[54] the constitutional issue may be highlighted by examining a hypothetical House of Commons. Suppose that a Labour Prime Minister, A, with an overall majority gives notice of his intention to retire as soon as a new Leader is elected (following the Wilson precedent of 1976). The electoral college elects B,[55] mainly through trade union and constituency votes. But it is obvious, through public statements, media polls, and so on, not only that B would have fared badly under the old PLP electoral system, but that another MP, C, would have won convincingly under it, because in this example the PLP is to the right (or to the left) of the Party outside the House of Commons. B enjoys the full-hearted support of only a small percentage of the PLP. Assuming, as it seems safe to do, that the opposition parties would not support B as Prime Minister in the Commons, his parliamentary majority just does not exist. What 'right' would B have to become Prime Minister? One plausible result might, of course, be that the PLP would make the best of it, tolerating B as their Leader because he was the choice of the Party. The consequences of rejecting him could be (a) a fatal split in the Labour Party as a whole; (b) an utterly confused state of party politics in the Commons; and—most serious of all in the immediate term for Labour—(c) the danger that the Queen might refuse to appoint B Prime Minister because of his obvious lack of a Commons majority. Constitutional development could be thrown back to before 1965, with the Queen exercising the prerogative of choice based on the best advice available to her. No one in the Labour Party would want that; the Party outside Parliament would be outraged;[56] the Sovereign would be seen, however unavoidably, to be taking sides. And there would be no solution in appointing a Labour Prime Minister conditionally on a request for a dissolution, because were Labour to be returned to power the Leadership question would still be there.[57] A compromise (which by definition would not satisfy everyone)

---

[54] One direct result was the emergence of the Social Democratic Party in April 1981, 12 sitting Labour MPs initially joining it, and several others defecting to it later.

[55] Candidates must be a 'Commons Member of the Parliamentary Labour Party': S.O. 5(2) (b) (1981).

[56] See above, note 18, about the Party's insistence that no one should become a Labour Prime Minister without first having been elected Leader of the Party.

[57] For the Queen to appoint the Leader of the Opposition as Prime Minister conditional on such a request would be a gambler's throw indeed, for what if Labour were to win the general election? This can be distinguished from the Whitlam affair in Australia in 1975 only because the Opposition Leader *did* win the election. Again, what would have been the consequences if the dismissed Labour Prime Minister had won? See further P. G. Polyviou, *Annual Survey of Commonwealth Law* (1976), p. 16; Sir John Kerr, *Matters for Judgment* (1978); Gough Whitlam, *The Truth of the Matter* (1979); and Gareth Evans (ed.), *Labor and the Constitution 1972–1975* (1977).

can be suggested. It would avoid, on the one hand, the use of the prerogative of choice in appointing C as Prime Minister (not as Leader of the Party but as the Leader of the majority of the PLP) and, on the other, an automatic use of prerogative of appointment to install B (as Leader of the Party) , knowing that he had no Commons majority. The PLP could conduct a poll of its members to test which man had the greater support.[58] Presumably, in the hypothesis presented, C would win[59] and he would become Prime Minister. Even as this is written, howls of anger from Labour ranks can be imagined, but every political party must remember that it cannot.effect changes in British constitutional law or practice merely by changes in its internal rules if the consequence of those changes clashes with clear constitutional practice.[60]

A second difficulty could arise from the Labour Party rule (again dating from 1981) that a Leader in office as Prime Minister can be challenged for the Leadership at a Party conference if an election is requested by a majority of the conference on a card vote.[61] Now it could be argued that this likelihood is so remote as not to be worthy of consideration. After all, the Conservative Party has had provision for electing a new Leader while in office since 1975[62] and it has not been used in that circumstance. In 1975, Mr Heath, as Leader, accepted amended rules which had been drawn up under Lord Home's chairmanship[63] and announced that the first ballot would be held on 4 February 1975 (the Party, of course, then being in opposition). Of relevance here is the rule that a ballot for the Conservative Leadership *must* take place if the post is vacant, or within twenty-eight days of the beginning of *every* session, or between three to six months after the opening of *every* new

---

[58] There is now no provision at all in the Labour Party's constitution for this. To the contrary, in November 1981 the Parliamentary Labour Party accepted new standing orders which included the provision that the P L P should accept as its Leader and Deputy Leader the people voted into those positions by the electoral college. Yet what the P L P does it can undo.

[59] Admittedly *he* might not have a Commons majority either, because those who were loyal to B would not support C. In that case, the Queen would have to take an active role in consulting party Leaders. But to invite the Leader of the Opposition to form an administration on condition that he recommend a dissolution would be unwise: see note 57 above.

[60] The adoption by Labour of the election of its Leader by the P L P, and by the Conservatives of such a system based on Conservative MPs in 1965, constituted changes in internal rules but did not offend against constitutional practice—unless the old-fashioned view is adhered to that the royal prerogative should remain absolutely free in this matter, a view which I emphatically reject, as do other modern writers.

[61] *Standing Orders* (1981), S.O. 5(3) (*d*)(i). See also note 53 above.

[62] *Procedure for the Selection of the Leader of the Conservative Party* (1975): see Appendix B.

[63] The Conservative Party had first adopted rules for the election, rather than the 'emergence', of a Leader in 1965.

Parliament.[64] (In the event, Mr Heath, who had lost three general elections, lost the 1975 ballot to Mrs Thatcher.[65]) There is thus a Conservative *requirement* of an annual election—although, of course, if there is no challenger, no election will be necessary. The Conservative Party has no record of loyalty to failed Leaders or Prime Ministers. So is it safe to be sanguine about Labour's procedures, given the mood which deepened in the early 1980s and which strives for even greater accountability in the Labour Party, of which this rule is an example? I suggest that an attempt may well be made at some future Labour Party conference to dislodge a Labour Prime Minister. If it were successful, he would have to resign as Prime Minister. Whether his successor took over smoothly would depend on the issues discussed above in relation to the Leadership changing hands in a hypothetical House of Commons.

The last major problem potentially caused by changes in Labour rules in 1980 is that every Labour MP must undergo a reselection process.[66] This must happen once in each Parliament, usually not later than thirty-six months after the last general election.[67] It is very unlikely that a Labour Prime Minister would be deprived of his seat in this way, but it deserves to be noted that, however unwittingly, a piece of machinery has been created which could be used locally to deprive a Labour Prime Minister of his seat. *If* this were ever done, then unless some other constituency took him on board in time for the general election, or perhaps unless he stood and won in his constituency as some kind of independent Labour candidate with at least PLP support, then, on the declaration of the result in his constituency, he would lose any right to remain Prime Minister. Labour might be in the extraordinary position of winning a general election with its Leader outside Parliament.

---

[64] 1975 Rules 1 and 2 (my italics).

[65] On the first ballot on 4 February 1975, Mrs Thatcher obtained 130 votes to Mr Heath's 119 and Mr Hugh Fraser's 16. Mr Heath (and Mr Fraser) immediately withdrew. But because Mrs Thatcher had not obtained the required majority, a second ballot was held, in which Mrs Thatcher scored 146 votes, Mr Whitelaw 79, Sir Geoffrey Howe 19, Mr Prior 19, and Mr Peyton 11. Mrs Thatcher was declared the winner as she had received 7 votes more than those needed, that is, an overall majority of those entitled to vote plus 15 per cent more of the votes of those so entitled than any other candidate.

[66] *Rules for Constituency Labour Parties and Branches* (1980), cl. XIV.

[67] Ibid., cl. XIV (7). The National Executive Committee of the Labour Party has advised constituency parties that a short list of one (i.e. the sitting MP) should not be acceptable to the general management committee of the constituency if there is another candidate or candidates.

Conclusions

From this survey, three broad conclusions may be drawn.

(1) The idea that the role of the Queen has been reduced in the selection of a new Prime Minister to that of cypher is in many instances correct. The political parties have quite legitimately taken over some of the choices which the Sovereign has previously had to make, sometimes in controversial circumstances.

(2) It is, however, wrong to assume that the prerogative of choice of a new Prime Minister is as limited today as might have been supposed. Although some ways have been suggested in this chapter in which procedures might be adapted to ensure an element of democratic choice so that so far as possible the prerogative of choice could be kept in the background, a number of instances have been outlined where its use would be difficult to avoid. These are where:

(*a*) a coalition is needed, either as a matter of extreme urgency (so that there is no time for any party election), or when Parliament is dissolved;

(*b*) the Labour Party's electoral college chooses a Leader when Labour is in power who is rejected by the Parliamentary Labour Party;

(*c*) a Labour Prime Minister is ousted from the Leadership by the electoral college, and

(*d*) a Labour Prime Minister is denied his parliamentary seat through the mandatory reselection procedure and no other seat can be found for him in time for the next general election.

(3) Thus, although there has undoubtedly been a shift of constitutional responsibility from the Sovereign to the political parties, enhancing the dignity of the head of state while, where possible, making the choice of a head of government more democratic, there remain sufficient possible circumstances in which the Queen would have to exercise her prerogative of choice unaided by the parties. It is much too soon to consign that part of the royal prerogative to the lumber room wherein lie discarded bits of constitutional law and practice.

It is to the tricky question of how a Prime Minister is chosen on the return of a hung Parliament that attention is turned in the next chapter.

3

Government Formation from a Hung Parliament

The election of a hung Parliament[1] presents a broad range of possible procedures and resulting government structures: there are precedents this century which provide a dazzling array of choice.[2] So a Prime Minister, having failed to secure a majority at the general election, might resign immediately,[3] or stay in office to negotiate a coalition,[4] or wait to meet Parliament to have his fate decided on the motion on the loyal address in reply to the Queen's Speech.[5] The Sovereign might take some part in the resolution of the crisis,[6] or none.[7] There could be a protracted succession,[8] or a resolution almost as speedy as if the electorate had returned a majority government.[9] The administration which emerged could vary in its composition from a minority government enjoying no support from other parties,[10] to a minority government with negotiated aid from others so as to ensure some degree of stability,[11] to a majority coalition of two[12] or three parties,[13] or even a national coalition of all the main parties.[14] And behind all that would be another uncertainty: if the

[1] Two important books are Vernon Bogdanor, *Multi-party Politics and the Constitution* (1983) and David Butler, *Governing Without a Majority: Dilemmas for Hung Parliaments in Britain* (1983).

[2] The main precedents will be evaluated later.

[3] As did Baldwin in 1929.

[4] As did Mr Heath in February 1974.

[5] Baldwin took this course in 1923.

[6] As did George V, indirectly through his Private Secretary, in 1923–4.

[7] The Queen did not have to intervene following the election of the February 1974 hung Parliament.

[8] The longest this century lasted from the 6 December 1923 general election to the appointment of MacDonald at the head of the first and minority Labour government on 22 January 1924, a period of 6 weeks.

[9] As in February–March 1974, a period of only 4 days.

[10] Such as the minority Labour governments of MacDonald (January to November 1924) and Wilson (March to October 1974).

[11] Like the Lib.-Lab. pact which sustained the minority Callaghan government in office from March 1977 to July 1978. The pact did not follow a general election, nor did the governments indicated in notes 12–14.

[12] As with the Conservative-Liberal Unionist government from 1900–5 (although over-whelmingly Conservative).

[13] The 'National Government' of 1931 to 1940.

[14] The wartime coalition of Lloyd George of 1916 (which lasted until 1922) was formed from a hung Parliament, but not that of Churchill (1940 to 1945).

successor government were to be defeated on an early vote of confidence, would the Queen be obliged to permit a further turn of the constitutional roulette wheel by granting a second dissolution of Parliament?

It seems from all this that there are no 'rules' about government formation from a hung Parliament. Such uncertainty in an area of major importance in the constitution may cry out for regulation, but the only 'rule' in such circumstances is open-ended and unhelpful, namely that in choosing a Prime Minister the Queen should commission that person who appears best able to command the support of a stable majority in the House of Commons, or, failing such a person, that politician who seems able to form a government with a reasonable prospect of maintaining an administration in office.[15] This does not take us very far. How, for example, could the Queen identify that person who *might* command a majority in the House of Commons of minority parties, and how would she resolve the possible and conflicting claim of the Leader of the largest minority party to form a minority government?

Moreover, the precedents—especially those in which a minority administration was formed—have to be approached with caution, as they were (as will be explained later) political accommodations arrived at as the result both of the political realities of the day and of the personal relationships between the party Leaders. Such relationships have varied and will vary greatly from time to time, making inter-party co-operation more, or less, likely.[16] Accordingly, those precedents should not be considered as being rule-constitutive.

The likelihood today of achieving agreement in advance of an inconclusive general election about relevant rules is remote, given the attitudes of the Leaders of the parties. The Leaders of the Conservative and Labour Parties have insisted at recent general elections that, as their respective parties would win an outright majority, discussions about a hung Parliament would be pointless—although Mr Kinnock has said that if Labour were to emerge as the largest minority party after an election he would be entitled to form a minority administration after the resignation of the Conservative government. The SDP/Liberal Alliance,

---

[15] See the formulations given in, for example, S. A. de Smith, *Constitutional and Administrative Law* (5th edn., 1985 by H. Street and R. Brazier), pp. 173–6; E. C. S. Wade and A. W. Bradley, *Constitutional and Administrative Law* (10th edn., 1985 by A. W. Bradley), pp. 236–9; O. Hood Phillips, *Constitutional and Administrative Law* (7th edn., 1987 by O. Hood Phillips and P. Jackson), pp. 318–22.

[16] Baldwin's animosity towards Lloyd George contributed to his part in the break-up of the latter's government in 1922. It would be difficult to envisage a peacetime coalition between Mrs Thatcher and Mr Kinnock.

however, actively campaigned for a coalition government to be formed from any hung Parliament and rejected the formation of a minority administration out of hand.[17] Given the absence of all-party agreement on appropriate government formation procedures, the setting up of an inter-party conference or a Royal Commission to work towards agreed rules would not be worth while.[18] Equally, it would be astonishing if the Queen were to publish what her attitude would be in such a crisis, partly because it would be wholly outside any previous practice, but mainly because a pre-condition of such publication would be ministerial advice to make it, which in the light of the stance of Mrs Thatcher and Mr Kinnock would not be likely to be forthcoming.[19]

These matters expose the Queen to pressure to decide political questions, with the inherent risk of criticism however she might answer them. In the absence of rules about forming an administration from a hung Parliament the present purpose is to suggest a number of procedures which would help to preserve the perceived political neutrality of the head of state, ensure that as far as possible politicians would take responsibility for the resolution of political issues, and facilitate the effective continuance of government during any period of crisis. The first stage to be considered concerns the political negotiations which might take place after an inconclusive election but before the Queen became involved to any significant extent.

The political negotiations

After a general election in which the electorate records a decisive verdict the political debate may slacken. After the election of a hung Parliament, however, that debate will intensify: the political parties could well disagree on the type of government which should be installed; some party activists might be ready to denounce the heresy of co-operation or (worse) coalition with the adversaries of the late campaign; evidence of bias against one party or for another on the Queen's part might be sought—all to be relayed to the nation by the media. In such a situation

---

[17] For an analysis, see R. Brazier, 'An Alliance Veto of a Minority Government?' [1985] *Public Law* 545.

[18] Those two devices are suggested by David Butler, op. cit., p. 105.

[19] Butler, op. cit., pp. 132–3 suggests that the Queen could publish 'during a time of political peace' what her response would be to a request for a dissolution by a minority Prime Minister, but he does not address my point about the need for ministerial advice being obtained for such publication.

it is suggested that the guiding light ought to be that the political crisis should if possible be resolved by politicians—in a phrase, that there should be political decisions, politically arrived at. If followed, such a guiding light would help to refute any allegation that a non-elected head of state had imposed a particular solution on the elected House instead of allowing that House, through the party Leaders, to arrive at a conclusion. It would also enhance the Queen's impartiality as between the political parties and between individuals,[20] which would be crucially important if a political compromise were to prove impossible, when only the Queen could end the succession crisis.

Support for such a guiding light can be obtained from the aftermaths of three hung Parliaments that have been elected this century,[21] in 1923,[22] 1929,[23] and February 1974.[24] In May 1923 Baldwin succeeded the dying Bonar Law as Prime Minister and, although the government which he took over had a majority of thirty-seven seats and had only been elected in the previous November, he obtained a dissolution to seek a mandate for protection against the import of foreign manufactures. The Conservatives secured only 258 seats in the December 1923 general election, with the free-trade parties obtaining 191 seats (for Labour) and 159 seats (for the combined Asquith and Lloyd George Liberals, reunited against protection). Several outcomes were theoretically possible: a minority Conservative government, as being the largest minority; a Liberal-Labour free-trade coalition; a Liberal-Conservative coalition (or at least co-operation between them in the House) so as to keep out Labour (which had never held office before), or a minority Labour government. Baldwin decided to stay in office and to meet the new

[20] The Queen's inevitable interventions in the fight for the succession to Macmillan in 1963, and to a lesser extent in choosing a successor to Eden in 1957, raised accusations that she had been forced to choose between contenders within the Conservative Party. For the published accounts see above, chapter 2 note 2.

[21] The two general elections of January and December 1910 resulted in hung Parliaments, but as Asquith's government remained in power throughout they are not helpful in this analysis and are disregarded here.

[22] For detailed accounts of the 6-week succession crisis in 1923–4, see David Marquand, *Ramsay MacDonald* (1977), pp. 296–305; Kenneth Rose, *King George V* (1983), pp. 324–7; Sir Harold Nicolson, *King George V* (1952), chapters 22 and 23; Vernon Bogdanor, op. cit., pp. 91–107. George V caused soundings to be made by his Private Secretary after the 1923 election about what his attitude should be if a request for a further dissolution were made, but his direct intervention in the government formation after that election was non-existent.

[23] See David Marquand, op. cit., pp. 483–91.

[24] See Harold Wilson, *The Governance of Britain* (1976), pp. 25–6 and *Final Term: The Labour Government 1974–1976* (1979), pp. 9–11.

Parliament.[25] The Labour Party would not countenance coalition.[26] Baldwin would not join a coalition—after all, he had played an important role in destroying Lloyd George's coalition government in 1922 and, in his words, he had 'killed one coalition and would never join another'.[27] The Liberals would offer no support to the Conservative Party which had fought the election to end free trade; and, as Asquith put it, if there were to be a Labour government for the first time it would be in a minority and 'it could hardly be tried in safer circumstances'.[28] A minority Labour government was inevitable, and Labour and the Liberals combined to defeat Baldwin's government by seventy-two votes on the King's Speech. Baldwin resigned, and George V—in his first personal intervention in the crisis—appointed MacDonald Prime Minister in January 1924.[29] The outcome had been dictated by the politics of the day and by the attitudes of the party Leaders, not by the King.[30] The second hung Parliament was returned in 1929. Labour became the largest minority party, with 288 seats, with Baldwin's second government obtaining 260 seats and the Liberals 59 seats.[31] Several of the factors which had militated against coalition only five years earlier were still present, and Baldwin resigned immediately.[32] The King accordingly sent for the

[25] His first inclination, having lost what his critics claimed was an unnecessary general election, was to resign forthwith as Prime Minister and Leader of the Conservative Party, but he subsequently changed his mind, perhaps at the King's urging. 'The Prime Minister came to see me and I asked him not to resign but to meet Parliament and see what happens': George V's diary for 10 December 1923 (quoted in Kenneth Rose, op. cit., p. 324). Vernon Bogdanor thinks that Baldwin had already decided to stay before that audience, so that the King's role in the episode has been exaggerated: op. cit., p. 97.

[26] The National Executive Committee resolved on 12 December 1923 that the '. . . Parliamentary Party should at once accept full responsibility for the Government of the country without compromising itself with any form of coalition': The Times, 14 December 1923.

[27] Quoted in Sir Harold Nicolson, op. cit., p. 495. He could not foresee 1931.

[28] Quoted in R. W. Lyman, The First Labour Government (1957), p. 86.

[29] MacDonald, as Leader of the second-largest party after the 1923 general election, was Leader of the Opposition. Sir Ivor Jennings has written in his Cabinet Government (3rd edn. 1959), p. 32 that 'The rule is that on the defeat and resignation of the Government the Queen should send first for the Leader of the Opposition.' This rule, however, fails to take account in a hung Parliament of a possible majority coalition which might or might not include the Leader of the Opposition.

[30] George V's Private Secretary, Lord Stamfordham, had acted as an important channel of information from the party Leaders to the King.

[31] The Conservatives had a larger share of the popular vote than Labour, 38.2 per cent to 37.1 per cent, a phenomenon repeated at the February 1974 election of a hung Parliament (Conservative 37.9 to Labour 37.1).

[32] He told the King's Private Secretary that 'He was beaten and he accepts it and thinks this sporting attitude will count in his favour next time. If he hangs on they will say, "Here is a man clinging to office, he won't take his defeat, he is trying to prevent the Labour Party from enjoying their victory" ': Keith Middlemas and John Barnes, Baldwin (1969), p. 527. By 1929 there was a readier recognition that universal suffrage meant that seats won in Parliament represented the will of the electorate more closely than had been the case before that suffrage.

Leader of the Opposition from the previous Parliament, MacDonald, who formed his second minority administration: beyond formally appointing MacDonald, George V was required to perform no function. Strong support for the suggested guiding light of political decisions, politically arrived at, is provided by the most recent instance of a hung Parliament, that of February 1974. A Conservative majority of sixteen at the dissolution disappeared at the polls, Labour becoming the largest minority with 301 seats, the Conservatives second with 296, the Liberals with fourteen and the United Ulster Unionists with eleven.[33] Mr Heath had an audience of the Queen on the day after the election to inform her of the political situation, and saw the Leader of the Liberal Party, Mr Thorpe, over the weekend to offer Liberal places in a coalition Cabinet and a Speaker's Conference on electoral reform.[34] The Liberals in the event rejected the offer, and on Monday 4 March Mr Heath resigned and, as the Labour Shadow Cabinet had already made it publicly known that it was prepared to form a minority administration with no help from the other parties,[35] the Queen appointed Mr Wilson Prime Minister. Once again the new government had emerged from a hung Parliament with no recourse to the Sovereign.

In 1923, 1929, and 1974 the party Leaders resolved the crises. In each case the result happened to be a minority government. In the circumstances, there was no alternative. But the situation has since changed in two respects. First, the SDP/Liberal Alliance has been adamant that a coalition and only a coalition be formed from a hung Parliament. A pre-condition for Alliance support of such a coalition would have been an agreement on policy, including the introduction of proportional representation. The Alliance view has been that the economic situation could only be addressed adequately by a coalition government, not by an 'unstable' minority administration.[36] If in such a Parliament the Alliance

[33] The Scottish and Welsh Nationalists achieved a total of nine seats, there were 2 Independents, a Social Democratic and Labour member from Northern Ireland, and the Speaker. The Ulster Unionists no longer took the Conservative whip.

[34] The Ulster Unionists might have been available—at a price—to join Mr Heath's proposed coalition, and had they done so he would have had a 9-seat majority: see Phillip Whitehead, *The Writing on the Wall* (1985), p. 113; Cecil King, *Diary 1970–1974* (1975), p. 348.

[35] Their statement was reported in *The Times*, 2 March 1974.

[36] See Brazier, ibid. The Alliance threat to vote down a minority government was not very convincing, because the other main opposition party (or a large section of it) would have to vote with the Alliance to achieve that result and that party would have to be prepared (as the Conservatives in 1974 were not) to face the financial cost of a quick second election and the possible antagonism of the electorate. The 'boredom factor' which might affect the electorate was in Harold Wilson's mind between the two 1974 general elections: see *The Governance of Britain*,

(or presumably now the Social and Liberal Democrats) could find support from MPs in other parties so as to constitute a majority in the House, then the consensus for minority government which was forced on the parties in 1923, 1929, and 1974 would no longer exist, and if the traditional parties of government clung to their anti-coalition positions[37] a conflict would be produced which the Queen would have to end. The second change is that, if some of the political parties were to embrace the idea of a coalition, a pre-condition might be a change in the party leadership on the part of a potential coalition partner. One analogy, not involving the aftermath of a general election, comes from 1940, when neither the Labour Party nor the Liberals would join a coalition under Chamberlain, who eventually resigned to make way for Churchill.[38] In the 1983 and 1987 general election campaigns the Alliance parties indicated that a change in the Leadership of the Conservative Party might have to take place before they would join a Conservative-Alliance coalition.[39] If a party challenged in that way stood by its Leader, a minority administration might have to result. Alternatively, if it agreed to change its Leader, there would be a significant delay in forming the successor coalition until the change in Leader had been made. That delay would be exacerbated by the formal Leadership election procedures which all the parties have. All involve formal nominations, secret ballots, and, in the Conservative rules, a requirement of a weighted absolute majority over all other candidates for victory, achieved by a knock-out system and renomination. The Liberals and the SDP had postal ballots of their entire memberships, and the Social and Liberal Democratic Party will follow suit. The Heath–Thatcher transfer in 1975 took seven days; the

---

p. 39. Nevertheless, in 1986 the Alliance took out an insurance policy at Lloyds under which the Alliance would receive several hundred thousand pounds if there were a second dissolution within six months of a general election. The premium was very low because the Alliance was doing badly in the opinion polls at that time: *The Times*, 26 March 1987.

[37] Conservative antipathy can be traced back to Baldwin's hatred of Lloyd George. The Conservatives have only taken part in coalitions this century in wartime and at a time of financial emergency—the 'National Government' of 1931. Mr Heath suggested a 'Government of National Unity' in the October 1974 manifesto *Putting Britain First* but the idea died with his loss of the Conservative Leadership in 1975. Labour's antagonism was perhaps historically class based and was bitterly reinforced by MacDonald's break-up of the Labour Party in 1931.

[38] Churchill was Prime Minister for 5 months before reluctantly accepting the Leadership of the Conservative Party: see Martin Gilbert, *Finest Hour: Winston Churchill 1939–1941* (1983), pp. 347–8, 829, 835–7.

[39] As the Leader of the Liberal Party put it: '. . . we cannot get rid of Thatcherism without getting rid of her. So she would have to step down to make way for a new Tory leader more in the "one nation" mould of Winston Churchill or Harold Macmillan': speech at Westminster to the Liberal Youth Day rally, 15 May 1985.

Wilson–Callaghan changeover in 1976 took three weeks.[40] Thus an embryo coalition might have a gestation period of some weeks before it could be born.[41]

I have argued that after an inconclusive general election the guiding light should be: political decisions, politically arrived at. If the party Leaders were to agree within a few days that a majority coalition could not be formed and that a minority government should take office (as in 1974) the succession question would be decided. The Queen, acting on the views of the party Leaders as published[42] and presumably as communicated to her by the Prime Minister, would perform without controversy her dignified function of receiving the outgoing Prime Minister's resignation and appointing his minority successor.[43] (The only constitutional problem which could later occur would be if the minority Prime Minister were to seek within a short time a further disolution: this is discussed later.) Alternatively, a majority coalition might turn out to be on the cards, with or without a change in the Leadership of one party, but the largest minority party might insist that it had a right to take office on its own.[44] In such a case of irreconcilable disagreement the suggested guiding light would be extinguished and the Queen would have to become involved. It is her role in that delicate situation which will now be examined.

The Queen

The King or Queen for the time being is not a mere piece of mechanism but a human being carefully trained under circumstances which afford exceptional chances of learning the business of politics.[45]

The Queen is clearly in a unique position to observe the business of politics. She has been head of state for thirty-six years, during which time she has presided over ten general elections and has seen eight

[40] See Patrick Cosgrave, *Margaret Thatcher* (1978), chapter 2; Harold Wilson, *Final Term*, pp. 236–9.

[41] The party election rules are in given in Appendix B. Labour's electoral college system could prove the longest by far. The resultant delay would enhance the need for a caretaker government, a point which is developed later.

[42] As they were in 1923 and 1974: see above, notes 26 and 35.

[43] It might be, of course, that the Prime Minister was going to succeed himself.

[44] It is unlikely that the parties representing a majority of seats would both fail to agree on a coalition *and* seek to vote down a minority government at the earliest opportunity.

[45] Sir William Anson, *The Law and Custom of the Constitution* (4th edn., 1935), ii. 61.

different Prime Ministers.[46] She is well informed, receiving all Cabinet papers and minutes and Foreign and Commonwealth Office telegrams. Her former Prime Ministers have paid tribute to her assiduity, her knowledge of national and international problems, and her accumulated political knowledge and experience, all of which became apparent to them through their weekly audiences.[47] It is therefore possible greatly to exaggerate the extent to which the Queen would need to seek advice as to what steps she should take following the election of a hung Parliament.

Her closest adviser would in the first instance be her Private Secretary, currently Sir William Heseltine. The office of Private Secretary[48] was created by Queen Victoria in 1861 and the holder has become a major source of professional advice, knowing the leading politicians and absorbing published and other opinions of constitutional writers. He is appointed personally by the Sovereign: there is no scope for political interference in the appointment. There is a precedent for the Private Secretary, following an inconclusive election, acting both as a conduit for the party Leaders' views and as an active gatherer of them. From the general election of December 1923 until the Conservative landslide of 1924, George V's Private Secretary Lord Stamfordham[49] conducted informal and confidential talks which helped to install MacDonald's first government and to inform the King of the attitude of the Leaders to any parliamentary defeat of it and of the issues involved in any consequent request for a dissolution.[50] Nevertheless, it would be doubtful, I suggest, whether today a Private Secretary should be asked to perform a similar function, partly because of the risk that the political left might regard him as an establishment figure rather than as a purely neutral conveyer of information to the Sovereign, and mainly because an intermediary who saw the Leaders privately would be an inadequate substitute for the Queen receiving their opinions personally and according to a fair

[46] She could say with even greater force than her grandfather, who reigned for 25 years, that 'My Ministers come and go and are relieved of their duties, but I am here always': George V to Lady Desborough, quoted in Kenneth Rose, op. cit., p. 106.

[47] See Harold Macmillan, *Riding the Storm* (1971), p. 344 and *Pointing the Way* (1972), p. 30; Lord Home, *The Way the Wind Blows* (1976), p. 201; articles by Lord Home, Lord Wilson of Rievaulx, and James Callaghan, *The Sunday Times Magazine*, 13 April 1986 (on the occasion of the Queen's 60th birthday).

[48] On the office, see Sir John Wheeler-Bennett, *King George VI: His Life and Reign* (1958), Appendix B; H. C. 29 (1971–2), pp. 30–41.

[49] He had been Private Secretary to the King since 1910.

[50] See above, note 22.

procedure.[51] Another potential adviser whom the commentators either overlook or rule out as being an inappropriate source of information is the outgoing Prime Minister. A Prime Minister who had failed to obtain a majority at a general election would be following precedents if he were to resign immediately,[52] or if he were to stay to see if he could form a coalition,[53] or if he were to wait and meet Parliament.[54] He is in theory entitled to remain in office until defeated on a vote of confidence.[55] Since MacDonald's resignation in 1924, however, none has waited to meet Parliament.

Three assertions have been made about an outgoing Prime Minister's constitutional position. First, that he is under no duty to give advice about his successor, but is under a duty to offer it if asked; secondly, that it would none the less be *improper* for the Queen to elicit his opinion, and thirdly that resigning Prime Ministers have not in modern times in fact sought to volunteer a view on the succession.

The first proposition must be right, especially if at his final audience he resigns and then speaks about his successor, for clearly his opinion could not be classified as ministerial advice but as the view of a former (albeit the most recent) Prime Minister.[56] As Harold Wilson has written: 'Contrary to widespread belief, there is no duty on the prime minister, still less any inherent right, to recommend the man to be sent for.'[57]

The second assertion, that it would be improper for the Queen to seek the outgoing Prime Minister's views, must be challenged. David Butler has written that

. . . there could be even greater problems if [the Queen] were obliged, in default of anyone else, to act on the advice of a lame-duck Prime Minister. It would be widely seen as outrageous if, in an essentially adversarial situation, the umpire had to act on the advice of one of the protagonists.[58]

[51] That suggested procedure will be outlined shortly. I do not consider the idea of an *informateur*, that is, a respected honest broker who might act on the Queen's behalf, to be worth consideration. Such an idea has received considerable criticism (see, for example, Butler, op. cit., pp. 88–91; Bogdanor, op. cit., pp. 129–33; and for implicit rejection, Marshall, *Constitutional Conventions* (1984), pp. 43–4), and no support.

[52] Baldwin (1929).

[53] Heath (1974).

[54] Baldwin (1923–4).

[55] On what is a vote of confidence, see P. Norton, 'Government Defeats in the House of Commons: Myths and Reality' [1978] *Public Law* 360 and below, chapter 9.

[56] This point was explained earlier.

[57] *The Governance of Britain*, p. 22. Similarly, he has put it in *Final Term*, p. 239 that 'Contrary to the views of some text-book writers, a retiring Prime Minister does not advise the Queen who should be sent for, still less is there any truth in one proclaimed view . . . that if the Queen asks for advice she must accept it.'

[58] Op. cit., p. 80.

Vernon Bogdanor comments that 'It would be absurd, for example, [for the Queen] to ask a Prime Minister just defeated in the Commons or at the polls for advice as to his successor.'[59] But if a hung Parliament were elected, what could be more natural and less objectionable than the Queen asking the outgoing Prime Minister for the benefit of his experience over the next step? This would not be on the basis of seeking ministerial advice, as he would be resigning, but rather on the basis that that person had served the Queen as Prime Minister, perhaps for some years,[60] and that his opinion would be one piece of information which the Queen might wish to have. What weight she attached to it would be another matter. Just because a Prime Minister had lost a general election should not turn him into a pariah to be ushered from the Queen's presence as quickly as possible before he could add an inappropriate gloss on the bare act of resignation. The third proposition, that advice by a resigning Prime Minister has seldom been given in modern times,[61] must be qualified. The office of Prime Minister has changed hands twenty-three times since 1900. A perusal of the published materials shows that in five cases when the main opposition party won a majority at a general election it is not recorded whether advice was given,[62] perhaps because such advice was redundant, so that those cases can be ignored. Of the remaining eighteen situations, advice was definitely given in nine transfers—half that total.[63] There is no record either way in five other transfers;[64] advice was certainly not given in the remaining four.[65] Even if the five unknown cases shifted to the 'no advice' column, advice has actually been tendered as often as not this century in situations in which the succession was not automatic after a general election. I stress that this does not show any 'right' to advise, merely that, as a matter of published record, advice has been given more often than is sometimes recognized.[66]

[59] 'No Overall Majority: Forming a Government in a Multi-party Parliament' (Constitutional Reform Centre, 1986), p. 4.

[60] And perhaps having formed a close relationship: see, for example, the Queen's letter to Harold Macmillan after his retirement, quoted in his *At the End of the Day* (1973), pp. 518–9.

[61] See Butler, op. cit., p. 91.

[62] 1924 (MacDonald to Baldwin), 1951 (Attlee to Churchill), 1964 (Douglas-Home to Wilson), 1970 (Wilson to Heath), and 1979 (Callaghan to Thatcher).

[63] 1916 (Asquith to Lloyd George), 1931 (MacDonald succeeding himself), 1935 (MacDonald to Baldwin), 1937 (Baldwin to Chamberlain), 1940 (Chamberlain to Churchill), 1945 (Churchill to Attlee), 1955 (Churchill to Eden), 1963 (Macmillan to Home), and 1976 (Wilson to Callaghan).

[64] 1902 (Salisbury to Balfour), 1905 (Balfour to Campbell-Bannerman), 1922 (Lloyd George to Bonar Law), 1929 (Baldwin to MacDonald), and 1974 (Heath to Wilson).

[65] 1908 (Campbell-Bannerman to Asquith), 1923 (Bonar Law to Baldwin), 1924 (Baldwin to MacDonald), 1957 (Eden to Macmillan).

[66] The Queen could consult former Prime Ministers and senior Privy Councillors (as in 1957). George V's device of an all-party conference at Buckingham Palace, to which he resorted four

Thus if the result of the party Leaders' negotiations were to be anything other than a speedy agreement on a minority government, the Queen would have to intervene using her own knowledge and skill, with her Private Secretary at her elbow, and, if she wished, receiving the views of the outgoing Prime Minister. Her intervention would be to receive the differing opinions of the party Leaders and to commission a new Prime Minister.

Suppose that a general election were to give Labour 290 seats, the Conservatives 260, a third party eighty seats,[67] and others twenty.[68] As the largest minority, Labour might claim the right to form a minority administration, whereas the Conservatives (or most of them less their current Leader[69]) and the third party might be ready to form a majority coalition government. The precedents of 1923, 1929, and 1974 all point to Labour's solution, and so in that sense it would be prudent for the Queen to commission a Labour Prime Minister. But I have already argued that those precedents are not prescriptive. Accordingly, the Queen might consider it to be her duty to commission a Conservative-third party coalition as having the better prospect of reasonable stability, especially if those parties threatened to vote down a minority Labour government at the earliest opportunity. How should the Queen decide between those competing aims in a fair manner which would leave the political decisions to politicians?

It is suggested that the Queen should hear the views in audience of each party Leader in turn in order of their seat strengths in the new House.[70] So in the hypothetical example she would receive in turn first the Leader of the Labour Party, then the Leader of the Conservative Party, then the Leader of the third party, then the Leaders of the parties from Northern Ireland, and so on.[71] The outgoing Prime Minister

---

times, would not be apposite in choosing a new government from a hung Parliament. If such a conference were necessary, it could just as expeditiously take place away from Buckingham Palace and thus take away the media spotlight. The Queen could, moreover, inform herself just as well through an alternative procedure now to be discussed.

[67] Perhaps the Social and Liberal Democrats.

[68] Northern Ireland returns 17 MPs: Parliamentary Constituencies Act 1986, s. 3 and Schedule 2, para. 1(4). The overwhelming majority will be Unionists. The Scottish and Welsh Nationalists might account for the remaining handful.

[69] This scenario was discussed above.

[70] It would be a nice question who would go first if the two leading parties tied (as they did in December 1910). Personal convenience should, perhaps, dictate the order, and that would sensibly be made public.

[71] Any dispute about the number of seats held by any party could be resolved by whoever had been Speaker in the old Parliament (or a deputy if he were not re-elected): at this stage, before the new Parliament had met, there would be no elected Speaker. The Speaker can already be called upon

would be one of these. Such audiences would bear the advantages that the Queen would be following the electorate's choice as reflected in the seats given by it to the parties; no Leader could feel piqued at not being consulted, or at being consulted after some other Leader for no apparent reason, and the Queen would be informing herself personally of the Leaders' views, so tha〈 〉 one could allege that his views might have been distorted by an intermediary. The views of all the party Leaders, regardless of how few MPs they led, should be so obtained, for *not* to consult them all, especially in a close result, could be damaging: just a handful of votes in a Commons division could be crucial to the continuance of a government.

Let it be supposed after the hypothetical election result posed earlier that in the audiences the Labour Leader were to urge the Queen to appoint him Prime Minister of a minority government, and that subsequently the Conservative Leader[72] were to wish to see if an anti-Labour coalition could be formed with the third party, or perhaps were to tell the Queen that some Conservative MPs wanted to ally with that party and that time would be needed to test party opinion. In his later audience the Leader of the third party would make plain his enthusiasm for a coalition solution.[73] Armed with that information the Queen would be unwise immediately to commission anyone as Prime Minister—not the Labour Leader (because there could well be a Commons majority against him), not the Conservative or third-party Leader (because she would have an insufficient guarantee of a viable coalition to persuade her to take the novel step of appointing anything other than a minority administration from a hung Parliament). I suggest that it would be more prudent if, through the outgoing Prime Minister,[74] the Queen were to tell the Leaders that if she were to receive evidence (again through the outgoing Prime Minister) of a copper-bottomed agreement on a majority coalition, its leadership, proposed disposition of ministerial offices, and agreed Queen's Speech, together with an equally sound guarantee that that coalition government would not seek a dissolution within a reasonable time, then she would appoint the person agreed upon to be Prime Minister. The Queen should further stipulate that the package should be

---

to decide who is Leader of the Opposition by reference to numbers of seats (Ministerial and other Salaries Act 1975, s. 2(1)), and he might now be called upon to rule on the rights of opposition parties to Opposition Days, again based on seat strengths (Standing Order No. 13(2), (3)).

[72] One of these two Leaders may be assumed to be outgoing Prime Minister.

[73] There is no point in speculating here what might be the attitudes of the other parties.

[74] It will be argued shortly that he should remain in office throughout the succession crisis as caretaker Prime Minister.

endorsed by the relevant parliamentary parties before it is submitted to her so as to ensure that the leaderships are entirely in tune with their parliamentary colleagues,[75] and also that the ultimate agreement should be made public. Such intensely political negotiations on the package would then take place at Westminster between politicians, not at Buckingham Palace with the Queen. If the whole agreement on a majority coalition were achieved, then that fact would be communicated to the outgoing Prime Minister, who would see the Queen, recommend that she send for the coalition leader, and resign.[76] Again from caution, the older formula might be used of inviting the coalition leader to form a government and to report back on his success, rather than then and there appointing him Prime Minister, so that if, despite everything, he were unable to form a government the embarrassment of 'revolving door' Prime Ministers would be avoided.[77] Alternatively, if after the party negotiations no such copper-bottomed coalition agreement were to prove possible, the Queen should accept the outgoing Prime Minister's resignation and appoint the Leader of the Labour Party as minority Prime Minister.[78]

Such a process of audiences would, it is submitted, constitute a fair system that could be seen to be following the electorate's choice so far as practicable. It would leave the political responsibilities and decisions to the party Leaders, who would have to assure the Queen that, in appointing a coalition rather than a minority government, she would not be embarrassed by any early demise of that coalition or by an early request for another general election. The cost of such a process would be time: a coalition agreement could take several weeks to conclude. That prompts the question of how effective administration could be continued during such a hiatus.[79]

---

[75] This point is made by David Steel, *A House Divided: The Lib-Lab Pact and the Future of British Politics* (1980), pp. 153–4, in which, reflecting on the lessons of the Lib.-Lab. pact, he stresses that in any future inter-party co-operation the relevant parliamentary parties should be involved and their positive support achieved. The point was echoed in a joint letter from Mr Steel and Dr Owen to prospective Alliance parliamentary candidates before the 1987 general election.

[76] By the Queen acting on the advice of the Prime Minister, potential problems of Her Majesty acting on party Leaders' advice, rather than ministerial advice, would be avoided.

[77] This formula was last used in 1963. See Lord Home, op. cit., p. 185.

[78] If a *minority* coalition could be formed which had more seats than the largest single party, it would be entitled to form a minority government.

[79] Sir Humphrey Appleby's answer could be confidently predicted, no doubt drawing no distinction between the hiatus and any other time.

A caretaker government

The British post-election experience is that the defeated Prime Minister will resign and his successor will be appointed the day after the poll.[80] The electorate is used to television pictures of furniture vans in Downing Street the day after the election, moving out one head of government so as to make way for his successor. The formation of a coalition government from a hung Parliament, however, could be a lengthy process, but I suggest that a development of the use of caretaker governments would ensure continuity of administration. The governmental system, through what are in fact (though very rarely in name) caretaker governments, has regularly coped with succession uncertainties caused both by dissolutions and by resignations of Prime Ministers from governments which are to continue in office.

The operations of government are regularly suspended in large part for about three weeks from the announcement of a general election until after the result of it is known. Those periods of suspension have not caused the heavens to fall, and it is difficult to see why a longer period during which coalition negotiations were held after the return of a hung Parliament would invite catastrophe. The *period* itself is scarcely crucial: in 1979, for example, the suspension lasted five weeks from the fall of the Callaghan government to the return of its Conservative successor, and during that time the Labour government acted as a caretaker administration, introducing a minimalist Budget and Finance Bill after discussions with the Opposition. And in 1945 Churchill formed a caretaker Conservative government on the break-up of the war coalition which governed for two months until the overseas election results were declared. A closer analogy is in the six-week interregnum between the 1923 general election and MacDonald's appointment in 1924. In all three cases necessary administration continued. The other situation of suspension occurs when a Prime Minister wishes to resign so as to make way for a successor from his government. For example, the Wilson–Callaghan transfer in 1976 took three weeks,[81] and the Wilson government remained

---

[80] Was this expectation partly responsible for the opinion that Mr Heath's delayed resignation in 1974 was in some way 'unconstitutional'? See Lord Crowther-Hunt's letter to *The Times*, 4 March 1974. No one else thinks that Mr Heath acted other than with complete propriety.

[81] The Wilson precedent of 1976, not that of Macmillan in 1963, would be followed today given that all the parties have a system of secret ballots to elect their Leaders. I have explained above that, if a Prime Minister, perhaps through sudden illness, had to resign before the secret ballot could be conducted, a caretaker from his Cabinet could take temporary charge during the party election.

throughout effectively as a caretaker.

Thus a Prime Minister whose authority is in question by virtue of a dissolution or his impending retirement has been entirely able to preside over routine matters of government. All that would need to be accepted after the return of a hung Parliament and during any lengthy political negotiations would be that the defeated administration should stay in office as a caretaker government until the succession was settled.[82] The defeated Prime Minister would merely see the Queen to inform her of the political situation.[83] This would be a non-novel solution,[84] and indeed caretaker governments have worked well in Britain,[85] although we have not tended to recognize caretaker governments as such, rather as Monsieur Jourdain spoke prose most of his life without knowing it.

The second dissolution[86]

The election of a hung Parliament could set a constitutional time bomb ticking in that a resulting minority government might be defeated on a vote of confidence, or a coalition government might disintegrate, so that another general election might be sought, perhaps within a very short time of the inconclusive poll. Could—and would—the Prime Minister's request be refused? How could the existence and viability of an alternative administration in the existing House of Commons, the appointment of which might vitiate the need for another election, be tested? How could the Queen be assured that if she were to refuse a dissolution to one Prime Minister she would not be forced quickly to grant one to his successor? In addressing such questions I hope to suggest an approach which would throw most of the burden of responsibility on to the party Leaders.

It is beyond doubt that the Sovereign can refuse a request for a dissolution of Parliament: the difficulty lies in identifying the situations in which such action would be constitutionally appropriate. That identi-

---

[82] Of course, if the Prime Minister insisted on resigning he could not be required to stay in office.

[83] As did Mr Heath on the day after the February 1974 general election.

[84] Sir Ivor Jennings has written that 'It is essential to the parliamentary system that a Cabinet should be formed, and the Cabinet must remain until its successors have been appointed': op. cit., p. 57.

[85] See Butler, op. cit., chapter 4.

[86] On dissolution generally, see B. S. Markesinis, *The Theory and Practice of Dissolution of Parliament* (1972); Eugene A. Forsey, *The Royal Power of Dissolution of Parliament in the British Commonwealth* (1943), especially chapters 3 and 4; H. V. Evatt, *The King and His Dominion Governors* (1935).

fication is made more awkward by the fact that no dissolution has been refused this century, something which could wrongly be seen as evidence that any refusal would become an acceptance if pressed. But this negative fact proves no more than that no Prime Minister has improperly requested a dissolution, and that therefore the Sovereign has had no reason to refuse. George V certainly considered that the granting of a dissolution was not automatic, so that the cardinal convention of the constitution that the Sovereign acts on ministerial advice was subject to this exception at least.[87] That view is underpinned by the weight of opinion of writers,[88] politicians,[89] and a King's Private Secretary.[90] Few today would assert that the Sovereign has no discretion in the matter—although the prudence of normally granting a dissolution rather than refusing is rightly stressed. And three Governors-General have provided dramatic evidence of actual refusal, in Canada,[91] South Africa,[92] and Australia.[93] Apart from the South African case, acute controversy was caused.

[87] In November 1910, according to one account, he was thought to have decided to refuse any request for a dissolution but to have changed his mind having discussed the issue with senior Ministers: see Jennings, op. cit., p. 424, but cf. Sir Harold Nicolson, op. cit., pp. 125–39 and 150. He was also prepared to refuse a dissolution in 1916 if Bonar Law had succeeded Asquith and had sought one: see Nicolson, op. cit., chapter 18, sections (1) and (2).

[88] See, for example, de Smith, op. cit., pp. 129–31; Wade and Bradley, op. cit., pp. 239–41; Hood Phillips, op. cit., pp. 148–51; Geoffrey Marshall, op. cit., pp. 35–44; Lord Blake, *The Office of Prime Minister* (1975), pp. 60–2.

[89] Harold Macmillan has written 'I ventured to impress upon [Her Majesty] that a P.M. had no right to "advise," a dissolution. "Advice", in the long run, the Crown must today accept. The P.M. "asks" for a dissolution, *which the Crown can agree to or not*': *Riding the Storm*, p. 750, quoting his diary (my italics). Mr Edward Short, as Leader of the House of Commons, wrote a letter, quoted in *The Times*, 11 May 1974, to reject some Labour MPs' opinion that the Queen could not refuse a general election, saying, 'Constitutional lawyers of the highest authority are of the clear opinon that the Sovereign is not in all circumstances bound to grant a Prime Minister's request for a dissolution.'

[90] Sir Alan Lascelles, Private Secretary to George VI, writing as 'Senex' to *The Times*, 2 May 1950.

[91] In 1926 the Governor-General, Viscount Byng, refused Mackenzie King's (the minority Liberal Prime Minister) request, believing that Meighen, the Conservative Leader, could form a government with a majority. Meighen's new government was defeated four days later on a vote of confidence, and he was granted what Mackenzie King had been denied. The Liberals won the general election.

[92] In 1939 the Governor-General, Sir Patrick Duncan, rejected Hertzog's request for a general election. Hertzog wanted a mandate for South Africa to remain neutral in the Second World War; the majority of his Cabinet, led by Smuts, favoured a declaration of war. Hertzog resigned; Smuts became Prime Minister; war was declared, and Smuts remained securely in office for four years before seeking and obtaining a dissolution.

[93] In 1975 the Governor-General, Sir John Kerr, refused Whitlam's request for a Senate, rather than a general, election. The Governor-General subsequently dismissed Whitlam's government and appointed the Leader of the Opposition as Prime Minister, and he recommended a general election which he won. See further Gough Whitlam, *The Truth of the Matter* (1979); Sir John Kerr, *Matters for Judgment* (1978); Gareth Evans (ed.), *Labor and the Constitution 1972–1975* (1977).

Against that background I wish to make three propositions.

(1) If a government continues in office as a minority administration after an inconclusive general election obtained by its Prime Minister and is immediately defeated on an amendment to the loyal address in reply to the Queen's Speech, there is no precedent for such a Prime Minister seeking a second dissolution; rather, there is ample precedent for him to resign. Baldwin resigned in just that circumstance in 1924. Any such request would be improper because it would smack of an attempt to get a recount of the electorate's first decision (a decision recorded at the Prime Minister's asking). If any such request were made, it would rightly be rejected. Such a refusal of ministerial[94] advice could be said to involve the indirect dismissal of the government.[95]

(2) If either a minority or coalition government is formed from a hung House of Commons and the new Prime Minister had not obtained the first dissolution, then a request by him at any time for a general election should be granted—although I will argue shortly that the alternative course of the Queen seeking another administration should not be ruled out. The first part of this proposition can be demonstrated from the 1974 hung Parliament. Harold Wilson clearly assumed that, since he had formed the minority Labour government in March 1974, a dissolution was his for the asking at the time of his choosing (and certainly if the opposition parties were to defeat his government on a vote of confidence).[96] That assumption, it is submitted, was entirely right. His predecessor Mr Heath had been granted the February 1974 dissolution, so that Mr Wilson's request would be his first; and Mr Heath and Mr Thorpe had shown in their abortive talks in February that a Conservative-Liberal coalition could not be formed from that House. A Prime Minister in a position similar to that of Harold Wilson would, like him, have a clearer right to a dissolution the longer the hung Parliament were to last, as that Parliament would have done its job for a period and there could be no convincing allegation that he was really seeking an improper recount[97]. Equally, the Queen would not want to look for an alternative government in such a case.

---

[94] Geoffrey Marshall, op. cit., chapter 3, powerfully challenges the assumed right of a Prime Minister alone to recommend a dissolution without Cabinet approval.

[95] By analogy with the events leading to Edward VIII's abdication: if the King had insisted on marrying Mrs Simpson contrary to the government's advice the government would have felt obliged to resign. Might a government which had been refused a general election decide in certain circumstances to accept that refusal and stay in office?

[96] See his speech at High Wycombe, 14 March 1974.

[97] In the event the February 1974 Parliament lasted seven months.

(3) If a Prime Minister of either a minority or a coalition government in a hung Parliament were to ask for a general election, even for his first time, in order to forestall another majority and workable grouping supplanting his administration, then again refusal would be defensible if that alternative grouping in fact existed. Suppose that, after an inconclusive general election, a Conservative-third party coalition were formed but that eventually a disagreement on some central issue arose. Suppose further that the third party threatened to resign and join a willing Labour Party in a new majority coalition in return for an agreed programme. The Conservative-third party Prime Minister might recommend an immediate election to thwart the coup. The Queen would be required to reconcile two conflicting constitutional principles, the one being that she must accept ministerial advice (here, to dissolve), the other being that a person with a parliamentary majority behind him has the right to be Prime Minister (here, the head of the proposed new coalition). In favour of Her Majesty applying the second principle would be the facts that the Prime Minister would be seeking a dissolution with the improper motive of trying to prevent his ouster from office by an adverse parliamentary majority, and also that a new majority government could be installed without the need for a general election. If the Queen were to apply that second principle and refuse a dissolution, the government would resign and the new Labour-third party administration would take office.

Inherent in the second and third propositions is the question of the presence of an alternative majority government in the existing House of Commons. One major reason in favour of the 'automatic theory' of dissolution is the predictable allegation of bias which would be made against the Queen if she were to refuse a general election to the Prime Minister in the mistaken belief that another government could be formed, and could carry on without an election, when in the event that new government were forced to seek, and was granted, the very thing which had been denied its predecessor.[98] I suggest that, as with the primary decision whether to commission a minority government or a coalition on the return of a hung Parliament, those party Leaders who were wanting to form a majority coalition (so as here to remove the need for dissolution) would have to make public an agreed and watertight package concerning the majority government in waiting. Nothing less than that would do if the Queen were to feel sufficiently confident to

[98] As with Lord Byng: see note 91 above.

take the novel course of refusing a dissolution of Parliament and of bringing about a new administration. This would, in a way, be an example not of revolutionary royal interventionism but of the Queen giving effect to the wishes of Members of Parliament—it would once again be the proper recognition of political decisions, politically arrived at.

Events in Ontario in 1985 give significant support for my approach. Ontario has a system of government which, within the Canadian federation, is similar to Britain's. Elections to the 125-seat Legislative Assembly have to take place every four years, but earlier dissolution is possible. The Premier is appointed by the Queen's representative in the province, the Lieutenant-Governor, and is usually the Leader of the majority party in the Assembly: indeed, the Progressive Conservative Party had enjoyed such a majority for decades. In 1985 the Premier, Mr William Davis, asked for a dissolution from the Lieutenant-Governor, Mr John Black Aird, which was granted. The result gave the Progressive Conservatives fifty-two seats, the Liberals forty-eight, and the New Democrats twenty-five. Mr Davis decided to form a minority government; the Liberals and the New Democrats, meanwhile, formally agreed on a two-year programme of government, including an agreement that there should be no general election within that period. The Conservatives' Speech from the Throne was duly defeated and a motion of no confidence in Mr Davis's government was passed. The Lieutenant-Governor had caused it to be made clear informally that, if the Premier were to ask for a second dissolution, that request would be denied as there was a viable alternative government waiting in the Assembly which, as the result of its public pact, would have a very fair prospect of governing for a least two years. Not surprisingly, Mr Davis made no such request, but resigned, and the Leader of the Liberal Party was appointed Premier.

This Ontario episode shows, perhaps, in the British context that the 'automatic theory' of dissolution is dead (assuming that it ever lived); that a minority government, having received one dissolution, will not receive another dissolution, if beaten on an early vote of confidence; that a published copper-bottomed party pact on an alternative government can avoid any embarrassment of having to grant a dissolution to one head of government having refused it to his predecessor; and that an informal communication of the Queen's attitude, in response to the published agreement of some party Leaders prepared to take over the government without a dissolution, avoids, among other things, the general embarrassment of the tendering of formal ministerial advice and its formal rejection.

Of course it would be less controversial for the Queen to accept a request to dissolve Parliament than to seek an alternative. I have, however, posed three cases which could arise in a hung Parliament in which a royal refusal would be possible.

Conclusions

I have tried to develop several themes in this chapter. One is that the Queen is ideally placed to moderate between any competing wishes of party Leaders in a hung Parliament, and indeed that she has ample expertise at her disposal to enable her to do so. Another is that procedures which would scarcely be radically new could be followed so as to enhance the neutrality of the head of state and to continue the historical responsibility of politicians to resolve political questions posed by an inconclusive general election. If, for example, they wanted to achieve the unusual results of either a coalition administration, or the refusal of a sitting government's request for a dissolution and the appointment of a replacement government from the existing House, then the burden would be on the party Leaders involved to present the Queen with a public, watertight guarantee of a successful outcome before she would be justified in making such novel constitutional departures. A linked theme is that, in any prolonged succession crisis, it would be part of the politicians' duty through a caretaker government to ensure the efficient discharge of government until that crisis was ended.

Whenever a hung Parliament is elected, prudence, the current attitudes of the Conservative and Labour Leaders, together with potentially misleading precedents might well produce a minority government rather than a coalition, and consent to a requested second dissolution rather than a refusal of it. But new factors (such as significant political opinion in favour of the coalition of parties in a hung Parliament) might combine with old truths (especially that party Leaders are transient and that MPs prefer office to opposition) so as to make different outcomes possible.

4

The Transfer of Power

Before a new Prime Minister or government can take office the outgoing Prime Minister or administration must resign. Such resignations will arise in one of a number of ways. First, if a government is unambiguously defeated at a general election and one opposition party is returned with a majority of seats in the new House of Commons,[1] the modern practice is for that government to resign without waiting to meet Parliament. Secondly, a Prime Minister may be forced to quit through illness or old age, or may die in office; or he may voluntarily decide to retire, there being no question of a change in the party in power. In the last thirty years the Churchill, Eden, Macmillan and Wilson administrations have ended in this way. Lastly, the resignation of a Prime Minister and his immediate reappointment may be used as a device to show that the whole political basis of the government is to change. So in 1915 Asquith resigned in order to form a coalition government, so as to prosecute the war better than his Liberal administration could have hoped to do; in 1931 MacDonald resigned so that he could form the 'National Government' immediately to succeed his minority Labour government, and in 1945 Churchill resigned on the break-up of the war coalition so that a caretaker Conservative government under him could be installed pending the general election.

The constitutional consequences of those three political scenarios are very different. In the first (where the whole government is to resign after electoral defeat) the Prime Minister will obtain an audience of the Sovereign and resign. This carries with it the resignation of the entire administration, and his colleagues will cease to operate as Ministers and will leave their departments as soon as they have cleared their desks. In the second case (where only the Prime Minister, as an individual, is to go) as soon as the procedures for selecting a successor have been accomplished[2] the Prime Minister will see the Queen and resign—but that act does not cause or signal the resignation of any other Minister. In

---

[1] The consequences of the return of a hung Parliament were considered in chapter 3.
[2] See chapter 2.

this context Harold Wilson somewhat misstated matters in a letter to all his former Cabinet colleagues after he had resigned in 1976. He wrote that he had resigned that day, and continued:

. . . as you will know, this carries with it the resignation of the whole of the present Administration. This does not require other Ministers to tender their individual resignations to Her Majesty; but they should, of course, regard their offices as at the disposal of my successor. Meanwhile, I ask all Ministers to carry on the necessary administration of their Departments until a new government is formed.[3]

Mr Wilson's resignation did not, however, carry with it the formal resignation of the whole of his government, as indeed the last sentence of his letter quoted makes clear. Unless they were reshuffled or dropped, all Ministers stayed in the same offices under his successor. Their offices were at Mr Callaghan's disposal in a political sense, certainly: but Ministers did not leave office unless they were actually disposed of, and even then, because all Ministers are appointed by the Queen, they did not cease to be Ministers until they had resigned in the prescribed manner. Most of Mr Wilson's Ministers continued in the same offices under Mr Callaghan and they did not have to be reappointed to office. In the third—and unusual—situation (in which the Prime Minister is to stay but the whole basis of his administration is to change) the Prime Minister will resign and be reappointed, but there is no uniform practice on whether all the other Ministers, too, will resign in the first instance. In 1945, after the Labour Party had decided that the war coalition should be dissolved and that a general election should take place, Churchill decided to form a caretaker Conservative government. He resigned at noon on 23 May, and was reappointed at 4 p.m.[4] Churchill had not asked Ministers to place their posts at his disposal or to resign. Many of the Conservative coalition Ministers were in fact confirmed in the new administration, so appointments or reappointments were not needed for them; Labour and Liberal Ministers, of course, left office. On the other hand, when Asquith was in effect forced in 1915 to accept a coalition so as to stave off a potentially ruinous Conservative attack on the conduct

---

[3] I am grateful to Lord Wilson of Rievaulx for permission to quote from his letter.

[4] Churchill's romantic view of the royal prerogative ensured this time interval so as to emphasize the King's freedom of choice in selecting a Prime Minister: see Sir John Colville, *The Fringes of Power* (1985), p. 601. As the Conservatives had a majority of 180 at the time, Churchill was scarcely risking the loss of his office. He recommended for the same reason that a whole day elapse on his retirement in 1955 before the Queen sent for Eden—even though Eden had been his nominated heir since 1942: Anthony Eden, *Full Circle* (1960), p. 266.

of the Admiralty,[5] the Prime Minister asked for the resignations of all his colleagues.[6] And in 1931 the Labour Cabinet told MacDonald to inform the King that they had placed their resignations in his hands.[7] Clearly if a Prime Minister is to reconstruct the political basis of his administration he does not (like Asquith) need to obtain resignations because all members of the unreconstructed government will regard their portfolios as being at his disposal.

When Ministers are to leave office so as to clear the way for a transfer of power, it is, of course, the substance that excites interest, not the formalities of how and when the resignations of politicians take place. The media will ensure that the public knows, for example, that a government rejected by the electorate in effect removes itself once the Prime Minister has resigned, or that after an ailing Prime Minister has retired his successor will decide which of his inherited pack to keep and which to discard. But how as a matter of law do Ministers cease to hold office?[8] A resignation may be express or implied. So a Minister leaving the government will submit a formal letter of resignation, but the resignation of one who is merely being reshuffled is implicit on his appointment to the new post. In the case of those ministerial appointments which require some formal document to give effect to them (a point which will be explained later), that document will include an express revocation of the previous holder's appointment. The Lord Chancellor and the Chancellor of the Duchy of Lancaster alone now retain the right of audience of the Queen to surrender their seals. The earlier practice by which other resigning Ministers who had seals of office would personally deliver them up to Her Majesty has been discontinued, and their seals are simply collected by the Privy Council Office. Private audiences for such Ministers are, however, usually arranged later as a matter of courtesy so that thanks may be offered and farewells made.

The Prime Minister takes office

The Prime Minister is always a Privy Councillor.[9] Since 1961 every new Leader of each of the main political parties in opposition on or soon after

---

[5] See Roy Jenkins, *Asquith* (Fontana edn., 1967), p. 402.

[6] See J. A. Spender and Cyril Asquith, *Life of Lord Oxford and Asquith* (1932), ii. 164–6.

[7] See David Marquand, *Ramsay MacDonald* (1977), p. 635.

[8] I am most grateful to the Clerk of the Privy Council, Mr G. I. de Deney, for his kind help on the questions how in law and practice Ministers cease to hold, and take up, office. With his permission, a memorandum which he wrote for me appears in a slightly edited form as Appendix C.

[9] On the Privy Council, see S. A. de Smith, *Constitutional and Administrative Law* (5th edn., 1985 by H. Street and R. Brazier), chapter 7.

his election as Leader has been admitted to membership of the Privy Council (if not already a member) on the advice of the Prime Minister.[10] And if a Cabinet colleague is to take over a resigning Prime Minister's administration, he too will be a Privy Councillor by virtue of his membership of the Cabinet. Thus today every person who is likely to assume the office of Prime Minister will normally possess this qualification.[11] When a party Leader receives the sweet summons to Buckingham Palace[12] to take office, he will be orally appointed Prime Minister, and sometimes will kiss the Queen's hand to signify his acceptance and his loyalty: the kissing of hands may be taken as read.[13]

He will have achieved the supreme prize: but other gifts attach to it, namely the offices of First Lord of the Treasury[14] and Minister for the Civil Service.[15] Most Prime Ministers have taken the title of First Lord of the Treasury: indeed, the last not to was Lord Salisbury from 1895 to 1902, when his nephew Arthur Balfour led the House of Commons and took the title of First Lord. In practical terms, the Prime Minister resides at 10 Downing Street as First Lord of the Treasury; and since 1937 no Prime Minister would wish the other office on to someone else unless he wanted his own services to be offered free during his incumbency, because the Ministers of the Crown Act of that year provided an annual salary of £10,000 for the 'Prime Minister and First Lord of the Treasury'. The equivalent provision today is in the Ministerial and other Salaries Act 1975.[16] Despite this statutory recognition of the fact that those two posts will always now be combined, a Prime Minister will formally receive the title of First Lord of the Treasury by taking the oath of office as First Lord at a later ceremony at which his first batch of Ministers are sworn in.[17] Since the creation of the Civil Service Department in 1968—and despite its abolition in 1981[18]—the Prime Minister

[10] This may be seen partly as an honour and partly as a means whereby the party Leaders can be briefed by the Prime Minister on defence or other sensitive matters 'on Privy Councillor terms'— that is, on the understanding that they do not reveal the details of the briefing to others. Mr Robert Maclennan was not, however, made a Privy Councillor when he became Leader of the SDP in 1987.

[11] The last not to was MacDonald in 1924. Labour had never held office before, and the King formally admitted him to membership some hours before appointing him Prime Minister: Marquand, op. cit., p. 304.

[12] Other venues are possible: in 1908 Asquith had to travel to Biarritz where Edward VII was holidaying in order to be appointed Prime Minister.

[13] Harold Wilson, *The Labour Government 1964–1970: A Personal Record* (1971), p. 2.

[14] On that office, see Harold Wilson, *The Governance of Britain* (1976), chapter 5.

[15] Another Minister is charged with day-to-day civil service matters.

[16] Section 1(1) and Schedule 1.

[17] Harold Wilson, *The Labour Government 1964–1970*, p. 7.

[18] See 1968 S.I. No. 1656; 1981 S.I. No. 1670.

has also taken the title of Minister for the Civil Service. This gives him significant powers and duties in relation to the civil service, and it is unlikely that any Prime Minister, in the absence of further institutional change, would forgo it. In normal circumstances a Prime Minister would today take on no other additional departmental responsibility, given the vast burdens which he must carry as head of the government; there is, however, no legal or conventional reason why he should not take to himself a number of other offices if he wishes. When Prime Ministers have done this in modern times, peculiar conditions have persuaded them to do so: thus Asquith temporarily became Secretary of State for War in 1914 during the Curragh crisis;[19] Baldwin retained the office of Chancellor of the Exchequer for five months after becoming Prime Minister in 1923 during McKenna's convalescence;[20] MacDonald was his own Foreign Secretary in 1924 largely because he considered no one else to be qualified;[21] Churchill throughout his war premiership, and from 1951 to 1952, and Attlee for the first seventeen months of his premiership in the aftermath of war were both Minister of Defence. The nearest any other Prime Minister has come this century to taking on another department of state was in 1967 when Mr Wilson, in order to strengthen the position of the Department of Economic Affairs, took personal charge of it with a Secretary of State to assist him. In the event, he relinquished that charge the following year and the Department was wound up in 1969.[22]

Matters legal, conventional, and political

Once he has been appointed to office, the first task facing a new Prime Minister is the selection of personnel for his administration. In 1900 the total number of salaried Ministers was sixty; by 1950 that number had risen to over eighty; today it is 105.[23] Filling all those posts is obviously a

[19] See Jenkins, op. cit., chapter 19.

[20] In the event Neville Chamberlain took the post because of insuperable difficulties which McKenna had in finding a seat.

[21] See Marquand, op. cit., pp. 299–300. In 1929 he reluctantly agreed to make Henderson Foreign Secretary.

[22] For an explanation of his decision, see 762 HC Deb. 1585–8 (11 April 1968).

[23] On the various ministerial titles, see chapter 7. There are additionally a number (currently 40) of Parliamentary Private Secretaries, each appointed directly by a Minister from the back benches of his party. They act as general parliamentary (but not ministerial) assistants. The consequences of acceptance of the job of PPS is to bind the holder by the doctrine of collective responsibility, breach of which can lead to dismissal by the Prime Minister. The total number beholden to the Prime Minister is, as a result, nearly 150.

major operation (although as will be explained later the formation of a Cabinet is normally straightforward).

The main legal (although in practice not particularly irksome) restraint concerns the total number of MPs who may be appointed Ministers. So as to impose some limit on prime ministerial patronage, by statute not more than ninety-five MPs may sit and vote in the Commons and hold ministerial office at any one time, whether paid or not.[24] If a Prime Minister wishes to exceed that number of Ministers in the Commons, he must procure the passage of legislation.[25] As far as pay is concerned, it is true that individual Ministers occasionally take office without drawing a salary—as did Lord Young in Mrs Thatcher's Cabinet—but this may be regarded as somewhat exceptional. For all the rest the Ministerial and other Salaries Act 1975 provides[26] that specified salaries may be paid to no more than 105 Ministers at any one time.[27] Should this provision not prove adequate, a Prime Minister could still properly fill additional offices without pay and provided that not more than ninety-five Ministers were MPs, or he could invite Parliament to legislate afresh. For the rest, the choice of Ministers will be made in deference to convention, politics, and (to a limited extent) the Queen.

By convention, all Ministers must be or must become members of the House of Commons or of the House of Lords;[28] a Minister without a seat may be appointed, but he must obtain a seat in one or other House within a reasonable time or resign. The broad mass of potential Ministers to whom power is to be transferred will have been returned to the House of Commons or will be peers, or could quite quickly be made peers. Problems can, however, occur where the seatless individual concerned is to remain or become a Minister in the Commons. Thus Ramsay MacDonald was Lord President of the Council and his son Malcolm Colonial Secretary under Baldwin at the general election of November 1935, at which they both lost their seats; they remained in office and were returned at by-elections the following February. But there can be a risk in relying on a by-election. Thus Frank Cousins, the general

---

[24] House of Commons Disqualification Act 1975, s. 2(1). If the limit is exceeded, those appointed in excess may not sit or vote in the Commons until the excess is reduced to 95: ibid., s. 2(2).

[25] As happened in 1964 when the Ministers of the Crown Act 1964 raised the number from 70 (which it had been since 1957) to 91; there was a further increase by the Ministers of the Crown Act 1974, to the present level of 95. As a temporary measure, those appointed in excess could continue as Ministers but not sit or vote in the Commons.

[26] Section 1(1) and Schedule 1.

[27] Which may be altered (which in practice means raised) by Order in Council: ibid., s. 1(4).

[28] General Jan Smuts was Minister without Portfolio in Lloyd George's war coalition from June 1917 to January 1919 without a seat in either House, but that is explained by the exigencies of war.

secretary of the Transport and General Workers' Union, was not an MP when in October 1964 he was appointed to the Cabinet in the new post of Minister of Technology; Patrick Gordon Walker had lost his seat at Smethwick at that election but was none the less translated from his shadow post to be Foreign Secretary. Two sitting Labour MPs were persuaded to accept, with some reluctance, life peerages in order to cause by-elections which the new Ministers fought; Cousins was returned at Nuneaton, but Gordon Walker lost Leyton and a government majority of almost 8,000, the electors not responding as kindly as their counterparts further north to such a device.[29]

Two special cases historically have been the Lord Advocate and the Solicitor-General for Scotland. As a result of a shortage of Scottish MPs or peers with appropriate legal and other qualifications, particularly under Labour governments, appointments have been made to those offices from time to time from people outside Parliament. Since 1969, however, the Lord Advocate, as the senior Scottish Law Officer, has been given a life peerage when not an MP, and from 1974 to 1987 both Ministers were members of one or other House. But what was becoming an expectation that the usual convention of parliamentary membership would apply to both Ministers received a check when Mr Peter Fraser remained Solicitor-General for Scotland despite having lost his seat at the 1987 general election.

Again by convention, if the ministerial head of a department is in the Lords then at least one of his ministerial team will be in the Commons to represent him there. So, for example, when Lord Young was appointed Secretary of State for Employment in 1985, the Paymaster General, Mr Clarke (who was also in the Cabinet) was designated as his representative in the Commons (an arrangement which was continued when Lord Young was switched to be Secretary of State for Trade and Industry, and Mr Clarke Chancellor of the Duchy of Lancaster, in 1987). But there is no equivalent rule for the bulk of Ministers who are departmental heads in the Commons: the small band of Ministers in the Lords must do the best they can to put the government's case in the upper house. This can stretch the abilities of even the most able Minister who will have to answer well outside his own portfolio.

This leads to the question, resolved through a mixture of convention,

---

[29] Gordon Walker took Leyton at the 1966 general election and returned to the Cabinet as Minister without Portfolio. Sir Alec Douglas-Home was Prime Minister in 1963 without a seat between the disclaimer of his peerages and winning the Kinross by-election.

political convenience, and a small dash of law, of which Ministers are required to sit in one House rather than the other. Most Ministers will perforce sit in the Commons. That House is the representative chamber; party political dogfights take place there; the government will need as much persuasive influence as possible from its ranks in the Commons the better to present its case; the Commons has asserted its superiority (at least since 1911) over the Lords (even though the latter body is still, confusingly, referred to as the upper house). In short, political reality will ensure that all (or practically all) sensitive ministerial posts will be held by MPs. The Treasury team[30] will all be in the Commons, for that House has total control over finance. But what of the Foreign Secretary? The appointment of a peer as Foreign Secretary is always unpopular with the Opposition, but it cannot be said that any convention now subsists (even if it ever existed) which requires the holder of that office to be in the Commons. After all, Lord Halifax was appointed Foreign Secretary in 1938 at a critical time in European affairs;[31] and the appointments of Lord Home from 1960 to 1963 and Lord Carrington from 1979 to 1982 demonstrate that, if a Prime Minister is prepared to withstand Opposition criticism, there is really no substantial reason why the Foreign Secretary should not be in the Lords,[32] especially as appropriate ministerial arrangements are always made in the Commons.[33] Equally, there is no reason why other senior, non-Treasury Ministers like the Home Secretary or the Secretary of State for Defence should not be peers.[34] The Lord Chancellor, by the custom of the ages, will, however, be a member of the House of Lords. This is assumed to be the case by the Ministerial and other Salaries Act 1975[35] which provides that he shall be paid 'at such a rate as together with the salary paid to him as Speaker of the House of Lords' will amount to a specified sum. So if a future government wished

[30] The Chancellor of the Exchequer, Chief Secretary, Financial Secretary, Economic Secretary, and Minister of State.

[31] Chamberlain was, it is true, largely his own Foreign Secretary, and he took Foreign Office questions in the Commons himself.

[32] A significant advantage for him is the reduced amount of parliamentary work in that House. Other Foreign Secretaries in the Lords this century have been Lords Lansdowne (1900–5), Curzon (1919–24), and Reading (1931).

[33] For example, Sir Ian Gilmour and Humphrey Atkins were both successively the senior Foreign Office Minister in the Commons as Lord Privy Seal under Lord Carrington and were both in the Cabinet.

[34] They have been more rarely than the Foreign Secretary—only Viscount Cave from 1916 to 1919 (Home Secretary) and Lord Chatfield for a short period in 1939 (Minister for Co-ordination of Defence—although the Service Ministers were not infrequently peers before the creation of the unified Ministry of Defence under a Secretary of State in 1964).

[35] Section 1(2).

to create a new office of Minister of Justice in the Commons with the Lord Chancellor fulfilling that role,[36] legislation would be needed to remove the judicial functions from him[37] and to amend the 1975 Act so as to place his salary on a par with other Cabinet Ministers: obviously he could no longer be paid the amount now provided for the Lord Chancellor as Speaker of the House of Lords. The Prime Minister will need to make other ministerial representation in the House of Lords. At least one Cabinet Minister other than the Lord Chancellor will need to be a peer so as to be Leader of the House of Lords, the government's business manager there. Other junior Ministers will also be appointed in the Lords, although the total number of salaried Ministers in that House will rarely exceed twenty out of a total administration of slightly over a hundred.

Particularly following a general election which produces a change of party government, a new Prime Minister may wish to make alterations in the machinery of government to reflect the introduction of fresh policies.[38] So, for instance, the return of the Labour government in 1964 after thirteen years in opposition not surprisingly heralded several changes in the governmental machine—in particular, the introduction of four new departments of state each headed by a Cabinet Minister,[39] one other new department outside the Cabinet,[40] and a number of alterations of status at junior ministerial level.[41] Mr Heath entered office in 1970 also committed to major changes in the machinery of government, especially the merger of a number of ministries into giant departments, and the creation of a Central Policy Review Staff.[42] Not all new Prime Ministers, it is true, succumb to the temptation to make structural changes so as to presage significant alterations in policy from that of their predecessors: after all, no one would deny that Mrs Thatcher made radical changes in

[36] On a possible Ministry of Justice, see the end of chapter 11.

[37] For example, as President of the Supreme Court, ex officio judge of the Court of Appeal, and President of the Chancery Division (Supreme Court Act 1981, ss. 1(2), 2(2), 4(1), and 5(1)); and his ability to sit in the judicial House of Lords and the Judicial Committee of the Privy Council would have to be abolished (Appellate Jurisdiction Act 1876, s. 5 and Judicial Committee Act 1833, s. 1).

[38] See generally Sir Richard Clarke, 'The Machinery of Government' in William Thornhill (ed.), *The Modernization of British Government* (1975), pp. 63–96.

[39] The Department of Economic Affairs, the Ministry of Technology, the Ministry of Overseas Development, and the Welsh Office.

[40] The Ministry of Land and Natural Resources.

[41] For example, the appointment of a 'Minister of Disarmament' (a Minister of State at the Foreign Office); another Minister of State at the Foreign Office was also the Permanent Representative at the United Nations.

[42] See 'The Reorganization of Central Government', Cmnd. 4506 (1970).

policy from that of her predecessor after 1979, but only one department represented in the Labour Cabinet (Prices and Consumer Protection) was abolished by her and no new department was created.[43] In these matters an innovative Prime Minister will have advice available to him from the Secretary to the Cabinet. Indeed, in a typically British arrangement in 1964, Harold Wilson as Leader of the Opposition had a secret meeting, with the Prime Minister's approval, with the Head of the Civil Service three months before the general election, during which he outlined some of his ideas for changes in departmental responsibilities, and received helpful comments and advice.[44] This courtesy is probably now extended routinely to the Leader of the Opposition before each general election; in 1987 it was offered to Dr Owen and Mr Steel as well. Within the Cabinet Office there is a permanent machinery of government division which is available to the Prime Minister and the Secretary to the Cabinet for detailed information and advice about any proposed rearrangements.[45] The days are long gone since primary legislation was needed to give effect to such changes. A more efficient procedure was introduced in 1946[46] and today is contained in the Ministers of the Crown Act 1975. An Order in Council may provide for the transfer to any Minister of any function previously exercised by another Minister, or for the dissolution of any government department and consequent transfer of functions;[47] it may make changes in the departments of the office of Secretary of State, or changes in the functions of a Secretary of State;[48] and it may change the style and title of a Minister. Provision is made for parliamentary scrutiny of such Orders.[49]

A device open to a Prime Minister to allow one of his Ministers to pursue a particular policy or carry out some function without even the use of such subordinate legislation is the deployment of a senior Minister holding a sinecure. Thus the Lord Privy Seal in MacDonald's second government was responsible for unemployment; the Paymaster-General from 1985 in Mrs Thatcher's Cabinet was also unofficially (and more

---

[43] The Departments of Trade and of Industry, which had been separated in 1974, were remerged in 1983; the Civil Service Department and the Central Policy Review Staff were abolished, in 1981 and 1983 respectively. There has been speculation recently that the Department of Health and Social Security might be split into two departments.

[44] Harold Wilson, *The Labour Government 1964–1970*, p. 4.

[45] I am grateful to the Cabinet Office for confirmation on this point.

[46] Ministers of the Crown (Transfer of Functions) Act 1946.

[47] Ministers of the Crown Act 1975, s. 1(1).

[48] Ibid., s. 2

[49] Ibid., s. 5. See further chapter 7.

positively) styled Minister for Employment as Commons representative of the Employment Secretary; there are many other examples. It is invariably more controversial when such a Minister holds a party office as well: the Chairman of the Conservative Party is not infrequently a Minister.[50]

The Cabinet chooses itself

The Cabinet today largely selects its own membership. Despite the evolution of prime ministerial government, a new Prime Minister has strikingly little freedom of choice in ordinary circumstances in picking his first Cabinet. Whether this should worry him to any significant degree, however, as possibly restricting the way in which he is able to govern is, as will be explained in the following two chapters, highly doubtful.

Which departments must be represented in the Cabinet? It is possible to identify three distinct periods this century. The first, which may be styled the all-inclusive period, carried over from the nineteenth century up to the outbreak of war in 1914. In that time, filling all the available ministerial offices was to make the Cabinet, as customarily the only offices excluded from it were the Law Officers and the Royal Household appointments.[51] All central government functions could be represented in a Cabinet of up to twenty people—even including some Ministers without departmental responsibilities, such as the Lord President of the Council, the Lord Privy Seal, and the Chancellor of the Duchy of Lancaster. The war made necessary an increase in the number of ministries;[52] the expanding welfare state added others,[53] so that a second, selective period developed in which some offices had to be excluded if the Cabinet were to remain a manageable body. That selection became the more necessary after the return of the 1945 Labour government, with its major extension of governmental responsibilities.[54] This meant that from

[50] Mr Tebbit, for example, was Chancellor of the Duchy of Lancaster from 1985 to 1987 in Mrs Thatcher's Cabinet and also Chairman of the Conservative Party.

[51] At various times between 1900 and 1915 the Chief Secretary for Ireland or the Postmaster-General or the First Commissioner of Works were also left out. The Law Officers and the holders of Household appointments (who are Government Whips) are only rarely in the Cabinet: an example was Sir Gordon Hewart, the Attorney-General, from 1919 to 1922.

[52] Some creations were only temporary, like Blockade and Food Control.

[53] Such as Pensions (1916), Labour (1916), and Health (1919).

[54] So in 1945 the Ministries of Civil Aviation, Food, Pensions, National Insurance, Information, Town and Country Planning, Supply, and (from 1946) the three Service Ministries were not included in the Cabinet.

the First World War up until the 1970s, Prime Ministers had to decide
which departments to exclude from the Cabinet. But with the creation
of giant departments through the merger of existing ministries which
took place from 1968 to 1983[55] there has been a return to an all-inclusive
type of Cabinet of from eighteen to twenty-four members. All departments of state since the early 1970s have been included in the Cabinet.
Since that time, therefore, a Prime Minister has had only peripheral
decisions to make about the exclusion of offices from the Cabinet, really
only involving Overseas Development and Transport.[56]

Thus today a Prime Minister must, on the face of it, be concerned not
with which departments to include in his Cabinet but with which of his
colleagues to ask to join it, although again freedom of action may be
illusory. Some people could hardly be left out, by virtue of their position
in the government party and experience in office and opposition: it
would have been impossible for, say, Mr Whitelaw, Sir Geoffrey Howe,
Mr Prior, Mr Pym, or Sir Keith Joseph at least not to be included in
Mrs Thatcher's first Cabinet. The Shadow Cabinet,[57] too, will find itself
transferred into the substantive Cabinet. The Parliamentary Labour
Party (P L P) elects a fifteen-strong Parliamentary Committee each year
when in opposition to which the Leader has, since 1955, added other
MPs so as to form the Shadow Cabinet, each member having a particular
shadow responsibility. There is a requirement in Standing Order E of the
P L P that all elected members of the Parliamentary Committee be given
seats in the Cabinet, and there is an unwritten expectation in the P L P
that the other members of the Shadow Cabinet will be included as well.
In 1964 and 1974 the entire Shadow Cabinet was given Cabinet office; in
1964 one non-Shadow Cabinet member was brought in, Frank Cousins.[58]
After the 1945 Conservative defeat, Conservative Privy Councillors
were deployed in debates as the occasion seemed to demand: only in a
loose sense did particular Privy Councillors routinely shadow particular

---

[55] Those giant departments are the Foreign and Commonwealth Office (created 1968), Department of Health and Social Security (1968), Department of the Environment (1970), and Department of Trade and Industry (1970)—the latter being split in 1974 and remerged in 1983, the
Department of Energy having been created from it in 1974. The responsibilities of nine former
departments are now carried out in those five, together with (since 1976) a separate Department of
Transport. See further Appendix D.

[56] The Ministry of Overseas Development finally came to rest as the Overseas Development
Administration in the Foreign and Commonwealth Office in 1979.

[57] On which see John Mackintosh, *The British Cabinet* (3rd edn., 1977), pp. 259–61, 536–40.

[58] 1945 is not comparable, as Labour had not been in opposition during the war. From 1940–5
the PLP had elected an Administrative Committee of 12, plus peers' representatives, none of whom
was a Minister.

Ministers. Members were added to the Shadow Cabinet but never sub-tracted; formal minutes were not kept.[59] But under Sir Alec Douglas-Home and Edward Heath the Conservative Opposition adopted fully the Labour strategy of having a formal Shadow Cabinet, with each member discharging a specific shadow responsibility. Thus was the modern Shadow Cabinet system settled in the two main parties by 1964. And since 1964 new Prime Ministers have relied overwhelmingly on their shadow team to make up the Cabinet: its members will, after all, usually have had some years' experience in opposition mastering their shadow departmental duties, and there would need to be a pressing reason why someone should receive a portfolio for which he had had no training in opposition. Although the Leader of the Conservative Party has no party rules to bind him about whom to choose for the Shadow Cabinet, his reliance on that team when the Conservatives come to power can be seen by the inclusion in Mr Heath's Cabinet in 1970 of only two people who had not been in the Shadow Cabinet, and in Mrs Thatcher's Cabinet in 1979 of only three.[60] Moreover, although a Labour Prime Minister is not obliged to give a Minister the portfolio which he has shadowed, it is the occasion when this has not happened that has caused surprise. So, for instance, Richard Crossman and Michael Stewart were each appointed in 1964 to the post which the other had shadowed in opposition.[61] Even under the Conservative system, it has become unusual for shadows to be switched on appointment: Quintin Hogg, for example, had been Shadow Home Secretary before the 1970 general election, and was surprised after it to be given the woolsack by Mr Heath instead of the Home Office.[62]

A Prime Minister taking over a government from a party colleague will find himself a little less circumscribed than if he had just led his party from opposition to power; but he might conclude that widespread changes at what will always be a politically difficult time would not be sensible. Thus the changes made to his predecessor's Cabinet by Eden in 1955 were minimal because he had decided on an early dissolution; Lord Home's had to be a little wider given that two Cabinet Ministers, Enoch Powell and Iain Macleod, refused to serve under him;[63] Mr Callaghan's

[59] See Robert Rhodes James, *Anthony Eden* (1986), pp. 317–8.

[60] Mr Noble (President of the Board of Trade) and Mr Thomas (Secretary of State for Wales); Mr Walker (Minister of Agriculture), Lord Soames (Lord President), Mr Howell (Secretary of State for Energy).

[61] Housing; Education and Science.

[62] See Lord Hailsham, *The Door Wherein I Went* (1975), p. 244.

[63] Harold Macmillan had more room for manœuvre in 1957 as a number of Eden's Ministers wished to retire from politics.

in 1976 were somewhat more extensive, including the settling of an old score by dropping Mrs Castle[64]—but even so nearly all of Mr Wilson's Cabinet stayed in the new Cabinet.

One special case in which prime ministerial appointments to senior office will have external restraints is on the formation of a coalition government, when the views of the Leaders of the other coalition party or parties plainly must be taken into account. So Asquith had to consult Bonar Law in 1915, as did Lloyd George a year later; MacDonald had to rely heavily on Baldwin and Samuel for men and advice in 1931 when forming the 'National Government' (as only nine National Labour men joined him in the entire new administration), and although Churchill in 1940 told Attlee the names of four of the latter's senior colleagues whose services in the government were immediately required, he also asked Attlee for a list of Labour names to consider.[65] Such consultations would be relevant today especially if a hung Parliament were returned and a coalition government were to emerge: any coalition Prime Minister would have to consult and cajole his prospective partner or partners to agree on the disposition of offices.

The Sovereign's influence

During the transfer of power the Sovereign has to perform two roles, the one formal, the other influential. Her formal role is to appoint Ministers to office. Ministers are the Queen's Ministers: by virtue of the prerogative they hold their offices at her pleasure. Of course, the prerogative is overladen by convention, but the prerogative gives her the formal legal power to appoint and to dismiss. That formal position was underlined in a characteristically helpful memorandum which George V wrote for MacDonald when he first came to office in 1924: 'No change', he wrote, 'is made in the constitution of the Ministry until the King's approval has been obtained.'[66] Without appointment by the Sovereign, a Minister in charge of a department of state does not hold office.

The Sovereign's influential role is less easy to gauge. A Prime Minister's audiences of the Sovereign take place with no one else present; no record is kept; what passes is confidential between Monarch and Minister, although the Queen's views, if appropriate, will be conveyed to the

[64] See Barbara Castle, *The Castle Diaries 1974–1976* (1980), pp. 724–5.
[65] See Martin Gilbert, *Finest Hour: Winston Churchill 1939–1941* (1983), p. 315.
[66] See Sir Harold Nicolson, *King George V* (1952), p. 388.

Cabinet.[67] We have to wait for guarded political autobiographies and biographies for scraps of information, and even longer for royal biographies. Undoubtedly the Sovereign may express a view about proposed appointments; but it must be stressed that, although the Sovereign appoints and the Prime Minister merely recommends appointments, the Queen must defer in the end to the Prime Minister's advice. That follows from the cardinal convention of the constitution that the Queen must act on ministerial (and usually prime ministerial) advice.[68] If, unthinkably, she were implacably to resist a particular appointment and the Prime Minister were to refuse to give way, the only (and unreal) alternative open to her would be to dismiss him and to find a more congenial replacement. Constitutional monarchy has come too far for such a retrograde lunge into a mid-Victorian view of royal power.[69]

In exercising her undoubted rights to be consulted, to encourage, and to warn, however, the Queen does comment on proposed ministerial appointments, if only by way of approbation. Harold Macmillan has described the Queen's reaction to the list of his proposed Cabinet in 1957.[70] '[She] seemed to approve the changes. She is astonishingly well informed on every detail. She particularly liked the decision about the Foreign Office[71] and was interested in what I told her about Percy Mills.'[72] On the other hand, while giving way in due course to the Prime Minister's wishes, the Sovereign may require him to justify a nomination. There are three documented instances of this. In 1918, Lloyd George, in reconstructing the coalition after the December general election, submitted the name of F. E. Smith, then Attorney-General, to be Lord Chancellor. George V demurred. He caused his Private Secretary to write to the Prime Minister inviting him to reconsider, on the grounds that Smith was only 47 and had only been Attorney-General for three to four years, so that his appointment would come 'as somewhat of a surprise to the legal profession'. Lloyd George replied that many distinguished Lord Chancellors had attained the office between 30 and

---

[67] Especially if they concern the Sovereign personally, such as the Queen's insistence, contrary to the initial decision of the Cabinet, that her Coronation be televised: see Sir John Colville, op. cit., p. 648.

[68] See chapter 8.

[69] For that reason, examples of Queen Victoria's refusals to accept nominations of Ministers are of interest but of no precedential value today. For them, see Sir Ivor Jennings, *Cabinet Government* (3rd edn., 1959), pp. 62–5.

[70] *Riding the Storm* (1971), p. 189, quoting his diary.

[71] That is, to retain Selwyn Lloyd there despite Suez.

[72] He was an industrialist whom Macmillan brought in as Minister of Power with a peerage.

40, and pressed the appointment: the King replied that 'in the circumstances he could only follow your advice'.[73] The second example comes from 1940 when Churchill recommended the Canadian Lord Beaverbrook as Minister of Aircraft Production. George VI plainly disliked Beaverbrook, and was moved to write a special letter to Churchill on the very day he had been appointed, so taking up the Prime Minister's time with the matter even when military defeat could have been imminent.

... I would like to warn you of the repercussions, which I am sure will occur, especially in Canada, at the inclusion of [Beaverbrook]. You are no doubt aware that the Canadians do not appreciate him, and I feel that as the Air Training Scheme for pilots and aircraft is in Canada, I must tell you this fact. I wonder if you would not reconsider. ... I fear that this appointment might be misconstrued.[74]

Churchill defended his choice, and Beaverbrook was appointed. But there could scarcely be a clearer instance of a royal warning to a Prime Minister over a Cabinet appointment. The final example is both the best known and the least clear. What role did George VI play in suggesting to Attlee in 1945 that Bevin should become Foreign Secretary and Dalton Chancellor of the Exchequer, rather than the other way around?[75] Attlee subsequently denied that the King's advice had moved him;[76] the accuracy of his recollection has, however, been doubted,[77] and Dalton's official biographer devotes a whole chapter to 'the switch' and concludes that it is 'reasonable to suppose that the King's advice was an important factor' in transposing the two nominations.[78]

From these examples it is equally reasonable to conclude that the Sovereign can, and occasionally does, ensure that a nomination to office is reconsidered, thus causing a delay in which a Prime Minister can

---

[73] See 2nd Lord Birkenhead, *The Life of F. E. Smith, First Earl of Birkenhead* (1959), p. 332; Kenneth Rose, *King George V* (1983), p. 233. Rose points out that Smith was actually 46, and that the only Lord Chancellor who had held office under the age of 40 was Jeffreys in 1685, aged 37.

[74] Martin Gilbert, op. cit., p. 316. Churchill recorded that Beaverbrook was at first reluctant to take the job, and that the Air Ministry disliked losing its supply functions—and 'there were other resistances to his appointment . . . [but] I persisted in my view': *The Second World War*, vol. ii, *Their Finest Hour* (1985 Penguin edn.), p. 12.

[75] See Sir John Wheeler-Bennett, *King George VI: His Life and Reign* (1958), p. 638. There is support for the view that the King played a crucial role in Robert Rhodes James, op. cit., pp. 310–11.

[76] *Observer*, 23 August 1959.

[77] By Tom Driberg (1969) 50 *Parliamentarian* at 165.

[78] Ben Pimlott, *Hugh Dalton* (1985), chapter 24 at p. 415. Beginning with George V the Royal Family had disliked Dalton—George VI said that he could not abide him—and that dislike has been suggested as a reason why George VI did not want him as Foreign Secretary: ibid., pp. 414–22.

ponder anew, change his mind, or defend his choice so as to secure the proposed appointment.

Ministers take office

The appointment of over a hundred people to a new administration will always take a few days. If there is urgency in the transition, such as the financial crisis in October 1964, the Prime Minister may secure the appointment of the most senior members of his Cabinet quickly and before the others; otherwise, the whole Cabinet will be selected first, followed by the other Ministers.

Junior Ministers[79] are those who are not in charge of a department of state. Given the all-inclusive nature of modern Cabinets[80] the term 'junior Ministers' today encompasses almost all Ministers outside the Cabinet. Whether a particular junior Minister is actually chosen by the Prime Minister or by the ministerial head of the department in which he is to serve varies from one government to another. Attlee, for example, chose all junior Ministers himself, although he consulted senior Ministers about them, because he thought that a senior Minister might not recognize his own deficiencies and that the Prime Minister should construct a departmental team to take account of them.[81] Macmillan followed suit. He has written that the factors which weighed with him were candidates' suitability and merit; the need to represent different parts of the country and different groups of party opinion; the desire to reward loyalty (but not to punish sincere disaffection); and the need to reflect the views of the senior Ministers in whose departments the junior Ministers would work.[82] Mrs Thatcher appears to have done likewise in appointing all junior Ministers.[83] By contrast, at least at the formation of his last government in 1974, Harold Wilson gave some Cabinet colleagues, like Roy Jenkins and James Callaghan, a free hand to make their own appointments—even to the extent in Mr Callaghan's case of

[79] See Kevin Theakston (1986) 57 *Political Quarterly* 18—an excellent discussion on junior Ministers; and below, chapter 7, for definitions and discussions.

[80] This was discussed above.

[81] Quoted in Kenneth Harris, *Attlee* (1982), p. 406.

[82] Harold Macmillan, op. cit., pp. 189–91.

[83] So, for example, when James Prior as the new Employment Secretary readily agreed to have Patrick Mayhew as an Under-Secretary of State, Mrs Thatcher was pleased, characteristically adding, 'I'm determined to have *someone* with backbone in your department': see James Prior, *A Balance of Power* (1986), pp. 113–14.

agreeing to obtain a peerage for an MP who had just lost his seat so enabling him to become a Minister of State at the Foreign and Commonwealth Office.[84] The names of new junior Ministers are formally submitted to the Queen; their appointment takes effect forthwith on her formal approval of them.

Once his name is approved a new Minister may go at once to his new department.[85] Any formal appointment will come later. There used to be a legal distinction between Cabinet Ministers, who would be sworn of the Privy Council (so as, it was sometimes thought, to apply the Privy Councillor's oath to them and so ensure the confidentiality of Cabinet proceedings[86]), and other Ministers, who were not. If the Sovereign were advised to admit an individual to the Privy Council, that was tantamount to his joining the Cabinet. That distinction is no longer helpful, because since the 1970s even some Ministers of State have been made Privy Councillors.

Ministers achieve office in law in a variety of ways.[87] The Promissory Oaths Act 1868, sections 3 and 5, and Orders in Council made under that Act,[88] require that those Ministers specified in Part I of the Schedule (as amended) to it must take the oath of office. Members of the Cabinet take the oath of office before the Queen in Council. To do so, the person concerned must be a Privy Councillor; if he is not one already, he must be sworn a member of the Council before taking the oath of office:[89] the provisions of the 1868 Act therefore make it a legal requirement that Cabinet Ministers be members of the Privy Council—a case, for once, of law imitating convention. Having taken the oath of office, the new Cabinet Minister kisses the Queen's hands as a courtesy. Other Ministers, specified in Part I of the Schedule and in an Order in Council,[90] take the oath of office before another senior Minister, usually the Lord

---

[84] See James Callaghan, *Time and Chance* (1987), p. 294. According to Mr Wilson's former Senior Policy Adviser, in March 1974 many of the other junior appointments were selected at the suggestion of the Prime Minister's personal staff over lunch: see Bernard Donoughue, *Prime Minister: The Conduct of Policy under Harold Wilson and James Callaghan* (1987), p. 48.

[85] Assuming that he knows where it is. On being nominated Minister of Health in 1952 Iain Macleod left 10 Downing Street and drove to a telephone box to look up the Ministry's address in a phone book: Nigel Fisher, *Iain Macleod* (1973), pp. 85–6.

[86] The oath was not relied on by the Attorney-General in the Crossman diaries case: *Attorney-General* v. *Jonathan Cape Ltd.* [1976] QB 752, and see below, chapter 7.

[87] For the details see Appendix C.

[88] The main one is the Promissory Oaths Order 1939, SR &O. 1939 No. 916.

[89] See Richard Crossman, *Diaries of a Cabinet Minister*, vol.i (1975), p. 29 for an amusing account of the swearing ceremony.

[90] Promissory Oaths Order 1939, SR & O. 1939 No. 916.

President of the Council. Some Ministers receive seals[91] or some other token of their offices; others are appointed by Letters Patent; yet others by a warrant under the sign manual.[92] They do not legally assume office until these requirements have been satisfied. If there are no such requirements in relation to any given office (and junior Ministers fall into that category), the holder of it is legally appointed at the moment when the Queen approves the Prime Minister's list recommending the appointment, and he does not see the Queen in order to assume his office.[93] All Cabinet appointments must be published in the *London Gazette* in order that the Ministers may be paid the appropriate enhanced salaries.[94]

Thus is the administration completed and the Prime Minister may bend himself to his other tasks.

---

[91] When Richard Crossman examined the seals which he had received as the first Secretary of State for Social Services in 1968 he discovered that they had been the seals of the newly defunct Commonwealth Office, with sticky tape over them to change their character: op. cit., vol. iii (1977), p. 233.

[92] That is, a warrant signed by the Queen. See further Appendix C.

[93] Except for the Government Whips who hold Royal Household appointments—Treasurer, Comptroller, Vice-Chamberlain (in the Commons), Captain of the Gentlemen at Arms, and Captain of the Yeoman of the Guard (in the Lords).

[94] Ministerial and other Salaries Act 1975, s. 1 and Schedule 1.

5

The Prime Minister

A careful reading of histories and biographies makes me feel that the power of a Prime Minister has steadily grown. . . . [T]he very complexity of affairs leads to a concentration of authority in his hands (Harold Macmillan, writing in 1972.)[1]

My own conclusion is that the predominantly academic verdict of overriding prime ministerial power is wrong. It ignores the system of democratic checks and balances, in Parliament, in the Cabinet, and not least in the party machine and the party in the country (Harold Wilson, writing in 1976.)[2]

Those conclusions of two former Prime Ministers, the one more or less following the other into office, disclose a divergence of view in the debate about whether Britain has prime ministerial rather than Cabinet government.[3] Both conclusions contain the error which is sometimes made in that debate of offering a final judgement which purports to hold good for the foreseeable future. In practice, however, several variables affect the argument, chiefly the personality of any given holder of the office of Prime Minister. Thus the dogmatic assertion, based on Mrs Thatcher's period in office, that prime ministerial government has finally triumphed over Cabinet government might look most odd after her successor, with perhaps a very different personality and approach, had moved into Downing Street. Any catalogue of a Prime Minister's powers which apparently makes him pre-eminent over his colleagues must always be read with the warning in mind that matters could alter rapidly on a change of Prime Minister.

If the Prime Ministers since 1945[4] are considered for a moment, any

---

[1] *Pointing the Way* (1972), p. 33.   [2] *The Governance of Britain* (1976), p. 8.

[3] On that debate see (arguing the prime ministerial thesis) Richard Crossman, Introduction to Walter Bagehot's *The English Constitution* (1963)—although he was more ambivalent in his 3-volume *Diaries of a Cabinet Minister* (1975–77); Humphrey Berkeley, *The Power of the Prime Minister* (1968); and see (opposing that thesis) Herbert Morrison, *Government and Parliament* (3rd edn., 1964); Patrick Gordon Walker, *The Cabinet* (revised edn., 1972); Harold Wilson, op. cit., Forward and passim; and (for a balanced view) A. H. Brown, 'Prime Ministerial Power' [1968] *Public Law* 28 and 96.

[4] This chapter is broadly confined to that modern period. For a discussion down to 1951 see Sir Ivor Jennings, *Cabinet Government* (3rd edn., 1959), pp. 177–99, and for an enlightening exposé of Cabinets since 1945 see Peter Hennessy, *Cabinet* (1986).

views as to the supremacy or otherwise of the Prime Minister must take
account of very different incumbents: there is no such thing as an
'average' Prime Minister. At one extreme, Winston Churchill from
1951 to 1955 treated Cabinet meetings as great occasions and colleagues
with deference, rarely seeking to rely only on his office to obtain his own
way in defiance of any contrary majority opinion.[5] Then there have been
the relaxed and amusing yet businesslike approaches of Prime Ministers
like Harold Macmillan[6] and James Callaghan,[7] or the efficient styles
epitomized by Clement Attlee or (to a lesser extent) Sir Alec Douglas-
Home, both of whom preferred short Cabinet meetings and an absolute
minimum of unnecessary talk.[8] Then at the opposite extreme to the
peacetime Churchill has been Margaret Thatcher, who according to
ex-colleagues among others is the apotheosis of the imperious style.[9]
Future Prime Ministers will bring their own stamps to bear, thus making
analysis even more imprecise. This chapter will, therefore, largely be
concerned with identifying the sources of any Prime Minister's power
and then with those factors which may collectively be termed his weaknesses, and in that process the nature of the office will be analysed.

The electorate's choice

A Prime Minister has the invaluable political authority of being the
choice (directly or indirectly) of the electorate, an advantage which

[5] See Anthony Seldon, *Churchill's Indian Summer: The Conservative Government 1951–1955*
(1981), p. 106. Churchill's physical and mental powers were in any case in decline: see Lord
Moran, *Winston Churchill: The Struggle for Survival* (1960), chapters 34 ff.; Sir John Colville, *The
Fringes of Power: Downing Street Diaries 1939–1955* (1985), Part IV.

[6] For a description of Macmillan as Prime Minister, see for example Lord Home, *The Way The
Wind Blows* (1976), pp. 191–2; Hennessy, op. cit., pp. 58–60; and his own autobiographical
version in Macmillan, op. cit., chapter 2.

[7] See Phillip Whitehead, *The Writing on the Wall* (1985), chapter 9; and for his own version, see
James Callaghan, *Time and Chance* (1987), chapters 13–17. Mr Callaghan's style was epitomized in
the way in which he arranged the discussion of the terms of the International Monetary Fund loan
in 1976—9 Cabinet meetings over 3 weeks, during which Ministers in effect convinced themselves
that the view of the Prime Minister and the Chancellor that the terms had to be accepted was
inescapable, even though initially the government might have broken up over the issue: see
Callaghan, op. cit., pp. 427–42.

[8] See Kenneth Harris, *Attlee* (1982), pp. 401–18, 427–8, 567: '[H]is object was to get the
meeting over as soon as possible' (ibid., p. 403); Hennessy, op. cit., p. 64 (interview with Lord
Home on his Cabinet style): '. . . the great thing is to be short. People can't bear [waffle].'

[9] Three of her former Cabinet Ministers have attested to this: Francis Pym, *The Politics of
Consent* (1984), chapter 1; James Prior, *A Balance of Power* (1986), pp. 114–19, and chapter 8; Sir
John Nott, speaking on the BBC *Panorama* programme, 4 January 1988.

neither his party nor any other Minister can claim. A general election is today the machinery through which a Prime Minister is chosen. Since the 1945 general election at the latest voters have been offered a choice—sometimes stark—between very different party Leaders: they will vote to keep Mr A in office, or to put in Mr B in his stead.[10] At some elections the personification of a government in its leader will be stronger (as for instance with Macmillan in 1959, or Mr Wilson in 1966, or Mrs Thatcher in 1983 and 1987) than at others (as, say, with Sir Alec Douglas-Home in 1964). But now that general elections are firmly established in the United States presidential mould and are projected to a mass television audience it is most unlikely that any party would now try to win an election by offering a collective leadership with its Leader buried somewhere in it. No party returned to power this century could claim with any justice that it had won despite its Leader—rather, the victorious political parties will acknowledge that, while the nation's boredom with the late government,[11] perhaps exacerbated by that government's loss of steam,[12] taken with the attraction of the successful party's alternative policies, all played their parts, the personalities of the Leaders were vitally important. That concentration of attention on the successful Leader can clearly be seen in most of the six general elections since 1945 at which there was a change of government, and in the 1970 contest a case has been made that Mr Heath won almost despite his party.[13]

Even when someone becomes Prime Minister by succeeding a resigning colleague or at the formation of a coalition, he can still be regarded as the indirect choice of the electorate, for he must be able to count on the support of the existing House of Commons returned by that electorate. Since 1945 Eden, Macmillan, Sir Alec Douglas-Home, and James Callaghan did not come initially to office in the wake of electoral victory, but they became accepted quickly by the majority party in the Commons[14] (and in Mr Callaghan's case he had been elected by a majority of the

[10] This proposition clearly cannot be sustained when a hung Parliament is returned.

[11] The view that 'it's time for a change' will obviously become stronger the longer a government has been in office.

[12] The 1945 Labour government suffered in this way, but it was also physically exhausted by the Conservative Opposition tactics in the 1950 Parliament of keeping Ministers in the House late each night: see Harris, op. cit., chapter 25: 'Struggling On'.

[13] For example, by *The Economist*, 20 June 1970; Whitehead, op. cit., pp. 49–51.

[14] In the case of Eden and Macmillan, both successfully fought general elections as Prime Minister. Sir Alec Douglas-Home (narrowly) and James Callaghan lost the only elections they fought as Prime Minister; in Mr Callaghan's case for most of his premiership he had no parliamentary majority, but until the 1979 vote of no confidence no Commons majority was prepared to assert itself so as to bring about a dissolution.

Parliamentary Labour Party[15]). From his first moments in office, therefore, a Prime Minister is imbued with authority conferred personally (albeit sometimes indirectly) by the electorate.

Power over Ministers

Patronage in relation to Ministers is the most important political power enjoyed by a Prime Minister, for it establishes his supreme place in the eyes of his government and parliamentary party. No one will achieve ministerial office without his approval; his continuing favour is essential to keep office; the deference which this can cause in many cases is clear. It was noted in chapter 4 that at an initial transfer of power to a new Prime Minister there are constraints on his freedom of action. But even at that stage it is possible for a Prime Minister who is both exceptionally determined and sure of his power base to set his policy stamp on his government. The outstanding example is that of Neville Chamberlain in 1937 who, when taking over the 'National Government', was ruthless in excluding anyone who might be an uncongenial colleague—in particular, anyone who might want to resist the dictators and to rearm more quickly. Thus men who were to give full-hearted support for appeasement were appointed—Sir John Simon to Chamberlain's old place at the Treasury, Sir Samuel Hoare to the Home Office, the anodyne Sir Thomas Inskip confirmed as an undemanding and largely ineffectual Minister for the Co-ordination of Defence. Eden was retained at the Foreign Office, but Chamberlain was always his own Foreign Secretary, directing foreign policy from Downing Street advised by a civil servant;[16] and Eden only lasted nine months, resigning in the end over Chamberlain's insistence on negotiating with Mussolini.[17] Chamberlain summed up his appointments policy in the words, 'I won't have anyone who will rock the boat'.[18] Of course, he was exceptional: most Prime Ministers want to begin with an administration which reflects the various strands of opinion in their party, but Chamberlain showed what

[15] See chapter 2.

[16] Briefly from January 1938 by Sir Robert Vansittart as Chief Diplomatic Adviser, then by Sir Horace Wilson. On the conflict between Chamberlain and the Foreign Office, see Viscount Templewood, *Nine Troubled Years* (1954), pp. 259–61.

[17] At the crucial Cabinet on 19 February 1938 it is instructive that 14 Ministers supported Chamberlain's proposed initiative and only four expressed any reservations: Robert Rhodes James, *Anthony Eden* (1986), p. 193.

[18] Quoted in R. J. Minney (ed.), *The Private Papers of Leslie Hore-Belisha* (1960), p. 130.

can be done; and (as will be seen later) Mrs Thatcher achieved the same result of having an agreeable Cabinet within a couple of years of coming to power.

In making his first appointments to office a Prime Minister will decide on the relative seniority of Cabinet Ministers—the 'pecking order'—and whether to have a deputy. It is not unnatural for Ministers in the Cabinet to wish to be seen near the top of it so as to reflect not only their individual importance but also the importance in the government of the departments which they head.[19] The pecking order can now be seen[20] in the list of Cabinet Ministers published fortnightly in *Hansard*. Occasionally the ranking can stretch credulity, as for example in 1985 when Mrs Thatcher transferred Mr Leon Brittan from the Home Office to the Department of Trade and Industry; this move was regarded by everyone save the Prime Minister and Mr Brittan as a demotion, caused by her desire to bring in new blood to the upper reaches of the Cabinet in the shape of a new Home Secretary, Mr Douglas Hurd: but Mr Brittan remained ranked fifth as he had been as Home Secretary.[21] Some Ministers can be sensitive about their rankings: one such was Michael Stewart in 1966 who, when moved to the Department of Economic Affairs from the Foreign Office to make way for George Brown, insisted on remaining at number three in the Cabinet.[22] The pecking order is reflected in the seating arrangements at the Cabinet table. The most senior Ministers sit to the Prime Minister's right[23] and left and also directly opposite him, the others being seated further away with the most junior at the ends. A purely practical advantage which this gives to Ministers sitting near to the Prime Minister is that it is easier to catch his eye[24] and to hear and be heard.[25] No doubt this can irritate junior members, but it is a physical

[19] An incidental consequence is that if two Ministers are to meet, the more junior is expected to offer to travel to the other's department: Wilson, op. cit., p. 23, note 1.

[20] It was formerly seen in a List of Ministers and Heads of Public Departments published regularly by HMSO.

[21] When Mr Brittan resigned in 1986 following his part in the Westland affair, his successor as Secretary of State for Trade and Industry was ranked bottom of the Cabinet list.

[22] On the other hand a minority of Ministers claim to be unconcerned by the order, and Mr Wilson wrote (op. cit., p. 23, note 1) 'In Attlee's Government I did not even know what my pecking-order position was.'

[23] The Secretary to the Cabinet sits on his immediate right.

[24] Prior, op. cit., p. 117. There is some room for prime ministerial manoeuvre: one day Lord Home found the Cabinet Secretary changing the places at the Cabinet table; and he explained that '[t]he Prime Minister cannot stand Enoch Powell's steely and accusing eye looking at him across the table any more, and I've had to move him down the side': Lord Home, op. cit., p. 192.

[25] This is why the Cabinet table was altered into a coffin-shape in 1961 so that those at the ends could be a little less out of affairs.

reminder of the Prime Minister's ability to put them away from, or near, the centre of authority.

The designation of a Minister as deputy to the Prime Minister has caused some controversy and even denials that any office of Deputy Prime Minister exists.[26] That agitation will be allayed if the reasons for nominating a deputy are more carefully analysed than is usually the case. There are three different reasons why an identified deputy to a Prime Minister may be appointed. The first—and, today, illegitimate—reason could be to indicate that Minister who is recognized by the Prime Minister as the crown prince who would in due course succeed him. Such a designation has become pointless since 1965, which was the year in which the Conservative Party came into line with the Labour and Liberal Parties in establishing a formal election procedure to choose a successor to a resigning Leader. But such a designation must be noted here because it was that sort of attempt to establish a succession which first caused the objections to be voiced that appointment to the office of Deputy Prime Minister was 'unconstitutional', and it has clouded the office ever since.

When Churchill returned to Downing Street in 1951 he included in his list of Ministers submitted to the King the name of Anthony Eden as 'Secretary of State for Foreign Affairs and Deputy Prime Minister'. George VI immediately instructed that the second title be deleted on the ground that the '. . . office . . . does not exist in the British constitutional hierarchy', and because it could be seen as an attempt to restrict his prerogative of choice,[27] especially as it was generally assumed that Churchill would retire within a short time—he was, after all, 76 in 1951.[28] The King's objection was sustainable in the days when royal rather than party choice was (as least in theory) the norm, although even then it should be remembered that it was George VI who had asked Churchill in 1942 formally to record whom he should send for in the event of Churchill being killed by enemy action.[29]

[26] For example, R. A. Butler in the House of Commons stated that 'the office of Deputy Prime Minister is not known to our constitution': 561 H. C. Deb. 1448–9 (6 December 1956); in 1961 Macmillan noted in his diary that '[t]he Queen has in the past rightly pointed out that there is *no* such official post': *At the End of the Day* (1973), p. 41. For George VI's objections, see below.

[27] Sir John Wheeler-Bennett, *King George VI: His Life and Reign* (1958), p. 797.

[28] No one would have predicted a premiership lasting 3½ years. In the event Churchill's succession by Eden was entirely uncontroversial—'No two men have ever changed guard more smoothly', was Churchill's assessment, recorded in Eden's *Full Circle* (1960), p. 265.

[29] The King's request had been prompted by Churchill's impending (and scarcely safe) flight to see Roosevelt in Washington. Churchill had recommended that Eden be sent for in the event of his death: Martin Gilbert, *The Road to Victory* (1986), p. 125.

The second reason for nominating a deputy arises in the Labour Party, where the post of Deputy Leader is recognized by the party's constitution.[30] There will, therefore, always be a Labour Deputy Leader, and he will naturally be second only to a Labour Prime Minister when the Deputy Leader is in the government. Thus in Attlee's Cabinet, Morrison was Attlee's party and ministerial deputy,[31] and in Mr Wilson's first Cabinet, George Brown was his deputy[32] until Brown resigned from the government in 1968,[33] as were Edward Short and later Michael Foot in the 1974 to 1979 Labour Cabinets.[34] Given the elective nature of the Labour Deputy Leadership it would be difficult to imagine the holder being other than deputy to the Prime Minister.

George VI raised no objection to Attlee receiving the formal style of Deputy Prime Minister in 1942.[35] This is partly explicable[36] as an example of the third reason why a Prime Minister might nominate a deputy: administrative efficiency and convenience. As Churchill's wartime unofficial and later official Deputy Prime Minister, Attlee exercised broad authority in home and economic affairs, leaving Churchill to concentrate on the prosecution of the war. More generally, someone must chair the Cabinet, and Cabinet committees normally taken by the Prime Minister, and answer his questions in the House of Commons,[37] in his absence; perhaps even (according to a Prime Minister's taste) more formally taking charge of the government while he is away. R. A. Butler fulfilled that role from 1955 in a variety of offices in the Conservative government,[38] as did Mr (later Viscount) Whitelaw in Mrs

[30] *Labour Party Constitution* (1981), cl. VI; *Standing Orders*, No. 5(?)–(4). See Appendix B. The Deputy Leader becomes Acting Leader automatically if the Leader, for whatever reason, becomes permanently unavailable, and retains that position until a new Leader is elected at a party conference.

[31] As Lord President of the Council and Leader of the House of Commons, and then as Foreign Secretary 1951.

[32] As First Secretary of State and Secretary of State for Economic Affairs, and then as Foreign Secretary.

[33] Brown was Deputy Leader from 1960 to 1970. On his resignation from the government in 1968, Michael Stewart was moved up to number two in the pecking order.

[34] Edward Short was Deputy Leader 1972–6, Mr Foot from 1976–80. Both were Lord President and Leader of the House of Commons.

[35] Attlee was first Lord Privy Seal in 1940 in the War Cabinet, then Deputy Prime Minister from 1942 to 1945, being also Dominions Secretary (1942 to 1943), and Lord President (1943 to 1945).

[36] The King had already taken advice about the succession: see note 29.

[37] When Mrs Thatcher's deputy William Whitelaw went to the Lords in 1983, the Leader of the House of Commons was charged with taking her parliamentary questions in her absence.

[38] Lord Privy Seal 1955–9, Leader of the House of Commons and Home Secretary 1957–62, First Secretary of State 1962–3.

Thatcher's Cabinet.[39] Arrangements which promote efficient continuity of government are plainly beneficial, and no objection can be made to the use of a deputy for such a purpose.

The actual title accorded to a deputy has varied. Some deputies to the Prime Minister have had to rely on their second place in the pecking order with no distinctive title (such as Lord Whitelaw, first as Home Secretary, then as Lord President of the Council). Only Attlee has actually enjoyed the formal title of Deputy Prime Minister, from 1942 to 1945: the style which has been used more frequently is that of First Secretary of State, invented in 1962 by Macmillan for Butler. That title denoted Butler's superiority over any other Minister while avoiding the objections which had been raised eleven years earlier to the style of Deputy Prime Minister.[40] On the succession of Sir Alec Douglas-Home in 1963 the office of First Secretary of State was left vacant;[41] on Labour's return to power the following year George Brown, as Deputy Leader, was appointed to the Department of Economic Affairs with the additional rank of First Secretary of State. It was subsequently held by two other Ministers in that Labour government,[42] but has not been used since 1970.

In summary, the arrangement of a general pecking order of Cabinet Ministers and the singling out of one of them as a deputy to the Prime Minister provide yet another reminder to Ministers that the Prime Minister is chief among them.

As a government ages its personnel will naturally change. Some Ministers will wish to leave for personal reasons, perhaps as the result of illness, or to start or resume another career.[43] Additionally, a Minister

[39] Mr Whitelaw had been nominated Deputy Leader of the Conservative Party in 1975 by Mrs Thatcher on her election as Leader, that Deputy Leadership being appointive. He remained Deputy Leader after his resignation from the government in 1988. There has only been one other Deputy Leader, Reginald Maudling (from 1965–72).

[40] Butler recorded in his memoirs that '. . . I was named First Secretary of State and invited to act as Deputy Prime Minister, a title which can constitutionally imply no right to the succession and should (I would advise, with the benfit of hindsight) be neither conferred nor accepted': *The Art of the Possible* (1971), p. 234.

[41] Perhaps because Butler had twice been deputy and on neither occasion became Prime Minister, which no doubt contributed to his view (note 40 above) of the value of the title. He was ranked second to Sir Alec, as Foreign Secretary.

[42] Michael Stewart 1966–68 while also Secretary of State for Economic Affairs and then as Foreign Secretary, and Barbara Castle 1968–70 as Secretary of State for Employment and Productivity. The title was, however, debased on both occasions as neither was deputy to the Prime Minister.

[43] A recent example was afforded by James Prior, who retired from Mrs Thatcher's Cabinet in 1984 to become chairman of GEC.

may need to be moved to another post, possibly because he has become stale; or a Minister may need to be removed from the government because he has ceased to be an asset (although he may be the last to recognize it). Again, a reshuffle may be needed to give the administration a fresher, and perhaps younger, look, and to give promotion to junior Ministers and talented back-benchers. Thus must be played a game of musical ministerial chairs in which some unlucky contestants lose their places. For these reasons a Prime Minister's power over the futures of his colleagues increases as time passes.

In a draft for his Introduction to Bagehot's *The English Constitution* Richard Crossman wrote that a Prime Minister can liquidate the political careers of his rivals as effectively as any Soviet leader.[44] A Minister holds office at the Prime Minister's sufferance: he holds office at the will of the Crown and can be removed at any time on the Prime Minister's recommendation. Yet there are political limits within which any reshuffle must be set: to say with Crossman that the Prime Minister's power in this context is absolute is to overstate the case. Some Ministers are essential to the very continuance of a government, and could not be dropped even if the Prime Minister wanted to do so: thus, for example, the acceptance by Butler of Sir Alec Douglas-Home as Harold Macmillan's successor in 1963 was crucial to the latter's success in forming a government. Butler was guaranteed a place for as long as he wanted it. Michael Foot's personal relationships with trade union leaders throughout the 1970s, too, ensured him office in the 1974 to 1979 Labour government, dependent as it was on its concordat with the unions. Moreover, at junior ministerial level, no Prime Minister could possibly have personal knowledge of all potential Ministers, and he will have to lean heavily on the Chief Whip, and perhaps the Leader of the House of Commons, for information about candidates' suitability for office, parliamentary performance, particular strengths, and so on. No Prime Minister could begin to reshuffle an administration of over a hundred people from a total pool usually of over 325 government MPs free of such dependency. That advice could deny a Prime Minister the chance to bring in a favourite, whether at Cabinet or junior level. A prime example can be seen in Mrs Thatcher's scarcely concealed desire to restore Mr Cecil Parkinson to her Cabinet as quickly as possible after his resignation from it in 1983: the advice of her deputy Lord Whitelaw and

---

[44] His publishers protested: he cut out the sentence: three years later, after he had been a Cabinet Minister, that deletion was his only regret about the Introduction: John Mackintosh, *The British Cabinet* (3rd edn., 1977), p. 439.

of the Chief Whip not to do so (on the ground that it would encourage the media to give him and thus the government unfavourable publicity) delayed until his return until after the 1987 general election.[45] A Prime Minister will also normally need and wish to maintain the political and geographical balance of the Cabinet and administration. Moreover, the complexity of a general reshuffle must be borne in mind: however much a Prime Minister wishes to replace X, move Y, and bring in Z, the pieces at the end must fit. Harold Wilson has described any substantial reshuffle as 'a nightmarish multidimensional jigsaw puzzle'.[46]

Some Prime Ministers have relished and others have dreaded reshuffles: the undoubted power to move colleagues into, about, and out of the administration is subject to the incumbent's attitude towards the task. It was Asquith who first described as a vital attribute of a Prime Minister the ability to be a good butcher, in the sense of being able to remove ineffective colleagues without hesitation. In modern times Attlee has been acclaimed the best butcher. Always a man of few words (for example, when asked during a cinema newsreel interview whether he had anything further to say about the impending general election, he replied 'No'), he was rarely drawn into an explanation for a requested resignation. Once he did bluntly explain that a Minister was going 'Because I don't think you are up to the job';[47] very occasionally he might use a metaphor from his beloved cricket that the Minister concerned had had a good innings and it was time to go back to the pavilion and hang up the bat.[48] Mrs Thatcher may now be ranked with Attlee. Her 1979 Cabinet, based on her own choices for the Shadow Cabinet, was a balance between monetarists and non-monetarists, 'one of us' and 'wets'.[49] Yet by the end of 1981 five 'wets' had been shuffled out,[50] leaving only Mr Walker and Mr Prior to represent the liberal Conservative tradition (and by 1984 Mr Prior had retired from politics). Mrs Thatcher's increasing confidence meant that after two years of her premiership she was able to be as ruthless as Neville Chamberlain in

[45] See further chapter 7.

[46] Op. cit., p. 34. When planning one reshuffle he found that he had to find an office for a Yorkshirewoman, but the only vacancy was at the Welsh Office, and he had to start again.

[47] Mackintosh, op. cit., p. 440.

[48] Quoted in Wilson, op. cit., p. 34.

[49] James Prior believes that Mrs Thatcher was responsible 'for pinning this name on her opponents. . . . In due course it became a badge of honour, but it was hardly conducive to loyalty in Cabinet': op. cit., p. 134.

[50] Lord Soames, Sir Ian Gilmour, Mr St. John-Stevas, Mr Howell, and Mr Carlisle. Lord Carrington and Mr Atkins, who tended to 'wetness', left the government in 1982 over the Falklands: see chapter 7.

excluding possible rockers of the boat. And her style could be as direct as Attlee's in making changes: Mr Pym records that her first words to him after the 1983 general election were, 'Francis, I want a new Foreign Secretary.'[51] Harold Macmillan, on the other hand, would probably not have rejected the title of the worst butcher since 1945. He regarded the duty of asking colleagues and friends to leave the government as very disagreeable;[52] possibly his requests for the resignation of a record seven Cabinet Ministers in 1962 in an attempt to restore the fortunes of his faltering government might never have come to pass had he found it easier to move colleagues more regularly.[53] The title of intermediate butcher could be accorded to Harold Wilson. He seemed reluctant to lose ministerial colleagues entirely, moving them instead from one job to another with the result that Ministers only had an occupancy of any given department of about eighteen months. So, for example, from 1964 to 1970 Mr Wilson had three different Secretaries of State for Economic Affairs, four Foreign Secretaries,[54] three Home Secretaries, and six Lord Privy Seals.[55]

Now in a reshuffle it is rare for the language of dismissal to be openly employed. If a Minister is to go, he is asked for his resignation. An advantage of this courteous approach is that such a Minister can save face by giving his own reasons for his departure (ill health, a desire to return to private life, and so on). None of Macmillan's 1962 purge was called a dismissal: even Selwyn Lloyd stuck to the euphemistic usage in his resignation letter when he wrote to the Prime Minister, 'You have told me that you would like me to resign and this I willingly do'—a sentence which aptly shows that the line between dismissal and resignation is in

[51] Op. cit., p. ix.

[52] *Pointing the Way*, p. 32.

[53] For his account, see *At the End of the Day*, pp. 84–98. He concluded that it was a serious error to try to mask the blow to Selwyn Lloyd (who was asked to resign as Chancellor) by combining his resignation with a general reshuffle.

[54] Michael Stewart held the office twice. Mr Wilson lost his first Foreign Secretary, Patrick Gordon Walker, when he failed to win a by-election following the loss of his seat at the general election.

[55] Lords Longford and Shackleton each held the office twice. Richard Crossman wrote in 1968 that 'I am now convinced that one of Harold's greatest mistakes is his constant reshuffling. Too many job changes in three years means a tremendous decline in the power of the politician over the Civil Service machine. . . . The truth is that a Minister needs eighteen months to get real control of his Department. . . . It's the constant fiddling with Ministers and shifting them round which has undermined the central strategy of this Government.' *Diaries of a Cabinet Minister*, vol. iii (1977), p. 78. Colin Turpin in his excellent *British Government and the Constitution: Text, Cases and Materials* (1985), pp. 128–9, records that from 1918 to 1971, seven leading offices were each held for an average of 27 months; that from 1964 to 1970 the median tenure of office was 19 months; and that of 85 Ministers appointed in 1979, 60 had been moved at least once by 1983.

some cases a truly fine one. Dismissals actually so called are, however, rare: Sir Ivor Jennings identifies a number from Victorian times, but none in this century.[56] Two dismissals have occurred since Jennings's last edition. In 1975 Mr Eric Heffer, Minister of State for Industry, broke the terms of the Cabinet's 'agreement to differ' over the referendum on continued membership of the EEC [57] by making a speech in the House of Commons (significantly from the back benches) urging the electorate to vote to withdraw:[58] Mr Wilson immediately wrote to him to say that 'I am . . . informing the Queen that you have ceased to be a Minister.' And in 1981 Mr Keith Speed, a junior Minister in the Ministry of Defence,[59] made a public speech against cuts in naval spending which he knew the Cabinet had approved but which had not been announced. He was sacked.[60] Both dismissals were dramatic demonstrations of the ability of a Prime Minister to dispense with a ministerial colleague who is not prepared to toe the line.

Resignation can, of course, come from a Minister for political reasons: he may decide that he can no longer accept collective responsibility, and leave the government of his own volition, making a parliamentary statement and other explanations of his reasons.[61] The resignation can, in part, be designed to bring about a change in government policy or, at the least, to cause the Prime Minister and government to defend its policy and perhaps cause it embarrassment in doing so. But history shows that such resignations are never fatal to a government, and usually result (after a few days or weeks) in the resigner entering the political wilderness for good. It would, after all, take an exceptional memory that could reconstruct even a partial list of Ministers who have resigned in the last

---

[56] Op cit., pp. 209–14.

[57] On which see chapter 7.

[58] 889 H. C. Deb. 1325–32 (9 April 1975).

[59] He was Parliamentary Under-Secretary of State for Defence for the Royal Navy; a consequence of this episode was the Prime Minister's decision no longer to have junior Ministers representing the three separate Services.

[60] In a letter from Mrs Thatcher of 19 May 1981.

[61] Jennings, op. cit., p. 267 asserts a convention that '[a] Minister who resigns from the Cabinet usually desires to make an explanation in Parliament. Since this involves an explanation of Cabinet discussions, he must secure the Queen's consent. For this purpose he asks permission through the Prime Minister.' A similar formulation was given more recently in the Report of the Radcliffe Committee of Privy Counsellors on Ministerial Memoirs, Cmnd. 6386 (1976). I doubt, however, whether this is still the case. Mr Michael Heseltine, for example, made a very full press statement of the reasons for his resignation on 9 January 1986, including details of what had taken place in Cabinet meetings, and made a speech indicating his reasons during a debate on the Westland affair: 89 H. C. Deb. 1098–1107 (15 January 1986). But he has told me in a private letter that he 'was neither aware nor made aware of such a convention'.

forty years on policy grounds;[62] most never held ministerial office again, Harold Wilson and Sir Edward Boyle providing the two exceptions thus far;[63] even the resignations of the Chancellor of the Exchequer and two Treasury Ministers in 1958 because they could not persuade the Cabinet to accept further cuts in government spending could be shrugged off by the Prime Minister as 'little local difficulties'. And the refusal of Iain Macleod and Enoch Powell to join Sir Alec Douglas-Home's administration in 1963 did not affect his ability to form a government: Macleod later became Chancellor of the Exchequer in 1970, but Enoch Powell never held office again.

In the hands of a confident Prime Minister, therefore, the power to appoint, reshuffle, and discard Ministers is, for his ambitious parliamentary colleagues, essential to the inception and continuation of their ministerial lives. It gives the Prime Minister an authority over them which is unrivalled by any other person or body.

The extent to which any Prime Minister controls Cabinet meetings[64] and decisions will in large part again turn on his disposition and political strength. By custom the agenda for the weekly meeting, normally held on Thursday, is decided by the Prime Minister, and the order of items is fixed by him in consultation with the Secretary to the Cabinet. John Mackintosh believed that this procedure enables the Prime Minister to keep any item which he does not wish discussed off the agenda indefinitely.[65] Harold Wilson, on the other hand, while accepting that in theory that could happen denies that it could take place in practice, because any Minister could raise an issue orally under either of the two standing first items on the regular agenda, namely parliamentary affairs,

---

[62] A full list can be compiled from David and Gareth Butler, *British Political Facts 1900–1985* (1986), pp. 85–6, and John Mackintosh, op. cit., p. 448, and by adding the names of Ian Gow (who resigned as Minister of State at the Treasury in 1985 over the Anglo-Irish Agreement) and Michael Heseltine (who resigned as Secretary of State for Defence in 1986 over aspects of the Westland affair).

[63] Perhaps Mr Heseltine may prove a third exception.

[64] There are descriptions of Cabinet meetings in, for example, Harold Wilson, op. cit., pp. 45–62; John Mackintosh, op. cit., chapter 21; Patrick Gordon Walker, op. cit., chapters 2, 6, and 9.

[65] Op. cit., p. 449. He cites as evidence (for example) Attlee's refusal to tell the Cabinet about British work on atomic weapons until tests had taken place (an example disputed by Gordon Walker, op. cit., pp. 87–91); Chamberlain's attempt to raise House of Lords reform at a meeting in June 1927, which Baldwin thwarted by leaving the room and thus ending the Cabinet; and Hore-Belisha's wish to circulate memoranda in April 1939 advocating partial mobilization, which Chamberlain forbade (although later he allowed him to raise the issue orally). See also Jennings, op. cit., pp. 245–9.

and foreign and Commonwealth affairs.[66] Those views are not in such conflict as they may seem to be, for a resolute Prime Minister who possesses enough authority could both direct that a particular item be not put on the agenda, and also stop a Minister who tried to raise it orally dead in his tracks; conversely, of course, a less secure chairman might be able to do neither. Take as an illustration the 'great unmentionable' during the first three years of the 1964 Labour government, devaluation. No Minister who took the view that the possibility of devaluation ought to be discussed—not even George Brown—could challenge Mr Wilson's implacable determination (fully buttressed by his Chancellor of the Exchequer) that it was not an option open to the government: such a Minister could neither have had the issue put on the agenda nor have raised it orally, for to do so would have invited immediate rebuff and a request for his resignation. That Cabinet's agenda was totally controlled in the sense that such a request or attempt would just not have been made, not in the sense that one was actually made and rejected. A contemporary analogy might be that of a member of Mrs Thatcher's Cabinet who might wish to have debated an alternative economic or industrial strategy, plainly at odds with that of the Prime Minister and a clear majority of her Cabinet: it would be pointless—perhaps politically fatal—for him to seek to do so. On the other hand, a Prime Minister who saw that support for a particular policy of his was ebbing away simply could not take such an autocratic view and would find it increasingly difficult to block discussion.

Naturally, the lower down the agenda an item might be the less likely it is that sufficient time would be available to take it; that knowledge will obviously weigh with a Prime Minister in approving the order of business. Cabinet Ministers are absurdly overworked people[67] and they will have other pressing matters to get to (including lunch); the nearer the clock moves to 1p.m. or 1.30 p.m. the more amenable they will be to a suggested adjournment. Equally, a Prime Minister would be pushing his luck too far if an important matter appeared very low on the agenda, was deferred, and reappeared in the same place at a subsequent meeting.

It does not tell us very much about the position of a Prime Minister in relation to his Cabinet to note that only the former has the authority to summon a meeting of the latter, and that without the Prime Minister's

---

[66] Op. cit., pp. 47–8. A. H. Brown agrees with Mr Wilson on the ground that no Minister whom he had interviewed could recall a suggested item being kept off the agenda: [1968] *Public Law* at 51.

[67] Exhaustion is frequently referred to in the Crossman and Castle diaries.

consent no meeting of Ministers is able to make Cabinet decisions,[68] for if enough Cabinet colleagues were to insist on a meeting it would be inconceivable that their chairman would refuse to call one. But a *consequence* of that authority is of great importance, namely a Prime Minister's decision on the frequency with which the Cabinet should have regular meetings. In the premierships of Attlee and Churchill the Cabinet regularly met twice a week during the parliamentary session.[69] At the latest by 1964 those regular meetings had been halved to one a week, and that remains the frequency today. Now the pressure of government business has not slackened so as to permit fewer Cabinet meetings—indeed, the amount of business has at the very least remained the same as it was from 1945 to 1955. The reason for the cut in the number of Cabinet meetings is the increased use of Cabinet committees and *ad hoc* groups of Ministers. That development is best explained in the context of a full examination of the Cabinet as an institution, which will be undertaken in the next chapter.[70] Here it must be stressed that that development for two reasons represents a significant expansion of prime ministerial power. First, the fewer Cabinet meetings held, the fewer opportunities there will be for Ministers to raise and to discuss issues that the Prime Minister would prefer not to be raised and discussed: the occasions are fewer at which the Prime Minister may have to justify and defend his actions (or inactions). Secondly, the use in particular of informal, *ad hoc* groups allows a Prime Minister to select colleagues who would be likely to further his preferred solutions. An example has been reported of the way that Mr Heseltine's attempt to get additional spending for the inner cities after the 1981 riots was thwarted by the use of a packed *ad hoc* group of Cabinet Ministers. Prime Ministers have apparently altered the machinery of government so that Cabinet government has about half as many opportunities to represent an irritant or even a challenge to the Prime Minister as was the case thirty years ago.

[68] When an emergency Privy Council meeting was summoned late at night on 14 March 1968 to approve an Order in Council proclaiming a bank holiday during a gold crisis, George Brown (who did not know what was going on) arranged a meeting of Ministers and asked the Prime Minister over the telephone to join them. The Prime Minister retorted that if a Cabinet meeting was wanted 'they should come over to No. 10 for a properly convened one', which they did: Harold Wilson, *The Labour Government 1964–1970: A Personal Record* (1971), pp. 508–9. George Brown, *In My Way* (Pelican edn., 1972), chapter 9. Brown resigned over the incident.

[69] Peter Hennessy, op. cit., pp. 99–100. The Secretary to the Cabinet refused to give him statistics on the frequency of Cabinets since 1955. Gordon Walker notes that the Conservative Cabinets from 1951 to 1959 met twice a week, but that Harold Wilson reduced the regular meetings to once a week: op. cit., p. 101.

[70] See especially the second section of that chapter.

A Prime Minister's ability to influence discussion and decisions at Cabinet meetings will, yet again, vary according to his character and his personal authority. The various styles since 1945 were indicated at the beginning of the chapter. The prime ministerial thesis seems triumphant (so far) in the person of Margaret Thatcher—utterly clear in her opinions, putting her views on any given topic first so that the Cabinet knows her position from the start, not wishing to waste time having arguments,[71] tending to the authoritarian.

Votes may be taken at Cabinet meetings on minor procedural matters but not normally otherwise: rather, the Prime Minister sums up and states what he takes the Cabinet's decision to be.[72] A Prime Minister, however, could scarcely use a summing up, however skilful, to disguise by sleight of hand a Cabinet opinion one way as a decision in the opposite sense. There can, though, be a little more leeway in the compilation of the minutes.[73] The main responsibility for drafting the minutes lies with the Secretary to the Cabinet or his deputy, who bases them on notes made by him at the meeting. The minutes are promptly circulated to Cabinet Ministers. Harold Wilson has written that the Prime Minister does not see them before that circulation, and that the Prime Minister will only be consulted at the drafting stage in cases of doubt over what had been decided.[74] But Richard Crossman is not entirely alone in asserting that the minutes may bear only a loose relationship to what was actually said or concluded.[75] Mr Michael Heseltine objected that the Secretary had not recorded his protest at a Cabinet meeting over the cancellation of a Cabinet committee which he had understood was due to take place to discuss an aspect of the Westland affair.[76] As a result, the Secretary issued a brief correcting note, but in the minutes 'as finally issued' there was still no reference to his protest.[77] This was not a minor matter, as the cancellation of that committee meeting was an important factor in Mr Heseltine's resignation as Defence Secretary; but when those Cabinet minutes are made public there will, presumably, be no

[71] A phrase she had used in an interview in the *Observer*, 25 February 1979, before becoming Prime Minister.

[72] Clement Attlee, 'The making of a Cabinet' in Anthony King (ed.), *The British Prime Minister*; Harold Wilson, *The Governance of Britain*, p. 55; Edward Heath, the *Listener*, 22 April 1976 (who, speaking for his premiership and for those of Eden, Macmillan, and Douglas-Home, in whose Cabinets he had sat, confirms this statement).

[73] The formal term is 'Cabinet conclusions'.

[74] Harold Wilson, *The Governance of Britain*, p. 56.

[75] See *Diaries of a Cabinet Minister*, vol. i (1975), pp. 103–4.

[76] See chapter 6.

[77] He made this point in public statements explaining his resignation.

reference in them to that protest and a little piece of history will have been rewritten by the Cabinet Secretary, who could have understood the Prime Minister's wishes without consulting her at all.

Through his authority over the Cabinet agenda, the frequency of Cabinet meetings, the use of Cabinet committees and *ad hoc* groups of Ministers, his chairmanship, and to some extent through his influence over the minutes, a Prime Minister is able to guide the decision-making of the Cabinet.

The highest profile; patronage; dissolution

A Prime Minister's power is greater than the sum total of his powers, and a significant reason for this is that his profile is higher than any other Minister's. In Parliament, he answers Prime Minister's Questions every Tuesday and Thursday, whereas other Ministers have a chance to shine only once every three to five weeks. His skill at such frequent gladiatorial contests can enhance his prestige with Ministers and back-benchers[78]— and, through television and radio news reports (and the occasional live radio broadcast), with the general public. The Prime Minister will also decide when to intervene in debates, unlike all other Ministers who will normally only speak in debates touching their departmental responsibilities. In that sense a Prime Minister has no portfolio and every portfolio and can put his personal prestige behind an issue or a particular Minister. In the country, the Prime Minister can frequently be news: his visits and speeches, these days carefully arranged into 'photo opportunities' for newspaper photographers and television cameramen, concentrate attention on his doings and sayings. If he wishes to make an announcement over television or radio by ministerial broadcast, he can do so. Abroad, Prime Ministers have represented the country in personal attempts to improve international relations, a development started with Chamberlain's visits to Hitler and accelerated by the onset of easy air travel. The epitome was Harold Macmillan, who during his premiership clocked up a tour of the Commonwealth, a visit to Moscow, meetings with Presidents Eisenhower and Kennedy, and the 1960 Paris summit; others, since, have made similar though not such extensive journeys. Today, if the Prime Minister wants to discuss an issue at length with the

---

[78] All Prime Ministers who have written of their time in office have explained the intense preparations which are made for Question Time.

President of the United States, it is taken for granted that he will fly to see him. At the many regular international gatherings, too, the Prime Minister will represent the United Kingdom—the biennial Commonwealth heads of government meetings, European Council gatherings, economic meetings of the western industrialized nations, and so on. Additionally, important visitors from abroad are received personally by the Prime Minister.[79] The electorate must be forgiven if it concludes that the Prime Minister *is* the government, a conclusion which the Prime Minister might not wish to correct.

It is, of course, important to a Prime Minister that his pre-eminence be appreciated by the public, and to that end he controls his party's public relations. To Attlee and Churchill in the pre-television age[80] any such notion as public relations would have seemed entirely foreign. Eden's suspicion of the BBC led to television being kept at arm's length during his premiership. Macmillan was the first Prime Minister to appreciate the need to communicate his policy and to project himself to the voters through television. He also appointed the Minister without Portfolio in his Cabinet to co-ordinate government information from the various departments. Edward Heath took responsibility for this into Number 10, employing Donald Maitland, a career diplomat, as head of his Press Office.[81] The Prime Minister can control which Ministers appear on the media to put the government's case and also which journalists are favoured to receive personal guidance over and above his Press Secretary's briefings 'on lobby terms'.[82] General elections have increasingly been fought through the medium of television, the 1987 contest being totally geared by all the main parties to the communication of image through 'photo opportunities'. Labour's election campaign was generally agreed to have been its most effective ever, and even better on television than that of the Conservative Party. That the government still convincingly won the election shows that policies remain vital, but Prime Ministers will clearly have to communicate to the best possible effect through television if they are to succeed electorally.

[79] The greatest coup in this respect was when Macmillan persuaded President Eisenhower to appear in a live television broadcast from 10 Downing Street in which the President gave him his personal endorsement shortly before the 1959 general election.

[80] A film was shown during the television programme *Television and Number 10* on 12 November 1986 of the only television screen test to which Churchill agreed. It was appalling.

[81] A Labour Prime Minister is more hemmed in by committees on these matters.

[82] This is the cosy system under which journalists accredited to the Westminster Lobby receive whatever information the government's spokesman (frequently the Prime Minister's Press Secretary) wishes to give out; the quid pro quo is that the source be not exactly identified. *The Guardian* and *Today* newspapers withdrew from the Lobby in 1986; the *Independent* did not join it.

The Prime Minister's supremacy is also marked out by his unique relationship with the Sovereign. That relationship will be explored in chapter 8: here it will suffice to note that his right of audience enjoyed once each week during the parliamentary session is not shared by any other Minister.

Another area of a Prime Minister's power concerns patronage and honours. In 1977, Mr Callaghan listed in a written answer in *Hansard* those public appointments which were either in his gift, or which he recommended, as Prime Minister. The reply exceeds four columns[83] and even then excludes ecclesiastical appointments, the choice of Ministers of the Crown and certain civil service appointments. At a Prime Minister's effective disposal is a dazzling range of jobs. That range must entail the seeking of advice about possible candidates—he could not know them all—but, having received that advice the patronage is his alone.

His patronage in relation to Ministers has already been discussed.[84] Senior civil servants—Permanent Under-Secretaries of State[85] and other senior officials—need his approbation for their appointment and promotion. In the judiciary[86] the Lords of Appeal in Ordinary, Lords Justices of Appeal, the Master of the Rolls, the Lord Chief Justice, the Vice-Chancellor, and the President of the Family Division are all appointed by the Queen on his advice[87]—although the importance of the Lord Chancellor's view should not be underestimated.[88] In the Church, 384 appointments are made by the Crown on the Prime Minister's advice when vacancies arise.[89] Other appointments include the Chairman and governors of the B B C , the Comptroller and Auditor-General,[90] the Parliamentary Commissioner for Administration,[91] the Chairman of the Police Complaints Authority,[92] the Regius Professors, and so on. All

---

[83] 932 H. C. Deb. *232–6* (written answers 19 May 1977).

[84] See also chapter 4.

[85] 'Permanent Secretaries' if their Minister is not a Secretary of State.

[86] For the details, see chapter 11.

[87] To date it has fallen to Mrs Thatcher to recommend the appointment of all the Law Lords except one, the entire Court of Appeal, the Master of the Rolls, and the Lord Chief Justice.

[88] Lord Hailsham of St. Marylebone L C has written that '. . . in practice the Lord Chancellor greatly influences [the Prime Minister's] decision': *The Door Wherein I Went* (1975), p. 254.

[89] I am grateful to the Secretary for Appointments at 10 Downing Street for help on this point. He is puzzled by the figure of 700 given by Jennings, op. cit., p. 453, which is more than double the current number.

[90] National Audit Act 1983, s. 1(1): he is appointed by the Queen on an address from both Houses, the motion requiring to be moved by the Prime Minister with the consent of the chairman of the Public Accounts Committee.

[91] Parliamentary Commissioner Act 1967, s. 1(2).

[92] Police and Criminal Evidence Act 1984, s. 83 and Schedule 4.

this patronage can clearly encourage the deference shown to any Prime Minister.[93] Formally, the Queen is the fountain of honour and all peerages and honours are conferred by her. But (with a few exceptions[94]) those grants are made on ministerial advice.[95] Appointments to honours from peerages down to the humblest British Empire Medal are made on the Prime Minister's advice.[96] To some, honours are very important, and to them the Prime Minister's patronage will be important, too.[97]

The Prime Minister's ability to dissolve Parliament is often described as an important element in his personal power. I think that this is misleading. Although the legitimacy of the Prime Minister's sole right to recommend a dissolution, rather than any recommendation being the collective advice of the Cabinet, has been challenged,[98] it is now so generally accepted by Ministers of all parties that only the acceptance by a future Prime Minister of a most unlikely self-denying ordinance could possibly restore the pre-1918 position[99]—and even then it would be hard to see how that would bind his successors. Of course, the ability to choose an election date strengthens the Prime Minister's hand in relation to the opposition parties, for ideally he will opt for a time when he is most likely to win. But is anyone really taken in by the claim that the dissolution power strengthens the Prime Minister in relation to his Cabinet and party? That claim has it that, because the Prime Minister has the personal right to recommend a dissolution, then he can threaten to obtain a general election so as to bring to heel the rebellious in his administration and his parliamentary party; and government MPs with vulnerable majorities would be restrained from voting so as to bring about an early election, just as turkeys would never vote for an early Christmas. He could *threaten*, certainly, just as Mr Wilson threatened in January 1968 at a PLP meeting;[100] but the weapon would never be fired, save like a state with nuclear weapons ready to commit suicide, for the electorate would see the unattractive picture of a government in

[93] See also Tony Benn (1980) 33 *Parliamentary Affairs* 7.

[94] Appointments to the Orders of the Garter, the Thistle, the Royal Victorian Order, and the Order of Merit are in the Queen's hands.

[95] Report of the Royal Commission on Honours, Cmd. 1789 (1922), vol. ii, p. 99.

[96] Or on the Foreign and Commonwealth Secretary's advice for appointments to the Order of St. Michael and St. George in the Diplomatic Service.

[97] The Political Honours Scrutiny Committee reports on the suitability of persons to be recommended for titles and honours at CBE level and above (whether for political or any other services), and it was highly critical of some of the recommendations in the Wilson Resignation Honours List in 1976.

[98] Notably by Geoffrey Marshall, *Constitutional Conventions* (1984), chapter 3.

[99] Namely, that a request to dissolve came from the Cabinet collectively.

[100] Gordon Walker, op. cit., p. 82; Mackintosh, op. cit., pp. 606–7.

disarray, its Leader in open warfare with his own troops. The opposition parties would enjoy a field day, and electoral victory would be likely for them. The notion of a 'penal dissolution' should be forgotten.

Although fourteen Prime Ministers since Lloyd George have enjoyed the power which he assumed to recommend a dissolution off his own bat, the more modern practice[101] has been for the Prime Minister to consult senior Ministers and party officials both to help to pick a date *and* to involve them in collective responsibility for it. Mrs Thatcher's approach to this matter has been typical of recent Prime Ministers. Before the announcements of the 1983 and 1987 dissolutions she conferred with a group of senior Cabinet Ministers and the Chief Whip; the discussion led to a 'provisional' decision, on which the Prime Minister slept; a full Cabinet was summoned the following day to be informed of her final choice (which confirmed the provisional date); the Prime Minister saw the Queen and a public announcement from Downing Street followed. If a Prime Minister, alone, chooses a date and wins, well and good for him; but if he loses, having chosen the wrong date,[102] or the wrong issue,[103] or the wrong campaign[104] (or all three), he could inflict a wound on himself from which he might never recover. It is, therefore, far better for him to rely on his right of personal choice but also to involve at least some senior colleagues—his potential rivals—in the decision so that they are implicated if all goes wrong. Such a practical consideration must detract from the idea that a Prime Minister has unrestricted personal power in the matter, for if he were in a minority in that consultation it would be risky to press ahead despite the opposition: if electoral defeat resulted, the silence of his colleagues could not be guaranteed over the manner in which the decision had been made. This is not to deny that as the decision is the Prime Minister's and as the

---

[101] See Marshall, op. cit., pp. 51–3. According to James Prior, op. cit., p. 149, when Mrs Thatcher was deciding on the date of the 1983 general election she consulted the Cabinet in small groups.

[102] One example was, perhaps, Mr Heath's timing in 1974 (in which the entire Cabinet concurred: see Lord Hailsham, op. cit., p. 298). Another was, certainly, Mr Callaghan's: he had consulted the Cabinet in August 1978 about the date of the election, and according to one eyewitness account a majority of Ministers favoured a dissolution that autumn, but the Prime Minister and his closest colleagues were opposed to that: see Bernard Donoughue, *Prime Minister: The Conduct of Policy under Harold Wilson and James Callaghan* (1987), pp. 160–3. Mr Callaghan delayed into 1979, by which time the 'winter of discontent' had destroyed any chance of his being returned: for his account, see Callaghan, op. cit., pp. 514–18.

[103] Such as Baldwin in 1923—protection. He was back in office as Prime Minister in 1924 and again in 1935.

[104] Like Mr Wilson's of 1970.

announcement one way or the other comes from him,[105] attention will yet again naturally be focused on him when an appeal to the country seems near.

The direction of departments

A Prime Minister's authority reaches into every department of state. In an ideal administration a Prime Minister will leave his colleagues to get on with running their departments within the framework of the government's policies. As head of the government he has the natural right to intervene if necessary to ensure that decisions are carried out, in a way that no other Minister outside his department may do.[106] If, like Eden, he fretfully interferes, too much and at inconvenient times,[107] it will do him no good in the long run. According to one account[108] Mrs Thatcher would really like to run at least the major departments herself, and (even though that would be impossible) presumably her presence is felt in them. On the other hand, if like Macmillan or Harold Wilson[109] a Prime Minister takes charge of a particular matter for a time because his authority needs to be brought to bear, well and good. Prime Ministers who always sit in the back seat, however, can upset Ministers as much as the compulsive driver. Baldwin favoured long weekends at Chequers, refused to have papers sent there, and made little attempt to control his colleagues. He was accessible, loyal, and friendly, but neither intervened in departmental matters nor was much help when Ministers sought his advice.[110] A typical example occurred when Austen Chamberlain was working towards the Locarno Pact and took certain fundamental issues to Baldwin, who listened attentively and then replied, 'Well, Austen, do what you think fit and I will support you.'[111] What Chamberlain wanted was a second opinion from his chief, not a gratifying expression of loyalty.

[105] Such as Mr Callaghan's television broadcast on 7 September 1978 announcing that there would be no dissolution recommended until 1979.

[106] Unless, of course, he has a co-ordinating role between two or more departments.

[107] As R. A. Butler put it, 'I was . . . at the receiving end of those innumerable telephone calls, on every day of the week and at every hour of the day, which characterized his conscientious but highly strung supervision of affairs': op. cit., p. 184.

[108] Pym, op. cit., p. 17.

[109] Macmillan had to take over the writing of a White Paper on incomes policy in 1962 as a result of delay by the Chancellor and Treasury: *At the End of the Day*, p. 89. Mr Wilson took personal charge of the Department of Economic Affairs for a time from 1967–8.

[110] Keith Middlemas and John Barnes, *Baldwin* (1969), pp. 482–3.

[111] This incident was recounted by Chamberlain to Jennings, op. cit., p. 189.

The Foreign and Commonwealth Office is in a special position because of the frequency with which politically important matters occur: the Prime Minister and the Foreign Secretary must be left to implement Cabinet policy without constant references to other Ministers. Some Prime Ministers—like Lloyd George, MacDonald, Chamberlain, Eden, and Macmillan—have taken a keen personal interest in international affairs and some of them have tended to treat the Foreign Secretary as their own Under-Secretary. Mrs Thatcher, obviously, is concerned in particular with Anglo-American relations and certain E E C matters. If a Prime Minister has the will to do so, then (unless the Foreign Secretary is strong enough to resist) he himself can direct major Foreign Office policies. Such close direction of home departments is much less common (save, as already indicated, on a single issue). Here, as in other areas, the office of Prime Minister is what the individual is willing and able to make it.

In order to enjoy the fruits of his office to the full a Prime Minister must have adequate information. He has in fact at his disposal a machine so responsive to his needs that, although it is not in a unified organization or styled such, he has in effect a Prime Minister's department.

A major part of that organization is the Cabinet Office,[112] headed by the Secretary to the Cabinet. He may be likened to a Permanent Secretary to the Prime Minister.[113] As well as servicing Cabinet meetings the Cabinet Office and Secretary in theory service all Cabinet Ministers, but Ministers naturally tend to rely principally on their departmental civil servants, whose first loyalty is to their departments and to their Ministers for the time being; in the result it is for the Prime Minister primarily (and certain Ministers without portfolio[114]) that the Cabinet Office and Cabinet Secretary work. The Office can get whatever information the Prime Minister needs from the departments: any request made in his name will obviously be given priority. The Prime Minister's Private Office at Number 10 is his inner sanctum of advisers, dealing with his immediate needs.[115] It is small, with three or four civil servants seconded from the major departments to act as Private Secretaries to the Prime Minister. A primary task for the Private Office is to sort out essential

---

[112] See chapter 6.

[113] Especially, perhaps, Sir Robert Armstrong under Mrs Thatcher.

[114] Thus Mr Tebbit as Chancellor of the Duchy of Lancaster from 1985 to 1987 was based in the Cabinet Office: see 105 H. C. Deb. *39* (written answers 17 November 1986); he received no pay as a Cabinet Minister.

[115] For a description, see Callaghan, op. cit., pp. 405–6; Bernard Donoughue, op. cit., pp. 17–26.

items for the Prime Minister to see from the mass of paper which daily threatens him. The Private Office also co-ordinates the Prime Minister's engagements, assembles materials for speeches, ensures that he is properly briefed before meetings, liaises with Ministers' Private Offices, acts as a link with the Queen's Private Secretary, and as a filter for visitors. The Policy Unit[116] in Downing Street was created by Harold Wilson in 1974 to advise him on all matters, and it has been continued by his successors. Its staff are not civil servants but individuals who are in tune with the Prime Minister's political ideology. It is thus party political, supplying the Prime Minister with systematic policy analysis. It is that political counterbalance to civil service advice which Prime Ministers have found invaluable over the past fifteen years. Mr Callaghan considered that the information with which the Unit supplied him enabled him to test and challenge departmental proposals, especially from the Treasury, much more effectively than otherwise would have been possible.[117] The Political Office at Number 10[118] is made up of party members, again not civil servants, paid for by funds which the Prime Minister or his party must find. Its functions vary according to which party is in power: a Labour Prime Minister, for example, will use the Political Office to maintain contact with the National Executive Committee of the Labour Party, with constituency parties, and with the trade unions. No Prime Minister has tried formally to establish a Prime Minister's Department because he already receives all the help he can use through existing structures, especially from the Cabinet Office.[119]

A Prime Minister's weaknesses

The trappings of power and the prestige of the office of Prime Minister ensure that ministerial colleagues and back-benchers acknowledge the Prime Minister's supremacy through the deference shown to him.

---

116 See Mackintosh, op. cit., pp. 517–21; Callaghan, op. cit., pp. 404–5; Donoughue, ibid; Hennessy, op. cit., p. 194, who asserts that, with the abolition of the Central Policy Review Staff in 1983 Mrs Thatcher's Policy Unit was expanded 'into a shadow Whitehall with each of its members . . . covering a clutch of subject areas'.

117 See Callaghan, op. cit., p. 404.

118 See Callaghan, op. cit., p. 406.

119 Mackintosh, op. cit., p. 520; Harold Wilson, op. cit., p. 82. See also Sir Kenneth Berrill, 'Strength at the Centre: The Case for a Prime Minister's Department' (Stamp Memorial Lecture, 1980), and (for a case against) Sir Douglas Wass, *Government and the Governed* (1984), pp. 32–4. Mr Callaghan decided against such a department partly on the ground that it would duplicate existing machinery and would add an unnecessary layer of administration: see Callaghan, op. cit., p. 408.

When (as is usually the case) the Prime Minister has a parliamentary majority behind him his political power will be the envy of dictators. But there is another aspect to consider, namely what might be collectively termed a Prime Minister's weaknesses. These will now be briefly sketched.

An unavoidable weakness of every Prime Minister and government in Britain is that they are temporary (although, as Mrs Thatcher has shown us, some are less temporary than others). However complete may be his superiority in the Cabinet and party the Prime Minister must in peacetime face a general election no more than five years in the future, and his tenure of office may be abruptly ended. And Prime Ministers and administrations do not only leave office after rejection at the polls: a Prime Minister's ill health may force resignation;[120] governments occasionally break up (as in 1931); a Prime Minister may be required to make way for a coalition (as in 1916 and 1940). Prime Ministers come and go for a variety of reasons, and statistical averages on lengths of tenure are accordingly meaningless. They are, however, salutary reminders for any Prime Minister of the transience of power. The longest continuous premiership this century has been Mrs Thatcher's, which in January 1988 overtook the previous record held by Asquith (of eight years and eight months).[121] The longest administration was the thirteen-year Conservative government from 1951 to 1964—but that was under three Prime Ministers. Six Prime Ministers have held office for less than three years,[122] with Sir Alec Douglas-Home achieving one year and Bonar Law only seven months. The average period of office since 1902 (leaving Mrs Thatcher out of account) has been four years nine months.[123] On that record a Prime Minister will be exceptional if he enjoys more than seven or eight years in office—less than two full Parliaments.

If the governments over the last thirty years are considered, it is possible to formulate the maxim that a Prime Minister will be relatively strong when things go well, but that when affairs go badly his authority will wane and perhaps come under challenge, and if his luck deserts him he may well be finished. Such a statement may be objected to as being too uncertain, but a number of examples illustrate that it is fundamentally correct.

[120] As it has this century with Campbell-Bannerman, Bonar Law, Eden, and Macmillan.

[121] The longest interrupted totals are those of Churchill (8 years 8 months) and then Wilson (7 years and 9 months).

[122] Callaghan, Chamberlain, Campbell-Bannerman, Eden, Sir Alec Douglas-Home, Bonar Law.

[123] Aggregating all separate terms where individuals held the office more than once.

Sir Anthony Eden, Churchill's golden crown prince, popular, respected, a major figure in diplomacy, succeeded Churchill in 1955 and speedily consolidated his position at the general election of that year, increasing Churchill's majority of sixteen to one of sixty. Eden's authority was such that critical decisions over Suez were taken by him and the small Egypt Committee of the Cabinet.[124] But the divisions which the invasion of Egypt caused in the Conservative Party and in the country, and the collapse of his health (rarely strong since a surgical misfortune in 1953[125]), brought about the end of his premiership in January 1957 after only twenty-one months, after he had been Churchill's heir for thirteen years.[126] His successor Harold Macmillan achieved a remarkable feat in so restoring the Conservative government's morale and political fortunes that at the 1959 general election Eden's parliamentary majority was increased to almost one hundred. 'Supermac' was ascendant from 1957 to 1962, when many things started to go wrong—security lapses, by-election reverses, the 'night of the long knives' in 1962, failure of the initiative to join the E E C, the Profumo scandal, and Macmillan's illness and resignation. Harold Wilson, elected as Leader of the Labour Party in 1963 partly as a direct contrast to Macmillan, was to achieve two general-election victories in a row, with the second increasing his Commons majority—a first for this century.[127] Enforced devaluation in 1967 in flat contradiction of three years' toil to maintain the parity of the pound, and repeated financial and economic crises, sapped his credibility as an astute Prime Minister; his 1970 general election strategy was a misjudgement of the electorate's mood in offering a Baldwinesque 'safety first' campaign. True, he was back in office four years later, but the personification of a government in its head in the 1964 Labour administration was seen to be an electoral asset of uncertain value. Edward Heath's government, whatever its successes, was finished by the 1973–4 miners' strike and three-day working week, and possibly by a mistiming of his appeal to the electorate.[128] In James Callaghan the Labour Party had a Prime Minister who could do business with the trade unions which had in effect ruined Mr Heath—a conciliator who had built up close relationships with trade union leaders over the years, who

---

[124] See Robert Rhodes James, op. cit., pp. 459–62, 496ff.

[125] Rhodes James, op. cit., pp. 361–9.

[126] Whatever his health, Eden could not have survived the Suez debâcle. The Cabinet urged him on 17 December 1956 not to resign—but then they had to make the best of things, and, when the dust had settled, he would have been pushed out.

[127] Mrs Thatcher repeated the achievement in 1979 and 1983.

[128] Prior, op. cit., pp. 91–3.

had opposed 'In Place of Strife'[129] (and who reminded everyone of it on becoming Prime Minister by dropping its author Mrs Castle from the government). Yet the great inflation of the 1970s and the 'winter of discontent' of 1978–9 with its damaging public-sector strikes seemed to show that his touch had deserted him; and his attempt to last to the end of the October 1974 Parliament without a majority proved fatal. Mrs Thatcher remains in a strong personal position, her political authority undiminished, a record this century of three consecutive general elections won; if she were to retire without electoral defeat she would establish a record of political success unparalleled this century.

Each of those Prime Ministers from Eden to Callaghan might have thought in the early months of their governments that, with luck, a long and successful administration lay ahead. Yet as much as anything it was luck which deserted them, and that annoyingly unquantifiable ingredient must be set in the balance to weigh against any theory of supreme prime ministerial authority.

The Cabinet is not a body of twenty or so politicians unquestioningly committed to the Prime Minister's success. At any time there will be up to five overlapping elements in the Cabinet which can weaken a Prime Minister's authority.

There will be, first, the potential successors who must demonstrate their own departmental successes and (within the limits of collective responsibility) distance themselves from the Prime Minister in anything which smacks of political failure. Sometimes the number of potential successors will be greater than at other times, so that, for example, in the last Wilson Cabinet from 1974 to 1976 there were several, whereas in his first 1964 Cabinet there had been initially none (if previous ministerial experience and position in the party were taken as the main criteria). Secondly, there will be those who will never themselves be contestants for the premiership but who will none the less put the success of the party above the unquestioned continuance of any particular Prime Minister. Such a grouping is easier to discern in the Conservative Party—the grandees, or the 'magic circle'. Thirdly, some senior members of any Cabinet will owe their membership of it not to the Prime Minister's patronage but to their position in the party or to their indispensability to the Prime Minister. Thus the Deputy Leader of the Party in a Labour Cabinet, defeated rivals in a Party Leadership contest, and senior figures in a Cabinet of any colour could not realistically be excluded, and none of

[129] That is, the 1969 White Paper introduced by the Labour government as the basis for legislation (which was ultimately withdrawn).

them necessarily owes any personal loyalty to the Prime Minister. Fourthly, some members of a Cabinet will have a different political philosophy or will represent a different strand of party opinion from the Prime Minister. They may believe that the Prime Minister's time will eventually run out and that their time will come—not necessarily through a particular individual succeeding to the premiership but perhaps by means of their political position once more becoming mainstream government philosophy. It is for instance clear that Mrs Thatcher's 1979 Cabinet was a coalition in economic policy terms, of monetarists and the so-called 'wets'. The latter might have hoped that their outlook would carry the Cabinet, but in that particular case the monetarists were triumphant by the time of the 1981 reshuffle.[130] Lastly, there will be those—probably a majority of every Cabinet—who want to survive politically, so that as long as things go well they will support the Prime Minister to the limit; but if things go wrong, if the Prime Minister starts to lose his grip, or if the opinion polls swing away from the government and stay away, they will become the more ready to question and on occasion challenge the Prime Minister. Those five groups will thus usually give a Prime Minister conditional support at best. They will be prepared when it is in their interests to do so to act to overrule the Prime Minister on particular issues[131] or to force a change of style of government.[132] The Cabinet in that case will assert itself: Cabinet government, at least for a time, may again rival government by Prime Minister.

Any Prime Minister who has a small or no majority in the House of Commons will necessarily appear feebler than one with a comfortable majority, partly because there may be a general expectation of an early reference to the electorate, partly because he will have no guarantee that his government's legislation will pass. Since 1900 governments have had no majority, or one in single figures, for a total of seventeen years. In the first hung Parliament of this century, returned at the January 1910 election, the Liberal government depended on the Irish members for its continued existence; in the last hung Parliament from 1977 until 1978

[130] Another example might be those members of the 1974–9 Labour Cabinet who favoured an alternative economic strategy, a 'siege economy'.

[131] Gordon Walker (op. cit., pp. 91 ff.) and Harold Wilson (*The Labour Government*, pp. 184, 269, 396, and 513) cite examples.

[132] For example, in July 1966 Mr Wilson conceded that too much economic policy was being decided by too few Ministers, and established a more widely based Cabinet committee on the subject; and in 1986, in the immediate aftermath of the Westland affair, there was some evidence of a move back towards collective Cabinet government for a time.

the Labour government depended on the Lib.-Lab. pact for its life.[133] And that government either lost legislation entirely or obtained it in a form which was far from ideal from its point of view. Clearly, such a Prime Minister, and indeed a Prime Minister presiding over a coalition, will be less effective than one with a homogeneous majority, as (say) both James Callaghan and Lloyd George found to their costs at the end of their premierships.

The potential vulnerability of a Labour Prime Minister under the Party's 1981 constitution was noted in chapter 2, in particular (a) the danger that Labour's electoral college might choose a Leader who was unacceptable to the PLP, (b) the possibility of a Labour Prime Minister being challenged for the Leadership, and (c) the possibility that he might be denied his seat. These remain theoretical weaknesses—thus far. But Prime Ministers *have* been removed from office, not usually by formal party votes[134] but by more subtle pressures exerted by their parties and in Parliament. Both world wars produced such casualties, Asquith and Chamberlain. Those might be dismissed as being special to wartime, but there are other examples which show how vulnerable a Prime Minister can be when he is seen as a liability. Churchill was, in effect, levered out in 1955, by which time his advanced old age and increasing infirmity had become major political disadvantages. No one seriously asserts that, had Eden been fully fit, he would have continued in office after the Suez debâcle: the efforts which had been brought to bear on his predecessor would have been deployed more quickly and ruthlessly to show Eden that he no longer had the confidence of the Conservative Party as a whole or of the government. So a removal *can* occur even in peacetime; it would be unusual, certainly, but the threat is there to remind any Prime Minister that he relies ultimately on his parliamentary party.

Conclusions

Through this analysis of a Prime Minister's strengths and weaknesses both generally, and particularly in relation to his Cabinet and parliamentary party, the main features of the office have become clear. His authority can make him, in theory, an elective dictator. The powers actually exercised certainly give him a superior role in British central

---

[133] See chapter 9.

[134] The formal Conservative vote at the Carlton Club in 1922 to end the Lloyd George coalition was a notable exception.

government, undoubtedly transcending that of the Cabinet. Some Prime Ministers since 1945 have been more superior than others; even the mightiest, however, have succumbed to forces some of which are no less real for being irritatingly imprecise.

6

The Cabinet

No one writing a book about the practice of British central government today would entitle it (as Sir Ivor Jennings did his work) *Cabinet Government*. Although opinions are not unanimous about the nature of the modern Cabinet, all agree that the Cabinet as a body is not what it once was. The two principal reasons behind the change in its position are the enhanced powers of the Prime Minister,[1] and the increased decision-making outside Cabinet meetings which has taken place at least since the Second World War (whether by the Prime Minister consulting a few ministerial colleagues, or by Cabinet committees, or by informal ministerial groups). It is that second aspect to which particular attention will be paid in this chapter.

Some topics which traditionally appear under the heading of the Cabinet are treated elsewhere in this book. Thus, for example, the choice and composition of the Cabinet were dealt with in chapter 4; the Cabinet's agenda, procedure, and minutes as they relate to the Prime Minister's authority were examined in the previous chapter; and ministerial responsibility will be looked at in the next chapter, as that notion does not vary according to whether a Minister is or is not a member of the Cabinet.

Cabinet business

Six years after the Cabinet Office had been established Bonar Law contemplated its abolition.[2] But he soon realized that during that time the Cabinet Office had shown its value in making central administration more efficient, and it is indeed astonishing to think today of the amateur way in which the Prime Minister and the Cabinet governed Britain and the Empire before 1916.[3] The Cabinet would meet without a written

---

[1] On which see chapter 5.

[2] He originally thought that it was an undesirable relic of Lloyd George's War Cabinet, and planned its abolition—or at least a radical reorganization—after the 1922 general election.

[3] See generally Lord Hankey, *Diplomacy by Conference: Studies in Public Affairs 1920–1946* (1946), pp. 52, 62–9.

agenda; no one acted as secretary and no minutes were taken—indeed, in some Cabinets, Ministers were forbidden to take notes in an attempt to maintain secrecy.[4] The only official account of deliberations was contained in the letter which the Prime Minister sent to the Sovereign, keeping his own copy. Not surprisingly Ministers were not always at all clear what had been decided, a situation aptly encapsulated in the well-known letter from Lord Hartington's Private Secretary to his opposite number at 10 Downing Street in 1882.

Harcourt and Chamberlain have both been here this morning and *at* my Chief about yesterday's Cabinet proceedings. They cannot agree about what occurred. There must have been some decision, as Bright's resignation shows. My Chief has told me to ask you what the devil *was* decided, for he be damned if he knows. Will you ask Mr G. in more conventional and less pungent terms?[5]

That method of doing business continued into Asquith's coalition, but ended abruptly in 1916 with the advent of Lloyd George. He used the Secretariat of the Committee of Imperial Defence as the basis for his new Cabinet Office and Secretariat,[6] with that Committee's Secretary, Colonel Maurice Hankey, becoming Secretary to the Cabinet. Lloyd George's wartime organization of the Office was approved by the Haldane Committee on the Machinery of Government[7] and its functions have broadly remained the same ever since.

The five secretarial functions of the Cabinet Office are (*a*) to compile the agenda for the Cabinet (under the Prime Minister's direction) and for Cabinet committees (under the direction of their chairmen); (*b*) to summon members to meetings; (*c*) to take and circulate Cabinet and Cabinet committee minutes, and to draft reports of those committees; (*d*) to circulate memoranda and other documents for the Cabinet and its committees;[8] and (*e*) to file and maintain Cabinet papers and minutes. As

[4] Such a ban existed under Lord Salisbury and under Asquith: see Lady Gwendolen Cecil, *Life of Robert, Marquess of Salisbury* (1921), ii. 223; Lord Oxford and Asquith, *Fifty Years of Parliament* (1928), ii. 197.

[5] Quoted by Viscount Hailsham during a House of Lords debate on the disclosure of Cabinet secrets: 86 H. L. Deb. 529 (21 December 1932).

[6] On which see Sir Ivor Jennings, *Cabinet Government* (3rd edn., 1959), pp. 242–5; Patrick Gordon Walker, *The Cabinet* (revised edn., 1972), pp. 47–55; John Mackintosh, *The British Cabinet* (3rd edn., 1977), pp. 517–21; R. K. Mosley, *The Story of the Cabinet Office* (1969); S. S. Wilson, *The Cabinet Office to 1945* (1975). The organization of the Cabinet Office under the 1974–9 Labour government is described in Bernard Donoughue, *Prime Minister: The Conduct of Policy under Harold Wilson and James Callaghan* (1987), pp. 26–30.

[7] Report, Cd. 9230 (1918).

[8] Such papers also go to any Minister in charge of a department who is not a member of the Cabinet.

was indicated in the previous chapter, the Cabinet Office serves all Cabinet Ministers, but it is really a vital part of what was termed in that chapter the Prime Minister's 'department' and thus of his personal authority, providing him with information and advice; the Secretary to the Cabinet has claim to the unofficial title of Permanent Secretary to the Prime Minister.[9] The Cabinet Secretary is the most important member of the civil service,[10] and, since 1981, has been the Head of the Home Civil Service as well.[11] During the Wilson and Callaghan administrations the Cabinet Secretariat each week issued the Secretary to the Cabinet with its proposals for Cabinet and Cabinet committee business for the following fortnight. Each Thursday the Private Secretary to the Cabinet Secretary discussed it with the Prime Minister's Private Secretary: this constituted the provisional programme of Cabinet and Cabinet committee business for the following two or three weeks. From it the Cabinet Secretary produced a forward programme of business which, when approved by the Prime Minister, became the specific arrangements for government business in the following week.[12]

Of the three functions of the Cabinet identified by the Haldane Committee in 1918,[13] one remains an accurate description of the Cabinet's main role today, namely the final determination of the policy to be submitted to Parliament. Meeting only once a week for a couple of hours with a full agenda, and being composed overwhelmingly of Ministers with heavy departmental responsibilities, the Cabinet could not possibly now be the forum either for the close control of the activities of government or for the co-ordination of the departments of state (essentially the other two functions ascribed to it by the Haldane Committee). As will be seen, much detailed work on policy matters is done outside Cabinet meetings; the Cabinet will consider decisions referred to it by

[9] A title suggested by Gordon Walker, op. cit., p. 54.

[10] Sir Robert Armstrong, Cabinet Secretary 1979–87, was perforce brought into the public eye more than his predecessors had been through his roles in the Westland helicopter affair in 1985–6 (on which see chapter 7), and in the action brought in the Australian courts in 1986–7 by the British government to prevent the publication of the memoirs of a former MI5 spy, Peter Wright.

[11] This combination of offices has caused some controversy. The Commons Select Committee on the Treasury and Civil Service recommended that the posts should in future not be held by the same person: see 7th Report from the Treasury and Civil Service Committee, Civil Servants and Ministers: Duties and Responsibilities, H. C. 92 (1985–6), para. 5.44. The government rejected that view in its response: Cmnd. 9841 (1984), para. 42; the Committee persisted in its view: see 1st Report from the Treasury and Civil Service Committee, H. C. 62 (1986–7), para. 3.1; the Prime Minister later announced that the next Cabinet Secretary, Robin Butler, would hold both posts.

[12] See Bernard Donoughue, op. cit., pp. 27–8.

[13] Cd. 9230 (1918), p. 5.

extra-Cabinet decision-makers; its role perforce is largely to ratify or to disapprove decisions taken elsewhere. In that way perhaps the Cabinet has developed another function: to provide the personnel for those Cabinet committees and similar bodies which make up the contemporary Cabinet system.[14]

It would obviously be a profitless exercise to try to list all those matters which in theory could be discussed by the Cabinet. It is, however, instructive to consider those issues which as a matter of practice are not normally taken by the Cabinet, and to note exceptional cases.

In his memoirs Asquith recorded three topics which in his day were not discussed by the Cabinet. These were recommendations concerning the exercise of the prerogative of mercy, the personnel of the Cabinet, and patronage.[15] This was incorrect even when written. The prerogative of mercy is exercised by the Sovereign on the Home Secretary's recommendation, and the Home Secretary acts more judicially than politically in making any recommendation.[16] Partly to underscore that role it is understood that he would not usually take such a question to the Cabinet, where the discussion would tend to be more political than legal. Exceptionally, however, cases under review will have political implications. So, in 1916, the question of whether to recommend a reprieve for Sir Roger Casement was discussed at four Cabinet meetings;[17] and, in the late 1950s, the Cabinet may well have debated the death sentences passed on a number of Cypriots during the struggle for independence, because executions would have affected both world opinion and negotiations about the island's future.[18] Today, it would be entirely right that the Cabinet (or at least a committee of it) rather than any single Minister should decide any question about the use of the prerogative to free prisoners in response to a terrorist ransom demand or to reprieve anyone convicted of treason, for the political connotations

[14] Although that statement is not entirely satisfactory because Ministers outside the Cabinet are also appointed to full membership of Cabinet committees.

[15] Lord Oxford and Asquith, op. cit., p. 194.

[16] The phrase 'the prerogative of mercy' encompasses pardon and remission of sentence as well as reprieve: it is not, therefore, of historical interest only. See A. T. H. Smith, 'The Prerogative of Mercy, the Power of Pardon and Criminal Justice' [1983] Public Law 398, and R. v. Foster [1985] Q.B. 115. For a former Home Secretary's account of his task in reviewing death penalty cases see Lord Butler, The Art of the Possible (1971), pp. 201–2.

[17] Roy Jenkins, Asquith (Fontana edn., 1967), pp. 452–4. The Cabinet decided against recommending a reprieve. Jenkins comments that 'There can be few other examples of a Cabinet devoting large parts of four meetings to considering an individual sentence—and then arriving at the wrong decision.'

[18] Mackintosh, op. cit., p. 415.

would warrant decisions at Cabinet level. Asquith was also incorrect to write that the personnel of the Cabinet (in the sense of who should be members) is a matter not discussed by it. Of course, such questions are pre-eminently for the Prime Minister.[19] But again there are exceptions, many during Victoria's reign when Prime Ministers consulted ministerial colleagues over whether to give office to individuals,[20] but also this century, such as Baldwin's acceptance in 1923 of his Cabinet's opinion that neither Birkenhead nor Austen Chamberlain should be brought in, whether as Ministers without Portfolio or in any other capacity.[21] Should a Prime Minister wish to consult the Cabinet collectively about possible Cabinet appointments there is no reason why he should not do so. Asquith was, however, right that patronage (in the sense of recommendations for non-ministerial jobs, honours, and so on) traditionally remains for the Prime Minister,[22] although again only as a matter of practice.[23]

Three other areas may be identified in which, again, the modern Cabinet normally has no role. Just as the prerogative of mercy at the end of the criminal process is not usually an issue for the Cabinet, nor is the decision to prosecute at the beginning of that process. That decision today lies initially with the police and, if they feel that there is evidence to justify a prosecution, they will refer the case to the Crown Prosecution Service.[24] The Director of Public Prosecutions is head of that Service; the Attorney-General's role is limited to appointing the Director, to determining his salary (with Treasury approval), and to the 'superintendence' of the Director.[25] The Attorney-General's consent is required before certain prosecutions may be started;[26] he may also enter a *nolle prosequi* to stop any prosecution. He is expected to exercise an independent judgement in all these matters, not dictated by his colleagues in the

---

[19] See chapter 5.

[20] Jennings, op. cit., pp. 66–8.

[21] Keith Middlemas and John Barnes, *Baldwin* (1969), p. 174.

[22] Or the Foreign and Commonwealth Secretary for the Diplomatic List.

[23] In a House of Lords debate on the Report of the Royal Commission on Honours, Cmd. 1789 (1922), Lord Curzon went so far as to say that '. . . the idea that [the Prime Minister] should bring before the Cabinet the question of honours is one utterly foreign to our whole constitutional procedure': 53 H. L. Deb. 286–7 (7 March 1923).

[24] Prosecution of Offences Act 1985, Part I.

[25] Ibid., ss. 1(1)(a), 2(1), (3), 3(1). There is no indication yet of what that 'superintendence' may amount to, but under the former system the Home Secretary (who appointed the DPP) did not attempt to control the ways in which the DPP discharged his office, and that should not change.

[26] For example, for certain offences under the Official Secrets Act 1911, the Prevention of Terrorism (Temporary Provisions) Act 1984, and the Public Order Acts 1936 and 1986.

government, although naturally he may seek their views on any case which has implications which exceed the legal or judicial and which enter the political arena. So, for example, when the War Cabinet purported to give Sir Frederick Smith instructions about certain prosecutions during the First World War he vigorously protested at the impropriety of this action;[27] on the other hand, Sir Gordon Hewart properly consulted the Home Secretary in 1919 over a prosecution for sedition.[28] The danger inherent in the Cabinet exercising any influence over prosecution policy was manifest in the Campbell case in 1924, where it was assumed that the Attorney-General, Sir Patrick Hastings, had bent to Cabinet pressure in withdrawing a prosecution for sedition against the editor of the *Workers' Weekly*;[29] as a result a vote of censure was carried against the government.[30] The decision in 1985 to prosecute Mr Clive Ponting under section 2 of the Official Secrets Act 1911 for leaking confidential information about the sinking of the warship *General Belgrano* during the Falklands conflict aroused much controversy, but the Attorney-General was able to assert that it was his decision, not the Cabinet's.[31] Similarly, the Attorney-General's decision to request the Director of Public Prosecutions to investigate possible breaches of the Official Secrets Act 1911 arising out of a *New Statesman* article in 1987 on the background to a secret British intelligence satellite, 'Project Zircon', led to controversial searches of the responsible journalist's home and of BBC headquarters in Glasgow, where a programme about 'Project Zircon' had been made. Questions were also raised about who in the government had asked or instructed whom to do what in the affair.[32] The prudent course

[27] 177 H. C. Deb. 614–15 (8 October 1924).

[28] 177 H. C. Deb. 598–9 (8 October 1924), described by the then Attorney-General Sir Patrick Hastings.

[29] See J. Ll. J. Edwards, *The Law Officers of the Crown* (1964), chapters 10 and 11, and *The Attorney-General: Politics and the Public Interest* (1984), chapter 11; David Marquand, *Ramsay MacDonald* (1977), pp. 364–77, 385.

[30] 177 H. C. Deb. 581–704 (8 October 1924).

[31] See 73 H. C. Deb. 737–830 (18 February 1985). Mr Ponting was acquitted: *R*. v. *Ponting* [1985] Criminal Law Review 318; Clive Ponting, *The Right to Know* (1985). The decision not to prosecute Mr Chapman Pincher under the same section following publication of his book *Their Trade Is Treachery* was, oddly, not taken by the Attorney-General, who insisted in 1986 that that fact be made publicly known. Sir Michael Havers—the longest-serving Attorney-General (1979–87) in modern times—was also reported in a colourful phrase to have threatened to 'send the police into No. 10 Downing Street' if there were no inquiry into the leak to the press of the Solicitor-General's letter to Mr Heseltine in 1985—a good example of an Attorney-General's independence from his ministerial colleagues. There was such an inquiry: see further below note 110 and chapter 7.

[32] See 109 H. C. Deb. *330* (written answers 29 January 1987), and the emergency debate on the matter at 109 H. C. Deb. 815–62 (3 February 1987). The Home Secretary said in that debate that

for a Cabinet must be to leave responsibility for initiating and abandoning prosecutions to the Attorney-General, and to be reticent in offering him advice even if he asks for it.

Perhaps the best-known topic which is routinely and regularly handled so as to provide as little opportunity as possible for Cabinet discussion is the Budget. The Chancellor of the Exchequer's proposals are of major political importance, but they are only disclosed to the Cabinet on the morning of the day on which they are to be presented to the House of Commons;[33] for practical purposes, the Budget is presented to Ministers as a *fait accompli*. Indeed, the time at which the Cabinet is informed has changed so as to allow for only a minimum of Cabinet influence over the strategy and details of the Budget: by 1936 on average four or five days elapsed between the Budget Cabinet and the Chancellor's delivery to the Commons[34]—short enough, but better than today's delay of a few hours. The reason advanced to support this apparently cavalier treatment of the Cabinet is the need for secrecy: a practical effect is to put the government's economic and financial policy in the hands of the Chancellor of the Exchequer and the Prime Minister. Thus it is said that the less time there is between a Cabinet Minister hearing these secrets and the publication of them, the less chance there will be of a damaging leak, and it could be argued that since J. H. Thomas's regrettable lapse in 1936[35] no Cabinet Minister (other than the Chancellor himself, Hugh Dalton, in 1947[36]) has admitted to leaking any Budget secret. Would it be too cynical to ask what is so unique about Budget facts as to make Cabinet Ministers untrustworthy of them? Does anyone fear that Ministers will either openly leak any of them (for were they to do so they would, like Thomas and Dalton, lose their jobs) or use the information for personal financial gain?[37] It is odd that no modern Cabinet seems to have rebelled

---

'. . . questions of prosecutions are never discussed collectively between Ministers . . . [The Attorney-General] does not consult his colleagues—indeed, he debars himself from consulting his colleagues on any matter relating to a prosecution': ibid., col. 823. That is plainly not correct.

[33] The Chancellor of the Exchequer traditionally dines with the Queen the evening before and outlines his Budget to her.

[34] Sir Maurice Hankey's evidence to the Budget Disclosure Enquiry (1936), Minutes of Evidence, p. 25.

[35] See Middlemas and Barnes, op. cit., p. 934; Gregory Blaxland, *J. H. Thomas: A Life for Unity* (1964), chapter 30.

[36] See Ben Pimlott, *Hugh Dalton* (1985), pp. 520–48.

[37] And the financing of social security *is* disccussed in the Cabinet: see, for example, Richard Crossman, *Diaries of a Cabinet Minister*, vol. i (1975), pp. 34–5. Of course no one could improperly use information about that to influence the money markets or to make a personal financial gain.

at a system which calls into question Ministers' honour, especially since the main source of unattributable leaks[38] in recent years has been Tresury Ministers themselves—an assertion for which the evidence is that only through such leaks could the accurate and detailed predictions appear in the media as they do almost routinely several days before each Budget statement. Cabinets have objected, certainly, but have not in the end kicked over the traces. In 1981, for instance, Sir Geoffrey Howe's Budget was rigidly deflationary and therefore highly controversial at a time of recession, but the strategy behind it was not discussed in the Cabinet, being revealed as usual to the Cabinet on Budget day itself, to the dismay of the Cabinet 'wets', whose protests, in the main, did not lead to changes, or to resignations.[39]

Now a number of correctives must be entered in order to avoid drawing a misleading picture about the background to the Budget. First, Cabinets have brought about changes of detail—although published instances are few and far between and do not amount to significant alterations in the structure of the relevant Budgets. For example, Mr James Prior claims that at the 1981 Budget Cabinet he and like-minded colleagues defeated the Chancellor's original proposal not to increase state retirement pensions in line with inflation, although significantly Mr Prior managed to convince the Prime Minister of the rightness of his case, thus making the Chancellor's defeat much easier.[40] Again, in his 1945 Budget, Dalton intended to make a change in the fuel oil tax but the Cabinet refused to accept it and the Chancellor deleted that item,[41] and in 1951 Hugh Gaitskell's idea for a differential fuel tax was dropped in view of the Cabinet's objections.[42] Secondly, Chancellors can and do accept changes during the committee stage of the Finance Bill, presenting them as concessions to party opinion and to representations from interested groups: the opinions of their ministerial colleagues could be taken into account then as well as anyone else's. Thirdly, it is of course wrong to imagine that a Chancellor acts entirely outside the government's economic strategy or that he is immune to ministerial opinions offered during the pre-Budget purdah into which he goes after Christmas. He will naturally frame his ideas within the government's overall policy, and Ministers will naturally speak and write privately to the

---

[38] These are discussed later.

[39] Francis Pym, *The Politics of Consent* (1984), p. 18.

[40] James Prior, *A Balance of Power* (1986), p. 130.

[41] Hugh Dalton, *High Tide and After* (1962), p. 25.

[42] Harold Wilson, *The Governance of Britain* (1976), p. 59.

Chancellor (especially to seek more money for their departments). He may not, therefore, always come to the Budget Cabinet with tablets of stone carved during a period of total deafness towards his colleagues. Fourthly, the disagreement caused by the 1981 Budget produced a procedural change: it was agreed that the Cabinet would in future meet in January or early February each year for a full discussion on economic policy before the Chancellor went into purdah.[43]

The final area usually outside the Cabinet's formal decision- making is the timing of a recommended dissolution of Parliament. This was discussed in the previous chapter.

Cabinet committees and ministerial meetings[44]

There is nothing new in Prime Ministers using a few senior Ministers, rather than the whole Cabinet, to keep a general oversight of the government's progress and to deal with particular questions. In the 1929 Labour government MacDonald held informal weekly meetings with Henderson, Thomas, Snowden, and Clynes to discuss parliamentary business and Labour Party affairs,[45] and in the 'National Government' after Snowden's resignation in 1932 until MacDonald's retirement in 1935 the Prime Minister relied heavily on Thomas, Simon, Runciman, Baldwin, and Chamberlain.[46] During 1936 Baldwin kept four colleagues informed of the progress of his audiences with Edward VIII about the King's plans to marry.[47] In the following year his successor Chamberlain used the Foreign Policy Committee of the Cabinet, made up of nine or ten Ministers, to advise him on his approaches to the dictators; by 1938 he abandoned that Committee in favour of discussions with Halifax, Simon, and Hoare, the 'guilty men' of Munich.[48]

It is entirely natural that a Prime Minister should talk to those Ministers whom he finds particularly congenial about issues facing the

---

[43] Prior, op. cit., pp. 140-1.

[44] Jennings, op. cit., pp. 255-61: Mackintosh, op. cit., pp. 521-9: Gordon Walker, op. cit., pp. 38-47; Wilson, op. cit., pp. 62-8. My debt to Peter Hennessy's *Cabinet* (1986) for some of the information in this section is obvious.

[45] Marquand, op. cit., pp. 489-95.

[46] Marquand, op. cit., p. 737.

[47] As Baldwin was to tell the Commons: 318 H. C. Deb 2180 (10 December 1936).

[48] Jennings, op. cit., pp. 241-2. Chamberlain did not consult that group or the Cabinet or any Cabinet committee before signing the Munich declaration in 1938.

government, sometimes formally as to an inner Cabinet[49] (like, for example, Harold Wilson's Parliamentary Committee of the Cabinet[50]), sometimes informally, perhaps late at night over a drink. Such ways of doing business, however, raise important questions. One concerns the ability of a Prime Minister to divert decision-making away from the full Cabinet to a few selected Ministers, either leaving the Cabinet entirely out of account or presenting it with a decision which, for practical purposes, it can only ratify. As was indicated in the previous chapter and will be explained shortly, this has greatly enhanced the Prime Minister's authority over his Cabinet. Another question concerns the status of decisions arrived at outside the full Cabinet compared with decisions of that body, for that question of status is frequently relied on to justify the astonishing secrecy which shrouds Cabinet committees and other extra-Cabinet groups. And then there is the matter of definition: what exactly is a Cabinet committee, as distinct from any other ministerial meeting? It is that question which will be explored first.[51]

The essential qualities of a Cabinet committee properly so called are that it is a committee of Ministers (which may include non-Cabinet and junior Ministers) established by the Prime Minister (whether or not chaired by him), with formal procedures and servicing by the Cabinet Secretariat. No grouping of Ministers will be a Cabinet committee unless (as with a Cabinet meeting) it is set up by the Prime Minister: there must be prime ministerial authority for a committee's existence. Cabinet committees follow procedures which are as formal as those of the Cabinet itself: each has a member of the Cabinet Secretariat assigned to it to be its secretary, and papers are circulated in the same way as for Cabinet meetings; minutes are kept, and if a committee's function is to report to the Cabinet, the chairman will do so, usually in writing. There is a further mark of recognition accorded to a Cabinet committee by the civil service: inclusion in the Cabinet Committee Book maintained by the Secretary to the Cabinet.

Three separate types of committee may be distinguished, ministerial, official, and mixed, only the first being a Cabinet committee proper. The ministerial committees are, in turn, of two sorts, standing and *ad hoc*. The best example of a standing ministerial committee is the Defence

---

[49] For a discussion of the terms 'inner' and 'partial' Cabinets, see Gordon Walker, op. cit., pp. 37–8, 88–91.

[50] This is considered below.

[51] It is largely ignored by most writers.

and Oversea Policy Committee,[52] which is concerned with defence and external affairs. It is standing in the sense that it exists on a permanent basis throughout any given administration and is not dissolved when that government leaves office (although its personnel will, of course, change). The Prime Minister is invariably in the chair because of the Committee's importance, and senior Cabinet Ministers will make up its membership. The Chiefs of Staff are invited to attend as required. Other examples of standing ministerial committees established under all governments will usually include a number on economic affairs (the main one, on economic strategy, normally being chaired by the Prime Minister); one on home affairs (which may take in social policy and education, as well as Home Office matters); legislation (which will consider departmental legislative proposals in principle, arrange provisional priorities, and later keep the parliamentary progress of Bills under review), and security.[53] *Ad hoc* Cabinet committees are established to deal with particular problems, and are disbanded when they have fulfilled the functions given to them: it is reasonable to assume that any important issue which falls for governmental decision may be referred to an *ad hoc* committee if there is no relevant standing committee. Examples of these are legion.[54] Because all *ad hoc* committees are dissolved when a government resigns, inevitably to be replaced by its successor with another elaborate set, they are for ease of identity designated in one administration 'Gen' (for 'General') and then 'Misc' (for 'Miscellaneous') in the next. Mrs Thatcher's are 'Misc'. Then there are official committees, which consist of civil servants either to shadow ministerial committees or to do preparatory work for ministerial committees.[55] There will be at least as many official as ministerial committees. Lastly, there may be mixed committees of both Ministers and civil servants. These were tried in particular by Mr Heath during his premiership, but were largely dissolved by Mr Wilson. A well-publicized mixed committee, dubbed 'The Seminar', was used by Mr Callaghan from 1977 to

[52] The existence and usual composition of the Committee were announced in the White Paper 'Central Organization for Defence', Cmnd. 2097 (1963). Originally the Prime Minister, First Secretary of State, Home Secretary, Chancellor of the Exchequer, Secretary of State for Commonwealth Relations, and Secretary of State for Defence were envisaged as members: ibid., para. 16.

[53] There is a chart in Gordon Walker, op. cit., pp. 174–5 indicating the main standing ministerial committees from 1914 to 1964. Mackintosh, op. cit., pp. 521–9 gives some examples of such committees.

[54] Examples are given in Mackintosh, ibid.

[55] Richard Crossman thought that it was through these official committees that '. . . Whitehall ensures that the Cabinet system is relatively harmless': op. cit., i. 198.

1979 to discuss sensitive and major decisions on interest rates and the level of sterling; it was made up of a few Cabinet Ministers and senior civil servants under the Prime Minister, and effectively took all the main decisions on those matters. Probably one of the few mixed committees still in existence is the Civil Contingencies Unit, which comes into play during industrial disputes which may threaten the essentials of life.[56]

There are sound machinery-of-government reasons which explain the growth of the Cabinet committee system. The full Cabinet cannot adequately cope with all questions which must be addressed by any government: pressure of business has required that a more efficient method of working be developed. Small committees of Ministers can settle preliminary issues so as to leave only fundamental points (or points of disagreement) for higher authority. Again, even with the merger of departments into the modern structure, problems do not always fall within the remit of any given department of state: it would be pointless to seek to tackle them within the four walls of one department: a committee of Ministers from several departments will frequently be needed. In short, good government requires a network of Cabinet committees.

That network has changed in various ways since 1945.[57]Attlee inherited a complex scheme of committees on coming to power, and used it to help to implement Labour's programme. An attempt in 1946 to rationalize and to reduce the number of committees was not very successful: by 1951 there were 148 standing and 313 *ad hoc* committees.[58] Lord Hunt of Tamworth has described Attlee's administration as '. . . government by committee—hundreds of them—rather than government by Cabinet'. He added: '[t]he system worked remarkably smoothly.'[59] Thus the general use of extra-Cabinet decision-making is not a recent phenomenon: it is at least forty years old. Churchill, with his traditional view of Cabinet government, disliked working through bodies inferior to the Cabinet, apart from the Defence Committee.[60] He authorized an assault on Attlee's structure, as a result of which the number of standing

[56] David Bonner, *Emergency Powers in Peacetime* (1985), pp. 29–35.

[57] Attlee had given a fairly detailed account of the War Cabinet committee structure to the House of Commons in 1941: see 361 H. C. Deb 769–70 (4 June 1940). Churchill did the same a year later: see 368 H. C. Deb. 261–4 (24 January 1941).

[58] Peter Hennessy and Andrew Arends, *Mr Attlee's Engine Room: Cabinet Committee Structure and the Labour Governments 1945–51* (1983), Stratchlyde Papers on Government and Politics, No. 26.

[59] Quoted in Hennessy, op. cit., p. 38.

[60] Anthony Seldon, *Churchill's Indian Summer: The Conservative Government 1951–1955* (1981), p. 117.

committees was cut and the number of *ad hoc* committees halved.[61] Only with the premiership of Harold Wilson were any significant innovations made in the Cabinet committee system. He established the Parliamentary Committee of the Cabinet in 1968, presided over by him and consisting of some ten Cabinet Ministers. (It was reduced to seven the following year.) It was serviced by the Cabinet Secretariat in the same way as any other Cabinet committee, but its terms of reference were vague: its declared purpose was to consider general political and parliamentary problems in a way that the whole Cabinet, through pressure of work, could not.[62] The Committee was not, however, continued in 1970 by Mr Heath, and there is no evidence of any subsequent resuscitation. Another alteration in procedure initiated by Harold Wilson was a rule that Cabinet committee papers could not be circulated to the full Cabinet if any dispute remained in the committee over facts. On the face of it a move to save Cabinet time, it actually had at least one political consequence: Douglas Jay's paper written as President of the Board of Trade asserting that British trade would suffer if the United Kingdom were to enter the European Economic Community was kept away from the Cabinet because some Ministers on the committee which was considering entry disputed some of Jay's facts.[63] The last of Mr Wilson's changes, again introduced in the spirit of greater efficiency, came towards the end of the 1964 government. In a 1970 *Minute on Cabinet Committee Procedure*[64] the Prime Minister decreed that if a Minister on a committee were dissatisfied with a committee decision, then he could only take the dispute to the Cabinet with the consent of the committee's chairman. Mr Wilson thought that far too many 'appeals' had been conducted and he believed that the chairmen, as experienced Ministers, would know when a disagreement was so politically sensitive that consent should be given.[65] In his turn Mr Heath reduced the number of Cabinet committees[66] and also designated some committees 'task forces' so as to allow senior civil servants full membership without disturbing the traditional Whitehall concept of Cabinet committees. So, for example, on the introduction of a prices and incomes policy, a 'task force', not a Cabinet committee, was established to supervise it, consisting not only

---

[61] Hennessy, op. cit., p. 50.
[62] Gordon Walker, op. cit., pp. 45–6.
[63] Mackintosh, op. cit., p. 528. It is not possible to discover whether that rule has survived.
[64] Quoted by Crossman, op. cit., iii. 861.
[65] Wilson, op. cit., pp. 65–6. This rule was also applied during the 1974–9 Labour government.
[66] An indication of some of his committees was published in *The Times*, 3 May 1973.

of the Prime Minister and four senior economic Ministers, but also of Sir
William Armstrong of the Civil Service Department and Ronald Mackintosh of the Treasury.[67] Too much should not be made of this development, for the line which divides civil servants who are merely invited to
attend Cabinet committees for particular items from persons enjoying
full membership may be more apparent than real, and the Chiefs of Staff
have attended the Defence and Oversea Policy Committee as required
(which could mean for most of the time).

It is generally assumed that Mrs Thatcher has significantly downgraded the status of the full Cabinet. What is the evidence? The Cabinet
meets only once a week, but that has been the case since the early 1960s.[68]
More importantly, we have it on the authority of her Foreign Secretary
Sir Geoffrey Howe that there are very few discussions of government
decisions by the full Cabinet.[69] According to Peter Hennessy the number
of standing Cabinet committees has been reduced by Mrs Thatcher to
between thirty and thirty-five, and *ad hoc* committees to about 120:
under Attlee the corresponding figures were 148 and 313.[70] Clearly the
extent of governmental responsibility cannot have declined to the extent
that weekly Cabinets and the smallest number of Cabinet committees
since before the Second World War can efficiently discharge it. It is
reasonably clear that Mrs Thatcher makes much greater use of discussions in small, informal groups of Ministers—not Cabinet committees,
and without civil service presence—and that Ministers in general use
direct interdepartmental correspondence to seek opinions and to arrive at
decisions outside any more formal machinery.[71] An example of that
method of working cited by Mr Hennessy[72] concerns Mr Michael

---

67 Mackintosh, op. cit., p. 516.

68 See chapter 5.

69 Interview in the *Daily Mail*, 6 February 1984. Almost 30 years before W. J. M. Mackenzie
and J. W. Grove had written that 'Much Cabinet business is now almost formal': *Central
Administration in Britain* (1957), p. 339.

70 Hennessy, op. cit., p. 101.

71 Lord Hailsham has testified to Mrs Thatcher's use of such groups. He believes that her
manner of working 'undermines the collegiate character of the Cabinet', and that it is 'handy' for
her because it 'reduces the discussions' in the Cabinet: see (1987) 1 *Contemporary Record* 58. He
developed his views in the Granada Guildhall Lecture 1987. Mr Prior goes so far as to say (op. cit.,
p. 133) that, since 1982, '. . . she has adopted ad hoc groups as one of her main methods of
government. . . . [T]he formal Cabinet committees were very much downgraded and she began
to operate very much in small groups dominated by her cronies. . . . This had obvious advantages
for those few on the "inside track", who came to regard meetings with their other colleagues as
increasingly unnecessary and time-wasting. But it is not at all good for the many, including Cabinet
Ministers, who are on the outside and who believe ad hoc groups can be weighted against them in
the way Cabinet cannot': op. cit., pp. 132–3.

72 Hennessy, op. cit., p. 102.

Heseltine's minute *It Took a Riot* in 1981, in which he urged greater government investment in the inner cities after the riots of that year. Mrs Thatcher convened an informal ministerial group, with a majority of members chosen by the Prime Minister who would be unsympathetic towards Mr Heseltine's proposals. The extra spending which was ultimately authorized was on nothing like the scale urged by Mr Heseltine.

All this directly raises the question of whether and if so how the increase in extra-Cabinet decision-making has enhanced prime ministerial power. Richard Crossman was convinced that the Cabinet committee system, particularly *ad hoc* committees, allowed the Prime Minister to get his own way more than he would through the full Cabinet. Thus he wrote in 1970 that the device of setting up hundreds of *ad hoc* committees to deal with specific problems, bypassing the relevant standing Cabinet committees, was important in helping Mr Wilson obtain decisions acceptable to him, primarily because he packed those committees with Ministers having views similar to his own.[73] Crossman also thought that the position of individual Ministers had been weakened by the 1970 rule limiting appeals from committees to the Cabinet.[74] The use of committees (especially the *ad hoc* variety) must certainly entail advantages for a Prime Minister over his Cabinet. First, it is the Prime Minister who has virtually absolute power over Cabinet committees. He alone decides whether to establish a particular committee at all. If he decides to do so, he decides on membership and who is to be its chairman,[75] within the limits of political prudence excluding those who might not further his own preferred solutions. He alone can decide on the terms of reference. He can (like Mr Wilson) lay down rules which restrict access from committees to the Cabinet. He can give a committee executive powers. He alone decides whether to wind up a committee. Secondly, the use of committees and informal ministerial meetings will in certain circumstances reduce the power of the Cabinet. Decisions taken by such bodies may be tantamount to a final Cabinet decision even if that decision goes to the Cabinet for approval. After all, the issue will have been examined minutely, frequently with access to expert official advice; those Ministers on the committee will often have relevant departmental expertise so

---

[73] Crossman, op. cit., iii. 860–1.

[74] Ibid. Gordon Walker, op. cit., p. 44, viewed the 1970 change merely as a way to relieve pressure on the Cabinet.

[75] During Mr Callaghan's administration the Cabinet Energy Committeee was chaired by the Secretary of State for Industry, Mr Varley, rather than the Secretary of State for Energy, Mr Benn: *New Statesman*, 21 July 1978.

that respect will naturally be accorded to their views by the rest of the
Cabinet; the committee or group will strive to be unanimous, for if it
cannot compromise the Cabinet would be unlikely to either; a Minister
who sought to hold up the smooth running of a Cabinet meeting by
insisting on a return to the first principles of an issue could not count on
being popular, and a non-member of the committee or group might
want to give its recommendations a clear run so that, when his turn
came, the proposals of his committee or group might be accorded an
equally clear run.

Now such assertions have been denied. Harold Wilson has described
this view of prime ministerial power exercised through Cabinet committees as being, for two reasons, 'facile'.[76] A Prime Minister, he writes,
could not try to go against a unanimous decision of a Cabinet committee
of seven or eight Ministers. That, however, sidesteps the Prime Minister's life-giving power over such committees already outlined, especially
the fact that he chooses whom to put on the committees in the first
place. Harold Wilson also prays in aid Lord Blake to underline the
benign nature of the committee system: Lord Blake had written that it
'. . . strengthens—by making more efficient—the Cabinet itself'.[77]
That, in its turn, does not do justice to the ways indicated earlier in
which the Cabinet's own decision-making power can be diminished by
that system. Gordon Walker makes assertions similar to Lord Blake's,
but offers no explanation or evidence.[78]

No one doubts the personal authority of Mrs Thatcher in the 1980s
over her Cabinet and administration. I have argued that any Prime
Minister has wide powers over the formal Cabinet committee system
and that that system must in many cases effectively reduce the Cabinet's
ability to reject solutions favoured by the committee. The well-
documented use of the more fluid and perhaps more malleable informal
ministerial groups by Mrs Thatcher must make her (and any like-minded
successor) even more powerful in relation to the Cabinet.

Some of the above is necessarily speculative. This is because the
Cabinet committee system is a holy of holies to which only the Prime
Minister and the Cabinet Secretary as its high priests have total access.
There is no official list of even the standing committees, their chairmen,
members, or terms of reference. Only two official revelations have been
made since 1945 about the mystery. In 1963 the existence and member-

[76] Wilson, op. cit., p. 65.
[77] *The Office of Prime Minister* (1975), p. 53.
[78] Op. cit., p. 46.

ship of the Defence and Oversea Policy Committee was announced in a White Paper on the reorganization of the Ministry of Defence and the abolition of the three Service Ministries[79]—a curious (though welcome) piece of government openness given that the Committee deals with the most secret matters. Then in 1979 Mrs Thatcher confirmed the existence of four key standing committees,[80] Defence and Oversea Policy, Economic Strategy,[81] Home and Social Affairs, and the Legislation Committee. The rest is silence. Why?

For Jennings the main justification for keeping Cabinet committees more secret than the Cabinet itself was that, if information were made available about particular committees, the responsibility of individual Ministers could be undermined. If the identity of a committee chairman became known, and if (as is usual) he had a number of departmental Ministers in his committee, '. . . the chairman, and not the departmental Minister, will be regarded as the expositor of Government policy'. Jennings thought that the danger had materialized in Churchill's ministerial overlord experiment.[82] Are there not two difficulties inherent in his reasoning? First, the Minister who will carry the can for the committee's decisions will be the one who has to defend it in Parliament: *that* is where the responsibility of a particular Minister will bite, not against whoever might have been the committee chairman. Indeed, in the confidential *Questions of Procedure for Ministers*[83] that very point is made: decisions 'reached by the Cabinet or Cabinet Committees are binding on all members of the Government. They are however normally announced and defended by the Minister concerned as his own

---

[79] Cmnd. 2097 (1963).

[80] 967 H. C. Deb. *179* (written answers 24 May 1979), repeated at 45 H. C. Deb. 7–8 (written answers 4 July 1983). The reason which prompted these answers is unclear.

[81] Mr Prior says that he won approval for his step-by-step approach to trade union reform in the Economic Strategy Committee, against the views of the Chancellor of the Exchequer, Sir Geoffrey Howe, who preferred a return to the wholesale approach which had been taken in the Industrial Relations Act 1971.

[82] Jennings, op. cit., p. 256. On the overlords, see chapter 7.

[83] On assuming office each Prime Minister updates and issues this paper to all his Ministers. It contains largely uncontroversial notes about, for example, the preparation of business for the Cabinet, attendance at the Cabinet, minutes, collective responsibility, precautions against unauthorized disclosure of information, the preparation of government statements and White Papers, accepting gifts, and private financial business. It remains secret. Copies are released under the 30-year rule provided in the Public Records Act 1958 (as amended by the Public Records Act 1967), and extracts from the 1952 version are given in Hennessy, op. cit., pp. 8–14. The 1976 version had 132 paragraphs, compared with the 1945 version of 37 paragraphs: Tony Benn, 'The Case for a Constitutional Premiership' (I W C Pamphlet No. 67, 1979). Extracts from the document (although not the then current version) were published in the *New Statesman*, 14, 21, and 28 February 1986.

decisions'.[84] Secondly, Jennings's view of committees is too narrow; many committees straddle several departments, and there could at the committee stage be no obvious departmental Minister who would bear primary responsibility for conclusions. For Sir Burke Trend, giving evidence as Cabinet Secretary to the Franks Committee on Section 2 of the Official Secrets Act 1911,[85] the justification for secrecy turned not on individual by on collective responsibility: it was essential that a government's decisions were perceived as being those of the Cabinet as a whole, not merely those of a group of Ministers. So if, for instance, it were known that a certain decision had been taken in a committee, then the impression could be created that named Ministers not on the committee were dissociated from it, or on the contrary that Ministers who had been on the committee were especially and closely associated with it.[86] It is hard to see why that objection would not be met by official confirmation of the obvious—that modern governments must work through Cabinet committees if administration is to be efficiently carried out, and that whether committees act for the Cabinet, or whether their recommendations are ratified by the Cabinet, the result is policy for which the whole Cabinet is responsible. The Trend worries seem based on the belief that the interested citizen would be unable to grasp that simple fact.

The most comprehensive prime ministerial statement of the reasons for secrecy over Cabinet committees is contained in Mr Callaghan's personal minute of 1978, *Disclosure of Cabinet Committees*.[87] Those reasons may be summarized in nine points; brief comments will be offered on each. (*a*)'The manner of deciding policy questions is essentially a domestic one for any government.' This is a singularly unconvincing, if not coy, reason because Cabinet committees and the like attract legitimate interest as vital aspects of the machinery of government. As Gordon Walker put it,[88] the public has a right to know at least the organization of the Cabinet and Cabinet committee system given their central role in the way the public is governed. (*b*) 'The status of a decision could be disputed if it

---

84 *Questions of Procedure for Ministers* (1976 version), para. 22.

85 Report, Cmnd. 5104 (1972), Minutes of Evidence, iii. 324–6.

86 Memorandum from the Cabinet Office to the Franks Committee, para. 5. This justification has also been given by Mrs Thatcher as Prime Minister to the Commons: see 974 H. C. Deb. *450* (written answers 26 November 1979).

87 This was leaked and published in the *New Statesman*, 10 November 1978. It is published in full in Colin Turpin's *British Government and the Constitution: Text, Cases and Materials* (1985), pp. 138–9. It is not insignificant that there is no mention of Cabinet committees in Mr Callaghan's memoirs.

88 Op. cit., p. 45.

were acknowledged to have been reached by a committee rather than by the full Cabinet.' That is essentially Sir Burke Trend's reason already doubted above. (c) 'The existence of some committees could not be disclosed for reasons of national security.' Within an understanding of national security somewhat narrower than that promulgated by the government in recent years, that must be right.[89] (d) 'The absence of a committee on a particular subject, such as poverty, does not mean that the government attaches no importance to it;' (e) 'the existence in particular of ad hoc committees should not be disclosed because they are ephemeral.' Both those points could be fully met by official explanation— and, in relation to the former, by a government's deeds in relation to the subject-matter. (f) 'Disclosure could reveal that sensitive things were under discussion,' and (g) 'that something was in train about which the government was not ready to make an announcement.' Now both points are really indirect ways of saying that publicity would be inconvenient for a government, as MPs and others might want to contribute to the arguments before a policy was agreed. (h) 'Disclosure of standing committees alone would give a misleading picture.' That could, again, be met by explanation, or by disclosure of all committees (national security permitting). (i) 'Any departure from the convention of non-disclosure would be more likely to whet appetites than to satisfy them.' That phrase encapsulates the regrettable view adopted by civil servants and Ministers down the decades that secrecy is the norm, information and explanation the exception. The case for complete secrecy over Cabinet committees remains in my view unproved.

Confidentiality of proceedings and papers

Obviously the Cabinet and its committees must be able to deliberate in private and with some certainty that neither their proceedings nor their papers will subsequently be made public. They could not function on any other basis. What are the main legal and conventional means by which that position is maintained?

---

[89] The definition of the term 'national security' as understood by the Prime Minister in 1988 was taken '. . . to refer to the safeguarding of the state and the community against threats to their survival or well-being': 126 H. C. Deb. 7 (written answers 25 January 1988). Some sensitive economic matters would also require that the existence of any *ad hoc* committee on them would not be acknowledged.

It used to be thought that the Privy Councillor's oath[90] was a legal check preventing disclosure by Ministers of what happened in the Cabinet.[91] In part the Privy Councillor swears (or affirms) in terms established in Elizabethan times that he 'will keep secret all matters committed and revealed unto [him], or that shall be treated of secretly in Council'. But a literal interpretation of those words does not support that earlier belief, for the Cabinet is not the Privy Council, nor a committee of it: as the Radcliffe Committee on Ministerial Memoirs acknowledged, the Cabinet is a body distinct from the Privy Council.[92] Nor was the oath relied on by the Attorney-General in the Crossman diaries case in seeking to restrain their publication.[93] The Official Secrets Act 1911, section 2,[94] probably could not be used either to prosecute Cabinet Ministers who disclosed Cabinet proceedings.[95] Mr Crossman originally thought that, if he were to persist in his plan to publish revelations about his ministerial life after his resignation, he might be prosecuted under section 2; but the Prime Minister and the Cabinet Secretary told him in 1969 that their legal advice was that section 2 could not be used in that way.[96] The Radcliffe Committee, in a one-sentence paragraph,[97] recorded that no Minister or former Minister had been prosecuted under the Official Secrets Act and clearly considered that fact to have legal significance. The reason for this ministerial immunity seems to be that, as the Franks Report on section 2 of the Official Secrets Act put it, 'Ministers are, in

[90] The relevant part of that oath is set out in the Report of the Radcliffe Committee on Ministerial Memoirs, Cmnd. 6386 (1976), para. 21.

[91] For example, by Jennings, op. cit., pp. 228–9: although he wrote by reference to other factors which produce ministerial discretion, he clearly thought that the oath itself had some legal effect.

[92] Cmnd. 6386 (1976), para. 22.

[93] *Attorney-General* v. *Jonathan Cape Ltd.* [1976] Q.B. 752.

[94] In summary, s. 2 makes it an offence, punishable with up to 2 years' imprisonment, to retain without permission, or fail to take reasonable care of, information obtained as a result of one's present or former employment under the Crown or a government contract; or to *communicate* information so obtained, or entrusted to one in confidence by a person holding office under Her Majesty, or obtained in contravention of the Act, to anybody other than a person to whom one is authorized to convey it or to whom it is one's duty to impart it in the interests of the State; or to *receive* such information, knowing or having reasonable cause to believe that it has been given in contravention of the Act.

[95] Others who received information from a Minister could be prosecuted, although this has happened only rarely. For example, Edgar Lansbury was prosecuted under s. 2 for publishing memoranda which had been submitted to the Cabinet by his father George Lansbury (who had been First Commissioner of Works in the 1929 Labour Cabinet): George Lansbury was not prosecuted: Sir William Anson, *The Law and Custom of the Constitution* (4th edn., 1935), ii. 122.

[96] Crossman, op. cit., iii. 898–9.

[97] Cmnd. 6386 (1976), para. 26.

effect, self-authorizing. They decide for themselves what to reveal.'[98] Section 2 makes it an offence (among 2,323 other crimes[99]) to communicate information to anybody other than a person to whom one is authorized to convey it; and Ministers are assumed to be able to authorize themselves to do so. (Assuming that to be a correct view of the law, it is not easy to see why anyone who has resigned office may authorize himself to disclose information, unless, perhaps, the very generous view is taken that as he had been authorized to communicate lawfully while in office, then there is no reason to deny him that facility out of office.)

The principles established in *Attorney-General* v. *Jonathan Cape Ltd.*[100] could, however, be relied on in an appropriate case to prevent by injunction a Minister from disclosing Cabinet and other official discussions. The Lord Chief Justice there held that the courts have power to prevent such publication if it would be a breach of confidence and against the public interest by prejudicing the maintenance of the doctrine of collective responsibility. He also held that a Minister could be restrained, if need be indefinitely, from making any publication which would adversely affect national security.[101] On the facts the Attorney-General was denied an injunction because the first volume of the diaries complained of dealt with events which had taken place ten years before: the confidential nature of the material had ceased to exist—there would be no breach of confidence—and no issue of national security arose.

Legal restraints (such as they are) are not, however, very important. Ministers do not keep secrets through fear of injunctions, and indeed, as will be mentioned shortly, they make disclosures regularly while in office. To the extent that they feel bound to keep matters confidential they do so for conventional reasons: the weight of tradition (and the tradition of governmental secrecy is very strong), loyalty to their colleagues, a desire not to inhibit frank discussion, and the ultimate political threat—dismissal. True, there are also the guidelines recommended by the Radcliffe Committee[102] and accepted by the then

---

[98] Cmnd. 5104 (1972), para. 18. According to *Questions of Procedure for Ministers*, however, Minsiters are invited soon after appointment to sign a declaration that they have read the relevant provisions of the Official Secrets Acts. The reason for this is rather obscure in the light of the Radcliffe and Franks Reports.

[99] Ibid., Minutes of Evidence, ii. 262 (appendix of evidence of the Bar Council).

[100] [1976] Q.B. 752. See also Hugo Young, *The Crossman Affair* (1976).

[101] Ibid., at p. 770.

[102] Cmnd. 6386 (1976).

government,[103] to which the overwhelming majority of Ministers and
ex-Ministers have adhered since 1976 (subject to a major proviso about
leaking). Those guidelines require that at least fifteen years should elapse
before certain types of material should be disclosed, and the guidelines
continue the practice under which a former Minister wishing to publish
material derived from his time in office should submit the full text in
advance to the Cabinet Secretary, who will check that it is in line with
the Radcliffe guidelines. And the Prime Minister of the day is the final
court of appeal over national security and external relations matters, so
that indefinite secrecy may be enjoined. Those guidelines have not, however, been followed by a number of former Ministers:[104] the public
interest is, perhaps, also served by the full inside story of any administration coming into the public domain sooner rather than later, and publishers are eager that such accounts should do so.

In all this there is a wide gap between constitutional myth and
political reality. The myth is that for conventional (and perhaps legal)
reasons Ministers maintain a discreet silence about all government secrets,
so that problems over disclosure do not arise until they wish to publish
memoirs after resignation. But the reality is that Ministers—and Prime
Ministers—'brief' and 'leak' while in office. Attention will now be
turned to that issue.

From time to time Ministers will want their views publicly known so
as to distance themselves from any Cabinet decision with which they do
not agree: they may thus let their supporters know their views, and
perhaps mobilize opinion against that decision: to do so they make an
'unattributable leak', they 'brief' —it comes to the same thing.[105] This

[103] The government agreed that legislation on the matter would not be wise and that the
obligations should be binding on Ministers as a matter of honour: 903 H. C. Deb. 521–3 (22
January 1976). According to Mr Wilson's former Senior Policy Adviser, the Cabinet Secretary
tried to persuade the Prime Minister to insist that Ministers bind themselves more restrictively than
the Radcliffe Committee had proposed. See Bernard Donoughue, op. cit., pp. 123–4.

[104] Notably by Crossman's literary executors, and by Barbara Castle, *The Castle Diaries
1974–1976* (1980), and Hugh Jenkins, *The Culture Gap* (1979). Mr James Prior felt that the
contents of his *A Balance of Power* 'did not justify submission' of the text to the Cabinet Secretary—
although it is a book of memoirs. Mr Pym's *The Politics of Consent* was not submitted as it is 'a
treatise on politics'. Mr Callaghan's memoirs were, however, vetted. I am grateful to those last
three named authors who kindly answered my queries about this.

[105] As Mr Callaghan has helpfully explained, 'Briefing is what I do and leaking is what you do':
evidence to the Franks Committee, Cmnd. 5104 (1972), Minutes of Evidence, iv. 187. Crossman
recorded in his diary in 1969: 'People brief against each other, letting malicious stories out about
who does what. There is a difference between these malicious and damaging announcements and
the things I do, which are all designed to put the Government in a decent light': Crossman, op.
cit., iii. 583. No doubt his tongue was firmly in his cheek. There was notorious competitive
leaking during the Westland affair in 1985–6 by Ministers, the majority of whom favoured a
United States rescue of the helicopter firm, the minority favouring a European solution.

has taken place for decades. For such a leak to take place a journalist will be given information on the condition that he does not reveal its source. The Minister's purposes are served and the journalist gets his story: it is a symbiotic relationship which has the advantage that the public is better informed than otherwise might be the case. Two well-known examples may be briefly cited. After the devaluation of the pound in 1967 there were several press stories showing how the Cabinet had divided over the consequent economic cuts; and in the early years of Mrs Thatcher's government the economic 'wets' made sure that their case was known outside the Cabinet even if (or especially because) they were to lose the argument there. Prime Ministers have become past masters of the game: the appointment after the Second World War of a Press Officer at Number 10 Downing Street 'made the leak in a sense normal and almost official'.[106] The process has developed further under Mrs Thatcher at the hands of her Press Secretary Mr Bernard Ingham.[107] For according to Mr James Prior she has been the most adept Prime Minister at handling the press since 1945,[108] and in Mr Francis Pym's view, '[t]he notorious leaks have emanated as much from Downing Street as from anywhere else. The press receives a very good service from Number 10, which is perhaps why so much of it is so uncritical.'[109] Prime Ministers work with the Westminster Lobby system, to which journalists are accredited and through which the Downing Street Press Secretary can twice a day put the Prime Minister's version of events on an unattributable basis. This is 'briefing', the more respectable form of 'leaking'—after all, the Lobby is formally organized, has rules, and even officers, keeping sources secret on their words as gentlemen.

One of the reasons why governments of all parties have readily embraced the view that Ministers can authorize themselves to disclose information without fear of the Official Secrets Act is that the contrary view would mean a risk to the continuance of leaking, and the Attorney-General would have the invidious duty of deciding whether to consent to the prosecution of his ministerial colleagues who leaked and were found out. That would be inconvenient and distasteful for all concerned.

A day rarely passes without some item in the newspapers giving

[106] Gordon Walker, op. cit., p. 31.

[107] Mr Prior claims that she even leaked against her own Cabinet and quotes an example from a newspaper which resulted from it: 'Premier Margaret Thatcher routed the "wets" in her Cabinet yesterday in a major showdown over public spending. She waded into the attack . . .': Prior, op. cit., p. 135.

[108] Prior, op. cit., p. 134. See also Michael Cockerell, Peter Hennessy, and David Walker, *Sources Close to the Prime Minister* (1984).

[109] Pym, op. cit., p. 18.

details of Cabinet or Cabinet committee business which could only have been obtained by a leak. Leaking is periodically and hypocritically condemned by Prime Ministers and Ministers; sometimes leak inquiries are set up under the Cabinet Secretary; civil servants and Ministers are questioned; usually nothing comes of them.[110]

In this examination of Cabinet confidentiality Cabinet papers call for separate treatment. Such papers include Cabinet and Cabinet committee agendas, memoranda, minutes, and reports, and papers originating from departments with Ministers' views and civil service advice.[111] The special issues to be canvassed here are the restraints which exist on publication of such papers additional to those already mentioned, the access which former Ministers have to papers which they saw when in office, and whether a government has any right to see its predecessor's papers.

Cabinet documents are the property of the Crown.[112] Anyone who wishes to reproduce any part of them when they are still in copyright is subject to the Copyright Act 1956, so that publication of Cabinet papers could be actionable as being in breach of the Crown's copyright. As far as former Ministers refreshing their memories are concerned,[113] they will have been asked on leaving office to leave for their successors Cabinet documents needed for current administration and to return all others to the Cabinet Office.[114] They may, however, at any time thereafter have access in the Cabinet Office to Cabinet papers issued to them while they were in office, although they may not retain them. This sensible arrangement allows former Ministers to write and broadcast more authoritatively, subject to the limitations already noted. Access to one government's papers by a successor is governed by understandings explained by a former Cabinet Secretary, Lord Hunt of Tamworth.[115] They are that (a) Ministers may not see the Cabinet papers of a previous government of a different party, because they may wish to use them for party political capital; (b) Ministers may normally see the papers of previous administrations of the same party, provided the need to do so

---

[110] An exception was the Cabinet Secretary's inquiry into the leak to the Press Association of parts of the Solicitor-General's letter to Mr Heseltine in 1985, which eventually caused Mr Brittan to resign from the government.

[111] In 1977, 1,800 such papers were circulated to all members of the Cabinet. I am grateful to Mr Tony Benn for that fact.

[112] *Questions of Procedure for Ministers* (1952 version), para. 18, makes that point, and (in para. 8) also forbids the photocopying of Cabinet documents other than in the Cabinet Office.

[113] See generally Lord Hunt of Tamworth, 'Access to a Previous Government's Papers' [1982] *Public Law* 514.

[114] *Questions*, para. 18.

[115] See note 113 above.

arises out of normal ministerial duties; and (c) in any case the current Prime Minister seeks the approval of the former Prime Minister concerned (or, if he is not available, the current Leader of the relevant party) for access to the papers of the previous government. Classes of papers excluded from these understandings include documents deemed to be in the public domain (such as Ministers' letters to MPs), papers sent to foreign governments (for example, concerning bilateral negotiations), and Law Officers' opinions (which are not political documents).[116] Those excluded papers may be freely seen by successor governments regardless of party. In all this the object of the civil service is to judge what papers may properly be shown to Ministers without causing political embarrassment to former Ministers.[117]

Conclusions

In the previous chapter it was postulated that the Prime Minister's power has increased in relation to the rest of his colleagues. In this chapter it has been explained how that process has been accelerated by the development of ministerial decision-making away from the Cabinet as a whole. The Cabinet in its classical form as the supreme organ of administration, executing policies prescribed (or acquiesced in) by Parliament, has become a dignified element in the constitution; the structure of Cabinet committees and ad hoc ministerial groupings which occasionally in name and sometimes in effect decide government policy is the efficient part. It is true that from time to time the Cabinet may assert itself as of old to seek to restrain, or to limit the damage done by, the unacceptable exercise of prime ministerial power. It is also true that, as the style and authority of Prime Ministers vary, a Prime Minister still to take office could try to put the Cabinet as a forum back in the centre of the political stage. Perhaps for both those reasons developments since 1945 should not cause undue concern. It would, however, be helpful if Prime Ministers and Cabinet Secretaries could be persuaded to be frank about the Cabinet system as it now exists and so remove much of the unnecessary secrecy which surrounds it.

---

[116] Lord Hunt, op. cit., p. 516.

[117] Cabinet documents may also be protected from disclosure in litigation by a claim that such disclosure would be contrary to the public interest: see generally S. A. de Smith, *Judicial Review of Administrative Action* (4th edn., 1980 by J. M. Evans), pp. 35–46.

7

Ministers and Departments

Ministerial titles

The titles enjoyed by Ministers in the British government must baffle foreigners (and a few Britons). Some titles are very old and give no clue to the holders' present ministerial responsibilities, such as the Lord Privy Seal or the Chancellor of the Duchy of Lancaster. The ministerial head of a department of state may be called a Secretary of State or (rarely, nowadays) a Minister; his deputy may occasionally have a quaint title, such as Chief Secretary to the Treasury, or Paymaster General, or he may be styled Minister of State (sometimes with an informal title as well, like Minister for Local Government); the most junior Minister in a depart-ment may be called the Parliamentary Under-Secretary of State, or simply the Parliamentary Secretary. And most ministerial styles are more of a mouthful today than they were in former times—for instance, the Minister of Defence as was is now the Secretary of State for Defence; the Minister of Education is now the Secretary of State for Education and Science; the Parliamentary Secretary, Ministry of Health, is now the Parliamentary Under-Secretary of State, Department of Health and Social Security; and so on.[1] Now none of this matters very much, but minis-terial nomenclature requires systematic explanation if it is to be under-stood at all clearly.

The statutory definition of a Minister of the Crown is '. . . the holder of any office in Her Majesty's Government in the United Kingdom . . .'[2]—but that is hardly pellucid. A more helpful description of a Minister is a Member of Parliament or peer who is a member of the party (or one of the parties) which forms the government of the day and who is appointed to and removed from political office by the Sovereign on the Prime Minister's advice (or, in the case of a junior Minister, by the Prime Minister directly). The various ranks of Minister may, for convenience,

---

[1] Mr Edward Heath probably had the longest collection of titles as Secretary of State for Industry, Trade and Regional Development and President of the Board of Trade, in 1963–4.

[2] Ministers of the Crown Act 1975, s. 8(1).

be placed in different groups.

The first group is made up of the historical offices—the First Lord of the Treasury (always held today by the Prime Minister[3]); the Lord Chancellor (whose predecessors go back to the reign of Edward the Confessor); the Lord President of the Council (an office dating from 1497); the Lord Privy Seal[4] (which can be traced back to the fourteenth century); the Chancellor of the Duchy of Lancaster; and the Paymaster General.[5] The last three offices involve few departmental duties,[6] and in a modern administration will have tasks allotted to their holders by the Prime Minister on an *ad hoc* basis. The office of Prime Minister needs no further elaboration here.[7] The only other very old title, however, that of Secretary of State,[8] does require full consideration, because Secretaries of State now head nearly all the most important government departments. Up to 1782 there was only one Secretary of State. In that year his responsibilities were divided between two Secretaries of State, one for domestic and colonial matters, the other for foreign affairs, thus marking the beginning of the offices of Home Secretary and Foreign Secretary. A Secretary of State for War was appointed in 1794; other Secretaries of State were added as governmental responsibilities expanded; today there are thirteen.[9] In legal theory there is only one Secretary of State,[10] and lip-service is still paid to that theory by the parliamentary draftsman who insists in legislation on using the word 'the' or 'a' Secretary of State, not describing which one he means, even when it is obvious which one is in his mind.[11] Again, although the office of a Secretary of State can be created by an act of prerogative, it is the usual modern practice to legislate for any new Secretary of State, to make him a corporation sole,

---

[3] See chapter 5.

[4] Neither the Lord President of the Council nor the Lord Privy Seal need be a peer. The Lord President is always charged with Privy Council Office matters.

[5] The title of Chief Secretary to the Treasury sounds old, but in fact it was invented in 1961 to give further ministerial support to the Chancellor of the Exchequer, and is frequently held by a member of the Cabinet.

[6] The Chancellor of the Duchy of Lancaster is responsible for the general administration of the Duchy; the Paymaster General, however, has only nominal departmental tasks because his duties are entrusted to an Assistant Paymaster General, who is a civil servant.

[7] See chapters 5 and 6. The post of Deputy Prime Minister was considered in chapter 4.

[8] See Sir William Anson, *The Law and Custom of the Constitution* (4th edn., 1935 by A. B. Keith), ii. 172–84.

[9] The highest number ever was 15 in the 1974 Labour Cabinet.

[10] Unhelpfully, the phrase 'Secretary of State' is defined in the Interpretation Act 1978, s. 5 and Schedule 1 as 'one of Her Majesty's Principal Secretaries of State'.

[11] An exception is in the Defence (Transfer of Functions) Act 1964, s. 2, which refers to the Secretary of State for Defence.

and to provide for his duties and powers.[12] The total number of paid Secretaries of State cannot now exceed twenty-one,[13] and a Secretary of State heads every major department except the Treasury, the Lord Chancellor's Department and the Ministry of Agriculture.

As the ministerial heads of all the main departments are usually now in the Cabinet, I suggested earlier[14] that it is permissible to classify all Ministers outside the Cabinet as junior Ministers. (Should a ministerial office now in the Cabinet—say the Secretary of State for Transport[15]—be excluded from that body, he would not under this classification thereby become a junior Minister, because he would still be the ministerial head of a department; but it is unnecessary to think of a separate term for such a Minister just to accommodate what will now be a fairly infrequent occurrence.[16]) So in my formulation the expression 'junior Ministers'[17] covers the bulk of the government—the Law Officers, Ministers of State, Parliamentary Under-Secretaries of State, Parliamentary Secretaries, and Government Whips. The number of junior Ministers has increased dramatically, from a total in 1900 of some thirty ministers outside the Cabinet, to just under seventy in 1950, and to some eighty-five in 1988. Two reasons account for this growth: the general increase in governmental obligations and (since the 1960s) the merging of departments which has reduced the number of Ministers as heads of departments but which has required a related increase in the number of junior Ministers in those departments. The different types of junior ministerial office may now be considered.

Each government will have four Law Officers as its chief legal advisers, the Attorney-General and Solicitor-General, and the Lord Advocate and the Solicitor-General for Scotland.[18] The Attorney-General deals with questions of law arising on Bills, and with issues of legal policy, and he is concerned with all major international and domes-

---

[12] Through a statutory instrument made under the Ministers of the Crown Act 1975, ss. 2, 3. See, for example, the Secretary of State for Transport Order 1976, S.I. 1976 No. 1775, especially article 4 (style, seal, and acts of Secretary of State for Transport).

[13] Ministerial and other Salaries Act 1975, s. 1(1)(a), Schedule 1, Part V, para. 2 (a).

[14] See chapter 4.

[15] Transport was not represented in the Cabinet from 1976–81.

[16] The phrase 'Minister of Cabinet rank (not in the Cabinet)' was used for some years after 1945 to classify such a Minister, but that phrase is meaningless.

[17] See generally Kevin Theakston, 'The Use and Abuse of Junior Ministers' (1986) 57 *Political Quarterly* 18; *Junior Ministers in British Government* (1987).

[18] See J. Ll. J. Edwards, *The Law Officers of the Crown* (1964); *The Attorney-General: Politics and the Public Interest* (1984).

tic litigation involving the government. He has statutory duties in relation to the Crown Prosecution Service.[19] The Solicitor-General handles matters delegated to him by the Attorney-General, and they both answer in the House of Commons for the Lord Chancellor's Department. There is a small Law Officers' Department to assist the English Ministers,[20] and a Lord Advocate's Department for their Scottish counterparts.

The next rank of the junior Ministers is that of the Ministers of State.[21] A Minister of State was first appointed in 1941—Lord Beaverbrook, who, having left the Ministry of Aircraft Production, stayed in the War Cabinet and began the task of creating a Ministry of Production. The title was subsequently held by a succession of Ministers, in effect as the equivalent of Ministers without Portfolio. In 1950 the Minister of State was put into the Foreign Office as an additional junior Minister. Since then the number of Ministers of State has increased sharply to twenty-seven by 1988,[22] and almost all departments now have at least one Minister of State.[23] No doubt a contributory factory in this increase is that 'Minister of State' sounds grander than the titles of the other junior Ministers, such as Parliamentary Secretary, and so could be more impressive particularly in international negotiations. All Ministers of State take charge of a particular section of a department, and are also given particular tasks by their ministerial chief. Their exact duties (and indeed those of all other Ministers) are published from time to time by the Cabinet Office in the pamphlet *List of Ministerial Responsibilities*. In order to make the individual duties of the Ministers of State clearer, the custom developed in the 1970s, and continues, of describing certain Ministers of State by informal, or 'courtesy', titles, as Mrs Thatcher aptly dubbed them.[24] So in Mrs Thatcher's administration a Minister of State at the Foreign and Commonwealth Office holds the courtesy title

---

[19] See chapter 6.

[20] In the 1974 Labour government a Parliamentary Secretary to the Law Officers' Department was appointed.

[21] The statutory definition for purposes of the House of Commons Disqualification Act 1975, s. 9(1) is '. . . a member of Her Majesty's Government in the United Kingdom who neither has charge of any public department nor holds any other of the offices specified in Schedule 2 to this Act or any office in respect of which a salary is payable out of money provided by Parliament under s. 3(1)(*b*) of the Ministerial and other Salaries Act 1975 . . .'.

[22] Including the Financial Secretary and the Economic Secretary to the Treasury, who are of Minister of State rank.

[23] The Lord Chancellor's Department and the Law Officers' Department are the main exceptions in having no Minister of State; the Foreign and Commonwealth Office has four.

[24] See 106 H.C. Deb. *419* (written answers 1 December 1986).

of Minister for Overseas Development;[25] in the Department of Health and Social Security they are styled the Minister for Health and the Minister for Social Security and the Disabled; in the Department of the Environment they are the Minister for Local Government, the Minister for Environment, Countryside and Water, and the Minister for Housing and Planning; in the Department of Trade and Industry they are the Minister for Trade and the Minister for Trade and Industry; in the Department of Transport the Minister of State is the Minister for Public Transport. The use of the phrase 'Minister for' discloses the exact status of the holder: they are merely Ministers of State, but in name they represent a reversion to simpler days before the major departmental amalgamations.

At the bottom of the departmental ministerial hierarchy are the Parliamentary Under-Secretaries of State (if the ministerial head is a Secretary of State) or Parliamentary Secretaries (if the Minister in charge is not a Secretary of State: the only Parliamentary Secretaries today are in the Ministry of Agriculture and in the Treasury).[26] A Parliamentary Secretary has been statutorily defined as including '. . . a person holding Ministerial office (however called) as assistant to a Member of Her Majesty's Government in the United Kingdom, but not having departmental responsibilities'.[27] Some give parliamentary and departmental help directly to a Minister of State; most are themselves given responsibilities for particular areas—so that, for example, the Parliamentary Under-Secretary of State at the Home Office in Mrs Thatcher's government deals with numerous matters ranging from the police to animal welfare, all subject to a Minister of State and the Home Secretary. Parliamentary Secretaries will naturally hope that they so conduct themselves as to earn promotion up the ministerial ladder.

Every modern administration will have about twelve Whips in the House of Commons and a further seven in the Lords. The Government Chief Whip in the Commons is the Parliamentary Secretary to the Treasury (who has no Treasury duties, and indeed no room in it; he and his fellow Whips use Number 12 Downing Street). Under him are six

[25] A Ministry of Overseas Development was first established by Harold Wilson in 1964, the Minister being in the Cabinet. In Mr Heath's government the Ministry became the Overseas Development Administration within the Foreign and Commonwealth Office under a Minister of State. A separate Cabinet Minister was again appointed by Mr Wilson in 1974 and held office for a year or so; Mrs Thatcher reverted to Mr Heath's arrangements.

[26] The civil service follows suit: the official head of a department is styled either the Permanent Under-Secretary of State or the Permanent Secretary.

[27] House of Commons Disqualification Act 1975, s. 9(1).

Government Whips with various formal titles[28] and five Assistant Whips. Apart from their main functions of conveying the views of government back-bench MPs to the government, and vice versa, and of issuing the weekly whip (and administering discipline for breaches of it), arranging pairs, obtaining names of MPs to serve on parliamentary committees, and helping to manage government time in the House, the Commons Whips, through the Chief Whip, are a vital source of intelligence for the Prime Minister as to potential Ministers from the back-benches—and the Number 12 Whips' Office itself provides a separate pool from which ministerial promotions are made.[29] In the Lords all the Whips have notional appointments in the Royal Household and suitably fine titles to mark them out.[30] Party allegiances not being so vigorously policed in the Lords, some Whips are additionally designated government departmental spokesmen there. No equivalent status is ever accorded their Commons counterparts, who have to take a vow of silence.[31]

Two other forms of parliamentary and political life must be distinguished from what has gone before. A Minister may appoint a Parliamentary Private Secretary (or Secretaries) from the ranks of government back-benchers.[32] A PPS acts as a general dogsbody, advising his Minister on the state of parliamentary opinion, acting as a two-way channel of communication between MPs and his Minister, and generally helping the Minister with whatever parliamentary work he requires. PPSs are not Ministers; they are not paid; they have no official departmental status—but they are bound by collective ministerial responsibility[33] and as a consequence swell the maximum 'ministerial' vote in the House of Commons to some 150.[34] In return for their labours PPSs will obtain experience of ministerial life and, all being well, ministerial office one day. Since the 1970s Ministers have also taken to appointing one or two[35]

---

[28] Treasurer of Her Majesty's Household and Deputy Chief Whip; Comptroller of HM's Household; Vice-Chamberlain of HM's Household; and three Lords Commissioners of the Treasury.

[29] All Chief Whips since 1951 have gone on to be Cabinet Ministers, and Edward Heath (Chief Whip 1955–9) became Prime Minister.

[30] Captain of the Honourable Corps of Gentlemen-at-Arms (Chief Whip—who may be a woman: Baroness Llewelyn-Davies was so appointed in 1974); Captain of the Queen's Bodyguard of the Yeoman of the Guard (Deputy Chief Whip); and five Lords (or Baronesses) in Waiting.

[31] Save in moving the terms of formal motions.

[32] See R. K. Alderman and J. A. Cross, 'The Parliamentary Private Secretary' (1967) 48 *Parliamentarian* 75.

[33] This is considered below.

[34] Currently 41 PPSs and 105 Ministers.

[35] Mrs Thatcher has restricted her Ministers to one each.

personal advisers.[36] These now fall into two separate groups. First, they may be political advisers, brought in from outside Whitehall to give the Minister help with implementing that part of the government's election programme for which he has direct responsibility. Political advisers are paid from party funds and are not civil servants. Secondly, special advisers may be engaged by a Minister to give independent, non-party political, advice. They are given terms of appointment similar to those of civil servants. All personal advisers leave the department with the Minister.[37] The view that Ministers must have strong, effective support in implementing party policy has gained ground in all the political parties, and, although the presence of personal advisers can cause friction between them and established civil servants, there is no doubt that they are here to stay.[38]

I turn now from ministerial titles to the government departments in which their holders will work.

Departments

A working definition of a department of state is that it is headed by a Minister, is staffed by civil servants, and is charged, through the Minister, with recommending policies to the Cabinet and Cabinet committees; and when those policies have been approved there (and perhaps by Parliament) the department then has the task of implementing the details of those policies.[39]

Until the late nineteenth century all the duties of government could be discharged by the holders of the historical offices. Up to that time, if new responsibilities were assumed, additional Secretaries of State were appointed: thus, for example, the Colonial Office was created in 1768, the War Office in 1794, and the India Office in 1858, each headed by a

---

[36] See Sir John Hoskyns, (1983) 36 *Parliamentary Affairs* 137 at 146; Harold Wilson, *The Governance of Britain* (1976), Appendix V. Harold Wilson gives two reasons for this development: the pressure of work on Ministers, and the need for the civil service to remain non-party political.

[37] See Joan Mitchell, (1978) 56 *Public Administration* 87; Mr Callaghan's explanations at 939 H.C. Deb. *913* (written answers 25 November 1977), 951 H.C. Deb. *142* (written answers 20 June 1978), and Mrs Thatcher's at 58 H.C. Deb. *155–6* (written answers 10 April 1984).

[38] In the 7th Report from the Treasury and Civil Service Committee, Civil Servants and Ministers: Duties and Responsibilities, H.C. 92 (1985–6), para. 5, the Committee took the idea of personal advisers further and recommended the creation of policy units for Ministers, staffed by non-civil servants.

[39] For a different formulation, see D. N. Chester and F. M. G. Willson, *The Organization of British Central Government 1914 to 1964* (2nd edn., 1968), p. 391.

Secretary of State. As the functions of government expanded, the Privy Council was used to provide new machinery of government, Boards of the Privy Council being established with a President as the Minister responsible. Thus the Local Government Board[40] was set up in 1871, the Board of Agriculture in 1889 and the Board of Education in 1900.[41] That nomenclature ceased to be fashionable after the turn of the century, and the first Ministry so called, the Ministry of Munitions, came into being in 1915, to be followed rapidly by others such as Pensions, and Labour, in 1916, and Agriculture,[42] Health, and Transport in 1919.[43] (Only one Ministry so called, with a Minister so called at its head, has survived to the present day—Agriculture, Fisheries and Food.) In 1964 the style changed again: from that year many new ministries were dubbed 'Departments',[44] beginning with the Department of Education and Science, to be followed later in the same year by the Department of Economic Affairs, and in subsequent years by the Departments of Health and Social Security, the Environment, Energy, and Prices and Consumer Protection. (Three 'Offices', headed by Secretaries of State, were also created from 1964—the Welsh Office, the Foreign and Commonwealth Office, and the Northern Ireland Office.) There is no legal significance in whether a department of state is designated a Board, Office, Ministry or Department; but since 1964 the descriptions Office and Department and the style Secretary of State have been reserved for the most politically important units.[45]

Prime Ministers will want to change the structure of government departments for various reasons—to establish a new department to implement a new government's policy;[46] to create machinery to cope with matters which can no longer be dealt with adequately within

[40] The Board became the Ministry of Health in 1919.

[41] There had been a Vice-President of the Committee of the Privy Council for Education since 1857.

[42] Succeeding the Board of Agriculture.

[43] These (and other departments to be mentioned) can be traced through Appendix D.

[44] Exceptions (also created in 1964) were the Ministries of Overseas Development, of Technology, and of Land and Natural Resources.

[45] Two oddities may be noted. When the Service Ministries were merged in 1964 into an expanded Ministry of Defence under a Secretary of State for Defence, the new department could logically have been styled the 'Department of Defence', or the 'Defence Office'. Possibly the old appellation was kept in 1964 because 'Department of Defence' might have sounded too Americanized. Then again, when the Department of Health and Social Security was created in 1968, the Secretary of State was styled 'Secretary of State for Social Services', not 'for Health and Social Security'.

[46] In 1964, for example, the new Labour Prime Minister created five new departments.

existing structures;[47] to abolish departments whose usefulness has passed,[48] or which have ceased to represent a governmental responsibility;[49] or to merge departments; or to change the titles of Ministers or departments to mark a fresh approach. Frequent departmental changes are, however, disruptive and costly, and that price may not always be set against the benefit which the Prime Minister thinks will be achieved at that cost.[50] Not surprisingly, changes in the machinery of government have tended to be greater under Labour than under Conservative governments.

The Ministers of the Crown Act 1975[51] provides the means of hatching, matching, and dispatching departments and ministerial titles. An Order in Council may provide for the transfer to one Minister from another of any function, or dissolve any government department and distribute any of its functions to another Minister or Ministers, or direct that any Minister's functions will be exercisable concurrently with another Minister (or cease to be so exercisable).[52] An Order in Council may effect changes in relation to Secretaries of State and their departments.[53] If, however, the Prime Minister wishes to create a new department (rather than merely transfer existing functions to it from elsewhere) with a 'Minister' at its head rather than a Secretary of State, the 1975 Act does not apply and a fresh statute must be passed for the purpose. Thus in 1964 the Ministries of Land and Natural Resources, of Overseas Development, and of Technology required such an Act.[54] This is a pointless complication: the 1975 Act should be amended to allow the creation of any new department (however called) and any new Minister (however styled) by Order in Council.[55] The main changes in ministerial

[47] So, the Northern Ireland Office was set up in 1972 because the Home Office could no longer adequately deal with the province's problems, and the Department of Energy was established in 1974 after the escalation in the price of oil and during the emergency caused by a miners' strike.

[48] A large number of wartime departments were abolished after both world wars; the Department of Economic Affairs and the Ministry of Land and Natural Resources were merged into existing departments in 1967.

[49] Such as the Irish offices after the creation of the Irish Free State, and the abolition of the office of Postmaster-General when the Post Office became a public corporation in 1969.

[50] Of the 28 departments created between 1960 and 1979, 13 had been wound up by 1981: see Christopher Pollitt, 'The Civil Service Department: A Normal Death?' (1982) 60 *Public Administration* 73.

[51] The original statute was the Ministers of the Crown (Transfer of Functions) Act 1946.

[52] Section 1(1). Other consequential provisions are contained in s. 1(2).

[53] Section 2(1). Property rights are dealt with in s. 3.

[54] Ministers of the Crown Act 1964, ss. 1, 2(1)(a). Their *abolition* was effected by Order in Council.

[55] Especially as s. 5 of the 1975 Act subjects Orders in Council made under it to parliamentary scrutiny.

titles and in the list of government departments since 1900 are indicated in Appendix D.

The use of non-departmental Ministers

Traditionally, the holders of offices such as Lord President of the Council, Lord Privy Seal, Chancellor of the Duchy of Lancaster and Paymaster General have been allotted particular tasks by the Prime Minister on an *ad hoc* basis within their own very small departments. So, for example, Harold Macmillan charged Charles Hill (as Chancellor of the Duchy of Lancaster) with general government publicity, and Lord Hailsham (as Lord President of the Council) to try to reduce unemployment in the north-east. As the importance of Cabinet committees grew, so non-departmental Ministers were given heavier loads of committee work, and such Ministers will always be a prime source of Cabinet committee membership.

There are, additionally, three other modern uses of non-departmental Ministers. First, the Lord President of the Council and the Lord Privy Seal will usually be the Leaders of the two Houses: this was the case throughout the Wilson, Heath, and Callaghan governments and for most of Mrs Thatcher's.[56] The Leaders of the two Houses have major responsibilities in ensuring the progress of government business in Parliament,[57] and in practice two members of any Cabinet will have most of their time taken up as Leaders of the House of Commons and of the House of Lords.[58] Secondly, the Chairman of the Conservative Party Organization since 1951 has frequently been appointed as a non-departmental Minister with a seat in the Cabinet.[59] The Opposition has routinely objected to this: the fact that the Ministers involved have drawn a reduced, or no, ministerial salary has not assuaged them. Thirdly, some Ministers holding traditional titles have been used since 1970 as deputies to departmental Ministers, or have been given a major

---

[56] Although the Leader of the House of Commons from 1979–81 was the Chancellor of the Duchy of Lancaster.

[57] See chapters 9 and 10.

[58] They are unlikely to be also departmental Ministers, as was the case in (say) the 1950s.

[59] Mr Norman Tebbit was Chancellor of the Duchy of Lancaster in the Cabinet from 1985–7 and Chairman of the Conservative Party: he remained Chairman for a few months after his retirement from the government in 1987. Lord Thorneycroft, however (Chairman 1975–81), was not given ministerial office in 1979; Mr Gummer (Chairman 1983–5) was made a Minister, but outside the Cabinet. The current Chairman, Mr Peter Brooke, is also a junior Minister at the Treasury.

responsibility within a department. So in 1970 the Chancellor of the Duchy of Lancaster was put in charge within the Foreign and Commonwealth Office of negotiating terms for the United Kingdom's entry into the European Economic Community; from 1979 to 1982 the Lord Privy Seal was placed in the Foreign and Commonwealth Office and the Cabinet as deputy to the Foreign Secretary, who was in the House of Lords; and in 1985 the Paymaster General was brought into the Cabinet and the Department of Employment as number two (and 'Minister for Employment') to the Secretary of State, who was a peer: the same two individuals were transferred to the Department of Trade and Industry in the 1987 reshuffle, as Chancellor of the Duchy of Lancaster and Secretary of State respectively.

Should the four traditional non-departmental offices not be enough for a Prime Minister's purposes, he may designate a colleague (or colleagues[60]) as Minister without Portfolio. The 1951 Conservative government had a Minister without Portfolio from 1954–64, and the 1964 Labour and 1970 Conservative governments for the whole of their lives; Mrs Thatcher, on the other hand, has had only one Minister without Portfolio, for about a year.[61]

Winston Churchill experimented with the use of non-departmental Ministers as co-ordinating Ministers or 'overlords', from 1951–3.[62] Three peers were so used: Lord Cherwell (Paymaster General) co-ordinated scientific research and development; Lord Woolton (Lord President of the Council) oversaw the Ministries of Agriculture and Fisheries, and of Food, and Lord Leathers (the first—and last—Secretary of State for the Co-ordination of Transport, Fuel and Power) superintended the Ministries of Transport, of Civil Aviation, and of Fuel and Power. The relevant departmental Ministers were not made members of the Cabinet. These arrangements were criticized in Parliament[63] on the grounds that they blurred the responsibility to Parliament of the departmental Ministers, giving some responsibility (or none of it: this was never satisfactorily explained[64]) to the 'overlords'.[65] The system was allowed to lapse in

---

[60] In 1963, 1964–6, and 1967–8 there were two Ministers without Portfolio.

[61] Lord Young, 1984–5. He was made Secretary of State for Employment in 1985 and then for Trade and Industry in 1987.

[62] See Sir Ivor Jennings, *Cabinet Government* (3rd ed., 1959), pp. 78–81; Anthony Seldon, *Churchill's Indian Summer: The Conservative Government 1951 to 1955* (1981), pp. 102–6.

[63] They were never supported by Sir Norman Brook, the Cabinet Secretary, or Sir Edward Bridges, Permanent Secretary to the Treasury: Seldon, op. cit., p. 102.

[64] Lord Woolton denied that he had *any* ministerial responsibility to Parliament: 176 H.L. Deb. 474–7 (30 April 1952).

[65] For Churchill's explanations, see 500 H.C. Deb. 188–96 (6 May 1952): in essence, he believed that the departmental Ministers remained individually responsible, while the co-ordinating Ministers shared in the collective responsibility of the whole government.

1953.[66] (Strangely, a significant motive behind the experiment has been understood to have been to reduce the size of the Cabinet. Churchill's Cabinet was smaller by one than Attlee's, but this was in fact achieved by Churchill being Minister of Defence and by the exclusion of the Chancellor of the Duchy of Lancaster.) Co-ordination by a single Minister of the work of two or more departments can, however, be very successful if it is the intention to merge those departments. In 1968 Richard Crossman as Lord President of the Council was given the task of merging the Ministries of Health and of Social Security, which was achieved later that year when he became the inaugural Secretary of State for Social Services.[67]

Ministers' conduct

The three aspects of ministerial conduct which now fall to be considered are collective responsibility, individual responsibility, and rules relating to Ministers' personal financial affairs.

'Bye the bye, there is one thing we haven't agreed upon, which is, what are we to say? Is it to make our corn dearer, or cheaper, or to make the price steady? I don't care *which*: but we had better all tell the same story.'[68]

The essence of Lord Melbourne's cynical observation holds good today. For the doctrine of collective ministerial responsibility[69] requires that all Ministers, and usually Parliamentary Private Secretaries, must accept Cabinet decisions,[70] or dissent from them privately while remaining loyal to them publicly, or dissent publicly and resign, unless collective

---

[66] There was a Cabinet reshuffle in September 1953: Lords Leathers and Cherwell left the government and their 'overlord' functions were not continued. Lord Woolton had left the Cabinet in 1952. Sir John Colville, Churchill's Principal Private Secretary, thought that the experiment had proved unsuccessful: see *The Fringes of Power: Downing Street Diaries 1939-1955* (1985), p. 633. Sir Douglas Wass has referred with approval to a possible 'overlord' scheme: *Government and the Governed* (1984), pp. 27–30.

[67] Duncan Sandys was appointed Secretary of State for Commonwealth Relations in 1960, and was also made Secretary of State for the Colonies in 1962. Separate Secretaries of State were appointed in the new Labour government in 1964, but the two offices were merged into a new Commonwealth Office in 1966. See Appendix D.

[68] Lord Melbourne, after his Cabinet had been deliberating on the Corn Laws, quoted in Spencer Walpole, *Life of Lord John Russell* (1889), i. 369.

[69] See generally S. A. de Smith, *Constitutional and Administrative Law* (5th edn., 1985 by H. Street and R. Brazier), pp. 191–7; E. C. S. Wade and A. W. Bradley, *Constitutional and Administrative Law* (10th edn., 1985 by A. W. Bradley), chapter 7; Jennings, op. cit., pp. 277–89; John Mackintosh, *The British Cabinet* (3rd edn., 1977), pp. 531–6; Geoffrey Marshall, *Constitutional Conventions* (1984), pp. 55–61.

[70] And Cabinet committee decisions taken executively on the Cabinet's behalf.

responsibility is waived by the Cabinet on any given occasion. If a Minister does not resign over an issue of policy or procedure he will be collectively responsible for it, in the sense that he will have to support it publicly through his votes in Parliament and through his speeches. It will be no defence or excuse for him to say that the decision was taken without his knowledge (because, for example, he was a mere Parliamentary Under-Secretary of State not privy to Cabinet discussions, or because he was absent from the relevant meeting), for the doctrine binds all members of the government from the lowest to the highest: it is for that reason misleading to refer to it as collective *Cabinet* responsibility. There are many examples of Ministers of all ranks resigning or being required to resign because they could not accept collective responsibility for some decision or other—Cabinet Ministers,[71] Ministers of State,[72] Chief Whips,[73] and Parliamentary Secretaries.[74]

If a Prime Minister wishes, he may extend (and since 1945 usually has extended) the doctrine to Parliamentary Private Secretaries as well. Both Attlee and Harold Wilson dismissed a number of PPSs who abstained on government legislation. Although it is individual Ministers who appoint their own PPSs, the consequence of accepting appointment is that they may be bound by collective responsibility, and may be dismissed by the Prime Minister if they fail to give the government the loyalty which he thinks it deserves. This is as it should be. True, they are not Ministers and they are not paid; but they are necessarily very close to Ministers and public dissent by a PPS could be taken as a sign that the Minister himself dissents. In 1967 the PPSs to the President of the Board of Trade and the Minister of Agriculture campaigned vigorously against possible entry into the European Economic Community, and were correctly seen as surrogates for their ministerial chiefs.[75]

Now it is wrong to view collective responsibility either as a notion which ensures ministerial solidarity of almost Soviet proportions or as a

---

[71] For example, Mr Heseltine as Secretary of State for Defence in 1986: this is considered below.

[72] For instance, Mr Ian Gow, Minister of State at the Treasury, resigned in 1985 because he could not defend the government's conclusion of the Anglo-Irish Treaty with the Republic of Ireland.

[73] Attlee's Chief Whip in the Lords described the government's handling of a dock labour dispute in 1949 as 'absolutely crazy', and had to resign.

[74] For example, Dr Jeremy Bray, Parliamentary Secretary, Ministry of Technology, in the 1964 Labour government wanted to publish a book on economic management and the machinery of government: Mr Wilson refused him permission, saying that as Prime Minister he had to uphold 'the collective responsibility of the Administration', and Dr Bray resigned: see *The Times*, 26–9 September 1969.

[75] Mackintosh, op. cit., p. 532.

weapon which the Prime Minister can use in deadly fashion if faced by a recalcitrant colleague. In order to preserve the essentials of the doctrine at all a number of safety valves have been developed in it. Of these the unattributable leak[76] is the life-saver of collective responsibility. A Minister puts his views in the Cabinet or Cabinet committee; it turns out that he is in a minority and the decision goes against him; the Minister can accept neither defeat nor the end of his ministerial career, so he stays in the government and briefs the press as to his opposition. The result is that all the world knows that he opposes the policy, just as if he had resigned, but by using an unattributable leak the façade of collective responsibility is maintained and Minister, press and Prime Minister are happy. The citizen, however, will be left rather puzzled. The leak has also had another general and beneficial side effect. Ministerial solidarity involves the stifling of open dissent: it thereby contributes to secrecy in government, for although questions may be strongly contested between Ministers, solidarity requires that they are not aired in a way that would enable public opinion to be expressed before decisions are reached. The argument 'goes on behind the screen of collective responsibility'.[77] The leak will, however, occasionally draw that screen to one side.

A second safety valve consists in the ability of a Minister to run very close to the boundary between ministerial solidarity and open dissent in the hope or knowledge that the Prime Minister will do precious little to rein him in. Frank Cousins, the trade union general secretary temporarily turned Minister of Technology and MP in the 1964 Labour government,[78] publicly expressed his 'delight' when his union voted to condemn both the government's prices and incomes policy and its attitude to the Vietnam war.[79] In 1969, the Home Secretary, James Callaghan, spoke in the NEC against the government's proposals for industrial relations legislation contained in the White Paper 'In Place of Strife'; his dissent was (as he would have wished) leaked; but the only penalty imposed was exclusion from the Parliamentary Committee of the Cabinet. Then again, during the contest for the Leadership of the Labour Party in 1976 on Harold Wilson's retirement, Tony Benn, Secretary of State for Energy, publicly advocated policies which ran counter to the government's actual or likely policies: I argued in chapter

[76] See chapter 6.
[77] Colin Turpin, *British Government and the Constitution: Texts, Cases and Materials* (1985), p. 147.
[78] See chapter 4.
[79] Mackintosh, op. cit., p. 532.

2, however, that this might be regarded as a special case. What was *not* in any sense special was Mr Benn's dissociation in the NEC from the Cabinet's policies which produced a rebuke from the Prime Minister and a minute to Ministers reminding them of the obligations imposed on them by collective responsibility—but no other sanction.[80] And during Mrs Thatcher's administration Mr Peter Walker has been widely regarded as using 'coded' public speeches, such as his Harold Macmillan Lecture in 1984,[81] to advocate 'wetter' economic and social strategies than those being collectively pursued by his colleagues. These and similar occurrences amply show that near or actual breaches of collective responsibility provoke no automatic penalty: much will turn on the particular Minister's political strength, his ability to brazen out any demands for his resignation, and the attitude of the Prime Minister.

A somewhat different safety valve may allow a Minister, or the Prime Minister, publicly to go beyond and extend the agreed policies of the government without prior authority; the result can be a falling into line behind the Minister concerned.[82] As Prime Minister, Lloyd George occasionally made policy in this way, one of the most notable examples being his announcement in 1916 to a journalist (an American journalist at that) of the strategy of the 'knock-out blow' against the Axis powers—a vast commitment of men to overwhelm the enemy—without prior consultation of any Cabinet colleague.[83] Ministers have even announced departures during parliamentary debates: for instance, Sir William Joynson-Hicks, the Home Secretary, replying to a debate on a Private Member's Bill in 1927, startled the Prime Minister and indeed the whole House by committing the government to introduce its own Bill to reduce the age at which women would get the vote.[84] The Cabinet had taken no such decision, but rather than drop his Home Secretary, Baldwin adopted the proposal as the lesser evil.[85] Mrs Thatcher, a past master at the television interview, has been judged to develop policy in that medium, for example on immigration: but then what can a modern Cabinet do other than acquiesce in such things, at least outwardly?

The last and uncommon and derided but in my view attractive device

---

[80] He had to repeat the exercise in 1974: see Wilson, op. cit., Appendix I.

[81] Published in 1984 by the National Young Conservatives.

[82] A number of examples this century are given by Jennnings, op. cit., pp. 287–8.

[83] See Lloyd George, *War Memoirs* (1933), ii. 856–7.

[84] Lord Birkenhead, *Life of the First Earl of Birkenhead*, vol. ii (1934), pp. 291–2.

[85] The qualifying age for women to vote had been set at 30 in 1918. The Representation of the People Act 1928—the result of Joynson-Hicks's pledge—reduced it to 21. Joynson-Hicks went into honourable retirement in 1929 as Viscount Brentford.

for holding a government together is the agreement to differ. The only three examples of such agreements this century are well known and will not be rehearsed in any detail here.[86] They were the 'National Government's' agreement to differ in 1932 over the introduction of a general tariff (without which four free-trade Cabinet Ministers would have resigned[87]); the Labour Cabinet's decision to suspend collective responsibility 'in the unique circumstances' of the 1975 referendum campaign (on whether the United Kingdom should continue to be a member of the European Economic Community) so that Ministers who dissented from the Cabinet's recommendation to vote to remain in could say so publicly—although outside Parliament;[88] and the further suspension in 1977 so that Ministers who could not support the introduction of direct elections to the European Assembly could vote against the second reading of the European Assembly Elections Bill.[89] These suspensions are usually regarded as some sort of affront to our system of government, not to be spoken of in polite society. Sir Ivor Jennings, for instance, wrote that the 1932 agreement was a 'strange device', but that 'no harm was done by the precedent of 1932 provided that it is not regarded as a precedent'.[90] MacDonald's resort to an agreement to differ is usually described as a failure. Now, partly no doubt because of their rarity, agreements to differ look bad. The contrast between government A, which keeps its disagreements discreetly private, and government B, which openly announces a disagreement, is sharp and provides political ammunition for the latter's opponents. And James Callaghan's announcement—at the time of the 1977 suspension—'. . . I certainly think that the doctrine [of collective responsibility] should apply, except in cases where I announce that it does not'[91]—was seen by some as a cynical exploitation of prime ministerial power. I find these objections

[86] See Jennings, op. cit., pp. 278–81; David Marquand, *Ramsay MacDonald* (1977), pp. 709–13; Wilson, op. cit., pp. 75–6, 194–7; Turpin, op. cit., 147–9; D. L. Ellis, 'Collective Ministerial Responsibility and Collective Solidarity' [1980] *Public Law* 367 at 383–9.

[87] Including the leading Liberals Sir Herbert Samuel and Sir Archibald Sinclair.

[88] See Mr Wilson's explanation at 884 H.C. Deb. 1746 (23 January 1975) and 889 H.C. Deb. 351 (written answers 7 April 1975); *The Governance of Britain*, pp. 194–7. Mr Heffer spoke *inside* the House of Commons against continued membership and was dismissed as Minister of State for Industry: see chapter 5.

[89] See Mr Callaghan's statement at 889 H.C. Deb. 1307 (23 March 1977).

[90] Jennings, op. cit., pp. 279, 281. Even Wade and Bradley, op. cit., p. 110 consider that this 'short-lived departure from the principle of unanimity has generally been regarded as demonstrating the virtues of that principle and justifiable, *if at all* [my italics], only in the special circumstances of a coalition government formed to deal with a national crisis.'

[91] 933 H.C. Deb. 552 (16 June 1977).

unimpressive. The 1975 and 1977 suspensions were not only undoubted successes for the governments concerned—the two administrations held together, which is the main aim of the exercise—but also the issues before Ministers and the country (particularly in 1975) were more fully aired and argued than otherwise would have been the case. Even the 1932 experiment bought the coalition government an extra eight months of continued free-trade support (both National Liberal and National Labour) which it otherwise would have forfeited, at a time when the maximum national solidarity was desirable.[92] More fundamentally, why in a mature democracy do we still insist on the maintenance of the fiction that all Ministers are agreed on everything all the time—or at least that they all loyally fall in unreservedly behind majority decisions? That they do not is eloquently attested to by leaks—themselves an accepted but dishonest ruse, more objectionable in my view than an occasional and open agreement to differ. Governments should be readier to announce majority decisions and should use suspensions of the obligations of collective responsibility more often. The electorate would see more of the reality of political life, and there would be some increase in public debate of major issues. Naturally, there would have to be limits: every government must officially hold together on essentials— monetarism (or whatever is the appropriate label) rather than traditional liberal Conservative orthodoxy in the 1980s, for example; and too many suspensions could be politically dangerous. Subject to that, I accept Dr Geoffrey Marshall's injunction in the same spirit in which it is offered, that 'Those who now esteem open government ought perhaps to encourage open disagreements, openly arrived at.'[93]

Despite the safety valves (which could alternatively be described as the weaknesses in the doctrine of collective responsibility) some Ministers will reach a point of unavoidable departure from the administration. The Westland affair is instructive.[94] The Westland company supplied helicopters to the Ministry of Defence and other NATO countries, and in

---

[92] Nine free-trade Ministers eventually resigned in September 1932 over imperial preference.

[93] Marshall, op. cit., p. 58.

[94] On which see Geoffrey Marshall, 'Cabinet Government and the Westland Affair' [1986] *Public Law* 184; Magnus Linklater and David Leigh, *Not With Honour: The Inside Story of the Westland Scandal* (1986); Dawn Oliver and Rodney Austin, 'Political and Constitutional Aspects of the Westland Affair' (1987) 40 *Parliamentary Affairs* 20; Defence Committee, Westland PLC: The Government's Decision-making, H.C. 519 (1985-6)—and the government's response, Cmnd. 9916 (1986); Treasury and Civil Service Committee, 7th Report, Civil Servants and Ministers: Duties and Responsibilities, H.C. 92 (1985-6)—and the government's response, Cmnd. 9841 (1986).

1985 was in urgent need of financial reconstruction. Two reconstruction programmes emerged, one supported by the United States-backed Sikorsky-Fiat group, the other by a consortium of European manufacturers. Mrs Thatcher has always maintained that her government's policy was to leave the decision about which to take up to the Westland company; Mr Michael Heseltine, the then Secretary of State for Defence, maintained throughout that both she and Mr Leon Brittan, the then Secretary of State for Trade and Industry, consistently urged the Sikorsky-Fiat scheme on Westland, whereas he believed that the European option should have been chosen.[95] The two sides, as they may fairly be described, did not subsequently agree on other important details, for example, whether the issues were ever fully considered by the Cabinet, and whether a meeting of an important Cabinet committee about Westland had been arranged and whether the Prime Minister had ordered its cancellation. Meetings of Ministers summoned by Mrs Thatcher had always, apparently, left Mr Heseltine in a minority, and at a Cabinet meeting on 12 December 1985 she refused him permission to raise the Westland issues.[96] On 9 January 1986 it was accepted by the Cabinet that all ministerial answers to queries about Westland should be referred to the Cabinet Office for clearance; Mr Heseltine could not accept that procedure, and resigned.[97] He variously described his reason for resigning as being the attempted censorship through the Cabinet Office clearance procedure, or as the 'breakdown of constitutional government'.[98] Throughout the saga the two sides heavily leaked: not even that safety valve, fully opened, could keep the government together, because Mr Heseltine considered the points of disagreement to be too vital, and none of the other safety valves described earlier could be resorted to.

Two very brief footnotes may be added to this discussion of collective responsibility. First, the rate of resignations, decade by decade, following an inability to accept some government policy or other has, on a very crude measure, remained fairly constant since 1950, at about ten in every ten years.[99] Secondly, collective responsibility has been imposed more

[95] His account was given fully in a public explanation of his resignation on 9 January 1986—a statement not previously offered to the Prime Minister for clearance, on which aspect see above, chapter 5.

[96] The Prime Minister's ability to control what is discussed in the Cabinet was examined in chapter 5.

[97] The Westland company subsequently adopted the Sikorsky-Fiat package.

[98] See his article in the *Observer*, 12 January 1986.

[99] The figures are 1951–60: 11; 1961–70: 10; 1971–80: 15 (despite two agreements to differ); 1981–8: 10.

and more on Shadow Cabinets, with resignation or dismissal as the penalty for any major rejection of it.[100]
Attention may now be turned to individual responsibility.[101] Broadly, each Minister is individually accountable for (a) his private conduct, (b) his general conduct of his department, and (c) acts done (or things left undone) by civil servants in his department. Responsibility for (a) and (b) is somewhat clearer than for (c).

It remains the case that a higher standard of private conduct is required of Ministers than of others in public life, a major reason for this today being that the popular press and the investigative journalism of its more serious rivals will make a wayward Minister's continuance in office impossible. The Profumo affair[102] in 1963 shows that a Minister who deliberately lies to the House of Commons cannot remain in the government. Mr John Profumo was Secretary of State for War, and his extra-marital affair with Miss Christine Keeler, who was also sharing her sexual favours with a Soviet naval attaché (in reality, a Soviet intelligence officer), additionally raised for some people possible security questions—certainly for the Opposition, which did not wish to found its attack openly on the morality of his sexual behaviour.[103] Mr Profumo denied in the Commons that there had been any impropriety between him and Miss Keeler:[104] he could not stand the strain caused by that lie, and later resigned.[105] Lord Lambton's[106] resignation as a Minister and MP ten years later, when it was revealed that he had used the services of prostitutes—of which encounters photographs and tape recordings existed—could again be linked to a possible national security risk: after all, he was Parliamentary Under-Secretary of State for Defence for the RAF at the time. The resignation the following day of Earl Jellicoe, the Lord Privy Seal and Leader of the House of Lords, who owned up to having done the same thing, had no obvious security

---

[100] For example, the Leader of the Labour Party, Mr Kinnock, dismissed Mr Norman Buchan as Labour arts spokesman in 1986 because he would not accept the party's policy on future ministerial responsibility for broadcasting.

[101] See generally de Smith, op. cit., pp. 187–91; Wade and Bradley, op. cit., pp. 112–17; Marshall, op. cit., pp. 61–6 and chapter 6.

[102] On which see Marshall, op. cit., pp. 95–101; Harold Macmillan, *At the End of the Day* (1973), chapter 13; Lord Denning's Report, Cmnd. 2152 (1963).

[103] Lord Denning thought that the danger had been in Profumo's susceptibility to blackmail; Christine Keeler denied that she had ever asked him about national security matters.

[104] For his personal statement, see 674 H.C. Deb. 809–10 (21 March 1963).

[105] He also left the House of Commons and asked for his name to be removed from the list of Privy Councillors.

[106] This was a courtesy title: he was an MP at all material times.

aspect,[107] but he clearly thought that he had fallen below the standard of personal conduct required of a Minister. Ten years later still Mr Cecil Parkinson resigned as Secretary of State for Trade and Industry. Into the public domain had come the fact that his former secretary was expecting his child, together with her assertion that twice he had promised to obtain a divorce and to marry her, and had failed to try to do so. At first the Prime Minister strongly maintained that this was an entirely private matter which had no bearing on Mr Parkinson's ministerial life, but the press cared nothing about his ministerial life and so hounded him about the affair that he could no longer function effectively as a Minister, and resigned. He was summoned back to the Cabinet in 1987. In a way the press has made it unnecessary to judge the morality of a Minister in Mr Parkinson's position.

In summary, if a Minister lies to Parliament, or so conducts himself as to raise an arguable case that national security could have been thereby compromised,[108] or conducts his financial affairs other than with scrupulous care,[109] or—though doing none of those things—through his behaviour makes it impossible for him to carry out his departmental duties because of the attentions of the press, then (regardless of how loyal the Prime Minister may be) he will have to go.

A Minister is responsible for the general conduct of his department: more precisely, he may have to pay the price for political misjudgement within it. What amounts to misjudgement may be a matter of opinion, and guidance can be difficult to formulate. A marginal case is provided by the preliminaries to the Falklands conflict. The Foreign Secretary, Lord Carrington, and two of his ministerial colleagues, Mr Atkins and Mr Luce, felt compelled to resign in 1982 after the Argentinian invasion of the Falkland Islands because they considered that the Foreign and Commonwealth Office had not adequately judged Argentina's intentions. The Prime Minister did not want to accept their resignations, but the three Ministers persisted and left the

---

[107] The Security Commission reported that there had been no danger to security in Lord Jellicoe's case (because he had entertained the girls in his own flat where there was no danger of photographs being taken, and he had used a false name); Lord Lambton, however, had taken cannabis during his sessions with prostitutes and there was a risk that he could have inadvertently revealed secret information: see Cmnd. 5367 (1973).

[108] In that second case, a Prime Minister could allow the Minister concerned leave of absence while the allegations were investigated. This has never been done, but it was urged as an alternative in the Profumo case by the First Secretary of State: see Anthony Howard, *RAB: The Life of R. A. Butler* (1987), pp. 298–9.

[109] Lord Brayley, Parliamentary Under-Secretary of State for Defence for the Army, had to resign in 1974 after an inquiry into his former business interests.

administration.[110] The subsequent wide-ranging inquiry by a committee of Privy Councillors[111] exonerated them: no blame could be attached to any individual (or to the government collectively). The three Ministers' belief that a fresh Foreign Office ministerial team was desirable from the onset of the invasion had provided them with an impetus for resignation which any misjudgement alone perhaps would not have done. A clearer case from earlier in the same year involved the Solicitor-General for Scotland, Mr Nicholas Fairbairn, who gave his reasons for not agreeing to a prosecution in a dreadful rape case to the press before going to answer questions about it in the House of Commons. He thereby offended the sensitivities of that House, and resigned. Mr Leon Brittan, the second Cabinet casualty of the Westland affair, has provided a further example of ministerial misjudgement within a department leading to resignation.[112] In January 1986 the Solicitor-General wrote a letter to Mr Michael Heseltine indicating some material inaccuracies in a letter which Mr Heseltine had sent to a merchant bank about Westland. Selective parts of the Solicitor-General's letter, damaging to Mr Heseltine, were soon telephoned to the Press Association by Miss Colette Bowe, Mr Brittan's director of information at the Department of Trade and Industry. There had been prior consultation between her and officials in the Prime Minister's office, and it was decided to use that rather curious method to put the Solicitor-General's views as quickly as possible into the public domain, in time for an important meeting of the Westland board. The Solicitor-General, however, had not been consulted, and was furious: not only are Law Officers' letters not leaked, but it is also a long-settled practice that even the fact of their opinions having been offered is never disclosed. The Cabinet Secretary was directed to conduct a leak inquiry. Mr Brittan was taken to have tacitly approved an inexpedient and improper leak; Mrs Thatcher agreed that, had she personally been asked for her view at the time, she would not have approved the precise form used to leak the Solicitor-General's views. Mr Brittan lost support among Conservative back-benchers, and resigned.[113]

The extent to which a Minister will carry the can for the errors of his

---

[110] The Secretary of State for Defence, Mr John Nott, also offered to resign but his resignation was refused on the ground that the Ministry of Defence had not been responsible for policy on the Falkland Islands or Argentina.

[111] 'Falklands Islands Review', under the chairmanship of Lord Franks, Cmnd. 8787 (1983).

[112] See G. Marshall [1986] *Public Law* 184.

[113] Some of the claims made by or on behalf of the Prime Minister and the Secretary to the Cabinet in this episode lend great weight to Mrs Thatcher's statement (in a television interview on Westland) that 'Truth is often stranger than fiction'.

civil servants is bound up with the aim of preserving the anonymity of civil servants, for only by making them reasonably secure from (and their political masters open to) public censure can they give frank advice to successions of Ministers. At one extreme a Minister's responsibility for his officials could be formulated as involving total responsibility for all the acts of his officials, however junior and even if he did not know of their existence. Thus on that view the resignation of Sir Thomas Dugdale as Minister of Agriculture in 1954 over the Crichel Down affair[114] was entirely correct even if he had had no knowledge of the maladministration of his senior civil servants—the better view being, however, that he had been personally involved in that maladministration and had failed to organize his department efficiently. At the opposite extreme, simple justice and the improved administration which could result from the rooting out of incompetent civil servants would require that individual officials be publicly named and disciplined for misconduct. Thus the judicial inquiry under the Tribunals of Inquiry (Evidence) Act 1921 into the collapse of the Vehicle and General Insurance Company in 1972[115] was, according to such a view, correct in blaming named civil servants in the Department of Trade and Industry for failing to set in motion a timely investigation of the company's affairs, and in exonerating the responsible Ministers. As far as ministerial responsibility in these matters is concerned, the middle way is normally taken, ignoring the two extreme paths. So the further the Minister was, geographically or hierarchically, from the people or events complained of, the less he will generally be expected to take the blame for mistakes and resign. That explains a number of ministerial non-resignations, from that of the Colonial Secretary, Mr Lennox-Boyd, in 1959 over the killing of fifty-two people by the security forces in Nyasaland[116] (were they not, to borrow Neville Chamberlain's phrase, a far away people of whom Mr Lennox-Boyd knew nothing?), to that of Mr William Whitelaw as Home Secretary in 1982 after an intruder had confronted the Queen in her bedroom (for how could Mr Whitelaw know about or direct security measures at Buckingham Palace?), to Mr Prior's and Mr Scott's as Secretary and Parliamentary Under-Secretary of State for Northern Ireland following the mass escape of thirty-eight prisoners from the Maze Prison in 1983 (for how could they be expected to control day-to-day

---

114 On which see Turpin, op. cit., pp. 77–8, 353–4, and references cited there.
115 H.L. 80, H.C. 133 (1971–2).
116 See Report of the Nyasaland Commission of Inquiry, Cmnd. 814 (1959); Harold Macmillan, *Riding the Storm* (1971), pp. 733–8.

prison security throughout the province?).[117]

Failure adequately to discharge an aspect of a Minister's individual responsibility will not lead inexorably to loss of office. The Opposition may overreact in its criticism, perhaps putting down a notion of censure: then the government may well decide to close ranks around the unfortunate Minister and stand or fall with him. Mr Henry Brooke was so placed as Home Secretary from 1962 to 1964, and survived. The Prime Minister in particular may stand firmly beside the Minister, defying the Opposition to defeat them—and government MPs not to support them. Sir Geoffrey Howe as Foreign Secretary was thus defended in 1983 when the Foreign and Commonwealth Office was discovered to have no more knowledge of the United States' invasion of the Commonwealth state of Grenada than the man in the street.[118] Conversely, of course, if the Prime Minister decides that the Minister's position is untenable, he will be finished: thus Baldwin realized that Sir Samuel Hoare's conclusion on his own initiative of the Hoare–Laval Pact in Paris in 1935, which would have given the Italian invaders of Abyssinia part of that country, was ultimately indefensible.[119] Or the Minister may be saved from resignation by being reshuffled to another post, or he may resign following his transgression but return to a less exposed and perhaps less important job when the dust has settled.[120] As Professor Finer has observed, an enforced resignation will usually only follow if the Minister is compliant, the Prime Minister willing to let him go, and the party insistent that he should resign.[121]

Some Ministers have to decide matters which will have an effect on industry, business, and the money markets. There are therefore sensible rules which are designed to ensure that no conflict arises between the conduct of their ministerial offices and their private financial interests.

The rules now in force were set out in an Annex to a Memorandum by the Secretary to the Cabinet to the Royal Commission on Standards

[117]Mr Prior's offered resignation was refused: James Prior, *A Balance of Power* (1986), p. 232.

[118] Prime ministerial support is not always enough, as Mr Parkinson's resignation showed.

[119] On being summoned by George V to receive the seals of office in succession to Hoare, Eden wrote that he was told by the King: 'I said to your predecessor: "You know what they're all saying, no more coals to Newcastle, no more Hoares to Paris." ' The King added that (not surprisingly) 'The fellow didn't even laugh'. The veracity of Eden's recollection has, however, been disputed: see Kenneth Rose, *King George V* (1983), p. 400.

[120] Thus Dalton resigned as Chancellor of the Exchequer after his Budget leak in 1947, but returned as Chancellor of the Duchy of Lancaster the following year; Hoare came back as First Lord of the Admiralty in 1936.

[121] S. E. Finer, 'The Individual Responsibility of Ministers' (1956) 34 *Public Administration* 337 at 393–4.

of Conduct in Public Life.[122] A copy of the rules is given to each Minister on his taking office. The main ones are as follows. (a) Ministers must not take an active part in any undertaking which may have contractual or other relations with any government department. This could arise not only if the Minister had a financial interest in such an undertaking, but also if he were associated with any body (even of a philanthropic character) which might have dealings or disputes with the government. More precisely, (b) on assuming office Ministers must resign all directorships which they hold in any company,[123] as well as any directorships or offices held in any philanthropic undertaking if there is any risk of conflict arising through such an undertaking. (c) Ministers who are partners in professional firms, such as solicitors or accountants, must on taking office cease to play any day-to-day part in their firm's affairs—although they do not need to dissolve the partnership or let any practising certificate lapse. (d) Ministers are not expected to dispose of all their investments, but if they hold a controlling interest in a company a conflict of interest could then arise similar to those attaching to a directorship, and such a controlling interest should be disposed of. If shares are held in any company which could have dealings with the Minister's department, then, again, there could be a conflict of interest and those shares should be sold. (Mr Basil de Ferranti had to resign as Parliamentary Secretary, Ministry of Aviation, within a few months of his appointment in 1962 because it proved impossible for him to divest himself of shares in his family business which had major contracts with that Ministry.) In less clear-cut cases it might be appropriate for Ministers to place shares in the hands of trustees. (This was done by Lord Cockfield in 1982 after his appointment as Secretary of State for Trade: he deposited the share certificates of a company in which he had a small investment at his bank and directed the bank not to deal in those shares as long as he was a Minister.[124]) (e) No Minister should accept a gift or services which would place him under an obligation to a commercial undertaking. (John Belcher, Parliamentary Secretary, Board of Trade, fell badly foul of this

[122] The Parliamentary Clerk at Number 10 Downing Street kindly supplied me with a copy of the Memorandum. It recorded that Campbell-Bannerman, Neville Chamberlain, and Winston Churchill had all made parliamentary statements on the matter, the latter formulation still being the basis for the current rules: see 496 H.C. Deb. 702–3 (written answers 25 February 1952). Rules added since 1952 include those on partnerships, 'names' at Lloyds, and pension arrangements. The complete rules are available to members of the government in 22 paragraphs of Questions of Procedure for Ministers (1976 version).

[123] Excluding directorships in private companies established to maintain private estates.

[124] See also 34 H.C. Deb. 955–62 (22 December 1982).

rule by accepting small gifts knowing that in return speedy and favourable licensing decisions were expected from the Board of Trade.[125]) In any case of doubt about any of these rules, Ministers should consult the Prime Minister, who will be the final judge, advised by the Secretary to the Cabinet.

The House of Commons maintains a Register of Members' Interests:[126] Ministers who are members of that House have to make annual returns as MPs: most Ministers, having followed the rules already explained, have nothing to register. On leaving office, Ministers are free to put their expertise to work immediately wherever they can, as company directors or otherwise. Checks similar to those which exist on senior civil servants who wish to leave government service for the private sector—the Cabinet Office vets their applications and can deny permission—do not apply and could not be imposed on former Ministers.[127]

Other, related rules are contained in *Questions of Procedure for Ministers*. Ministers may not publish books relating (even if only loosely) to the work of their departments.[128] They may, however, publish fiction while in office (as Mr Douglas Hurd has voluminously demonstrated[129]) or books on historical,[130] scientific, or philanthropic matters. Ministers may not write regular newspaper columns, although occasional contributions on any matter are permissible.[131]

Ministers' pay and conditions

Ministerial salaries are prescribed by Order in Council made under the Ministerial and other Salaries Act 1975, section 1(4).[132] As a matter of practice, such an Order will only be made after a report has been received from the Review Body on Top Salaries. The Act provides for *maximum*

---

[125] Report of the Lynskey Tribunal of Inquiry, Cmd. 7616 (1948).

[126] See chapter 9.

[127] Prime Ministers have consistently refused to lay down rules restricting former Ministers: see, for example, 667 H.C. Deb. 999–1000 (20 November 1962) (Macmillan); 766 H.C. Deb. 171 (written answers 20 June 1968) (Harold Wilson). Mr Norman Tebbit was criticized by Labour back-benchers for accepting a directorship in British Telecom when he ceased to be a Minister and Chairman of the Conservative Party because, as a Minister, he had helped to privatize the company.

[128] As Dr Bray discovered in 1969: see above.

[129] He published a number of political thrillers in the 1970s and 1980s while holding various ministerial offices.

[130] Baldwin sanctioned the publication by his Chancellor of the Exchequer Winston Churchill of *The World Crisis*, vols. 1–5 (1923–8).

[131] Such as book reviews: the Secretary of State for Energy, Mr Peter Walker, for example, published a review of his former colleague's, Mr Michael Heseltine's, book *Where There's A Will* (1987) in the *Independent*, 11 March 1987.

[132] The current one is the Ministerial and other Salaries Order 1983, S.I. 1983 No. 1128.

salaries, and less may be paid:[133] so for example Mrs Thatcher as Prime Minister and her Lord Chancellor[134] (both of whom are entitled to amounts in excess of other Cabinet Ministers) chose in 1979 to draw only the same as their Cabinet colleagues. Another consequence of that statutory provision is that the House of Commons may still in theory lawfully exercise its traditional right to reduce a Minister's salary as a censure upon him.[135] The current maximum salaries for Ministers sitting in the Commons[136] (with lower actual amounts drawn given in brackets) are as follows.

Prime Minister	Lord Chancellor[137]	Cabinet Minister	Minister of State	Parliamentary Secretary
£45,787	£83,000	£34,157	£23,887	£17,897
(£34,157)	(£52,058)			

Additionally, Ministers who are MPs are entitled to a reduced parliamentary salary, currently £16,900.

Some Ministers have the use of official residences, Number 10 Downing Street and Chequers for the Prime Minister, Number 11 Downing Street for the Chancellor of the Exchequer, Number 2 Carlton Gardens and Dorneywood for the Foreign and Commonwealth Secretary.[138] Ministers have chauffeur-driven cars from the government car pool for use on official business. On leaving office Ministers receive a pension achieved through contributions from their ministerial salaries made to the Parliamentary Contributory Pension Fund.[139] None of these arrangements could be fairly described as excessive, or even generous.

[133] 1975 Act, s. 4.

[134] His salary is governed by a separate Order: see Lord Chancellor's Salary Order 1987, S.I. 1987 No. 941.

[135] This last happened in 1976 when government whips prematurely released some of their MPs in the belief that the day's divisions had ended: the Opposition then carried a motion to cut the Secretary of State for Industry's salary by £1,000. Another vote restored it a few days later. See 905 H.C. Deb. 461–527 (11 February 1976) and 1133–1204 (17 February 1976).

[136] Cabinet Ministers in the Lords are currently entitled to a ministerial salary of £40,438.

[137] The Lord Chancellor's Salary Order 1987, S.I. 1987 No. 941, allows him a maximum salary of £83,000. Of that amount, £11,620 (14 per cent) is taken as being his salary as Speaker of the House of Lords—his 'woolsack' salary. The Lord Chancellor draws that 'woolsack' salary plus £40,438 as a Cabinet Minister in the Lords—a total of £52,058 actually drawn.

[138] According to James Callaghan (who has been Chancellor of the Exchequer and Prime Minister) the living accommodation at No. 11 Downing Street is superior to that of No. 10: see Time and Chance (1987), p. 229. The Prime Minister and the Home, Foreign, and Northern Ireland Secretaries also have constant Special Branch protection. This can scarcely be classed as a benefit.

[139] Former Ministers who sat in the Commons will also have contributed part of their MP's pay towards an MP's pension. Former Prime Ministers and Lord Chancellors receive a pension as of right which may be increased from time to time: Parliamentary and other Pensions and Salaries Act 1976, s. 5. Former Lord Chancellors receive an annual pension of up to £35,275; the maximum pension payable to former Prime Ministers is £15,709 a year.

8

Constitutional Monarchy

The Queen is a symbol of national identity, a focal point of national loyalty, transcending political partisan rivalry. She personifies the state and the nation, their history and continuity. Coronations, royal weddings and funerals, and an investiture of a Prince of Wales are great national occasions. The Queen is also the supreme governor of the Church of England and an exemplar of family life. Wide legal powers are vested in the Queen or Her Majesty in Council. A great many formal acts have to be done by her in a traditional manner and require her personal signature or approval. She also presides at Privy Council meetings and reads the Queen's Speech at the opening of each new Parliament or parliamentary session. She receives letters of credence from ambassadors and Commonwealth High Commissioners, receives homage from new bishops, and holds some two hundred formal audiences each year.[1]

The Queen additionally has a part to play behind the political scenes. The extent to which a particular Sovereign may have a major impact on public affairs will depend on the number and gravity of the political problems of his or her reign. It was not till near the end of his life that Edward VII was faced with a serious constitutional issue, the dispute about the proper relative powers of the two Houses. George V, on the other hand, not only inherited that problem but his reign also saw the Home Rule crisis of 1912 to 1914, the trauma of the First World War, the choice of Baldwin or Curzon to succeed Bonar Law in 1923, the first (and minority) Labour government in 1924, the General Strike, the economic depression, and the events of the summer of 1931. His handling of these, and many less weighty, issues set the pattern for modern constitutional monarchy. Edward VIII's was a single-issue reign: the whole of his kingship may now be seen as a preparation for his leaving of it. George VI was required to be a symbol for a nation at war for survival, and had to supervise a critical decision in 1940: fortunately,

---

[1] S. A. de Smith, *Constitutional and Administrative Law* (5th edn., 1985 by H. Street and R. Brazier), pp. 122, 134.

the choice between Halifax and Churchill as Chamberlain's successor was made for him. The Queen has been unavoidably involved twice in the succession to the office of Prime Minister, in 1957 and in 1963; otherwise political questions since 1952 have been answered by politicians. By 1988 she had experienced twenty-five years of government by the Conservatives and eleven by Labour—slightly more of the latter variety than the aggregate under all of her predecessors. Although we must wait for the authorized biography to be published after her death for reliable information about her conduct as a constitutional monarch, the indications are that she has matched her grandfather as an exemplary head of state.

Some matters have been considered elsewhere in this book and so will not be further rehearsed here, such as the Sovereign's role in the choice of a Prime Minister,[2] her influence and function in the formation of a new government,[3] and the circumstances in which she might exercise her right to refuse a requested dissolution of Parliament.[4] Rather, what may be called her usual powers to advise, to encourage, and to warn her Ministers will be examined in this chapter, as will her reserve powers (any of which would, if exercised, involve the rejection of ministerial advice), followed by the legal rules which ensure the smooth operation of monarchy when the Sovereign is in some way incapacitated, and which regulate the succession to the throne.

The Queen's usual powers

The Queen normally exercises her formal legal powers on ministerial advice.[5] Asquith admirably summarized matters in a minute to George V in December 1910.

The part to be played by the Crown . . . has happily been settled by the accumulated traditions and the unbroken practice of more than seventy years. It is to act upon the advice of the Ministers who for the time being possess the

---

[2] See chapters 2 and 3.
[3] See chapter 4.
[4] See chapter 3.
[5] Two routine exceptions are her Christmas Day broadcast to the Commonwealth and her Commonwealth Day message, neither of which are prepared or delivered on ministerial advice as they are made in her capacity as Head of the Commonwealth—a title which imports only a symbolic function, not a legal or constitutional one: see R. W. Blackburn, 'The Queen and Ministerial Responsibility' [1985] *Public Law* 361. Abnormal situations in which the Queen might act *contrary to* ministerial advice will be considered later.

confidence of the House of Commons, whether that advice does or does not conform to the private and personal judgement of the Sovereign. Ministers will always pay the utmost deference, and give the most serious consideration, to any criticism or objection that the Monarch may offer to their policy; but the ultimate decision rests with them; for they, and not the Crown, are responsible to Parliament.[6]

The Queen's usual powers are customarily encapsulated in the formula that she has the rights to advise, to encourage, and to warn Ministers.[7] These rights must be employed with scrupulous impartiality in relation to governments of different party colours: the Sovereign must be totally even-handed, colour-blind as between the parties. Royal biographies and political autobiographies show that these powers are routinely exercised and are generally welcomed by Ministers, so that the Sovereign may have a marginal but beneficial influence on governmental decisions. It is convenient to look first at the Sovereign's right to encourage a Prime Minister and Ministers who are in difficulty or who need a little help, for that right will be exercised in uncontroversial circumstances.

It is impossible to read the official biography of George VI[8] without perceiving how Neville Chamberlain must have been heartened by the King's letters and audiences, particularly in relation to the policy of appeasement[9]—or without understanding the equal succour which Chamberlain's successor received to help him prosecute the total opposite of Chamberlain's policy: indeed, George VI and Churchill developed a close, comradely relationship during the war.[10] The King's third and last Prime Minister, Attlee, and the post-war Labour Ministers were accorded similar friendly help and a good working relationship was soon established.[11] After the 1950 general election, at which Labour held on by a tiny majority and after which the Conservative Opposition did its best to grind down weary Ministers[12] by keeping them late in the House of Commons every night, the King was sympathetic (although not at

---

[6] Quoted in Colin Turpin, *British Government and the Constitution: Text, Cases and Materials* (1985), pp. 76–7. Asquith wrote in a similar vein three years later, but on that occasion emphasized that it was the King's *duty* to point out any objections he might have and to suggest alternatives: see Sir Ivor Jennings, *Cabinet Government* (3rd edn., 1959), p. 336.

[7] Bagehot's actual formulation was 'the right to be consulted, the right to encourage, the right to warn': Walter Bagehot, *The English Constitution* (1963 edn., with Introduction by Richard Crossman), p. 111. The ways in which the Queen is consulted were described in chapter 5.

[8] Sir John Wheeler-Bennett, *King George VI: His Life and Reign* (1958).

[9] Op. cit., Part III, chapters 3 and 4.

[10] Op. cit., Part III, chapters 6–9.

[11] Op. cit., pp. 650–4.

[12] Many Labour Ministers had been continuously in office since 1940.

the price of seeking to defer the inevitable second election). Occasion-ally, the Sovereign may offer encouragement to an individual Cabinet Minister, rather than to the Prime Minister or the government as a whole. An example from 1976 has been revealed recently. In that year James Callaghan as Foreign and Commonwealth Secretary was contem-plating an approach to the regime which had made an unlawful declara-tion of independence in Rhodesia in 1965, and he mentioned this to the Queen at a dinner. The following day Mr Callaghan received a letter from the Queen's Private Secretary stating Her Majesty's view that, despite the clear difficulties in the way of success, she thought that an approach along the lines indicated to her by the Foreign and Common-wealth Secretary would, in her opinion, be worthwhile. Fortified thus by such 'an authority on the Commonwealth', the initiative was made.[13] Any Minister will be gladdened by a sympathetic hearing and helpful words from someone above the party battle, with no political axe to grind, and who (in the Queen's case) has seen it all—or nearly all—before.[14]

It is when a Sovereign chooses to advise or to warn that necessarily a Prime Minister may hear things which he finds uncongenial. Although George V greeted the first-ever Labour Prime Minister fairly and in a friendly way,[15] and through an early memorandum[16] and through other means[17] helped the Labour Party to adjust to the responsibilities of government, none the less at MacDonald's very first audience the King told him that he objected to some of Lansbury's remarks about the Court, that the combination of being both Prime Minister and Foreign Secretary was too much for one man, that he hoped he would never have to receive a representative of the Soviet government which had murdered his cousin and the Tsar's family, and that he wished the Labour Party would stop singing the 'Red Flag'.[18] Baldwin, in his turn, was urged in

---

[13] James Callaghan, *Time and Chance* (1987), pp. 378–82. Like so many other attempts by governments of both parties to negotiate with the regime, it failed.

[14] Queen Victoria once gave Gladstone information which Wellington had given her about Pitt. It would be interesting to learn if the Queen has had occasion to give any of her Prime Ministers information which (say) Churchill had given her about Asquith.

[15] '[The King] has been considerate, cordially correct, human and friendly', MacDonald wrote in his diary: Kenneth Rose, *King George V* (1983), p. 329.

[16] It is set out in Sir Harold Nicolson, *King George V* (1952), p. 502.

[17] '. . . [F]rom the moment Labour took office, the King seized every opportunity to demon-strate his trust both in public and in private; and when old friends presumed on their intimacy to commiserate with him on the affliction of a socialist Government, they were sharply snubbed for their pains': Rose, op. cit., p. 328.

[18] Nicolson, op. cit., pp. 497–9.

1924 'to really close and powerful grips with such questions as housing, unemployment, the cost of food and education',[19] and was later warned against the dangers of undue provocation by the government during the General Strike. The best-known—and ultimately heeded—royal warning was that issued by George VI to Churchill in 1944: it was just short of a command that Churchill should not view the hostilities at the D-Day landings.[20] It took two letters from the King (with some arguments suggested by his Private Secretary Sir Alan Lascelles[21]) and an explanation from the Navy of the dangers which would be involved before Churchill abandoned his plan: 'I must defer to Your Majesty's wishes and indeed commands', as the Prime Minister put it in a letter to a relieved King.[22]

A constitutional monarch will remember, before voicing either advice or warning, that however long may be her experience she does not have to preside over what may be a far from compliant Cabinet; she does not have to defend herself to the public through the media; she does not have to manage the House of Commons, or eventually face the electorate. What may be seen as an ideal policy from Buckingham Palace may simply not be practical politics in the view from Downing Street. The Sovereign will understand, too, that some of the obligations owed to her may also be minor irritants or inconveniences from time to time: a hard-pressed Prime Minister may wish that ideally his weekly thirty-minute or hour-long audience could be missed in deference to other pressures on him (but it is nevertheless rare for that audience not to take place while Parliament is sitting). Some obligations also affect other Ministers: Richard Crossman, when Lord President of the Council, regularly recorded his annoyance in his diary[23] that he and three colleagues had to travel for Privy Council meetings to the Queen at Balmoral when she was on holiday there, rather than the Queen break her holiday and return to London so as to save four busy Ministers perhaps a night and a day away from their offices.[24] (It is difficult to understand why Privy Council

[19] Nicolson, op. cit., p. 520.

[20] Wheeler-Bennett, op. cit., pp. 601–6; Sir Winston Churchill, *The Second World War*, vol. v (1985 Penguin edn.), pp. 546–51.

[21] Including the point that the King himself had wanted to go too, and yet he had been prevailed upon not to.

[22] A convention may still exist which requires the Sovereign's consent for the Prime Minister to leave the United Kingdom, although Churchill implicitly denied it in that letter. Cabinet Ministers are required by a rule in *Questions of Procedure for Ministers* to seek the Queen's approval as well as the Prime Minister's for any absence from the United Kingdom.

[23] Richard Crossman, *Diaries of a Cabinet Minister*, vol. ii, pp. 44, 194, 490, 512; vol. iii, pp. 39, 52, 132.

[24] Three Privy Councillors constitute a quorum.

business could not be wholly conducted in writing during the Queen's absence from London.) In all these matters, therefore, the Sovereign needs an acute appreciation of her Ministers' circumstances and a deftness of touch so as not to cause antagonism in her dealings with them.

The existence of the rights to advise and to warn must mean that the Queen will have personal views about some political issues which will not coincide with those of the Prime Minister and the Cabinet. Indeed, the opinions of the Queen and of her government *could not* always be the same unless she were to undergo a very odd change of heart and mind on the main issues of the day with every change of party government. The Sovereign may urge her view on the Prime Minister, especially at the weekly audience (at which the two are alone and no formal record is kept)—but in strict confidence, and in the end normally deferring to any contrary view persisted in by the Prime Minister. Any public revelation of disagreement could be damaging to the existing and future relationship between head of government and head of state, for obviously if it became known that the Queen had criticized government policy, she might be taken to be biased against that government and to be in favour of another. In 1986 someone in Buckingham Palace (generally assumed to be the Queen's Press Secretary Mr Michael Shea) allowed the *Sunday Times* to publish a story[25] that the Queen was 'dismayed' by 'an uncaring Mrs Thatcher': the source had agreed with suggestions from that newspaper that the Queen disapproved of several major government policies. The Queen's Private Secretary Sir William Heseltine intervened in a rare letter to the press.[26] He made three points which must be correct. (*a*) The Sovereign has the right and duty to counsel, encourage and warn her government. She is thus entitled to have opinions on government policy and to express them to the Prime Minister. (*b*) Whatever the Queen's personal opinions may be, she is bound to accept and act on the advice of her Ministers.[27] (*c*) The Sovereign is obliged to treat communications with the Prime Minister as entirely confidential. Sir William totally denied that any member of the Queen's household would reveal the Queen's private views, and concluded that Her Majesty enjoyed 'a relationship of the closest confidentiality with Mrs Thatcher',

[25] *Sunday Times*, 27 July 1986. See Geoffrey Marshall, 'The Queen's Press Relations' [1986] *Public Law* 505.

[26] *The Times*, 29 July 1986. Rare, but not unprecedented. Sir Alan Lascelles had written under the pseudonym Senex about when a dissolution of Parliament could be refused: *The Times*, 2 May 1950, and see above, chapter 3.

[27] Sir William did not digress into the situations in which the Queen might be justified in using her reserve powers contrary to Ministers' wishes—an understandable omission in the circumstances.

emphasizing that reports purporting to be the Queen's opinions on government policies were 'entirely without foundation'. The *Sunday Times* stood by its story; Mr Shea left the Palace in March 1987 for a job in industry. Now whether the Queen actually held the views ascribed to her is unimportant, but the episode does amply demonstrate the complete truth of her Private Secretary's three points, especially that the Sovereign can only exercise her rights, and a political consensus will only remain in favour of her continuing to do so, if complete confidentiality is observed by both Buckingham Palace and Number 10 Downing Street.

The Queen's reserve powers

Prime Ministers and governments do not routinely request dissolutions of Parliament in circumstances in which the Sovereign feels constrained to refuse; the Sovereign does not insist on a general election when her government does not advise one; royal assent to legislation is not withheld; governments do not decline to leave office having lost a general election, or behave in any other outrageous or illegal way so that the Sovereign is moved to dismiss them from office. These things just do not happen in Britain: rather, the players observe the rules of the game. That the Queen however possesses in law what I term her reserve powers[28] which would enable her to behave in these ways is not disputed.[29] Analysis of them is, however, made rather unreal through the difficulty of proposing hypothetical facts which would not be brushed aside as fanciful, thus causing doubt whether those powers could ever be used. Still, that analysis must be tried, for it would be a very strange constitution which endowed a head of state with certain rights but which did not allow of any indication of the circumstances in which they might be used and the consequences of their use.

All the reserve powers share a common attribute: the deployment of any of them would involve the setting aside of the cardinal convention of the constitution that the Queen must act on ministerial advice; for in all cases what the Sovereign would be moved to do (or not to do) would run counter to that which her Ministers advised. One of the reserve powers—refusal of a recommended dissolution—has been discussed in

---

[28] Termed, less happily, by Jennings, op. cit., chapter 13, her 'personal prerogatives'; see also Geoffrey Marshall, *Constitutional Conventions* (1984), chapter 2.

[29] Save (at least in part) by those few who still adhere to the 'automatic theory' of dissolution, dismissed above in chapter 3.

chapter 3. So let the first reserve power to fall for consideration here be the Queen's right to insist, contrary to the government's wishes, that Parliament be dissolved. The Queen not only has the legal power to dissolve Parliament: Parliament cannot be dissolved without her intervention, for dissolution requires an exercise of the royal prerogative. The main circumstance customarily and correctly offered as a case in which the Queen would be justified in insisting that a general election take place is where a government has lost a vote of confidence in the House of Commons yet refuses either to recommend a dissolution or to resign; but then no government in Britain would ever behave in such an astonishing fashion. Another case sometimes and again correctly suggested would be where a government wished improperly to postpone a general election beyond five years after the previous one,[30] say through fear of rejection by the electors; but, again, it is entirely improbable that that would ever be contemplated.[31] It is worth noting, though, that in both hypotheses a forced dissolution would be for the Queen a lesser evil than dismissal of the government, for the electorate, not the politically neutral head of state, would be able to decide the political issue of whether that administration should be replaced.

The only situation in this context which is worth examining in any detail is one which actually came to pass earlier this century. If a government were to advise the Sovereign to create a large number of peers in order to secure the passage of legislation (perhaps legislation to abolish the House of Lords itself), the Sovereign could insist that the government's policy be first approved by the electorate.[32] Peerages are created on the Prime Minister's advice.[33] If the Queen thought that a mass creation was improper,[34] she *could* refuse to make such a creation, but the more prudent course would be not to refuse but rather to follow precedent and require that the government had the electorate's agreement

[30] Dissolutions were properly postponed with all-party agreement during both world wars. See Parliament and Registration Act 1916; Parliament and Local Elections Acts 1917 and 1918; Prolongation of Parliament Acts 1940 to 1944.

[31] Indeed, assuming that such an errant administration at least stayed within the law to the extent of persuading Parliament to pass a Bill to extend Parliament's maximum five-year term, the Sovereign's role would arise in the context of refusing her assent to that Bill, a reserve power considered later.

[32] For a technical reason to be explained later, however, I doubt whether a request for a mass creation of peers is likely ever to be made again.

[33] Save for two cases: peerages granted to members of the Royal Family (such as the earldom conferred on Princess Margaret's then husband, and the Dukedom of York to Prince Andrew), and the earldoms given to former Prime Ministers: see further below chapter 10.

[34] For example, because a Bill to abolish the House of Lords could be passed, despite the dissent of that House, under the Parliament Acts 1911 and 1949.

through the ballot box for what was proposed. In neither of the first two relevant precedents, in 1712 and in 1832, was any reference made to the electorate, but then they arose before the advent of universal male suffrage.[35] By the time of the latest precedent in 1910–11,[36] however, such suffrage was in place. Both Edward VII and George V in turn insisted—and Asquith's government accepted—that before either would use the royal prerogative to create enough new peers to ensure the passage of the Parliament Bill[37] (which would reduce the Lord's absolute veto to a suspensory veto), the electorate must first approve the government's policy. That approval was achieved at the second, December, general election of 1910.[38] The House of Lords subsequently passed the Parliament Bill after the King's conditional guarantee to create peers was made public. An insistence on a general election[39] on the issue of creating a large number of peers would plainly be in accordance with the 1910–11 precedent. The reason why the electorate's approval is considered so important is as apposite today as when the King's Private Secretary Lord Knollys wrote to Asquith in 1910.

[T]he King regards the policy of the Government as tantamount to the destruction of the House of Lords, and he thinks that before a large creation of peers is embarked upon or threatened the country should be acquainted with the particular project for accomplishing such destruction.[40]

It is unlikely since the enactment of the Parliament Acts 1911 and 1949 that any government would ask for a mass creation: it could,

---

[35] In 1712 Queen Anne created 12 Tory peers to provide the government with a sufficient majority in the House of Lords (of some 150 members) to approve the Treaty of Utrecht, and in 1832 William IV reluctantly agreed to create enough Whig peers to carry the Reform Bill: in the event, however, enough Tory peers abstained to allow the Reform Bill to pass without fresh creations. See generally Jennings, op. cit., chapter 13, section 4.

[36] On which see Roy Jenkins, *Mr Balfour's Poodle* (1954); Nicolson, op. cit., chapters 9 and 10.

[37] In Roy Jenkins, *Asquith* (1964), Appendix A is a list of some 250 people whom it was proposed to approach with a view to the submission of their names to the King if a mass creation proved necessary. It was probably not a complete list of all those who would have had to be recommended.

[38] The Liberals and Conservatives obtained 272 seats each, the Irish Nationalists 84, and Labour 42. In the January 1910 election the equivalent figures had been 275, 273, 82 and 40. The Irish and Labour generally supported the Liberal government in both hung Parliaments.

[39] Perhaps an acceptable alternative to a general election might today be a referendum. A referendum is uniquely suited (as a general election never is) to a single issue, and the experience is available of the 1975 referendum on continued membership of the European Community. A disadvantage would be that legislation to provide for a referendum would have to be enacted, which the government might not be prepared to secure.

[40] Quoted in J. A. Spender and Cyril Asquith, *Life of Lord Oxford and Asquith* (1932), i. 261.

perhaps, only occur if a government were not prepared to have any of its legislation held up by the House of Lords for the year allowed under the Acts[41] or if a government in the fifth year of a Parliament did not wish to allow a Bill introduced in that last year to be voted down by the Lords, thus effectively vetoing it in that Parliament. But there is a major, and so far insufficiently appreciated, barrier in the way of a government in a hurry hoping through a mass creation to produce a co-operative House of Lords. Every newly created peer must be introduced into the House of Lords before he may take his seat or vote.[42] However rapidly new peers could be created, the crucial question would be how quickly they could become voting members. The answer to this lies with the House of Lords itself, because it is the total master of its own internal procedures, and those procedures can only be altered (apart from legislation) by resolution of the House. The practice which governs the timing of the introduction of new peers is set out in the authoritative *Companion to the Standing Orders of the House of Lords*,[43] which states that usually 'not more than two introductions take place on any one day . . .', and only part of one day (often a Wednesday) a week is reserved for introductions. The maximum rate of introductions under that timing is thus *two a week*: it would therefore take a very long time to get a large number of new peers introduced and therefore able to sit and vote. That rate is currently adhered to even if more than two newly created peers are awaiting introduction: it was followed, for example, to introduce the seventeen peers announced in the 1983 Dissolution Honours List (although it was raised to four introductions a week on a few occasions to accommodate the 1987 Dissolution Honours List). The House of Lords, moreover, would not be likely to alter its internal procedures in order to accommodate a government which it saw as trying to cut legislative corners (and perhaps to abolish the House of Lords itself). Once that introduction procedure becomes more properly understood, the likelihood of any future recommended mass creation would become even more remote.

If, for whatever reason, a Sovereign were to insist on a dissolution which the government refused to recommend, the Sovereign would have to dismiss that government in order to achieve that dissolution. This is because the mechanics of dissolution require the essential participation of

---

[41] One month for money Bills: Parliament Act 1911, s. 1.

[42] See Erskine May, *Parliamentary Practice* (20th edn., 1983 by Sir Charles Gordon), pp. 470–1; Sir John Sainty, *Companion to the Standing Orders of the House of Lords* (15th edn., 1984), p. 7.

[43] Sainty, ibid.

the Lord Chancellor.[44] Parliament is dissolved by proclamation under the Great Seal, which is in his custody, and the proclamation is issued by the Queen in Council and announces that she has directed the Lord Chancellor to issue writs to returning officers to cause elections to take place to the new Parliament. If, taking his Prime Minister's line, the Lord Chancellor were to refuse to co-operate, the only way around the impasse would be for the Sovereign to dismiss the government and to find another.

A second reserve power is that of refusal of assent to legislation. Such a refusal would be signified by the Clerk of the Parliaments: when the title of the doomed Bill was read out in the House of Lords for royal assent he would reply 'La Reine S'Avisera'. Royal assent has not been withheld from legislation since 1707; that negative precedent might be wrongly taken to mean that royal assent must always be granted to a Bill which has passed Parliament; but all that it really signifies is that no case has arisen since 1707 in which a Sovereign has felt impelled to refuse. The legal power to refuse certainly subsists. There will, however, be government advice that royal assent be given to every Bill passed by both Houses (or by the Commons alone under the Parliament Acts).[45] That advice will attach to every government Bill as well as to legislation for which it has no responsibility but which has received parliamentary approval, such as a Private Member's Bill or a Private Bill. It follows that one situation in which a refusal of assent might be recommended by the government itself with little controversy would be where a Bill had been introduced by one government and had passed both Houses but a change of government had come about without a dissolution and before royal assent had been sought.[46] If the new government then advised that royal assent be withheld, the Queen would obviously be acting on ministerial advice in refusing. Another example[47] could occur if a Private Member's Bill were to pass both Houses, perhaps on a free vote in the Commons but against the government's advice to Parliament: the government

---

[44] A dissolution also requires a Privy Council meeting at which the Queen assents to an Order in Council effecting the dissolution. The Lord President of the Council usually arranges for the calling of such meetings, but this is only customary. For example, during the night of 14–15 March 1967 an emergency Privy Council was summoned by the Prime Minister to authorize a bank holiday, after he had informed the Lord President, who was detained in the Commons during an all-night sitting: Harold Wilson, *The Labour Government 1964–70: A Personal Record* (1971), pp. 506–9. If, in the example in the text, the Lord President refused to co-operate someone at Buckingham Palace (perhaps the Queen's Private Secretary) could on the Queen's behalf summon four non-party Privy Councillors to a meeting.

[45] Subject to possible special cases to be mentioned later.

[46] With a dissolution all public Bills fall.

[47] Suggested by Marshall, op. cit., p. 22.

might decide that the Bill was so inimical to the public interest that a royal veto should be recommended.[48] But what of the harder cases: veto in the face of ministerial advice?

(a) If an Act provided for mandatory procedures to be followed before given legislation could be enacted, and legislation were passed at the government's request but contrary to those requirements, then the Queen could claim to be acting as a referee upholding the law by vetoing the resultant defective Bill. So, if a Bill of Rights Act prescribed special majorities in Parliament or a referendum before it could be amended or repealed, and an amending or repealing Bill were passed notoriously without resort to the prescribed safeguard, the Queen might feel obliged to veto the Bill which had been passed in defiance of the law.[49] I think that such action on her part would, however, be unwise. I suggest that the two Houses of Parliament should themselves attract any public odium for legislating improperly; that the government which had initiated the defective legislation should be forced to take political, and perhaps electoral, responsibility for it; that the Queen should assent to the Bill and thus give the courts an eventual opportunity to decide whether it was a valid Act of Parliament,[50] and that those three consequences would be adequate to meet the case, rather than the Queen precipitating a political crisis through the exercise of her veto (perhaps involving the government's resignation following rejection of its advice that she assent to the measure[51]).

(b) If a government were to procure the passage of a Bill to prolong the maximum life of Parliament for no proper reason the Queen would certainly be acting as the ultimate guardian of the constitution if she were to veto the Bill. The democracy upon which the constitution is built requires regular general elections at the elapse of no more than five years,[52] and unless the country were at war a prolongation Bill would be properly vetoed. But such prolongation—particularly without all-party agreement—would, again, just not be contemplated by any British

[48] It would be unclear why, if that were the government's view, it would allow a free vote in the first place. Without a free vote it could use its majority to vote down the Bill in the Commons. Perhaps the example given might be more likely to happen in a hung Parliament.

[49] This is another example given by Marshall, op. cit., pp. 22–3. He thinks that the Queen might have to use her veto in that case.

[50] The courts would have to decide whether royal assent had cured any procedural defect. For consideration of the relevant issues see de Smith, op. cit., pp. 94–104.

[51] Of course, a government whose Bill had been vetoed could shrug its shoulders, abandon the Bill, and carry on. We must be careful not to assume that governments are looking for excuses to sack themselves.

[52] Parliament Act 1911, s. 7.

government. And what on earth would the House of Lords have been doing in failing to use its absolute veto over such a shocking measure?[53]

(c) A government Bill designed to achieve a permanent subversion of the democratic basis of the constitution[54] could be appropriately vetoed, but there would be problems which suggest to me that the Sovereign would be wiser either to assent (under vigorous protest) or to insist on a dissolution. So, a Bill might be designed to gerrymander the constituencies in the government party's favour, or to effect some fundamental modification of the electoral system to the same end. But there could be tricky questions of degree which might pit the Queen's judgement against that of her Ministers. What form of gerrymandering would justify the use of the veto? Not, presumably, the Orders in Council under the Parliamentary Constituencies Act 1986,[55] which adjust constituency boundaries to take account of population changes but which are regularly denounced by the Opposition as gerrymandering. What, then, would be a sufficiently offensive modification of the electoral system?[56] Would the attempted introduction of proportional representation, which would enhance the position of a third party in the Commons at the expense of the Conservative and Labour Parties, qualify? Surely not. What is needed is a somewhat more closely drawn formula which would restrict royal intervention to the worst case. That formula, I suggest, could be that if (i) the House of Commons were persuaded to pass a fundamentally undemocratic measure designed irreversibly to affect the electoral system in peacetime, and (ii) the Queen were satisfied that no reasonable person outside the government supported the measure, then she would be justified in rejecting ministerial advice to the extent of insisting on a dissolution[57] so that the electorate could decide the issue.

Legislation is the end product of the political process. As with the choice of Prime Minister, the modern constitution ought to require political decisions, and responsibility for them, to be taken by politicians and (where appropriate) the electorate, not by the head of state. The Queen would, therefore, be justified today in using her legislative veto only over a Bill designed to postpone, without all-party agreement, a

[53] Parliament Act 1911, s. 2(1): Bills to prolong the life of the House of Commons beyond 5 years are outside the Parliament Acts, and the Lords' absolute veto over them remains.

[54] This is Jennings's phrase, and the examples which follow are his.

[55] Formerly the House of Commons (Redistribution of Seats) Acts 1944 to 1979.

[56] No doubt not the suspension of the right to vote in local government elections (see the Local Government (Interim Provisions) Act 1984, s. 1) or the abolition of a tier of local democracy (see the Local Government Act 1985, s. 1.).

[57] Or a referendum: see note 39.

dissolution in peacetime. In all other cases her role should be restricted either to vigorous private protest (but ultimately assenting to the controversial Bill), or to insisting on a dissolution (but assenting to the Bill if passed again in the new Parliament).

The last reserve power to be examined is that of dismissal of a government. Dismissal could arise indirectly, through the Queen's insistence on a dissolution or through her refusal of assent to legislation: the government might take rejection of its advice as a ground for resignation.[58] Direct dismissal is much less likely.

(a) If a government lost a vote of confidence in the House of Commons and refused either to recommend a dissolution or to resign then (because a government's only basis for legitimacy is majority support for it in the House of Commons[59]) the Queen would in theory be justified in dismissing it, and no reasonable criticism could attach to her for doing so. A more cautious reaction, however, might yet again be to bring about a dissolution, so as to put the political question to the electorate. It would be comforting to assume that the electors would not take kindly to a government so blatantly breaking the rules and that it would elect a different administration.

(b) It has already been suggested that a government which procured the passage of outrageously undemocratic legislation should receive the royal reaction of insistence on a general election. A *dismissal* of such a government would be inappropriate because that would involve the Queen attempting to resolve a profoundly political argument.

(c) The circumstances of the dismissal of the Whitlam government in 1975 could scarcely occur in the United Kingdom.[60] The nearest analogy might be a confused political situation in which only minority governments had been formed after at least two general elections, and in which those governments could not persuade the Commons to pass essential Finance Bills. Even assuming that the parties were prepared to put perceived party advantage over the national interest, however, it is difficult to understand what reserve power could be deployed—not dismissal (for presumably any alternative grouping in the Commons which could have coalesced into a stronger alternative government would have done so), and not insistence on a dissolution (for what would

---

[58] Or it might not: see note 51.

[59] Or, in a hung Parliament, the absence of any majority against it prepared to vote it down.

[60] Because the House of Lords cannot reject money Bills. On the Whitlam affair, see Sir John Kerr, *Matters for Judgment* (1978); Gough Whitlam, *The Truth of the Matter* (1979); Gareth Evans (ed.), *Labor and the Constitution 1972–1975* (1977); Colin Turpin, op. cit., pp. 118–22.

be achieved if yet another hung Parliament were returned?). In such a volatile situation the Queen should confine herself to her traditional and usual powers—perhaps urging the possibility of a coalition of some kind being formed.

If, despite everything, a dismissal of a government were ever unavoidable, it would at least be easy to effect. The Queen would simply inform the Prime Minister that he and the government ceased to hold office. From that moment all ministerial posts would be vacant.[61]

Continuity and succession

Because of the tasks entrusted to the Queen in the government of the country, there must be provision for her contribution to be continued if she is personally unable to carry them out. There has been no need for a Regency since 1820; Counsellors of State, on the other hand, have been appointed frequently since provision was first made for them by statute in 1937, and they will be considered first.[62]

The Queen may (and will) appoint Counsellors of State if she intends to be absent from the United Kingdom or if she is suffering from an illness which is not so serious that a Regency is required.[63] Counsellors will have delegated to them by Letters Patent such royal functions[64] as are specified in order to prevent delay or difficulty in the dispatch of public business.[65] The only legal restriction on the Counsellors is that they cannot dissolve Parliament save with the Sovereign's express approval, and they cannot create peers.[66] Candidates to be Counsellors are Prince Philip (as the Sovereign's spouse), those four persons next in line of succession to the Crown,[67] and the Queen Mother.[68] Prince Charles has acted as a Counsellor of State when required since his eighteenth birth-

[61] See chapter 4.

[62] See Wheeler-Bennett, op. cit., Appendix A for an historical account of the provisions for a Regency and for Counsellors of State.

[63] Regency Act 1937, s. 6(1). None has been appointed during the Queen's reign on account of any illness of hers.

[64] These are defined, ibid., s. 8(2) as including 'all powers and authorities belonging to the Crown, whether prerogative or statutory. . .'.

[65] Ibid., s. 6(1).

[66] Ibid., s. 6(1), proviso.

[67] And who would be qualified to act as Regent (discussed below) and be present in the United Kingdom. The heir to the throne may be a Counsellor of State provided he is over 18: Regency Act 1937, s. 6.(2A) as replaced by the Regency Act 1943, s. 1.

[68] Regency Act 1953, s. 3.

day in 1966, thus giving him useful though strictly limited experience of the role he will one day fulfil alone. By custom, two Counsellors act jointly,[69] together holding Privy Council meetings, receiving people in audience, and so on.

A Regency would be required if (*a*) the Queen were so ill as to be incapable of performing the royal functions, or if (*b*) she were for any definite cause not available to perform those functions, or if (*c*) a Sovereign were under 18 on his or her succession.[70] In cases (*a*) and (*b*) a collection of notables[71] would have to certify the existence of the incapacity.[72] The person would then be Regent who was next in line of succession to the Crown, over eighteen and not disqualified because a Roman Catholic:[73] that person would today be Prince Charles.[74] A Regent's only legal disabilities are that he cannot assent to any Bill to alter the succession to the throne or which would repeal the Acts which secure the established Church in Scotland.[75]

It would be a worthwhile, though unprecedented, departure for the Queen to request a declaration of a Regency when she next has a lengthy overseas tour, rather than (as has been the invariable custom) to appoint Counsellors of State. By reason of that absence she would, in terms of the Regency Act 1937, be definitely not available for the performance of her royal functions, and there would be a practical advantage that Prince Charles as Prince Regent would enjoy a period actually doing the job to which he might not otherwise succeed until he was in his 60s. A further development which I offer for consideration is that in several years' time the Queen might seek the passage of a fresh Regency Act to create Charles Prince Regent during the Queen's old age. Some duties might be expressly reserved to Her Majesty, but the more onerous tasks would be devolved to her son. This would both lighten the Queen's load and advance the day when Prince Charles would perform a central constitutional role while at the same time being a more acceptable change than abdication for them both.

---

[69] No minimum number is prescribed in the Acts, but the delegated functions must be 'exercised jointly': 1937 Act, s. 6(3).

[70] Regency Act 1937, ss. 1, 2. If Prince Charles died after his accession and was succeeded by Prince William while he was still under 18, Prince Andrew would be Regent.

[71] That is, any 3 or more of the Sovereign's spouse, the Lord Chancellor, the Speaker, the Lord Chief Justice, and the Master of the Rolls.

[72] It also declares the termination of the incapacity: Regency Act 1937, s. 2(1).

[73] He must also be a British citizen and be domiciled in the United Kingdom: ibid., s. 3(1), (2).

[74] Had a child of the Queen succeeded when still under 18, Prince Philip would have been Regent: Regency Act 1953, s. 1(1).

[75] Regency Act 1937, s. 4(2).

The succession to the throne is based at common law and in statute on heredity, primogeniture (and not coparceny[76]) and on religious tests (Catholics and persons marrying Catholics[77] are excluded;[78] a Sovereign must also swear to maintain the established Church in England and Scotland and take the Coronation Oath[79]). Thus the succession now is in the line Prince Charles, Prince William, Prince Henry, Prince Andrew, Prince Edward, the Princess Royal, Peter Phillips, Zara Phillips—and so on.[80]

Apart from any future disqualification from that line which might be brought about by marriage into Catholicism, the only other remotely possible change this century might occur if the Queen decided to accelerate Prince Charles's accession by abdicating. Although that has been and remains an unlikely prospect it is, perhaps, best to be prepared. What would be required to give effect to such an abdication?[81] First, the Cabinet's agreement would have to be sought because the government would need to take consultative and legal steps. There is no reason to think that such agreement would be withheld. Secondly, with the Queen's consent the other party Leaders would be informed, partly as a courtesy and partly to secure all-party support for legislation. Thirdly, the Prime Minister would communicate with the governments of Australia and Canada to ask both for the assent of their Parliaments to the abdication[82] and for the request and consent by those Parliaments to the enactment of an Abdication Bill at Westminster.[83] Fourthly, the

[76] That is, an older daughter succeeds in preference to any younger daughter in the absence of a son.

[77] Prince Michael of Kent removed himself from the line on his marriage to a Catholic in 1978. Their children remain 20th and 21st in line because they were baptized and have been brought up as Anglicans.

[78] By the Bill of Rights 1689, the Act of Settlement 1701, and the Succession to the Crown Act 1707.

[79] Ibid., and the Accession Declaration Act 1910.

[80] Prince Andrew may not be as far away from the throne as the formal line indicates, given the habit of the Prince of Wales of travelling by air with both his sons.

[81] Most of the following is based on the 1936 precedent.

[82] The Preamble to the Statute of Westminster 1931 states: '. . . [A]ny alteration in the law touching the Succession to the Throne or the Royal Style and Titles shall hereafter require the assent as well of the Parliaments of all the Dominions as of the Parliament of the United Kingdom.' 'Dominions' are defined in s. 1: only Australia and Canada remain within that statutory definition. New Zealand formally caused the Statute to cease to have effect in her law from January 1987: see Constitution Act 1986, s. 26 (NZ). This recital of that convention would not seem to concern as a matter of law the fifteen states which have become full Commonwealth members since 1931 and which still recognize the Queen as head of state: but see below note 84.

[83] Statute of Westminster 1931, s. 4. In 1936 a majority of the Dominions agreed that Edward VIII should abdicate.Canada requested and consented, Australia and New Zealand assented, to it: Preamble to His Majesty's Declaration of Abdication Act 1936.

Queen would sign an instrument of abdication expressing her irrevocable determination to renounce the throne and asking that effect be given to it. That instrument would be put before Parliament and sent to the Parliaments of Australia and Canada.[84] Lastly, an Abdication Bill, along the lines of His Majesty's Declaration of Abdication Act 1936, would be introduced into Parliament, and, on its enactment, Charles would be King.

[84] And, as a courtesy, to all Commonwealth states in which the Queen is head of state so that they could make any necessary changes in their laws to provide for her successor to be their new head of state.

9

The House of Commons

Elections, Members and parties

The maximum life of a Parliament is five years from the day, fixed at the dissolution, on which it was summoned to meet after a general election.[1] Parliament would be dissolved automatically on the expiry of that time, but Parliament never ends in that way: it is, of course, dissolved by the Sovereign on the Prime Minister's advice. Only three Parliaments since 1945 have been allowed by the Prime Minister to approach the maximum span allowed by law;[2] six have been terminated after some four years.[3] The Prime Minister will usually bring about a dissolution in good time before the maximum duration of Parliament and at the best moment as he can judge it for his party to win: this is an unfair advantage for him, but one which the Leaders of the opposition parties in the main[4] hope to enjoy themselves one fine day.

After the Prime Minister has received the Queen's consent for the dissolution the news of it is released through a press notice issued from Number 10 Downing Street. The first the House of Commons itself hears of this will be by rumour at Westminster or through news bulletins, a discourtesy which causes a small but justified grievance among Members of that House who are, after all, the most intimately affected by the development.[5] Parliament will actually be dissolved some seven to ten days later.[6]

---

1 Parliament Act 1911, s. 7

2 Those of 1945, 1959, and October 1974.

3 Those of 1951, 1955, 1966, 1970, 1979, and 1983. The Parliaments of 1950, 1964, and February 1974 are left out of account because the government had very small majorities (and in the last case no majority) and the Prime Minister's freedom of choice was therefore more limited.

4 Though not the Leaders of the SDP/Liberal Alliance: their 1987 general election manifesto, *Britain United*, advocated fixed-term, five-year Parliaments.

5 Ironically, the House of Lords was informed by a Minister of the impending dissolution in 1987 straight after the Prime Minister's announcement: see 487 H.L. Deb. 422 (11 May 1987).

6 This delay enables some of the government's legislative programme to be salvaged and passed (especially any Finance Bill) following negotiations with the main opposition party. It would be open to the Opposition to say that, if the government chooses to dissolve Parliament for party advantage during a session, it must take the consequence of losing any remaining Bills. No Opposition has taken that stance, both because the government could respond by securing the

Dissolution[7] is effected by a royal proclamation under the Great Seal made by the Queen at a Privy Council.[8] The proclamation recites that Parliament is dissolved and that the Lord Chancellor has been directed to issue writs to individual returning officers to cause elections to a new Parliament to be held. In practice polling day[9] is fixed by the proclamation for about four weeks after dissolution, with the new Parliament being summoned to meet on a date specified in the proclamation some two weeks after the election. In law Parliament need only be summoned to meet once every three years.[10] In fact, whether after a dissolution or otherwise, it will meet in annual session because there is a natural expectation that (recesses apart[11]) Parliament should be at work, because the government needs to procure legislation year in, year out as the life-blood of its existence, and because some essential laws must be renewed every year.[12]

The newly elected MP[13] receives a fair, but scarcely generous, financial settlement. He or she[14] is paid an annual salary of £22,548.[15] He may

---

passage of guillotine motions to force the legislation through quickly, and because when the Opposition became the government it would not want *its* legislation held up, or lost, before a dissolution: Oppositions and governments subscribe to the maxim that dogs must not eat dogs.

[7] A prorogation ceremony customarily took place before dissolution, formally ending the parliamentary session with a short speech on the Queen's behalf summarizing the work achieved during that session. There was, however, no such ceremony before the 1979, 1983, or 1987 dissolutions. (The end of each annual parliamentary session always has a prorogation ceremony, the main practical effect of which is to cause all public Bills which have not completed all stages to lapse; private Bills may, on application from their sponsors, be suspended over into the next annual session.) See generally R. Blackburn, 'Prorogation or Adjournment Before a Dissolution of Parliament' [1987] *Public Law* 533.

[8] The last time Parliament was dissolved by the Sovereign in person was in 1818, by the Prince Regent on behalf of the King.

[9] The detailed rules concerning the conduct of parliamentary elections are outside the scope of this book. See *Halsbury's Laws of England* (4th edn., 1977), paras. 401–981; Erskine May's *Parliamentary Practice* (20th edn., 1983), chapter 2.

[10] Meeting of Parliament Act 1694.

[11] For summer, Christmas, Easter, and Whitsun. The House of Commons sits for about 175 days each year.

[12] Especially the Armed Forces Act (currently of 1986) (which regulates Army and RAF discipline) and the Naval Discipline Act 1957, which would expire without an annual Order in Council; and legislative authority to raise income tax and corporation tax.

[13] To be elected a person must be 21 or over (Family Law Reform Act 1969, s. 1(4), Schedule 2, para. 4) and a British citizen (which for this purpose includes a citizen of the Republic of Ireland: British Nationality Act 1981, s. 50(1)), and must not be subject to any disqualification (to be explained shortly).

[14] It is still slightly awkward to write of an MP in the feminine: the highest number of women MPs was 41 in the 1987 Parliament, whereas the usual number has been 20 or so.

[15] From 1988 the rate of MPs' pay is linked to a prescribed percentage of the salary received by a senior principal in the civil service so that as civil service pay rises, so will that of MPs: see 46 H.C. Deb. 329–52 (19 July 1983); 120 H.C. Deb. 295–341 (21 July 1987). This should avoid the previous embarrassment of legislators voting themselves pay increases.

currently claim up to £20,140 a year as an office costs allowance for out-of-pocket office, secretarial and research expenses; all his travel within the United Kingdom on parliamentary business is either free or qualifies for a car mileage allowance, and his phone calls and postage from the House of Commons are free.[16] He must find his own London accommodation if his constituency is too far away to allow daily commuting.[17] If he expects a room of his own in which to work he will probably be disappointed: less than half of all MPs have their own offices; others must share, or use a table in the Library or benches in the corridors. If he wants a secretary he must find one and pay the agreed salary out of his secretarial allowance. He will, at least, enjoy an excellent Library and Research Division.[18] For some MPs access to the media, particularly television, is a valuable fringe benefit; consultancy, or lobbying, can also bring in cash—although such activities must be entered in the Register of Members' Interests.[19] The hours of work are uncivilized: the House does not sit until 2.30 p.m.[20] (but 9.30 a.m. on Fridays[21]) and, although the notional time at which the Commons rises is 10 p.m. on Monday to Thursday, late night and occasional all-night sittings are the norm. It cannot be said fairly that the House has provided lavishly for the reward, comfort, or efficient working of its Members, but any of them who make a reasonable objection face the certainty of being sharply told by someone that there is no shortage of candidates to take their places.[22]

Should an MP wish for whatever reason to quit membership of the House he has to resort to an antiquated device in order to resign. He

---

[16] These provisions have effect by virtue of various resolutions of the House. The office costs allowance is indexed to the salary paid to a senior personal secretary in the civil service, so that each annual percentage rise in that salary is reflected in an equivalent increase in the allowance: 120 H.C. Deb. 340–1 (21 July 1987).

[17] MPs who stay in London overnight away from home are entitled to an allowance of about £8,000 a year. If they have an inner London constituency and live there they may draw £1,000 annually as a London supplement.

[18] See M. Rush (ed.), *The House of Commons: Services and Facilities 1972–1982* (1983).

[19] See The Register of Members' Interests on 12 January 1987, H.C. 155 (1986–7). The Register enumerates 9 separate classes of financial interests which all MPs should register, including directorships, paid employment, and sponsorships: Erskine May, op. cit., pp. 435–9. They must also register any paid lobbying activity in public relations, political and parliamentary advice and consultancy: 89 H.C. Deb. 216–54 (17 December 1985). Mr Enoch Powell consistently refused to make any entry while he was an MP, the only Member to do so.

[20] S.O. No. 9. (All Standing Orders of the House of Commons referred to are in the 1986 revision: see H.C. 1 (1986–7).

[21] S.O. No. 11.

[22] No MP is returned unopposed (not even the Speaker seeking re-election), and the number of candidates for the 650 seats must be multiplied considerably to represent the total number who sought selection in the various parties.

must seek the office of Steward and Bailiff of either Her Majesty's three Chiltern Hundreds of Stoke, Desborough, and Burnham, or of the Manor of Northstead. These nominal offices are in the gift of the Chancellor of the Exchequer, who gives one on demand to any MP who asks for it, and under the House of Commons Disqualification Act 1975[23] holders of those offices are disqualified and their seats are vacated.[24] Should an MP decide (as of course most do) to stay, he may be involuntarily removed from membership of the House in a number of ways[25]— defeat at the next general election; inheritance of a peerage;[26] adjudication of bankruptcy which lasts for six months or more;[27] sentence to prison for more than a year, or for life;[28] detention in a mental hospital for six months or more;[29] or expulsion by resolution of the House.[30] On ceasing

[23] Section 4 and Schedule 1.

[24] From the late 17th century acceptance of a paid office under the Crown was considered to incapacitate an MP from continuing to sit, because an MP receiving a salary from the Crown could not be reckoned to scrutinize independently the actions of His Majesty's government. This disability extended to Ministers so that, on accepting ministerial office, they were disqualified and had to fight a by-election in their former seats; that inconvenient rule was abrogated by the Re-election of Ministers Act 1919. The two Stewardships are held either (a) until the Chancellor appoints another applicant, each new appointment expressly revoking that of the previous holder: in that manner 15 Ulster Unionist MPs were able to leave the House of Commons on the same day, 17 December 1985, so as to cause by-elections in Northern Ireland on the issue of the Anglo-Irish Agreement; or (b) by the holder applying for release from it, which he might do if he wished to fight a by-election in his former seat (such as Mr Dick Taverne in 1973). The other ways of voluntarily leaving the House are to accept a disqualifying job so described in the House of Commons Disqualification Act 1975, s. 4 and Schedule 1, or to be ordained into the Church of England or Scotland or Ireland (House of Commons (Clergy Disqualification) Act 1801) or into the Roman Catholic Church (Roman Catholic Relief Act 1829, s. 9); Nonconformist clergy are not disqualified, a discrimination of which the numerous reverend MPs from Northern Ireland take full advantage.

[25] See Erskine May, op. cit., chapter 3.

[26] *Acceptance* of an offered peerage must be classed as voluntary (although some are less voluntary than others—such as one urged upon an MP to provide a by-election for a Minister without a seat). The Member is disqualified from the moment of inheritance, and cannot go back into the chamber even to retrieve property: for an illustrative incident see Lord Home, *The Way the Wind Blows* (1976), pp. 100-1.

[27] Insolvency Act 1986, s. 427. Being adjudged bankrupt disqualifies an MP from sitting or voting; that disqualification ceases on discharge, but if bankruptcy lasts 6 months or more the seat is vacated. The last MP so excluded was Mr C. Homan in 1928.

[28] Representation of the People Act 1981, ss. 1, 2. During a sentence of less than 1 year an MP may not sit or vote, but he could be expelled on the resolution of the House. Any sentence for treason automatically disqualifies. The Speaker is informed by the court of any MP imprisoned by it, and he informs the House. See, for example, 118 H.C. Deb. 36-7 (25 June 1987)—Mr Maginnis, imprisoned for 7 days for non-payment of road fund tax.

[29] Mental Health Act 1983, s. 141. The Speaker must be notified of any MP's detention under the Act: if it lasts 6 months or more his seat is vacated. The last MP so excluded was Mr C. Leach in 1916.

[30] This can be for any reason, although the House cannot stop the expelled MP from standing at a by-election.

to be an MP a former Member will be entitled to a pension if he has contributed to the Parliamentary Contributory Pension Fund; if he loses his seat at a general election, he may receive severance pay, known as resettlement grant.[31]

In the regulation of its affairs the House of Commons is firmly wedded to the two-party system, one party (usually with a majority of seats) forming the government, another party (usually with the second largest number of seats) forming the Opposition—entirely regardless of the number of votes which had been cast at the election for them or for other parties represented in the House. The status of Her Majesty's Opposition carries with it numerous advantages, and, in a two-party system, that is as it should be for the Opposition represents the alternative government and it should have certain rights to enable it to act as such. That proposition is, however, a little less self-evident after the last two general elections in which the SDP/Liberal Alliance polled a significant proportion of the popular vote but was rewarded with a tiny number of seats.[32] Nevertheless, in the present parliamentary system the Leader of the Opposition (who is the 'Leader of that party in the House in opposition to Her Majesty's Government having the greatest numerical strength in the House'[33]) receives an annual salary of £48,148 (which includes his parliamentary allowance), and is supplied with a car from the government car pool.[34] Other party Leaders receive no salary.[35] The Leader of the Opposition has the opportunity to put a number of

---

[31] On the pension, see Parliamentary and other Pensions Act 1972; Parliamentary and other Pensions Act 1976; Parliamentary Pensions etc. Act 1984; Parliamentary and other Pensions Act 1987. As an example, an MP aged 63 who retired at a general election after 20 years' service would receive some £6,300 a year, or some £7,000 if he retired through illness, or some £5,400 if he retired during a Parliament: 110 H.C. Deb. *628–30* (written answers 19 March 1987). Resettlement grant is based on age and length of service; it has been available since 1971 by virtue of a number of resolutions of the House.

[32] For the details, see note 182.

[33] Ministerial and other Salaries Act 1975, s. 2(1). In any dispute the Speaker decides: s. 2(2). The office was first recognized in a similar statute in 1937.

[34] The Opposition Chief Whip receives a salary of £40,798 a year and two Opposition Whips £31,738 each a year.

[35] Opposition parties, however, receive public money to help them with their parliamentary work, calculated on the number of seats and votes won at the previous general election: see 888 H.C. Deb. 1869–934 (20 March 1975); 71 H.C. Deb. 1095–1101 (23 January 1985); 123 H.C. Deb. 481–500 (26 November 1987). At present a party can receive a maximum of £490,000 a year. This provision is known as 'Short money' after the Leader of the House who introduced the concept. On political funding generally, see the Report of the Committee on Financial Aid to Political Parties, Cmnd. 6601 (1976); M. Pinto-Duschinsky, *British Political Finance 1830–1980* (1982); K. D. Ewing, *The Funding of Political Parties in Britain* (1987). Additionally, companies and trade unions help fund the Conservative and Labour Parties respectively.

questions at Prime Minister's Question Time each Tuesday and Thursday, whereas the Leader of the Liberal Party or the Leader of the SDP were allowed to put one question between them. It is the Leader of the Opposition who asks the Leader of the House each Thursday to state the business of the Commons for the following week, together with a supplementary question (invariably in the form of a protest) when he has received the answer. Subject to the understanding that the government must be able to get its essential legislation through the House and to the rule that (with exceptions) government business has precedence in the House,[36] the government and the Opposition 'through the usual channels' (that is, the Leader of the House and Government Whips, and their Opposition counterparts) are in regular contact about parliamentary business—the timing of debates on Bills, general debates and divisions, and so on.[37] The other parties are, however, merely informed of the results of those deliberations. In major debates the Leader of the Opposition will be called immediately after the Prime Minister; the other party Leaders are either called next, or must take their chances in catching the Speaker's eye along with other senior Privy Councillors on both sides of the House (by which time the lure of the tea room may have proved too great for many Members). The Opposition chooses the subjects for debate on seventeen days during the session; the third largest party has that privilege on only three days.[38] If the Prime Minister or other Minister makes a ministerial broadcast, the BBC and IBA will offer the Opposition the right to reply; other parties may or may not be favoured with equal time.[39] In all these ways the standing of the Opposition and its Leader is enhanced in the House of Commons and indirectly in the

[36] S.O. No. 13(1).

[37] Discussions though the usual channels take place 'behind the Speaker's chair', which is figurative rather than strictly geographic, meaning merely that the discussions are held outside the chamber. On these arrangements see Donald Wade, *Behind the Speaker's Chair* (1978).

[38] Opposition days are considered in more detail later.

[39] See generally Alan E. Boyle, 'Political Broadcasting, Fairness and Administrative Law' [1986] *Public Law* 562, especially pp. 575–87. The only regular ministerial broadcast is that of the Chancellor on the evening of his annual Budget. In 1987 the Chancellor, the Labour Shadow Chancellor, and the Alliance economics spokesman each had a 10-minute broadcast on successive evenings. Time is given for party political broadcasts and party election broadcasts by both the BBC and IBA in ratios agreed between them and the parties. In the 1987 general election campaign the broadcasting authorities gave equal time to the Conservative, Labour, and the SDP/Liberal Alliance; other news and current affairs time was broadly divided equally between those parties. For an unsuccessful attempt in 1985 to require the Broadcasting Complaints Commission to examine an allegation that the Alliance parties had received unfair treatment in news and current affairs programmes, see *R. v. Broadcasting Complaints Commission, ex p. Owen* [1985] 1 Q.B. 1153.

eyes of the general public, to the detriment of other parties represented there.

All parties in the House organize themselves for maximum efficiency. The Whips are of vital importance, especially to the government and the Opposition. They convey back-bench opinion to the leadership, and vice versa; they keep Members informed of forthcoming business through means of the weekly whip—a document in which business is underlined once, twice, or three times to denote how important attendance is;[40] they supervise pairs with MPs from other parties so that paired absences make no difference to the result of divisions; they make recommendations of back-benchers for promotion;[41] and they help to maintain party discipline. Then again, the parties have parliamentary machinery designed to tap back-bench views. The Conservative Party has its 1922 Committee for that purpose,[42] made up of all Conservative MPs not in the government or the Shadow Cabinet: it is an important focus of opinion and leading Conservative Party figures may defer to its views. All Labour MPs form the Parliamentary Labour Party, which operates similarly to the 1922 Committee but more formally and sometimes more aggressively towards its leadership. The Liberal Party and the SDP had looser arrangements, largely because they had far fewer MPs than the Conservatives or Labour.[43]

The Commons and the government

The role of the House of Commons in the system of government has been much analysed. Perhaps five functions, briefly stated, may suffice here. First, it is the House of Commons which gives the government its political legitimacy.[44] A party which secures 326 seats or more at a general election, or a coalition of parties with that representation, is entitled to form an administration. In a hung Parliament a minority

---

[40] Technically the whip is claimed by the parties to be an order to attend, but it is acknowledged to carry the implicit instruction (not always obeyed) to vote with the party as well.

[41] See chapter 5.

[42] So named from the meeting of Conservative MPs at the Carlton Club in 1922 which decided to end the Lloyd George coalition.

[43] The Parliamentary Committee of the SDP consisted of all SDP MPs and representatives of SDP peers. The Parliamentary Liberal Party was made up of all Liberal MPs. The Parliamentary Social and Liberal Democratic Party will consist of all MPs taking the whip, and will choose a Chief Whip.

[44] Just as appointment by the Queen, or with her approval, gives Ministers their legal status.

government obtains conditional legitimacy from the Commons: it takes up and retains office until that House removes its legitimacy by carrying a vote of no confidence in it. Secondly, the House provides a forum in which a continuing general election campaign may be fought. The pace of that campaign will slacken off after a decisive poll, but will quicken again as the years pass. Through that forum the parties in opposition seek to present themselves as the alternative and preferable government, and the government seeks to prove the opposite. This must be a rather daunting prospect for opposition parties, but then Parliaments cannot last more than five years (and four years is nearer the mark); even governments with very large majorities are only rarely returned by a majority of electors;[45] there is a sizeable floating vote, and only three times this century has a government won three consecutive general elections out of a total of twenty-four contests.[46] All governments are thus temporary—although as Mrs Thatcher has shown us, some are less temporary than others. Thirdly, the House of Commons is the mechanism through which the government will achieve its legislation. A party returned to power at a general election will have commitments to legislation in its manifesto, and will bring forward more as time passes and as exigencies require; on average some sixty to seventy public general Bills will be passed each session, most of which will have been introduced by the government. A government is, by virtue of its majority in the House of Commons, entitled to expect that House to pass its legislation within a reasonable time, assuming that it retains the support of its MPs for it. Fourthly, the House of Commons is a place in which grievances may be ventilated, at Question Time, in debates, by putting down amendments to Bills and 'early-day' motions,[47] and in other ways. The House is, however, not very well equipped to *redress* grievances: for that, the citizen may be better advised to ask his MP to write to the relevant Minister or other authority (who might prefer to put the matter right quietly without risking publicity) or to put his complaint to the Parliamentary Commissioner for Administration[48]or the Health Service

---

[45] In 1987, for example, the Conservative Party obtained a majority of 102 even though nearly 58% of the total votes cast went to other parties.

[46] In 1906 and the two elections of 1910; 1951, 1955, and 1959; and in 1979, 1983 and 1987.

[47] Any MP may put down a motion for debate 'on an early day', knowing that his chances of it being selected for debate are very slim, but so as to allow other MPs to show support for it by signing it. Over 1,200 early-day motions were tabled in the 1985–6 session. See further 3rd Report from the Procedure Committee, H.C. 254 (1986–7). (Figures from the 1986–7 session are not considered in this chapter because the dissolution of Parliament made it a short session.)

[48] Parliamentary Commissioner Act 1967.

Commissioner;[49] or to seek justice from the Commissioner for Local Administration;[50] or to conduct an appeal to the courts, or to seek judicial review; or to try to interest the media in his complaint. Fifthly, and just occasionally, the whole House will actually represent the views of and speak for most of the nation, in time of war or armed conflict,[51] or of natural or man-made disaster, or after a terrorist outrage, or on the death of a respected citizen, or at a time of national rejoicing.

No administration governs without being affected by influences outside both Houses of Parliament. Particularly as a general election approaches, evidence that the government is not faring as well as it might hope in opinion polls[52] will present a temptation to trim policies—or, in the more acceptable modern idiom, to improve the presentation of policies.[53] Such pressure will be subtle, but can be just as effective in producing changes in a government's thinking as any efforts by the opposition parties in the House of Commons. By-election results, too, may have the direct effect of bringing the government up with a start and perhaps encouraging shifts of emphasis, even though every government publicly dismisses adverse by-election results as being just by-election results which would not be repeated at the general election.[54] The views of the party loyalists outside Parliament will obviously be taken into account as well. For the Conservative Party this will be informally expressed through local constituency associations—but not at the annual conference, which is stage-managed to present a united party in the best light to the general public. For the Labour Party, extra-parliamentary party opinion will be voiced through the National Executive Committee,[55] the constituency parties, the trade unions, and, above all, through the annual conference, which has a constitutional role in the making of party policy.[56] For the Social and Liberal Democratic Party (as

49 National Health Service Act 1977, Part V.

50 Local Government Act 1974, Part III.

51 Such as during the Falklands conflict in 1982, although not during the Suez invasion in 1956.

52 A high standing in the opinion polls may clinch the timing of a dissolution for a Prime Minister, as it did in both 1983 and 1987 for Mrs Thatcher.

53 Involving, perhaps, a Cabinet reshuffle, or the appointment of a new Conservative Party Chairman, or the hiring of a different public relations agency.

54 This is a fair point. Of the seats lost by the government at by-elections in the last 20 years, 66 per cent were retaken at the subsequent general elections.

55 On which see *Constitution of the Labour Party* (1981), chapter 9. The NEC has places reserved for representatives from the trade unions, constituency parties, the Co-operative movement, the Young Socialists, and women, as well as for the Leader and Deputy Leader and Treasurer of the Labour Party.

56 For example, the annual conference adopts policies for the party which, if approved by a ⅔ majority on a card vote, are included in the 'Party Programme', from which the manifesto is drawn up jointly by the NEC and the Cabinet (or Shadow Cabinet): *Constitution*, clause V.

in the Liberal Party and the SDP), constituency opinion will probably be important, as will its Federal Policy Committee. Its biannual conference will be its sovereign representative body with the power to determine the party's policies which will bind its MPs.[57] All governments are pressed, too, by organized pressure groups, although their actual impact as measured through changes in policy or in legislation sponsored by any government may not be very great. International opinion (especially that of allies[58]), international obligations, and the international economic climate[59] will all exert their influences on any government.

It is, however, to the House of Commons that the government will look for its strength and legislation. A government with a majority of seats behind it is, in Lord Hailsham's famous and apt phrase, and with only some exaggeration, an elective dictatorship.[60] No majority government has been unambiguously voted out of office or forced to the polls by the House of Commons since 1895.[61] Such a government could only be put at risk if it were to be rent by an internal party split of such vehemence that enough of its supporters were determined to engineer a dissolution. But, as all the years since 1895 have shown, this is unlikely to happen because modern governments and government parties in the Commons are cohesive, being bound both by loyalty and by the knowledge that they sink or swim together. Potentially rebellious government back-benchers know that if by their votes they were to endanger the continuance of the government they could well be denied party endorsement at the general election and thus almost certainly lose their seats: that is a very high price for any MP to be prepared to pay. The endorsement of the Conservatives or Labour or a major third party is usually essential for election to the House of Commons,[62] as independent candidates are but

---

[57] See *Constitution of the Social and Liberal Democrats*, articles 5–7.

[58] Of which a spectacular manifestation in 1986 was the government's agreement to let the United States use United Kingdom air bases to launch a bombing raid on Libya in response to terrorism.

[59] Consider, for example, how the 1964 Labour government's economic policy was moulded by an initial decision to maintain the international parity of the pound, and by the need to try to correct an adverse balance of payments.

[60] Lord Hailsham, *The Dilemma of Democracy: Diagnosis and Prescription* (1978), pp. 9–11.

[61] In that year Lord Rosebery's Liberal government was defeated on a snap vote to reduce the salary of the Secretary of State for War, Campbell-Bannerman, by £100 because of an alleged shortage of ammunition and cordite, and resigned. Chamberlain's resignation in 1940 was largely brought about by the refusal of over 90 Conservative MPs to support him on the division after the adjournment debate on the conduct of the war.

[62] Selection of candidates is largely a matter for local constituency parties. In the Labour Party, a candidate is chosen locally subject to the endorsement of the NEC (which is not always forthcoming: Mr Kinnock, for example, persuaded the Committee to reject a number of candidates before the 1987 general election). Additionally, every Labour MP must submit to a reselection (or

rarely elected (although there is more room for success in the Nationalist cause in Scotland or Wales,[63] or in the sectarian parties in Northern Ireland[64]). That party endorsement is made even more valuable because the national campaigns of the major parties, seen mainly through television, are much more important for the election of individual candidates than the efforts and identities of those candidates in their constituencies. So a majority government controls its MPs and has great power in and over the House of Commons, and it may be likened to the possessor of almost dictatorial powers, albeit powers that are restrained by regular general elections and by notions of what is generally acceptable in a liberal democracy. It has legislative supremacy in the Commons: its business (subject to exceptions which will be examined later) has precedence at every sitting,[65] and it can invoke the closure[66] and the guillotine[67] to ensure that it gets its legislation. It will suffer adverse votes from time to time, but the mass of its legislative programme will be enacted as it wants despite the best efforts of the opposition parties.

Two correctives need to be added to this description. First, in *very* special cases a Prime Minister may be forced from office directly or indirectly by the House of Commons.[68] The only three examples since 1895, however, have occurred during world war (Asquith's replacement by Lloyd George in 1916, and Chamberlain's by Churchill in 1940) and during a coalition in which the Prime Minister had only a minority of

---

deselection) procedure once in every Parliament, and a number of Labour MPs, having been deselected, have indirectly lost their seats. The Conservative Party uses a lighter rein; disagreements between Conservative Central Office and the constituencies over candidates are infrequent, and locally chosen candidates are usually endorsed. The Social and Liberal Democratic Party will have a powerful central candidates' committee which will maintain a list of parliamentary candidates approved by it. Each local party will choose its candidate by secret ballot. Social and Liberal Democrat MPs will be subject to reselection.

[63] The maximum Scottish National Party presence in the House was 11, and Plaid Cymru 3, both after the October 1974 general election.

[64] Of the 17 Northern Irish MPs, most will be Protestant Unionists.

[65] S.O. No. 13(1).

[66] S.O. Nos. 35, 36. A Government Whip moves 'That the question be now put' and, unless the Speaker thinks that this is an abuse, that motion is immediately voted on; if it is carried with at least 100 MPs supporting it, the main question under debate is put and decided, so ending debate.

[67] S.O. Nos. 80, 81. The government may move an allocation of time, or guillotine, motion in respect of a controversial Bill, and that motion is debated for up to 3 hours. The motion will allocate time for the standing committee to spend on each clause of the Bill, and for the time to be spent on report and third reading: as a result, parts of it may not be examined at all in committee. In 1985–6, the guillotine was invoked over the Gas, Social Security, and European Communities (Amendment) Bills.

[68] As distinct from pressures within the government and government party, as with Churchill in 1955.

Commons seats and was always vulnerable to the majority party pulling the rug from under him (Lloyd George's ouster in 1922).[69] Secondly, a government backed even by a very large Commons majority may decide that the actual or feared resistance of its own back-benchers requires a change of course—not in relation to its core policies (for that might raise the question of whether the government continued to enjoy the confidence of the House), but in relation to less central matters over which the government may decide to change its mind. Even Mrs Thatcher's administration, whose lowest general election majority was forty-three in 1979, has altered its policies on a number of occasions, for instance on whether to compile a register of immigrants, the possibility of introducing local referendums, changes in green-belt policy, loans (rather than grants) to students, and the burying of nuclear waste at four planned sites. Changes of mind may thus be brought about by back-bench opinion without the spur of any formal vote.

Minority governments[70] are obviously less certain of the fate of their policies and legislation in the House of Commons. They are prone to defeat in the division lobbies at any time. They are liable to the passage of a vote of no confidence (although the opposition parties may not all be ready to precipitate a dissolution too near to the previous one[71]). They may be in difficulty at the committee stage of Bills (for, in nominating standing committees to examine them, regard is had to the party composition of the House,[72] so that the government will be in a minority on those committees). Nevertheless, even minority governments retain the power of dissolution,[73] which can be put to effective use, as the second 1974 dissolution showed.[74]

Every government (whether majority, coalition, or minority) and every House of Commons must know exactly what votes adverse to the government are fatal, in the sense of inevitably leading to a dissolution of Parliament or the government's resignation. Defeat on an unambiguous motion of confidence or of no confidence has been treated as fatal by all governments since 1832. So, when the House of Commons resolved on

[69] See chapter 2.

[70] On the parliamentary difficulties of the 1974 minority Labour government, see R. Brazier, 'The Constitution in the New Politics' [1978] *Public Law* 117.

[71] See chapter 3.

[72] S.O. No. 86(2).

[73] Assuming, as I have argued in chapter 3, that no other stronger grouping is ready to take over without a dissolution.

[74] The minority Labour government achieved a majority of 5 at the second 1974 general election.

28 March 1979 'That this House has no confidence in Her Majesty's Goverment',[75] James Callaghan immediately told the House that he would seek a dissolution the following day. Now it used to be the case that a defeat on a major matter had the same effect as if an explicit vote of no confidence had carried. Ramsay MacDonald expressed the essence of this to the Commons after he had formed his first minority administration in 1924.

> The Labour Government will go out if it is defeated upon substantial issues, issues of principle, issues which really matter. It will go out if the responsible leaders of either party or any party move a direct vote of no confidence, and carry that vote. . . . If the House on matters non-essential, matters of mere opinion, matters that do not strike at the root of the proposals we make, and do not destroy fundamentally the general intentions of the Government in intro-ducing legislation—if the House wish to vary our propositions, the House must take the responsibility for that variation—then a division on such amend-ments and questions as those will not be regarded as a vote of no confidence.[76]

That differentiation between, on the one hand, defeats on substantial issues which really mattered together with votes of no confidence (which were both taken as decisive) and, on the other hand, non-essential defeats (which could be ignored) survived down to the 1970s. During that decade a significant change occurred, perhaps as an understanding that there is no reason why an isolated defeat on even a substantial matter should call in question the government's right to go on. Despite an initial majority of thirty seats Mr Edward Heath's government from 1970 to 1974 suffered six Commons defeats including, for example, the loss of draft Immigration Rules.[77] His successor Mr Harold Wilson made an early statement to the House about the position of the new minority Labour government.

> The government intend to treat with suitable respect, but not with exagger-ated respect, the results of any snap vote or any snap division. . . . In case of a Government defeat . . . the Government will not be forced to go to the country except in a situation in which every Hon. Member of the House was voting knowing the full consequences of his vote. It is a vote of confidence about which I am speaking. . . . In other words, we shall provide a recount.[78]

75 965 H.C. Deb. 461–590 (28 March 1979).
76 169 H.C. Deb. 749–50 (15 January 1924).
77 846 H.C. Deb. 1343–459 (22 November 1972).
78 870 H.C. Deb. 71–2 (12 March 1974).

This marked a recognition that what was of account was not whether a particular matter was 'substantial' rather than 'non-essential', but rather whether a particular vote was recognized as being one of confidence in the administration. After this time only a division characterized by the government as a formal vote of confidence would, if lost, involve a general election, and the government would put down a motion of confidence if it suffered some other major loss in the division lobbies. This development had a wider parliamentary effect, because government MPs became readier to show their disapproval of their government's policies through abstentions and votes with the Opposition, a development which was accelerated during the 1974 Labour government.[79] So, in the short Parliament of 1974 the government lost seventeen divisions,[80] for example on industrial policy[81] and on an Opposition motion on the rating system;[82] and in the 1974–9 Parliament it suffered forty-two defeats before the final vote of no confidence was carried.[83] Those defeats were largely shrugged off by the government, and Ministers implied that if the opposition parties disliked that reaction the remedy was in their hands—to procure the passage of a vote of no confidence.[84]

In (say) 1960 the defeat of a government Bill at second reading would have raised the probability of a general election,[85] but no one could still hold that view by 1980. The 1974 Labour government lost several Bills, the main casualties being the Aircraft and Shipbuilding Industries Bill,[86] the Scotland and Wales Bill (which lapsed after the government failed to carry a guillotine motion[87]), the Reduction of Redundancy Payments Bill (which was lost on second reading[88]) and the Local Authority

---

[79] See generally P. Norton, *Dissension in the House of Commons 1945–1974* (1975), and *Dissension in the House of Commons 1974–1979* (1980).

[80] Norton, op. cit. (1980), p. 491.

[81] 875 H.C. Deb. 689–769 (20 June 1974). The House resolved to regret the government's damaging industrial policies based on massive nationalization and the control of individual companies.

[82] 875 H.C. Deb. 1750–876 (27 June 1974). The House called on the government to introduce fundamental reform of the rating system.

[83] See Norton, op. cit. (1980), 491–3.

[84] There were three unsuccessful motions of no confidence debated in the 1974–9 Parliament before the fatal one.

[85] '. . . [I]t is now assumed as a matter of course that any defeats in the House of Commons must be reversed or else lead to a Government's resigning or dissolving Parliament': Graeme Moodie, *The Government of Britain* (1964), p. 100.

[86] The Bill lapsed at prorogation in 1976 after Opposition tactics had delayed it in the Commons, and the Lords had insisted on wrecking amendments.

[87] 926 H.C. Deb. 1234–367 (22 February 1977).

[88] 925 H.C. Deb. 1183–9 (7 February 1977).

Works (Scotland) Bill (which fell at third reading[89]).[90] Even Mrs Thatcher's government has not been immune from actual or anticipated adverse votes in the House. The Protection of Official Information Bill, which was designed to change the law on official secrets, was withdrawn from Parliament in the 1979–80 session after it had received its second reading in the House of Lords: it was clear that the heavy criticism to which it had been subjected meant that its chances of ultimate survival in either House were small.[91] The draft Immigration Rules were defeated in the Commons in 1982.[92] Most spectacularly, the Shops Bill, which would have liberalized the rules on Sunday trading, was defeated at its second reading in 1986 by fourteen votes, sixty-eight Conservative MPs voting against it despite a three-line whip.[93] These examples show that no government, even with a sound or even huge majority in the Commons, can assume that elective dictatorship will carry all its legislation— although it must be stressed that the number of legislative defeats may well not be large, and the importance of the losses may be quite small.

So what adverse votes are fatal? The passage of a vote of no confidence[94] is always deadly, whether it be formally expressed as such or whether it is some other motion accepted by the government as testing the confidence of the House in it.[95] Defeat on any other major matter may cause the government to ask the House to approve a formal motion of confidence,[96] and to recommend a dissolution or to resign if that is lost. Any other adverse vote in the House of Commons will have whatever effect is prescribed by the terms of the vote, but no other.[97]

The real significance of the general requirement that a government retain the confidence of the House of Commons is not in the rare loss of a vote of confidence or in the somewhat more frequent legislative defeat,

---

[89] 935 H.C. Deb. 351–81 (12 July 1977).

[90] A motion on the government's public expenditure plans was also lost by 284 : 256, which led to a government motion of confidence being debated and carried the following day: see 907 H.C. Deb. 430–576 (10 March 1976); 907 H.C. Deb. 634–758 (11 March 1976). Numerous other provisions in various Bills were lost or amended contrary to the government's wishes.

[91] For the second reading debate, see 402 H.L. Deb. 608–80 (15 November 1979). The House of Lords does not usually reject a Bill at second reading but it may be emasculated or voted down in committee (customarily a Committee of the Whole House).

[92] 34 H.C. Deb. 355–439 (15 December 1982).

[93] 95 H.C. Deb. 584–702 (14 April 1986).

[94] Or, of course, defeat on a government motion of confidence.

[95] The 1924 Labour government declared the amendments to its motion on the Campbell case (the Liberal amendment, which was successful, demanding a select committee on the affair) to be tantamount to motions of no confidence: see 177 H.C. Deb. 581–704 (8 October 1924).

[96] As it did in 1976: see note 90.

[97] Frequent adverse votes will naturally cause any government embarrassment.

but rather that it obliges every government to defend itself, explain its policies, and justify its actions, to its own back-benchers, to the opposition parties, and through them to the country as a whole.

Members' influence on the government

The dramatic cases of the House of Commons forcing the government to seek a fresh term from the electorate may now be left to one side. What must now be examined are the routine opportunities enjoyed by MPs inside and outside the chamber to exert an influence on and to challenge Ministers and their policies.[98] Those opportunities will be looked at in turn, and it will become apparent that there is a major imbalance of advantage in favour of Ministers and against both individual MPs and the opposition parties, produced by the procedural rules of the House and by the government's ability to achieve its way in the end by deploying its Commons strength.

The parliamentary question[99] is exceptionally popular with MPs. Nearly 50,000 were put down in the 1985–6 session.[100] The attractions of the question for an MP are obvious. It is easy to put one down:[101] any MP (other than a Minister or, by convention, the Leader of the Opposition[102]) may give notice of his question to the Table Office of the House of Commons. The MP putting a question for oral answer is entitled, after the Minister has replied, to put a supplementary question of which no advance notice is given, and in the MP's inventiveness and

[98] For a good short account of the order of business both during a parliamentary session and on an average day, see T. C. Hartley and J. A. G. Griffith, *Government and Law* (2nd edn., 1981), pp. 204–20.

[99] See generally Sir Norman Chester and Nona Bowring, *Questions in Parliament* (1962); Sir Norman Chester, 'Questions in the House' in S. A. Walkland and M. Ryle (eds.), *The Commons Today* (revised edn., 1981); Erskine May, op. cit., 339–42.

[100] At an average cost of £75 to provide each oral answer and £45 for each written answer: 115 H.C. Deb. *56* (written answers 27 April 1987). If an MP wants a Minister to give an oral answer in the House he marks his question with an asterisk; otherwise he will receive a written answer printed in the daily *Hansard*: S.O. No. 17(4). Questions for written answer are usually designed to elicit purely factual information. Questions for oral answer which are not reached at Question Time receive written answers: S.O. No. 17(7).

[101] Subject to it being in order, which is explained shortly.

[102] The Leader of the Opposition uses the private notice procedure under S.O. No. 17(3): a question of an urgent character and which relates to matters of public importance or the arrangement of Commons business may be taken after Question Time provided the Speaker received it before noon, agrees that it satisfies those conditions and is told that the Minister has received notice of the question. Four or five private notice questions on average have been put each month in recent sessions.

in the Minister's quick-wittedness parliamentary reputations (so it is said) may be made or damaged. Moreover, more MPs contribute in the chamber by asking questions than otherwise manage to speak there: some forty to fifty Members will have the chance to shine during Question Time, which is more than will speak during an average debate.

Question Time is, however, more of an entertaining diversion than a method of parliamentary control of or influence over the government. Ministers only answer questions according to a rota which is agreed through the usual channels and in which the more important departments put up a Minister to reply roughly every four weeks.[103] Consequently, Members can only question a particular Minister when his turn in the rota comes round, however anxious they may be to grill him immediately. This is in stark contrast to Question Time in, for example, the Canadian House of Commons, during which any Minister (including the Prime Minister) can be asked any question on any day. (A British Minister who is not due to respond at Question Time may decide to make a statement after questions on an urgent or other matter,[104] and MPs may then question him on it: but if no statement is forthcoming MPs and the Speaker can do nothing about it.) The Prime Minister's rota requires his presence at the dispatch box for fifteen minutes every Tuesday and Thursday. These are occasions which many former Prime Ministers profess to have dreaded, but given the political ability which they must have to carry them to the top office together with previous ministerial[105] and Commons experience,[106] all Prime Ministers have tended to acquit themselves to the satisfaction of their supporters in the Commons.[107] Then again, Ministers have advance warning of the question which will appear on the order paper. A Member must give two

[103] Each major department is allocated to a particular day of the week, together with three or four others. When at the top of the rota, its Minister will be questioned first, and is likely to be questioned for the whole of the time available. In the following week he will be at the bottom of the rota, and in each successive week he rises a place, so that after three or four weeks he is back on top. Thus he can usually expect to answer questions for the best part of an hour once a month. Ministers with special responsibilities, or at the head of minor departments (like the Attorney-General) answer questions for 10 or 15 minutes on a specified day at regular intervals, usually every four weeks.

[104] The Speaker is informed of his intention, but neither his nor the House's leave is necessary.

[105] Ramsay MacDonald was the only man to become Prime Minister this century with no previous ministerial experience. The current Leader of the Opposition, Mr Neil Kinnock, would be the second.

[106] Sir Alec Douglas-Home had been in the Lords for 12 years when he became Prime Minister, and an MP again, in 1963.

[107] Even the open question (for example, asking the Prime Minister to state his engagements for the day, followed by a wholly unrelated supplementary) is taken in any Prime Minister's stride.

clear days' notice of the question to which he wants a Minister to give an oral answer.[108] A Member can put down a question up to ten sitting days before the Minister is due to answer, but not before that period,[109] a rule designed to prevent the order paper being filled up with questions which are stale by the time they come to be answered. But because of the large number of MPs who wish to question Ministers, an MP in practice must give notice on the first possible day to have any chance of his question being reached and given an oral answer. The effect of the rota and rules about notice is that on each day MPs are tabling questions to a particular Minister for a fortnight ahead. This gives the Minister's Private Office more than enough time to assemble all the information that the Minister will need and to work out what supplementary questions are likely to follow: no Minister should, therefore, go to the House to answer questions like a lamb to the slaughter.[110] In the result, as one writer has aptly put it, '. . . few Ministers are caught napping'.[111]

Moreover, a number of other procedural rules work in Ministers' favour. To be accepted by the Table Office and thus to appear on the order paper at all, a question must (quite fairly) relate to the public affairs with which the Minister is officially connected, to proceedings in Parliament, or to administrative matters for which the Minister is responsible.[112] So for instance the Table Office will not accept questions relating to local authority responsibilities, the remaining nationalized industries (save questions relating to a Minister's statutory responsibilities), the Stock Exchange, the banks, the police,[113] or which ask for an opinion on a point of law or for which, for whatever reason, the Minister has no responsibility. Erskine May's *Parliamentary Practice* sets out these exceptions over three pages of small print.[114] Additionally, a Minister will not usually answer any question (even if passed by the Table Office) which concerns confidential exchanges with other governments, or affects

---

[108] S.O. No. 17(4). The private notice procedure (see note 102) circumvents this, but is only of limited use. The requirement of two days' notice has the advantage that the text of the question is printed on the order paper, so that as each MP is called upon to ask his question, he merely states the number of it, rather than reading out the text, thus saving parliamentary time.

[109] S.O. No. 17(6).

[110] 'One evening I found Churchill at the Cabinet table. . . . "What are you doing, Prime Minister?" I asked. "Oh, parliamentary questions. Preparing improvisations! Very hard work!" ': Harold Macmillan, *Tides of Fortune* (1969), p. 496.

[111] Sir Norman Chester, op. cit., p. 185.

[112] Erskine May, op. cit., p. 336.

[113] The Home Secretary is the police authority for the Metropolitan Police district and can therefore be asked detailed questions about the conduct of that force.

[114] Op. cit. pp. 339–42.

national security, or involves commercial confidentiality, or which seeks information about individuals or companies for which he has no responsibility, or which would involve the disclosure of any advice given to him by the civil service.[115] MPs have, therefore, nothing like *carte blanche* to ask Ministers anything. If a Minister were embarrassed by a question which was in order he could (though rarely does) refuse point blank to answer: he is not obliged to say anything, but there are of course ways of speaking without saying anything, and if an MP is dissatisfied by a reply there is precious little he or the Speaker can do about it (the Speaker not being responsible for the quality of ministerial answers, as he reminds the House rather plaintively from time to time). Alternatively, and just as unhelpfully, the Minister may respond that he will write to the Member. Such a reply is offered periodically. As well as being sent to that MP, the Minister's letter is also made available in the House of Commons Library, indexed under the MP's name, but it is not published in *Hansard*. An MP seeking to joust with a Minister or looking for publicity through his question will be thwarted if the Minister resorts to this formula. Again, Ministers may, and sometimes do, decline to answer on the ground that the information sought could only be assembled at disproportionate cost, currently set at £200.[116]

Transcending all of those difficulties in the way of a questioning MP, however, is the imbalance of information and resources available to him, in contrast to the government, which is buttressed by all the resources of the civil service. No MP, however well served by the Research Division of the House of Commons Library or helped though the 'Short money' paid to his parliamentary party,[117] can hope to have at his fingertips the kind of detailed facts which could be deployed so as to make Question Time an effective exercise of parliamentary power. A Member will occasionally make a telling point, a Minister may occasionally stumble,[118] but both the procedural rules and expertise which is available only to Ministers mean that Question Time is not really much of a method of parliamentary control.

Each day one Member has the opportunity to speak in the adjourn-

---

[115] A list of 95 excepted matters is given in Appendix 9 to the Report from the Select Committee on Parliamentary Questions, H.C. 393 (1971–2).

[116] 79 H.C. Deb. 2 (written answers 13 May 1985).

[117] See note 35.

[118] A Minister who needs factual information which he does not have with which to reply to a question may be helped by civil servants from his department who will be on hand in a special box, technically outside the chamber, and who can pass notes to him. No Minister would want to be seen to be too reliant on that source.

ment debate.[119] This lasts for thirty minutes and is the final item of business. A ballot is held in the Speaker's office every Thursday, into which goes the name of every MP who wishes to speak on the adjournment together with the topic he wishes to raise.[120] The successful Member may then raise that issue—local or national, helpful to or critical of the government—and he will receive a ministerial reply[121] from a junior Minister (for after all the adjournment debate can take place in the small hours). The fundamental weakness of the adjournment procedure for the back-bencher who may wish to exert some influence over government policy is that he cannot question or reply to the Minister's speech: it is rather like Question Time without the right to put a supplementary, although sometimes the Minister gives way to interruptions and will then have to answer points made during them. And daily adjournment debates are thinly attended, partly because the matters raised may be of significance only to one constituency, and partly because of the timing.

Back-benchers have a less frequent chance to raise issues of concern to them during the adjournment debates which follow the passage of Consolidated Fund and Appropriation Bills, and during recess adjournment debates. The second and third readings of such Bills are formalities: the question that those readings be given is put without debate and they are passed;[122] a Minister then moves that the House adjourn, and the debate on the adjournment motion may go on until 9 a.m. the following day.[123] During that time Members 'debate' any topics they wish—although the word 'debate' is a misnomer, for each contributor speaks about his particular hobby-horse without reference to what was said before he got up, and after he has concluded perhaps one or two—but sometimes no—other MPs speak on the same topic, whereupon a junior Minister replies.[124] As in daily adjournment debates, that Minister's response cannot be queried or challenged; but at least a Minister is obliged to give a considered answer, and speakers can let off steam,

[119] S.O. No. 9(2)–(6).

[120] An MP dissatisfied by a ministerial reply to a question sometimes says he will seek an opportunity to raise the matter on the adjournment. The ballot is the means of doing so.

[121] Other MPs do not usually intervene.

[122] Uniquely for Bills, they have no committee stage.

[123] S.O. No. 54. Before 1982 those debates technically took place on second reading of the Bills, thus maintaining the fiction that the Consolidated Fund Bill and Appropriation Bill debates were exercises in parliamentary control of finance. The current procedure dates from the adoption of the recommendations in 1982 of the 1st Report of the Select Committee on Procedure (Supply), H.C. 118-I (1980–1), which were approved at 28 H.C. Deb. 117–84 (19 July 1982).

[124] The speeches during the debate following the passage of the Consolidated Fund Bill in 1987, for example, covered 12 wholly unrelated topics: 119 H.C. Deb. 754–952 (13 July 1987).

express a grievance, or urge the government to even better things. That contrasts quite sharply with the recess adjournment debate procedure.[125] When the government, in consultation with the Opposition, has fixed the timing and length of the next recess it puts down a motion to approve it. That motion may be debated for up to three hours—not that there will be any controversy over the matter, but so as to enable back-benchers who catch the Speaker's eye to raise any issue they wish. In the last fifteen minutes or so of the debate the hapless Leader of the House of Commons has to deal as best he can with all the contributions, mentioning each separately and usually in courteous terms, perhaps promising consideration of what each Member has said, but rarely conceding anything of substance.[126]

The government will hear from its attackers and defenders during Opposition day debates.[127] Twenty days[128] during the session are allotted to subjects chosen by the opposition parties, the Leader of the Opposition selecting the subjects on seventeen of those days while the remaining three are at the disposal of the Leader of the second largest opposition party in the House.[129] Fitting in those twenty days obviously affects the arrangement of the government's business. (The government must, additionally, find time to debate any motion of no confidence which the Opposition may put down: although the number of such motions has declined over the years, there will be from two to four in each Parliament.) Now the government will not normally be at risk of defeat on the invariably critical Opposition day motions, but the existence of such days helps parliamentary reputations to be enhanced or diminished and, yet again, obliges the government to answer criticism and thus provide interested electors outside the House with one more piece of information to weigh at the next general election.

A further ten Fridays and four other half-days are taken up by debates

---

[125] S.O. No. 22.

[126] See, for example, 113 H.C. Deb. 1279–318 (2 April 1987), in which 16 topics were raised by MPs, including the Shadow Leader of the House.

[127] The term Opposition day replaced the former (and ancient and latterly misnamed) Supply days in 1982. It was another change suggested in the Select Committee's recommendations accepted in that year: see note 123.

[128] The figure had been set at 19 in 1982, but was raised to 20 in 1985: see 79 H.C. Deb. 1246 (23 May 1985).

[129] S.O. No. 13(2). In the 1982 changes, all the Opposition days were given to the Leader of the Opposition; informal talks with the Liberal Party and the SDP ceded a few days to them *ad hoc*, but in 1985 the rights of the second largest opposition party were written in. The Liberal Party shared its days equally with its SDP Alliance partners.

on Private Members' motions.[130] For that purpose a ballot is held in which all back-benchers may take part, stating the matters which they wish to see discussed. In these debates, as well as in general debates on government motions and on Bills, the individual Member has the chance to challenge and to criticize; the reputation of particular MPs may go up or down, but it cannot be suggested that private Members' motions have any other significant effects.

It is in the process of legislation that the impotence of the opposition parties and back-benchers when faced by a cohesive majority government may be seen the most clearly.[131] As already noted, legislative defeats can be inflicted occasionally, but in the main most governments will get their legislation broadly in the form they desire. The Opposition cannot hope in the usual case to vote down a government Bill at second or third reading or on report, for government troops will be ready in the division lobbies to beat off attacks. The Opposition may try to amend the Bill in committee, but the government will have its majority on each standing committee,[132] so that if it does not want to accept any given amendment it can, if pressed, vote it down. In a detailed examination of the fate of amendments moved to government Bills in committee during three sessions of the 1964 Labour government, it emerged that of 3,510 amendments moved by back-benchers in standing committee only 171 carried, whereas of 907 amendments proposed by the government to its own Bills all save one carried.[133] There is no reason to believe that that pattern is untypical. Indeed, it is more accurate to classify the committee stage as an opportunity not for the Opposition to alter the terms of government Bills but rather for the government to incorporate its own second thoughts into its legislation; some of those second thoughts will result from representations from non-governmental quarters, and that is a far cry from a procedure permitting of detailed scrutiny and involving amendment of legislation by back-benchers.

The special standing committee[134] should be mentioned briefly here.

130 S.O. No. 13(7), (8). In recent sessions 8 full days and 4 half-days have been allocated so as to provide more time to consider private Members' Bills.

131 On that process of legislation, see S. A. de Smith, *Constitutional and Administrative Law* (5th edn., 1985 by H. Street and R. Brazier), pp. 286–94; D. R. Miers and A. C. Page, *Legislation* (1982); I. Burton and G. Drewry, *Legislation and Public Policy* (1981); and, for detailed rules, Erskine May, op. cit., chapters 21 and 24, section 3.

132 S.O. No. 86(2): in nominating MPs to standing committees, regard must be had to the party composition of the House so as to reflect it in the composition of each standing committee.

133 See J. A. G. Griffith, *Parliamentary Scrutiny of Government Bills* (1974).

134 S.O. No. 91. See H. J. Beynon, 'The House of Commons' Experiment with Special Standing Commitees' [1982] *Public Law* 193.

This is a very useful, but infrequently used, type of committee[135] which has the power to send for persons, papers, and records during its deliberations on a Bill, and may hold up to four morning sittings, at three of which oral evidence from interested individuals and groups from outside Parliament may be given in public. This horizon-broadening procedure should, I believe, be resorted to more often: it exposes the government not to defeat but to opportunities for wider debate and expertise than is otherwise the case, and thus to the emergence of legislation of a higher quality.

In the 1985–6 session seventeen Private Members' Bills passed into law. Just over one hundred had been introduced. Although the success rate is always low, some individual back-benchers do see their legislative proposals receive royal assent each year. There are three routes along which such back-bench Bills may progress, although only the first gives much prospect of eventual enactment. On ten Fridays each session Private Members' Bills have precedence over other business[136]—but in order to introduce a Bill on such a day a Member must be one of the twenty successful MPs in yet another ballot held for the purpose periodically through the session;[137] and he must also be at or near the top of those twenty for there to be sufficient time in the later arrangement of business for the Bill to be fully considered. Fortunately for back-benchers they do not have to indicate in that ballot the nature of the Bill which they want to introduce, for at that stage most have no idea.[138] A second route is through the ten-minute rule procedure,[139] through which a Member may give notice that he will seek the leave of the House to introduce a Bill on a Tuesday or a Wednesday (although only one MP may seek leave on any day, on a first come, first served basis[140]). The

---

[135] Such a committee was first established experimentally in 1980: see 991 H.C. Deb. 835–6 (30 October 1980). Only 5 Bills have been considered in special standing committee: the Criminal Attempts Bill (in the 1980–81 session), the Education Bill (in 1980–81), the Deep Sea Mining (Temporary Provisions) Bill (in 1980–81), the Mental Health (Amendment) Bill (in 1981–2), and the Matrimonial and Family Proceedings Bill (in 1983–4). The 2nd Report from the Select Committee on Procedure, H.C. 49 (1984–5), paras. 11–13 recommended that more use should be made of special standing committees, as virtually all the evidence which it had received about them had been enthusiastic—including evidence from Ministers.

[136] S.O. No. 13(4). In recent sessions 12 Fridays have been set aside for this purpose: see, for example, 118 H.C. Deb. 380 (30 June 1987).

[137] S.O. No. 13(6).

[138] MPs successful and high up in the ballot are much sought after by pressure groups keen to get them to take up their proposals, and to supply them with draft Bills and other help.

[139] S.O. No. 19.

[140] S.O. No. 19(2).

Speaker allows a brief explanatory statement from that MP, followed by one brief speech from any MP who opposes it, after which the question is put whether leave be given.[141] In general the use of the ten-minute rule procedure is not a serious attempt to legislate, but rather is a way of drawing attention to the need for a change in the law: only about twenty-five ten-minute rule Bills have actually been enacted since 1945. The final route—and the one chosen by most aspirant back-bench legislators—is merely to present a Bill after giving notice (but without needing the leave of the House): such a measure will be formally read a first time and will be set down for second reading on a specified Friday.[142] Any Member opposing the Bill—not infrequently a Government Whip—can postpone that second reading on that day simply by calling out 'object'. Even supposing that a Member is successful in the ballot,[143] or in getting leave under the ten-minute rule, or in avoiding an opponent uttering the deadly word, there may still be a major obstruction in his path—not the government using its majority to vote the Bill down, for that is something which governments refrain from doing—but rather that no Private Member's Bill is in order if it has as its main purpose the creation of a charge on public funds.[144] If a Member wishes to do that he must privately persuade the government to agree to a Minister signifying the Queen's recommendation that the Commons approve a financial resolution,[145] which is tantamount to the government adopting the Bill as its own (or to the government vetoing it if it refuses to do so). Large areas of public policy are effectively placed out of bounds to private Members by this rule. By contrast, the government will occasionally smile on a back-bench Bill and even, in a few cases, provide help in drafting it[146] and give up some of its time for it to be considered.[147] That a

[141] S.O. No. 19(1).

[142] S.O. No. 58.

[143] The top 10 MPs in the ballot may draw up to £200 each to help towards drafting expenses. Non-lawyer MPs may seek the help of friendly lawyer-MPs with drafting.

[144] S.O. No. 48. The government's use of a three-line whip in January 1988 to defeat Mr Richard Shepherd's Protection of Official Information Bill was unprecedented.

[145] S.O. No. 46; Erskine May, op. cit., chapter 30.

[146] For example, the Sexual Offences (Amendment) Act 1976.

[147] A list of private Members' Bills which have been given extra parliamentary time by the government since 1954 is given at 62 H.C. Deb. *367–72* (written answers 25 June 1984); 62 H.C. Deb. *495–6* (written answers 28 June 1984). Very occasionally the government may have to bow to parliamentary and public opinion and legislate itself as the result of a back-bench initiative. For example, Mr Austin Mitchell's Home Buyers' Bill, designed to end the solicitors' conveyancing monopoly, achieved its second reading and was only withdrawn when the government promised its own Bill with the same objectives; its legislative provision became the Administration of Justice Act 1985, Part II.

dozen or so Private Members' Bills become law each session is in the main attributable to luck and the acquiescence of the government—factors which in a wholly rational parliamentary system would not be the determinants for back-bench legislative initiatives.

In 1981 the Select Committee on Procedure (Supply) concluded that '. . . the House's financial procedures are antiquated and defective and need a thorough overhaul'.[148] Even after the adoption of that Committee's proposals, and others from the Public Accounts Committee,[149] neither the House as a whole nor individual back-benchers have much real control over the raising and spending of public money. Members of Parliament are the last to hear the Chancellor's Budget which is presented, more or less, as a *fait accompli*,[150] and the Finance Bill which is constructed on it passes into law without even marginal changes having been made to it at the insistence of the House. Members go through the motions of scrutinizing Finance Bills, but amendments are made almost entirely at the request of Ministers. (As already pointed out, there is no examination at all of Consolidated Fund Bills or of Appropriation Bills even though billions of pounds are spent each year by virtue of authority contained in them.) Nor is there any parliamentary control over the government's borrowing, even though this is a major source of any government's revenue. The House oversees the government's estimates as best it can through the three Estimates days on the floor of the House, during which Members debate, and vote on, the details of government expenditure;[151] but the Public Accounts Committee reported in 1987 that 'Parliament's consideration of the annual estimates—the key constitutional control—remains largely a formality.'[152] The Public Accounts Committee[153] itself is better placed. It is composed of fifteen MPs, selected to reflect party strengths in the House, with an Opposition MP as its chairman (and who is usually a former junior Minister at the Treasury). The Committee's task is to check that money has been spent according to Parliament's wishes, although it ranges more widely and

[148] H.C. 118-I (1980–1), para. 37.

[149] The Public Accounts Committee recommended (H.C. 115–I (1980–1)) in particular the creation of a National Audit Office in place of the Exchequer and Audit Department. It was through the efforts of Mr Norman St John-Stevas (as a back-bench MP, having resigned from Mrs Thatcher's Cabinet), that that proposal passed into the law in his Private Member's Bill which became the National Audit Act 1983.

[150] See chapter 6.

[151] S.O. No. 52. This was another 1982 procedural change adopted from H.C. 118-I (1980–1).

[152] 8th Report from the Public Accounts Commitee, H.C. 98 (1986–7), para. 2.

[153] See S.O. No. 122.

quite frequently discovers and reports on wasteful and extravagant expenditure and imprudent government contracts.[154] The Comptroller and Auditor-General[155] sits with the Committee, and its reports are treated with respect in Whitehall—but an inevitable weakness is that it can only report after money has been spent. All in all, as the Public Accounts Committee put it in 1987, '[p]ublic expenditure is constitutionally subject to the control of Parliament. At present this control is of doubtful effectiveness.'[156]

Back-benchers scrutinize and influence the government more successfully away from the chamber in the select committees which examine the expenditure, administration, and policy of government departments. These departmental select committees owe their existence to experiments in the 1966 Parliament,[157] the 1978 Report of the Select Committee on Procedure,[158] back-bench pressure, and a reform-minded and determined Leader of the House, Mr Norman St John-Stevas, supported by a commitment in the Conservative Party's 1979 general election manifesto.

The committees[159] oversee fourteen major departments.[160] (The Lord Chancellor's Department and the Law Officers' Department are, however, excluded because of fears that parliamentary inquiries into them might interfere with the independence of the judiciary, fears which in my view could easily be allayed by appropriately worded rules designed to exempt from investigation the essential meaning of the term judicial independence.[161]) Members are chosen by the Committee of

---

[154] It was reported in 1986, for example, that the Ministry of Defence had overspent by £938 million on 12 major defence contracts, and had paid out over £200 million in another 7 projects which had later been cancelled: 6th Report from the Public Accounts Committee, H.C. 104 (1986–7).

[155] See National Audit Act 1983, *passim*.

[156] 8th Report from the Public Accounts Committee, H.C. 98 (1986–7), para. 1.

[157] The Select Committee on Agriculture (which was allowed to lapse after two years), on Education and Science, on Science and Technology, on Race Relations and Immigration, on Scottish Affairs, and on Overseas Development.

[158] 1st Report from the Select Committee on Procedure, H.C. 588-I (1977–8).

[159] See Dermot Englefield, *Commons Select Committees: Catalysts for Progress?* (1984); Dilys Hill, *Parliamentary Select Committees in Action* (1984); Gavin Drewry (ed.), *The New Select Committees* (1985).

[160] See S.O. No. 130. The committees are: Agriculture; Defence; Education, Science and Arts; Employment; Energy; Environment; Foreign Affairs; Home Affairs; Scottish Affairs; Social Services; Trade and Industry; Transport; Treasury and Civil Service; Welsh Affairs. Each has 11 members.

[161] The Liaison Committee (see note 163) has pointed out that as a result substantial public spending on legal aid and court administration is not monitored: see H.C. 92 (1982–3), paras. 12, 85.

Selection[162] (which will hear informal advice from the Whips); each committee selects its own chairman (although by custom half the chairmen are from the Opposition); the committees choose what to investigate (subject to the Liaison Committee[163] which prevents duplication of inquiries); the Foreign Affairs, Home Affairs, and Treasury and Civil Service Select Committees may nominate subcommittees so that each may conduct simultaneous examinations.[164] The formal powers of the committees to send for persons, papers, and records are impressive but have only been used once:[165] an informal invitation usually does the trick. A refusal to comply with a select committee order would be a contempt of the House of Commons, and the committee concerned would refer it to the House to be dealt with.[166] The committees' power to send for persons embraces Ministers (even Prime Ministers) and civil servants (even the Head of the Home Civil Service and Secretary to the Cabinet). In setting up the committees in 1979 the government promised that Ministers would attend,[167] although the Prime Minister has occasionally directed a Minister to attend other than the one sought; and the Liaison Committee reported in 1982 that the physical attendance of Ministers was satisfactory—although that was before Westland[168] and two other incidents. In the aftermath of the Westland affair the Defence Select Committee wanted to examine named civil servants who had been involved in the improper leaking to the press of the Solicitor-General's letter to a Minister:[169] intense negotiations, at one stage of which the Committee made it clear that it was ready to use its formal powers and to respond to any obstruction by referring the

---

[162] S.O. No. 104. The Committee of Selection consists of 9 MPs: see Standing Orders of the House of Commons (Private Business), H.C. 130 (1983–4), S.O. No. 109. In nominating the select committees it reflects the party composition of the House—not by virtue of any standing order, but because the House as a whole approves motions to appoint to them and nominations are negotiated reflecting party strengths through the usual channels.

[163] The Liaison Committee comprises the 14 select committee chairmen: S.O. No. 131.

[164] S.O. No. 130(3). The Foreign Affairs subcommittee has concentrated on overseas development, the Home Affairs subcommittee on race relations and immigration, and the Treasury and Civil Service subcommittee on civil service matters.

[165] In 1982 when the Energy Select Committee made a formal order against Mr Arthur Scargill summoning him to give evidence before it. The Warrant Officer of the Serjeant at Arms served the order on Mr Scargill, with which he fully complied and gave his evidence.

[166] 1st Report from the Liaison Committee, The Accountability of Ministers and Civil Servants to Select Committees of the House of Commons, H.C. 100 (1986–7), para. 2; Erskine May, op. cit., chapter 10.

[167] See 969 H.C. Deb. 45 (25 June 1979).

[168] On the Westland affair generally, see chapter 6.

[169] Mr John Michell, Mr John Mogg, Miss Colette Bowe (all of the Department of Trade and Industry), and Mr Bernard Ingham (Chief Press Secretary to the Prime Minister) and Mr Charles Powell (Private Secretary to the Prime Minister).

matter to the House as a possible contempt, produced a compromise in which the Permanent Under-Secretary of State at the Department of Trade and Industry and the Cabinet Secretary attended instead.[170] Two years before that the government had refused to allow either the Director of the Government Communications Headquarters at Cheltenham or a trade union official working there to appear before the Employment Select Committee as part of its inquiry into the government's ban on trade union membership at GCHQ.[171] Then again, the Trade and Industry Committee was refused certain documents by the government, and civil servants appearing before it were instructed not to answer certain questions, so preventing it from reaching precise conclusions in its inquiry into the collapse of the tin industry in 1985.[172] At no stage in any of those episodes did the Committees accept any restriction on their ultimate legal powers to obtain whatever witnesses they wished. Now if compromise allows the select committees to get the witnesses they need and permits the government to uphold what it perceives as its legitimate rights, well and good; but if compromise fails the committees should, I suggest, assert their undoubted powers deliberately granted to them by the House of Commons itself in an attempt to redress the balance of advantage between legislature and executive.

It is one thing to establish machinery in order to elicit information more efficiently than through other forms of parliamentary inquiry: it is quite another actually to extract that information from witnesses. Broadly, this has not been a problem, but the government has been extremely cautious about allowing civil service witnesses to give certain kinds of evidence. Standing instructions[173] stress that when attending select committees civil servants remain subject to ministerial orders

[170] 4th Report from the Defence Committee, Westland plc: The Government's Decision-making, H.C. 519 (1985-6), paras. 225-33. The Committee recorded that the evidence of those two witnesses was hearsay; and it reiterated that a select committee's power to secure the attendance of witnesses remained 'unqualified': ibid., para. 228.

[171] 1st Report from the Employment Committee, H.C. 238 (1983-4), paras. 6-7.

[172] See 2nd Report from the Trade and Industry Committee, H.C. 305 (1985-6); Government Response, H.C. 457 (1985-6); 1st Report from the Trade and Industry Committee, H.C. 71 (1986-7); debate at 101 H.C. Deb. 72-118 (7 July 1986).

[173] Memorandum of Guidance for Officials appearing before Select Committees (1980), as supplemented by the Annex to the Government Response to H.C. 100 (1986-7), Cm. 78 (1987); The Duties and Responsibilities of Civil Servants in relation to Ministers: A Note by the Head of the Home Civil Service (Cabinet Office, 1985), especially para. 9. The latter document has been criticized by the Treasury and Civil Service Select Committee as being based on outdated principles: see Civil Servants and Ministers: Duties and responsibilities, H.C. 92-I (1986-7), para. 2.2. For the text of the Note as revised in 1987 see 123 H.C. Deb. 572-5 (written answers 2 December 1987).

(although they should actually withhold information only 'in the interests of good government'—a phrase of which Sir Humphrey Appleby would be proud). In any case civil servants must not give answers about advice given to Ministers,[174] interdepartmental exchanges on policy, advice given by the Law Officers, matters in the field of political controversy (but are not most governmental matters politically controversial?), sensitive commercial information, and sensitive negotiations with other states or with the European Community.[175] These are major exceptions, although in the main they do not seem to have caused too much interference with the committees' work.

The departmental select committees provide a means by which witnesses (Ministers, civil servants, and others) can be cross-examined at length and more thoroughly than in any other way now open to either House; their members have developed expertise and knowledge about the departments; the committees try to achieve, and usually do achieve, unanimous reports, cutting across party lines and thus carrying more weight than would any partisan document;[176] Ministers and civil servants may have to consider the committees' likely reactions to major new policies before they are finally formulated;[177] and the Liaison Committee has stressed that a markedly improved flow of information has been achieved from the departments to the House of Commons, not only through the committees' reports and published evidence but also through the government's responses to them published in White Papers in reply, so that overall the committees have become a valuable feature of parliamentary life.[178] But two drawbacks must be noted. First, only a

---

[174] 1980 Memorandum, para. 25.

[175] In its reply to the Defence Committee report on Westland (Government Response to the 3rd and 4th Reports from the Defence Committee, Cmnd. 9916 (1986), para. 44), the government stated that it would instruct civil servants in the future not to answer questions directed to their own or other named civil servants' conduct. The Treasury and Civil Service Committee, in H.C. 62 (1986–7), para. 5, termed that 'unfortunate'; the Liaison Committee considered it to be 'wholly unacceptable', and urged the government to reconsider its position 'without delay': 1st Report from the Liaison Committee, The Accountability of Ministers and Civil Servants to Select Committees of the House of Commons, H.C. 100 (1986–7), paras. 6, 11. The government, however, broadly stuck to its guns: it has directed that, if civil service witnesses are asked questions about the conduct of named civil servants with the aim of allocating individual criticism or blame, those witnesses should reply that such matters are for the relevant Minister; the Minister would then investigate, and report to the committee: Government Response to the 1st Report from the Liaison Committee, Cm. 78 (1987), paras. 9–12 and Annex.

[176] An unusual example of a select committee reporting on party lines was the Foreign Affairs Committee's report on the sinking of the *General Belgrano* during the Falklands conflict: that report was approved, and a Labour draft report rejected, by 6 votes to 4: see H.C. 11 (1984–5).

[177] A point made by Dilys Hill, op. cit., p. 29.

[178] 1st Report from the Liaison Committee, The Select Committee System, H.C. 92 (1982–3).

small minority of select committee reports are debated by the House itself. By November 1987 only ten had been debated substantively from a total of 565, while about sixty others had been relevant to the course of other debates.[179] Gathering information is an important exercise, but unless the House finds the time to debate such information and conclusions formed from it there is an obvious danger that select committee reports will merely take up shelf space in libraries. Secondly, Ministers and other witnesses are not obliged to answer questions, as Mr Leon Brittan's stonewalling showed during his appearances before the Defence Select Committee in its Westland investigations.[180] This failing must not be exaggerated, but as with Question Time it is an unfair advantage enjoyed by Ministers which the House as a whole has not adequately addressed.[181]

Reform of the Commons

An agenda for the possible reform of the House of Commons is easy to set down, with the aims of making that House more closely representative of the electors, giving back-benchers a more effective part to play and establishing fairer procedures for the smaller parties, while continuing to recognize the government's right to govern and to obtain its legislation. Changes to those ends could be both constitutional and institutional.

Constitutional change would hinge on the electoral system. The first-past-the-post system usually has the advantage of producing a majority government at a general election: it is decisive, simple, and familiar to the electorate. Yet it is also unfair. No one could say that a scheme which gives one political group three per cent of the seats from 22.6 per cent of the national vote, but which gives another party 36 per cent of the seats with a mere eight per cent more of the votes, does anything but violence to the concept of fair play as the British understand

---

[179] 1st Report from the Liaison Committee, The Select Committee System, H.C. 363 (1984–5); 122 H.C. Deb. 700 (written answers 20 November 1987). But the system, according to the Liaison Committee, remained 'a major, successful parliamentary reform': ibid., p. iv.

[180] H.C. 519 (1985–6), paras. 203, 204: the Defence Committee records a number of vital questions which it put to Mr Brittan and notes, 'He refused to tell us'. It could be a punishable contempt to refuse to answer select committee questions: Erskine May, op. cit., p. 145.

[181] Possibly again because today's Opposition MPs are tomorrow's Ministers.

it.[182] The present system also underpins elective dictatorship in a way that different electoral rules, which would return more MPs from third (and perhaps fourth) parties, would undermine. And we speak of 'majority governments' by reference to seats won in the House, but no government has been returned with a majority of the popular vote since 1935.[183] A linked issue is that of fixed-term Parliaments, which would remove the Prime Minister's unfair advantage of seizing on a moment to secure an election so as to maximize his party's electoral fortunes. If such a move were to be explored, plainly the relationship between a defeat on a vote of confidence (say in a hung Parliament) and dissolution before the expiry of the term fixed by law would need to be thought out. There has been no exploration of such core issues of the quality which only a Royal Commission can bring since the long-forgotten Report of the Royal Commission on Proportional Representation in 1918.[184] I suggest that the time has come for a new Royal Commission to be appointed so that the protagonists and antagonists could argue their cases rationally, away from the party political rhetoric which usually clouds these matters, and so that deliberations worthy of the subject could take place.

Possible institutional changes to be made by the House of Commons itself are, again, easy to adumbrate. It can only be for the House to decide whether, and if so in what ways, to change its procedures so as to add to the reforms of Balfour in the late nineteenth century, Crossman in the late 1960s, and St John-Stevas in the late 1970s. A better deal for back-benchers could include some real opportunity to scrutinize govern-

[182] This unfairness may be seen in the results of the last two general elections:

	Votes		Seats		
	%	No. (millions)	%	No.	Majority
1987					
Conservative	42.3	13.7	60	375	102
Labour	30.8	10.0	36	229	—
Alliance	22.6	7.3	3	22	—
1983					
Conservative	42.4	13.0	61	397	144
Labour	27.5	8.5	32	209	—
Alliance	25.4	7.8	4	23	—

[183] 1931 was the only other instance this century.
[184] Cd. 9044 (1918).

ment tax and borrowing policy, to allow more scope and time for legislative initiatives by private Members, for reform of standing committees to incorporate to some extent the attributes of special standing committees, and for more time for debate of departmental select committee reports. A fairer deal for smaller opposition parties would involve them being formally consulted in the planning of Commons business, provision of salaries for all party Leaders, and a further redistribution of Opposition days in their favour. In all of such matters the House might have to be prepared to concede (assuming for the moment that for whatever reason electoral reform were not forthcoming) that it ought to take some account of votes cast by electors as well as seats obtained by the parties—a principle already accepted to a small extent by the House in the allocation of 'Short money'.[185] The Opposition could be given improved facilities, primarily perhaps through the secondment to Shadow Ministers of civil servants to give it the kind of support which would begin to approach that available to the government.[186] Now such changes would rob the government of some of an invaluable asset, time. The hours of working of the House could obviously be reconsidered so as to afford some compensation, but there may not be much scope for the enlargement of the hours of daily sitting given the outside careers of many MPs and the committee and other work which must be fitted somehow into the parliamentary day. So, more modest alterations might be looked at, such as for example routine allocation of time to all major public Bills in order both to keep up a reasonable rate of legislation and to save the time now wasted on tedious three-hour debates on guillotine motions:[187] on average, an extra parliamentary day each session would be gained by that change alone. Another possibility would, of course, be to lengthen the parliamentary year.

[185] See note 35.

[186] See Sir Douglas Wass, 'Checks and Balances in Public Policy-Making' [1987] *Public Law* 181 at 191–2. As he concedes, this would be harder to arrange if a third party became much stronger in the Commons.

[187] The 2nd Report from the Select Committee on Procedure, H.C. 49 (1985–6), recommended the automatic acceptance of timetable motions for all Bills likely to take 25 hours or more in committee. The House rejected this proposal at the suggestions of both the government and the Opposition, who agreed that it would be an unwarrantable shift of advantage from the Opposition to the government: see 92 H.C. Deb. 1083–136 (27 February 1986). (It might be warrantable as a quid pro quo for some of the possible changes outlined above.) The Committee tried again, in its 10th Report, H.C. 324 (1985–6), this time recommending that each standing committee should, if it thought fit, recommend a timetable motion to the House after its sixth meeting on any particular Bill: it would be up to the House to debate and vote on those recommendations. No action has been taken on that report.

While such an agenda is easy to construct, the chances of major reforms being produced are not high while the traditional two-party system in the Commons continues. It is not dishonourable for the Conservative Party and the Labour Party each to wish to win the next general election with an outright parliamentary majority so that it could further policies in which each passionately believes, and as a consequence to resist changes which might thwart that goal. But respect for the views of people in other parties and in none—who are the *majority* who customarily vote against the government which is returned at the general election[188]—ought to count for rather more in our law and practice. There is a case to answer why opportunities should not be given to non-Conservative and non-Labour opinion to be more fairly reflected in the House of Commons, and more fairly taken into account there.

[188] Other than at the general elections of 1931 and 1935. Even Attlee's 146-seat majority in 1945 was won on 47.8% of the vote, and Mrs Thatcher's 144-seat majority in 1983 on only 42.4%.

10

The House of Lords

Acquiring and losing membership

The membership of the House of Lords consists of the Prince of Wales, hereditary peers, life peers, the Lords Spiritual and the Lords of Appeal in Ordinary.[1] In 1988 there were 790 hereditary peers[2] (including nineteen hereditary peeresses) and some 355 life peers (of whom only forty-five were women): that potential membership of over eleven hundred made it easily the largest chamber in any bicameral parliament in the developed world. The hereditary peerage is divided both by rank and by country of origin. Senior by rank are dukes (thirty-one in 1988), followed by marquesses (thirty-six), earls (191, plus five countesses in their own right), viscounts (125) and barons (463, plus fourteen baronesses in their own right[3]). Such peers are members of the peerage of England or of Scotland if their peerages were created before 1707; after the Union with Scotland, newly created peers became peers of Great Britain; since the Union with Ireland in 1801 newly created hereditary peers have been peers of the United Kingdom. Peers of Scotland whose peerages were created before the Act of Union sit as of right;[4] peers in the Irish peerage cannot sit at all.[5] Female hereditary peers have been entitled to sit in the House of Lords in their own right since 1963.[6] Members of the royal family may sit only if they have a peerage. Being merely a Prince or Princess of the United Kingdom does not qualify, and so Prince Edward is not a member; the five royal dukes (Edinburgh, Cornwall, York,

---

[1] House of Lords Standing Order No. 2, provided they are over 21.

[2] As will be explained shortly, some have leave of absence and so do not sit.

[3] A peeress 'in her own right' is one who holds her own peerage, rather than just having a title because her husband is a peer.

[4] Peerage Act 1963, s. 4. Before 1963 such peers elected 16 of their number to represent them in the House of Lords.

[5] *Re Earl of Antrim's Petition* [1967] 1 A.C. 691. Before 1922 peers of Ireland elected 28 of their number to represent them in the House; the machinery to elect them ceased to exist in 1922 on the creation of the Irish Free State. Peers of Ireland can, however, be elected as MPs and vote in parliamentary elections: Peerage Act 1963, s. 5.

[6] Peerage Act 1963, s. 6.

Gloucester and Kent) may sit, as may Princess Margaret's former husband the Earl of Snowdon, who received his earldom after their marriage in 1961.[7]

Not surprisingly, not everyone who might be willing to join the House of Lords found either the notion of heredity as a qualification or the social stratification inherent in the hereditary peerage acceptable. The Labour Party especially had insufficient people who were prepared to accept such peerages, and so it was conspicuously weak in the House of Lords. The Life Peerages Act 1958 has, however, helped. A life peerage in the rank of baron may be conferred on any person giving him membership of the House of Lords for life: the peerage expires on his death.[8] Even though the Act expressly states that a life peerage may be given to a woman,[9] life barons outnumber life baronesses by more than seven to one.[10] The Lords Spiritual sit in the House of Lords with the right to speak and vote, the Archbishops of Canterbury and York and the Bishops of London, Durham and Winchester being there ex officio, and twenty-one other Anglican bishops according to seniority of appointment to their sees.[11] All Lords Spiritual appointed since 1976 are subject to retirement at 70; on retirement the right to sit and vote is lost[12] and the next ex officio appointee or the next most senior bishop takes his place; by custom the Archbishop of Canterbury is given a peerage on his retirement.[13] Lords Spiritual are not peers:[14] it follows that (unlike peers) they may vote in elections to the House of Commons. The Archbishop of Canterbury exercised that right in the 1983 general election and caused a ripple of surprise by doing so.[15] The Law Lords, as they are

---

[7] No other commoner who has married into the royal family since 1961 has taken a peerage.

[8] Life Peerages Act 1958, s. 1.

[9] Section 1(3).

[10] The first list struck a slightly better ratio of 10 men and 4 women.

[11] But never the Bishop of Sodor and Man: Erskine May, *Parliamentary Practice* (20th edn., 1983), p. 5.

[12] Retired Lords Spiritual may, however, take full advantage of all the facilities open to peers outside the chamber: 4th Report from the House of Lords' Offices Committee, H.L. 173 (1970–1), para. 4.

[13] The Lords Spiritual consist of only Anglican clergy. Other clergy are given peerages very occasionally (such as Lord Soper), but peerages are not even given to the heads of other faiths, although there would seem to be every reason from Parliament's point of view why they should be. The Chief Rabbi received a peerage in 1988.

[14] See Erskine May, op. cit., p. 74 for the authorities.

[15] See Phillipa Hughes and Stephanie Palmer, 'Voting Bishops' [1983] *Public Law* 393. The government stated in reply to questions in the House of Lords that the issue whether Lords Spiritual were disqualified from voting in parliamentary elections had never been addressed in the courts, but at least by custom they had refrained from doing so. The Bishop of Derby, on behalf of

commonly styled, are made up of two distinct classes. Lawyers who are appointed Lords of Appeal in Ordinary receive life peerages and a salary on appointment and make up the two Appellate Committees of the House of Lords. To qualify for appointment they must have held high judicial office for at least two years, or have been called to the Bar for at least fifteen years.[16] In practice Lords of Appeal are appointed from the Court of Appeal. They are subject to a retiring age of 75,[17] but they may sit in the legislative House for life by virtue of their peerages. Up to eleven Lords of Appeal may be appointed;[18] that maximum number has, however, never been nominated: no more than ten have held the office at once. By convention two are always Scottish lawyers. The other class of Law Lord is those peers who hold, or have held, high judicial office,[19] that is the Lord Chancellor,[20] former Lord Chancellors,[21] and the Lord Chief Justice (who, though, sits full time in the Criminal Division of the Court of Appeal); and any Master of the Rolls, Lord Justice of Appeal, High Court judge, or judge of the Court of Session who holds a peerage[22] (but any who do will actually confine themselves to the work of their own courts).[23] In 1988 there were twenty-one Law Lords in total from both classes, although the Lords of Appeal in Ordinary make up the active membership of the Appellate Committees, each of which

---

all the Lords Spiritual, then announced that no Lord Spiritual would again do as the Archbishop had done: see 443 H.L. Deb. 243 (29 June 1983). The draftsman of the Parliament (No. 2) Bill of 1968-9 (which will be considered later) plainly thought that Lords Spiritual might have been barred by law from voting, as clause 16 stated that 'A person shall not be disqualified for voting at elections to the House of Commons—. . . (*b*) as being one of the Lords Spiritual.' This provision was not explained in the accompanying White Paper, 'House of Lords Reform', Cmnd. 3799 (1968), nor in the Commons.

16 Appellate Jurisdiction Act 1876, s. 6; Appellate Jurisdiction Act 1887, s. 5.

17 Because all the present Lords of Appeal in Ordinary have been appointed since the introduction of that retiring age in 1959.

18 Administration of Justice Act 1968, s. 1(1)(*a*).

19 Appellate Jurisdiction Act 1876, s. 25 and Appellate Jurisdiction Act 1887, s. 5.

20 Lord Hailsham (Lord Chancellor from 1970-4 and 1979-87) frequently sat in the Appellate Committee, and Lord Mackay of Clashfern has followed suit. Not all of their immediate predecessors, however, directed their energies in that way: see R. F. V. Heuston, 'Judicial Prosophography' (1986) 102 *Law Quarterly Review* 90 at 90-1.

21 Of whom there are currently four: Lord Gardiner (Lord Chancellor 1964-70), Lord Elwyn-Jones (1974-9), Lord Hailsham and Lord Havers (who had to resign on account of ill health having held the office for only four months in 1987).

22 Few do. In the Court of Session Lord Elmslie (Lord President) and Lord McCluskey (a former Solicitor-General for Scotland) hold life peerages (by virtue of their rank and former office, respectively); all other members of the Court of Session enjoy the courtesy prefix 'Lord'.

23 Lord Denning's peerage had been conferred on him in 1957 when he became a Lord of Appeal in Ordinary; he was appointed Master of the Rolls in 1962: the Master of the Rolls does not usually receive a peerage in right of that office, although the present incumbent was created a peer in 1988.

usually sits with five members.[24] The Law Lords can and do intervene in the general legislative work of the House, and are particularly helpful at the committee stage of Bills.

The formal creation of a peerage used to be effected by a writ of summons from the Sovereign to attend the House of Lords followed by the new peer taking his seat,[25] but the modern method is for the Sovereign to issue Letters Patent which actually create the peerage. Those Letters Patent state how the peerage, if it is hereditary, is to descend on death.[26] At the beginning of each new Parliament *all* peers who are entitled to sit receive an instruction to attend (also called a writ of summons). New peers by creation must be formally introduced before they may sit or vote; peers who have inherited their titles merely take their seats.[27] Peerages are created by the Sovereign on the Prime Minister's advice.[28] This is a valuable source of patronage for any Prime Minister:[29] for example, during the Labour governments of 1964 to 1970 and 1974 to 1979 nearly 300 new peers were created; during the Conservative governments of 1970 to 1974 and 1979 to the present 180 people have joined the House of Lords.[30]

A person will receive a peerage today through one of six entirely separate lists. First, a list of working peers is drawn up, usually once a year, consisting of new peers who are expected to take a full part in the parliamentary work of the House and who should see their peerages as a means to that end rather than primarily as honours. Such peers belong to a political party and sit with the peers of that party in the House of Lords. The list of working peers announced in February 1987 contained eleven names, six Conservative and five Labour, recommended by the Prime Minister after informal consultation with the Leader of the

[24] The judicial work of the House will not be considered further here. See Louis Blom-Cooper and Gavin Drewry, *Final Appeal* (1972); Robert Stevens, *Law and Politics: The House of Lords as a Judicial Body 1800–1976* (1979); Alan Paterson, *The Law Lords*(1982).

[25] See *Halsbury's Laws of England* (4th edn., 1981), vol. XXXV, paras. 820–2.

[26] Usually this would be to male heirs in direct line of descent. A hereditary peerage created by Letters Patent would only descend to a female if they contained a special limitation, which very few do. Older peerages created by writ of summons descend to heirs generally, male or female, lineal or collateral.

[27] S.O. No. 43. This could have an implication for any mass creation of peers: see chapter 8.

[28] Subject to possible minor exceptions noted below.

[29] See chapter 5. As with other honours, the Prime Minister's recommendations must first be considered by the Political Honours Scrutiny Committee to see whether the intended recipients are fit and proper persons to receive them.

[30] These figures omit the life peerages conferred on Lords of Appeal in Ordinary. Details of the 156 peerages recommended by Mrs Thatcher up to early 1987 are given at 120 H.L. Deb. *355–9* (written answers 23 July 1987).

Opposition—although not with any other party Leader.[31] These annual working peer lists are the largest regular source of new recruits to the Lords. Secondly, new peers may be included in the Queen's Birthday[32] and New Year Honours Lists, again on the Prime Minister's recommendation. Inclusion in them signifies mainly the bestowal of an honour, although of course such peers may take part in the proceedings of the House if they choose to do so. Thirdly, a Dissolution Honours List is issued early in the life of each new Parliament, primarily to honour former Ministers and MPs of all parties who did not seek re-election. Former Cabinet Ministers will normally receive a life peerage in that list.[33] The Prime Minister is, again, responsible for the list, and there will be consultations with other party Leaders. If the government changes as a result of the general election the new Prime Minister will take responsibility for his predecessor's list. In the 1987 Dissolution Honours List, by way of example, nineteen life peerages were announced; eleven went to former Conservative Cabinet Ministers, six to former Labour Ministers and MPs, one to a former Liberal MP, and one to Mr Roy Jenkins on the nomination of the Leader of the SDP. Additionally, four other former MPs received knighthoods, and Mr Norman Tebbit (who had retired from the Cabinet after the general election but who remained Chairman of the Conservative Party and an MP) was made a Companion of Honour. Fourthly, when a Prime Minister resigns other than following a general election, he will compile a Resignation Honours List, consisting only of members of his party and others who have served him, which his successor will recommend without amendment. It will normally contain a number of peerages.[34] Fifthly, special creations may be made infrequently and not necessarily on the Prime Minister's advice, though no

[31] The Leaders of the Liberal and Social Democratic Parties were particularly annoyed by their exclusion in 1987, especially as the first-ever and only life peer nominated by the SDP had recently died. The Liberal Leader stated that since taking office Mrs Thatcher's working peer lists had contained 29 Conservative, 20 Labour, but only 1 Liberal and 1 SDP, nominees: *Independent*, 13 February 1987.

[32] This falls on the second Saturday in June.

[33] Before 1964, retiring Cabinet Ministers received viscountcies and other former Ministers baronies, but now former Cabinet Ministers who are moved to the House of Lords mainly receive life peerages. This change dates from the period 1964–82, when no hereditary peerages were created; the old differentiation could, of course, be revived. Only 11 people who have left the Cabinet and the Commons since 1964 have remained outside the House of Lords. Former Ministers may receive honours other than peerages (because, for example, they may not wish to go to the House of Lords): John Nott was knighted on leaving the Cabinet in 1983.

[34] Harold Wilson's Resignation Honours List contained 8 new peers: it was very controversial: see Joe Haines, *The Politics of Power* (Coronet edn., 1977), chapter 7. Harold Macmillan's List in 1963 contained only one peer.

doubt with his knowledge. Members of the royal family who receive peerages may be so classified—such as Prince Andrew's creation as Duke of York in 1986, or Mr Armstrong-Jones's ennoblement in 1961 as Earl of Snowdon—and so may the peerages customarily conferred on former Prime Ministers. Since 1900 only six former Prime Ministers have remained commoners.[35] All the rest (apart from three) have received earldoms, the most recent being Attlee in 1955, Eden in 1961, and Harold Macmillan, who became Earl of Stockton in 1984 on his ninetieth birthday, twenty years after he had left the House of Commons. Sir Alec Douglas-Home was made a life peer on his retirement from the Commons in 1974, the only rank of peerage he could by law receive as he had disclaimed his hereditary peerages in 1963.[36] Harold Wilson and James Callaghan were created life peers in the 1983 and 1987 Dissolution Honours Lists respectively,[37] although they might of course both have declined hereditary peerages as they had recommended no such creations while Prime Minister. The attitude of the potential recipient and perhaps the personal intervention of the Sovereign in relation to the rank of peerage offered and accepted may be important,[38] and it seems safe to conclude that a former Prime Minister is entitled to be made an earl or a countess if that is what he or she wishes. Sixthly and lastly the Prime Minister may recommend a peerage for someone without a seat in either House in order that he may become a Minister. Thus Macmillan procured a peerage for Percy Mills on his being brought into the Cabinet from industry as Minister of Power in 1957, and Mrs Thatcher obtained a peerage for David Young on joining the Cabinet as Minister without Portfolio in 1984.

On first becoming Prime Minister in 1964 Harold Wilson decided to recommend no new hereditary peerages.[39] Edward Heath and James

---

[35] Campbell-Bannerman, Bonar Law, Chamberlain (all of whom died soon after resigning), MacDonald and Churchill (both of whom declined peerages), and Edward Heath (who is still an MP). Churchill had declined a dukedom: see Sir John Colville, *The Fringes of Power: Downing Street Diaries 1939–1955* (1985), p. 709.

[36] Peerage Act 1963, s. 3(2).

[37] As such their names were recommended by the Prime Minister and strictly their names do not belong in this category.

[38] At his resignation audience the Queen offered Eden an earldom 'when he wished': see Robert Rhodes James, *Anthony Eden* (1986), p. 595. She wrote to Macmillan in 1963 after his resignation that an earldom was his for the asking from her 'on her authority', that is, without ministerial advice: Harold Macmillan, *At the End of the Day* (1973), pp. 517–18.

[39] Sir Alec Douglas-Home's Dissolution Honours List was recommended by Mr Wilson: it had 6 hereditary creations in it, but this was an application of the principle that a new Prime Minister after a general election recommends his predecessor's List without amendment.

Callaghan followed suit, as did Mrs Thatcher for the first few years of her administration, so that between 1964 and 1983 only life peerages were created. A new convention seemed to be emerging that no new hereditary peers would be created, but Mrs Thatcher's recommendations of viscountcies for the former Speaker of the House of Commons, George Thomas, and for William Whitelaw[40] in 1983 showed that if such a convention were emerging it would, like many conventions, contain exceptions.

Disputes over the right to succeed to a hereditary peerage are rare.[41] The House of Lords itself resolves such disputes, invariably by accepting the recommendations of its Committee for Privileges,[42] which is made up for that purpose of up to sixteen peers together with three Lords of Appeal in Ordinary.[43] Given the complexity of peerage law it is natural that the Committee should be guided by the Lords of Appeal in Ordinary and that the House should accept the Committee's recommendations.

A peerage carries with it two disabilities: a peer other than the holder of an Irish peerage[44] may not vote in any parliamentary election,[45] and he may not be elected or sit as an MP. The first disability would have been removed by clause 16 of the unsuccessful Parliament (No. 2) Bill in 1968–9;[46] the second may be cast off by an instrument of disclaimer, a device which was introduced in 1963. Disclaimer may now be considered, together with other ways of losing membership of the House of Lords.

Before 1963 a peer could not divest himself of his peerage. Thanks chiefly to the efforts of Mr Tony Benn, who succeeded to the viscountcy

[40] He became Lord President of the Council and Leader of the House of Lords, remaining Deputy Leader of the Conservative Party and deputy to the Prime Minister.

[41] There could be no room for dispute over a life peerage.

[42] On which see S.O. No. 72.

[43] The last two claims resolved were the *Ampthill Peerage Claim* [1977] A.C. 547 and the *Annandale and Hartfell Peerage Claim* [1986] A.C. 319. In the latter the Earldom of Annandale and Hartfell was revived after having been in abeyance for nearly 200 years.

[44] See above, note 5. No new Irish peers have been created since 1898 when Curzon, not wishing to lose the possibility of returning to the House of Commons, was made a baron in the Irish peerage on his appointment as Viceroy of India: see Kenneth Rose, *Curzon* (1969), p. 331. There is no legal bar in the way of fresh creations should a latter-day Curzon be appointed to a similar post, although such a move is most unlikely.

[45] The House of Commons resolves at the beginning of each new Parliament that no peer 'hath any right to give his vote in the Election of any Member to serve in Parliament': see, for example, 118 H.C. Deb. 35 (25 June 1987).

[46] That Bill will be considered later. It was designated '(No. 2.)' to distinguish it from a Private Member's Parliament Bill which had already been introduced that session; 3 other back-benchers' Parliament Bills followed it in the 1968–9 session.

of Stansgate in 1960,[47] Harold Macmillan's government agreed to introduce what became the Peerage Act 1963. Under that Act anyone who succeeds to a peerage[48] may disclaim it for his life by delivering an instrument of disclaimer.[49] A succeeding peer has one year in which to make up his mind whether to keep his peerage; to be effective, any disclaimer must be made within those twelve months (or, if he is under 21 on his succession, within a year of reaching that birthday).[50] If an MP succeeds to a peerage, he has only one month in which to disclaim but he can sit and vote as an MP while he decides what to do.[51] A valid disclaimer makes the peer a commoner: it divests him (and, if he is married, his wife) of all right in and titles of the peerage, and all the disabilities that go with it;[52] the courtesy titles of any children are, however, unaffected[53] and any heir does not succeed to the peerage until the death of the disclaiming peer. There are two limitations. Anyone who agrees to be created a peer cannot later disclaim because he did not *succeed* to that peerage: if he has doubts, he should decline the offer. And if a peerage is disclaimed, no further hereditary peerage may be conferred on the former peer, although he may subsequently receive a life peerage.[54] Only fifteen peers from a potential total of some 790 have disclaimed: but the 1963 Act has removed a sense of injustice from a minority; it has allowed one peer to become Prime Minister and an MP (the Earl of Home); it has also allowed another peer to try to become Prime Minister and to be elected an MP (Viscount Hailsham);[55] and through it the most reluctant peer of them all, Mr Benn, was able to return to the House of Commons.

A peer may lose his right to membership of the House of Lords, but

[47] For his own account, see Tony Benn, *Out of the Wilderness: Diaries 1963–1967* (1987), chapter 1. And see Report of the Joint Committee on House of Lords Reform, H.L. 23 and H.C. 38 (1962–3); Lord Home, *The Way the Wind Blows* (1976), p. 179; Lord Hailsham, *The Door Wherein I Went* (1975), pp. 221–3; *Re Parliamentary Election for Bristol South-East* [1964] 2 Q.B. 257.

[48] Other than an Irish peerage: but then as it carries with it no practical disadvantage there is no reason why disclaimer should be available.

[49] Peerage Act 1963, s. 1(1) and Schedule 1.

[50] Section 1(2). Existing peers at the time of the passing of the Peerage Act 1963 had 12 months from the commencement of that Act in which to decide whether to disclaim: s. 1(3).

[51] Section 2(1). A succeeding peer who has been nominated, or is nominated subsequent to his inheritance, as a parliamentary candidate is deemed to succeed immediately after the declaration of his election result and has 1 month from then to decide whether to disclaim: s. 2(2).

[52] Section 3(1).

[53] Thus, for example, when the Earl of Durham disclaimed his earldom his heir remained known as Lord Lambton.

[54] Section 3(2).

[55] He became a life peer as Lord Hailsham of St Marylebone in 1970 on his appointment as Lord Chancellor.

not his peerage, in four other ways. Aliens are disqualified:[56] an alien may not receive a peerage, and if a British citizen became a peer and later renounced that citizenship he would have no right to sit. Adjudication of bankruptcy disqualifies a peer from sitting and voting unless and until the adjudication is set aside.[57] A conviction of treason disqualifies from membership until the sentence is served or a pardon is granted.[58] And peers under the age of 21 may not sit.[59] None of the other types of disqualification which affect MPs[60] affect peers, and the House of Lords (unlike the House of Commons) has no power to expel any member.

Now a person may be willing enough to succeed to a peerage while wishing to take no part in the proceedings of the House. Equally, it is right that such a peer, or one who sits rarely, should not turn up, as it were unannounced, and perhaps with others affect the outcome of a vote. This problem of backwoodsmen has been largely solved by the introduction of leave of absence.[61] At the beginning of each session of Parliament the Lord Chancellor writes to all those peers already with leave of absence and to those who did not attend at all in the previous session asking if they wish to have leave of absence for the new session. Leave is granted automatically for that session to peers who request it and to those who make no reply to the Lord Chancellor's inquiry. A peer with leave is expected not to attend, although he may cancel his leave by giving one month's notice; and if a peer sits and votes despite leave the House can do nothing about it.[62] Usually some 130 to 150 peers have leave; in the 1985–6 session the number was 135.[63] A new peer need never take his seat,[64] or having done so need never be seen in the House again: attendance is not compulsory and there are of course no constituents who might object.

---

[56] Act of Settlement 1701, s. 3. Commonwealth citizens and citizens of the Republic of Ireland are not aliens for this purpose: British Nationality Act 1981, s. 50(1).

[57] Insolvency Act 1986, s. 427(1).

[58] Forfeiture Act 1870, s. 2.

[59] S.O. No. 2.

[60] See chapter 9. Mental illness, for example, does not disqualify a peer, and compulsory detention under the Mental Health Act 1983, Part II, probably raises no issue of privilege: see Report by the Committee for Privileges on Parliamentary Privilege and the Mental Health Legislation, H.L. 254 (1983–4), especially para. 4; agreed to by the House at 455 H.L. Deb. 13–14 (23 July 1984).The Parliament (No. 2.) Bill, cl. 7, would have provided that such compulsory detention would disqualify a peer from sitting or voting or receiving a writ of summons during such detention.

[61] S.O. No. 20. For the background see Report from the Select Committee on Leave of Absence, H.L. 60 (1957–8).

[62] Report by the Select Committee on the Powers of the House in Relation to the Attendance of its Members, H.L. (7), (66-I), (67)(1955–6), especially paras. 29–39.

[63] Peers with leave of absence may still use the House of Lords Library, dining room, and guest room, thus continuing to enjoy what may be termed the club facilities of the House.

[64] Rather like Gerry Adams in the other House, who was elected as a Sinn Fein MP in 1983 and again in 1987 but has not taken his seat.

Organization in the House

Leaving out of account peers with leave of absence and those who are disqualified there is a House of about 980 potential members, of whom some two-thirds are hereditary peers. But a visitor to the public gallery on an average day would see a very different picture. The usual daily attendance is about 300, of whom life peers and hereditary peers of first creation will normally be in a small majority.[65] That same visitor might assume that the Conservative Party is always firmly in control of the House, but that assumption is not entirely correct. Once more leaving aside peers with leave of absence, in January 1988 the Conservatives had 444 supporters in the Lords, the opposition parties a total of 215 and the cross-bench, or independent, peers 250.[66] What is true is that the Conservative Party is the largest single group in the House on an average day, but even that (as will be seen later) does not make the House a supine body ready to do the bidding of a Conservative government in an unquestioning way.

Each year the House of Lords sits on about 150 days (compared with the Commons' average of some 175 days).[67] It only sits on Fridays at all regularly in the late spring and in summer when the volume of Bills sent to the Lords having passed the Commons increases sharply.[68] General precedence is given in the Lords to legislation,[69] but the actual business is arranged each day by the Leader of the House of Lords and the Government Chief Whip, in consultation with the other parties. The House as a whole regulates its proceedings and maintains the rules of order, in the light of which the Lord Chancellor's title of Speaker of the House of Lords is something of a misnomer, especially as it is the Leader of the House who advises peers on matters of procedure and who acts as the

---

[65] In the 1985–6 session the average daily attendance was 317. 813 peers attended at least once in that session; 268 attended on 100 days or more, and of those 268, 143 were life peers and 125 hereditary peers. The lowest average daily attendance in the last decade was 284 in 1981–2: information from the House of Lords Journal and Information Office. (Unless otherwise stated in this chapter statistics for 1982–3, 1983–4 and 1986–7 are omitted to avoid the distortions created by the 1983 and 1987 dissolutions.)

[66] Labour had 125 adherents, the SDP 45, and the Liberals 45: information from the House of Lords Journal and Information Office. See also the government's figures at 451 H.L. Deb. 1506–9 (17 May 1984) which confirmed the same sort of composition.

[67] The 1985–6 session was a heavy one, the Lords sitting on 165 days; the lowest annual total of sitting days in the last decade was 143 in 1980–1: information from the House of Lords Journal and Information Office.

[68] The House sat on 16 Fridays in the 1985–6 session.

[69] S.O. No. 37(4).

principal voice of the House in maintaining order. The House of Lords is a quiet and indeed rather relaxed legislative chamber, quite unlike the other House. If 'heat is engendered in debate' any peer may move that the Standing Order on Asperity of Speech be read by the Clerk, but no such motion has been moved in recent years. If a peer's speech is thought to be seriously transgressing the accepted practice of the House it is open to another peer to move that he be no longer heard, but that, too, is resorted to only exceptionally in a House which rightly prides itself on its civilized manner of conducting its affairs.[70]

Members of the House of Lords in general receive no salaries. All peers are, however, entitled to certain allowances and expenses in connection with their parliamentary work. They may claim up to £22 a day as general office, secretarial, and research allowance. A subsistence allowance of up to £20 a day (or £52 if an overnight stay in London is involved) is also recoverable.[71] And travel expenses within the United Kingdom on parliamentary business are reimbursed. A few peers are salaried: the Leader of the Opposition in the Lords receives £28,688 a year and the Opposition Chief Whip £25,618; as in the Commons, other party Leaders, including the Convenor of the Cross-bench Peers, receive no salary. The Lord Chancellor receives £11,620 of his £83,000 annual salary as Speaker of the House. The Lord Chairman of Committees and the Principal Deputy Chairman of Committees are paid £34,688 and £31,578 respectively as recompense for their heavy load in presiding over committees and in the Committee of the Whole House. Lords of Appeal in Ordinary each receive £74,500 as judicial salary. Ministers and Whips in the Lords, of whom there were twenty-seven in 1988, receive a ministerial salary. It had been envisaged in the 1968 White Paper 'House of Lords Reform' that in the planned new House life peers and hereditary peers of first creation would become voting peers and as such receive a salary:[72] £2,000 a year was mooted. That proposal was, however, so heavily criticized as an indefensible gilding on prime ministerial patronage (for the Prime Minister would have been able to distribute peerages *and* £2,000 a year!) that it was dropped.[73]

Peers are honour-bound to declare any personal financial interest

[70] The motion 'that the noble Lord be no longer heard' was, however, carried in 1985 against Lord Hatch of Lusby: see 459 H.L. Deb. 560–1 (29 January 1985).

[71] These rates were approved at 478 H.L. Deb. 906 (16 July 1986), and 488 H.L. Deb. 1529–46 (23 July 1987).

[72] Cmnd. 3799 (1968), para. 52.

[73] The Prime Minister's reasons for abandoning the proposal were given in the second reading on the Parliament (No. 2) Bill at 777 H.C. Deb. 54 (3 February 1969).

during debate, but there is no register of peers' interests. It is considered undesirable for a peer to speak or vote at all on legislation in relation to which he has been acting for payment or reward.[74]

The work of the Lords

No official and systematic statement of the actual or ideal functions of the House of Commons has ever been written, which is odd because that is easily the more important House, yet it is understandable because no government-sponsored attempt has been made for well over a century to reform it. The functions of the House of Lords, on the other hand, have been considered since 1900 to a greater or lesser extent by four official bodies.[75] So, for example, it was concluded in the 1968 White Paper 'House of Lords Reform' that the House has seven main functions: (a) to be the supreme court of appeal; (b) to provide a forum for debates on matters of public interest; (c) to revise public Bills passed by the House of Commons; (d) to initiate less controversial public legislation and private peers' Bills; (e) to consider subordinate legislation; (f) to scrutinize the activities of the executive; and (g) to consider private legislation.[76] That order of functions does not reflect their order of importance, and here the work of the modern House will be examined in relation to the consideration given to public Bills; general debates; scrutiny of the government through questions; and its scrutiny of the government and other work conducted through committees of the House of Lords.

The examination and amendment of Bills sent up by the Commons is easily the most important work of the House of Lords and takes up over half its time.[77] The Lords made over 2,500 amendments to public Bills

[74] There are special rules, the Addison Rules (so named after the then Leader of the House), which govern the contributions of peers who are members of public boards. The main points are that (a) Ministers alone are responsible to Parliament for public boards: that responsibility must not be assumed by peers who happen to be members of them; (b) such peers should not give details of day-to-day administration, as that is not a matter for Parliament; and (c) there is no duty on such peers to answer questions put to them in debate: see 170 H.L. Deb. 1241–2 (21 March 1951).

[75] See Report of the Conference on the Reform of the Second Chamber, Cd. 9038 (1918)—the Bryce Report; Agreed Statement on the Conclusion of the Conference on the Parliament Bill 1947, Cmd. 7380 (1948); 'House of Lords Reform', Cmnd. 3799 (1968); and Report of the Royal Commission on the Constitution, Cmnd. 5460 (1973), vol. i, para. 1073.

[76] Since then the House has set up machinery to scrutinize European Community legislation, which will be considered below. Functions (a), (e), and (f) will not be considered further here.

[77] It spent nearly 58 per cent of its time on such Bills in 1985–6. For ease of comparison, the approximate division of time in 1985–6 (as given in the Sessional Statistics) may be set out thus:

brought from the Commons in the 1985–6 session: this was an exceptionally high total,[78] but even so about 1,500 are made in an average session.[79] This is work well done as most Lords amendments are accepted by the government and the other House, but it is important to put the Lords' revising work into context. Anything from a half to two-thirds of public Bills brought from the Commons are passed by the Lords with no amendments of any kind. In the 1985–6 session, for example, a total of eight-seven public Bills passed the Commons: the Lords passed fifty-one of them entirely unamended.[80] Then again, of the hundreds of amendments which are made to government Bills from the Commons, most are proposed by Ministers who are prompted to do so by changes of mind during the passage of those Bills, or by ministerial promises to either House to reconsider particular matters, or sometimes as concessions to pressures in one or other House or from outside Parliament; the largest single category of Lords' amendments accepted by the government comprises those of a technical nature which improve drafting and which do not affect the policy underlying the legislation in any way. Such drafting help is naturally welcome and this is reflected in the government's (and therefore the Commons') acceptance of so many Lords' amendments. Amendments which are unacceptable to the

Topic	Time (%)
Public Bills from Commons	58
General debates	16
Unstarred questions (i.e. leading to debate)	5
Other questions	6
Ministerial statements	4
Subordinate legislation	4
European Communities Committee reports	2.5
Private Bills	0.5
Other	4
	100

[78] The Financial Services Bill 1985–6 alone accounted for 784 amendments.
[79] Information from the Public Bill Office of the House of Lords.
[80] The figures for earlier sessions are as follows:

Session	No. of Bills from Commons	No. passed unamended
1984–5	101	66
1981–2	82	61
1980–1	96	57

government may be voted down in the House of Commons.[81] The House of Lords gives a fair wind to Private MPs' Bills which have passed the Commons. They are usually approved so as to allow them to pass into law.[82]

Quite unlike the other House, the House of Lords takes the committee stage of public Bills in Committee of the Whole House.[83] Any peer may speak in committee and put down amendments, so that the opportunities for back-bench peers to influence the form of legislation are accordingly much better than those of their counterparts in the other House. Experiments in which Public Bill Committees[84] have taken the committee stage in order to save time in the chamber have been very limited: only six public Bills were dealt with in that way between 1968 and 1978, none was sent to a committee between 1978 and 1985, and only one in the 1986–7 session.[85] Such a procedure seems to be unpopular with peers, who prefer to keep the revision of public Bills in all their hands.

A factor in the ability of the House fully to consider and revise Bills is, obviously, the time available to the House to do so, which in turn is affected by the House in which Bills are first introduced. Most government Bills are introduced into Parliament in the House of Commons because they will be politically controversial and the elected House is where such controversies are fully argued; the Ministers responsible for the Bills will be in the Commons in most cases, and many Bills have a financial content over which MPs consider themselves supreme. So government business managers have to decide before and at the start of each session which public Bills may, within those constraints, safely be started in the House of Lords, and they manage to compile a list of about a dozen from a total of some fifty or so government Bills which are introduced into Parliament each year.[86] Law reform and revision Bills are invariably introduced into the House of Lords first.[87] Given the pre-

---

[81] Occasions on which the government has had to defer to the Lords over legislation are considered later.

[82] All such Bills have been passed by the Lords in the last few years.

[83] S.O. No. 45.

[84] See generally 3rd Report from the Select Committee on Procedure, H.L. 131 (1970–1), para. 6.

[85] It became the Pilotage Act 1987.

[86] Some significant Bills which have started in the Lords recently have included the Shops Bill in 1985–6 (which came to grief in the Commons: see chapter 9) and the Criminal Justice Bill in 1987–8.

[87] These are (a) consolidation Bills; (b) Bills presented under the Consolidation of Enactments (Procedure) Act 1949; (c) Bills to consolidate with amendments to give effect to Law Commission

ponderance of government Bills started each October or November in the Commons,[88] the Lords will have less legislative work to do in the first half of the session but its workload will increase dramatically each spring and summer as Bills emerge from the Commons. (Peers complain every year about this uneven level of work, and every year the Leader of the House of Lords hopes that things will be better ordered in the following session.) Government business managers in the Lords see prorogation as a deadline to be achieved if the government's legislation is to reach royal assent—and they must, of course, allow time for the Commons to consider any Lords' amendments, and for the Lords to react to the Commons' treatment of those amendments. Government Bills do normally pass in time, despite the complete absence of a legislative guillotine in the House of Lords, or of any power to allow the Lord Chairman of Committees to select only certain amendments for debate, and the rarity with which the closure is moved.[89]

Any back-bench peer may introduce his own Bill without giving notice, without going through any ballot, and without needing the leave of the House. He has much more freedom in that respect than his Commons counterpart. Given that the House of Lords has more time at its disposal, particularly in the first half of the session, and that there is no guarantee that any MP will take up a private peer's Bill, or that (even if one does) the Commons will pass it, the government does not oppose any such Bills which it finds uncongenial by forcing a division against them in the House of Lords. Between one and two dozen back-bench peers' Bills are introduced each session but no more than six of them usually pass into law, the high failure rate resulting from lack of opportunity to introduce them into the other House, or from opposition to

---

recommendations; (d) Law Commission Statute Law (Repeals) Bills to repeal enactments no longer of practical utility; (e) statute law revision Bills (which have largely been replaced by type (d)); and (f) statutory instruments to consolidate or revise Northern Ireland statute law. After second reading all such measures are referred to the Joint Select Committee on Consolidation Bills, which has 12 members from each House. After taking evidence from Parliamentary Counsel and sometimes from departmental sources the Bills are reported to the House with any suggested amendments. A Committee of the Whole House then considers them very briefly before passing them.

[88] Or in whichever month Parliament resumes after a dissolution.

[89] If it is moved, the Lord Chancellor or Lord Chairman of Committees is bound by standing order to read out—'slowly'—that the closure is a most exceptional procedure and that the House will not accept it save in circumstances where it is felt to be the only means of ensuring the proper conduct of business: see 1st Report from the Select Committee on Procedure, H.L. 129 (1960–1), para. 6; 6th Report from the Select Committee on Procedure, H.L. 169 (1970–1), para. 2. The closure motion 'that the question be now put' was first moved, amid considerable controversy, in 1926, and not again until 1961. The last attempt to move that motion was in 1985, when the Deputy Chairman declined to put it: see 464 H.L. Deb. 718–9 (4 June 1985).

them there.[90] The House of Lords spends about five per cent of its time on such Bills each session, and even those which get no further than that House allow public discussion of the ideas in them. Some controversial statutes have begun in this way, such as the Sexual Offences Act 1967 which made consenting male homosexual conduct in private no longer criminal.

Some twenty per cent of the time of the House of Lords is devoted to general debates. One day each week, usually Wednesday, is given over to debating a topic on a neutral motion calling for papers or on a motion to take note. There were seven five-hour debates and fourteen two-and-a-half hour debates in the 1985–6 session, the subjects for debate having been agreed through the usual channels. Additionally one day a month, again usually a Wednesday, up to the Whitsun recess is used for short debates, each up to a maximum length of two-and-a-half hours.[91] The right to select matters for short debates is entirely reserved to back-bench and cross-bench peers, the actual choice being made by ballot a few weeks before the day of the scheduled debate. It is common ground that the quality of general debate can be high, as it should be, given the diversity of the backgrounds of the life peers in particular, and the lack of any overwhelming desire (so common among MPs) to score party political points across the chamber. It was partly as a recognition of this quality that Professor Stanley de Smith stated his considered view that the House 'is the best second chamber in the Commonwealth and one which stands comparison with its counterparts in almost any developed country in the world'.[92]

Questions in the House of Lords are organized on a different, and in some respects more logical, basis than in the Commons. There are four different types of question. First, if a peer wishes to elicit factual information he may put down a starred question upon which no debate is permitted.[93] Such questions may be tabled on any day, although twenty-four hours' notice is required[94] and not more than four starred questions

---

[90] Thirteen such Bills were introduced in the 1985–6 session, of which 4 became law, the Gaming (Amendment) Act 1986, the Incest and Related Offences (Scotland) Act 1986, the Marriage (Prohibited Degrees of Relationship) Act 1986, and the Prevention of Oil Pollution Act 1986.

[91] S.O. No. 35. By Whitsun the rate of Bills coming from the Commons increases dramatically, and so short debates are abandoned from then.

[92] S. A. de Smith, *Constitutional and Administrative Law* (5th edn., 1985 by H. Street and R. Brazier), p. 310.

[93] S.O. No. 32.

[94] As against the 48 hours' notice required for Commons questions.

may appear on the order paper on any day. Supplementary questions may be asked, and some debating points do creep in. Up to twenty minutes a day are spent on starred questions as the first item of substantive business. Some 600 starred questions are dealt with in an average session, consuming about six per cent of the House's time. Should a peer not wish to put a supplementary at all he will table a different type of question, one for written answer,[95] and he will receive a reply in under two weeks. This is easily the largest category of Lords' questions, some 1,100 being tabled in an average session.[96] The third type is the unstarred question, which is designed to be the basis for debate. Such a question may be put down by any peer, but only one on each day,[97] and it is customary for the government Whips' Office to be consulted about a suitable date. It is taken as the final item of daily business; at the end of the debate a Minister or Whip will reply. Some forty unstarred questions are tabled each session, accounting for about five per cent of the time of the House. Finally, a peer may seek to put down a private notice question.[98] To do so he must try to convince the Leader of the House privately that it is a matter of urgency justifying an immediate reply: he will rarely succeed.[99] These procedures are superior to those of the Commons in two respects. There is no constraint of a ministerial rota for answering questions, as questions in the Lords are tabled to the government, not usually to a particular Minister,[100] and so peers may be able to raise a given issue through questions more quickly than may back-bench MPs. Moreover, the only distinction between questions in the Commons is between those for oral or written answer, both of which have the notional purpose of seeking factual information, although in the former debating points are scored in supplementary questions. The Lords' arrangements go beyond that rather crude distinction by recognizing that the purpose of some questions is to elicit facts (through Lords' starred questions and questions for written answer), and that of others is to spark off debate (Lords' unstarred questions).

[95] S.O. No. 42.

[96] It is, however, way below the Commons total which receive a written answer—about 30,000 in 1985–6.

[97] A second unstarred question may be put down if the day's business is exceptionally light.

[98] S.O. No. 33.

[99] Fewer private notice questions are allowed in the Lords than in the Commons. An example was the one which was allowed to be put to the Lord Advocate on the Special Branch raid on BBC headquarters in Glasgow over the planned 'Project Zircon' programme: see 484 H.L. Deb. 199 (4 February 1987).

[100] Questions may, however, be addressed to the Leader of the House on procedural and business matters.

Up to 1974 the committee work of the House of Lords was restricted to the procedure and administration of the House itself, together with the committee stage of Bills taken in Committee of the Whole House (which is a committee only in name). Since 1974, however, the use of committees has increased, although the House has not sought to set up committees to oversee the work of government departments. With very few exceptions (the most significant being the Committee of the Whole House) all Lords' committees are select committees.[101] Such committees can be appointed by the House to examine anything which in its view requires investigation. Once the House has agreed to establish a select committee the Committee of Selection[102] reports to the House the names of peers to form it, after consultations through the usual channels. There is no understanding as exists in the Commons that the government will have a majority of members. The select committee's scope of inquiry will be defined in its order of reference. Again unlike select committees in the Commons, any peer (whether or not a member of a given select committee) may attend and speak at its meetings, other than those at which a committee considers its findings. A select committee may call any witness it needs; ordinarily witnesses attend and documents are produced voluntarily, but if necessary the House itself could order witnesses to attend or papers to be delivered, and refusal or failure would be a contempt of the House.[103] Select committees report if necessary by a majority vote; as with the Commons' equivalents minority reports are not in order, but such reports may be moved and voted on. *Ad hoc* select committees have become influential since the 1970s, having been set up either to consider the merits of possible legislation or to investigate a particular matter which the House has thought needed detailed study. Some recent examples have included the Select Committees on a Bill of Rights, on Unemployment, and on Overseas Trade.[104] Advantages of investigations into particular topics lie in the expertise which can be brought to bear and in that there is no guarantee that a select committee will necessarily tell a government what it wishes to hear (thus echoing, as was seen in the last chapter, some of the Commons' departmental select committees). A good example of the latter point can be seen in the

---

[101] S.O. Nos. 61, 63–5.

[102] S.O. No. 61. The Committee consists of 11 peers from all parties and a representative of the cross-bench peers, with the Leader of the House as chairman.

[103] Erskine May, op. cit., chapter 10.

[104] For their reports, see respectively H.L. 176 (1977–8), H.L. 142 (1981–2), H.L. 238 (1984–5).

1982 Report of the Select Committee on Unemployment,[105] which called for major changes in the government's policies towards unemployment, including significantly increased government spending to try to increase the number of people in work. Sessional select committees[106] are greater in number and always include two Appellate Committees,[107] the Joint Select Committee on Consolidation Bills,[108] the Joint Select Committee on Statutory Instruments,[109] the Committee for Privileges,[110] the Procedure Committee, the Science and Technology Committee, and the European Communities Committee. The work of the last two is worth amplification.

The Science and Technology Committee was first set up in 1980 as a direct result of the House of Commons' decision not to appoint a successor to its Select Committee on Science and Technology when the fourteen departmental select committees were established. The Committee has about fourteen members who work through a general purposes subcommittee and two other subcommittees. Its terms of reference are simply 'to consider science and technology': subjects are chosen which concern areas where Parliament can stimulate the advancement and application of science and technology or in which the government is involved, or which involve issues over which there is public concern. The Committee appoints specialist advisers. On average the Committee produces two major reports a year: recent investigations have included ones on occupational health and hygiene services, education and training for new technologies, marine science and technology, civil research and development, innovation in surface transport, space policy, and priorities in medical research. The European Communities Committee was first established in 1974.[111] It has twenty-five members, but an additional eighty peers are usually co-opted and any other peer may

---

[105] H.L. 142 (1981-2), debated at 436 H.L. Deb. 425-513 (16 November 1982). A report critical of the government's civil research and development policy, 1st Report from the Science and Technology Committee, H.L. 20 (1986-7) was agreed to by the House at 484 H.L. Deb. 1251-332 (19 February 1987); the government accepted several of the Committee's findings, including the need for a new central structure for such work, in a White Paper, Cm. 185 (1987).

[106] That is, select committees regularly set up for the duration of each session.

[107] S.O. No. 82.

[108] S.O. No. 49; see above, note 87.

[109] Statutory instruments are subject to scrutiny by the Joint Select Committee on Statutory Instruments of 7 peers and 7 MPs which may draw any instrument to the attention of both Houses on any ground which does not impinge on its merits or on the policy behind it.

[110] S.O. Nos. 73-7.

[111] See the Report of the Select Committee on Procedure for Scrutiny of Proposals for European Instruments, H.L. 194 (1972-3); H.L. 62 and 139 (1973-4).

attend. Its purpose is to consider Community proposals (whether in draft or otherwise), to obtain all necessary information about them, and to report on those which in its opinion raise important policy questions or matters of principle or which for any other reason should be drawn to the attention of the House. The Committee may appoint subcommittees: at present there are seven.[112] The chairman refers Community proposals to the subcommittees, distinguishing between 'A-type' (which do not require parliamentary attention—usually some two-thirds of the total) and 'B-type' (which he thinks will require parliamentary scrutiny). The volume of paper which faces the Committee is daunting: some sixty-six Community documents, on average, are deposited each month. The Committee appoints specialist advisers, and has a legal adviser. It may confer with the Commons Select Committee on European Legislation. All reports which are recommended by the Committee for debate on the floor of the House are debated there, a total of a dozen or so every session.[113] In the 1985–6 session the Committee reported on, for example, nuclear power in Europe, Community forestry policy, indirect taxation, and the Single European Act. This is laborious and undramatic work which enhances the House's understanding of Community developments, and so indirectly the comprehension of interested individuals and groups outside Parliament.

Because the House of Lords has more time available than has the House of Commons, the Lords can and does debate all the reports from its committees—something which has proved impossible so far in the Commons, an inability which has detracted from the usefulness of Commons select committees. The efforts of both the Science and Technology Committee and the European Communities Committee have proved entirely worth while and, especially in the case of the former Committee, have allowed parliamentary work to be accomplished which otherwise would not have been undertaken. The types of inquiry into subjects conducted by *ad hoc* select committees, too, in no sense duplicate any efforts of the House of Commons. The decision not to set up departmental select committees has avoided pointless duplication and what would have been an intolerable burden on Ministers and civil servants. I suggest that a valuable development of the committee work of

---

[112] Subcommittee A (on finance, economics, and regional policy); B (on external relations, trade, and industry); C (on education, employment, and social affairs); D (on agriculture, food, and consumer affairs); E (on legal implications of European Community legislation); F (on energy, transport, technology, and research), and G (on environmental matters).

[113] Occasionally an unstarred question is also used to debate a Committee report.

the House would be the creation of a sessional Select Committee on Law Reform, made up of a Lord of Appeal in Ordinary (if he could be spared[114]) together with other Law Lords and peers with expertise or interest in legal affairs and the subject-matter of particular reform proposals. Such a committee could automatically consider the law reform reports as published of the Law Commission,[115] the Criminal Law Revision Committee, and the Law Reform Committee without waiting for any reference to it by the government. Its primary purpose would be to act as a pre-legislative stage on the draft Bills which are usually appended to such reports. Such detailed and expert committee work ought to reduce the amount of parliamentary time which would otherwise be needed for such proposals, and so might encourage governments to introduce more of them into Parliament.

Lords and government in conflict

The routine work of the House of Lords may now be left aside so as to consider conflicts which have arisen between that House and the government over legislation. The powers of the House over legislation were of course reduced by the Parliament Acts of 1911 and 1949 but were otherwise confirmed by those statutes. It is therefore possible to view the infrequent but sometimes dramatic conflicts between the Lords and the government as the exercise of authority expressly conferred by law on that House. The House's powers under the Parliament Acts may conveniently be considered in three groups: veto powers, Money Bill powers, and delaying powers.

The first of those groups, veto powers, is a ragbag in which are retained the pre-1911 prerogatives of the House of Lords over four disparate types of legislation. Thus the consent of the Lords remains necessary before royal assent may be given to a Bill to extend the maximum life of Parliament beyond five years,[116] or to a provisional order confirmation Bill,[117] or to a private Bill; and the Lords' veto over

---

[114] The eleventh Lord of Appeal in Ordinary provided for by statute has never been appointed, no doubt partly in the interests of holding down public expenditure.

[115] Apart from those currently considered by the Joint Select Committee on Consolidation Bills.

[116] Parliament Act 1911, s. 2(1).

[117] Ibid., s. 5. Both those veto powers would have remained under the 1968 proposals, the first because the reason for its existence was taken to be self-evident (see Cmnd. 3977, para. 56), the second on the ground that it was never likely to cause conflict between the government and the Lords (ibid., para. 55).

subordinate legislation remains as well.[118] The ability to ensure that general elections take place at least every five years is of great theoretical importance but of course no occasion has arisen on which the House of Lords has even had to consider using it. There would be nothing to prevent[119] a government removing any or all of these veto powers by causing a Bill to be passed under the Parliament Act procedure (that is, subject to a maximum Lords' delay of just over twelve months) to delete those powers and to substitute some (or no) delaying power. The second group of Parliament Act powers concerns Money Bills. In essence, the House of Lords may delay a Money Bill sent up to them by the Commons for up to one month (provided it reaches the Lords at least one month before the end of a session). If after that time the Lords have not passed it unamended the Bill may receive royal assent despite the absence of Lords' assent.[120] A Money Bill is one which, in the Speaker's opinion, has provisions which relate *only* to central government taxation, expenditure, or loans.[121] The definition of a Money Bill is narrow: indeed, most annual Finance Bills based on the Budget have not been certified as Money Bills.[122] To be valid the Speaker's certificate must be endorsed on a Money Bill before it leaves the Commons and is conclusive for all purposes.[123] The final group of powers—and in practice easily the most important—are the delaying powers of the House of Lords. These permit the Lords to hold up the passage of all other types of legislation

[118] The Parliament Act 1911, ss. 2 and 5 refers to 'Public Bills': private Bills and subordinate legislation are therefore not embraced. The last (and probably the first) Lords' veto of subordinate legislation was in 1968, when the House voted down the Southern Rhodesia (United Nations Sanctions) Order, largely on the ground that the economic sanctions which had been imposed against the regime which had made an unlawful declaration of independence in Rhodesia in 1965 had had little effect, and that mandatory UN sanctions would be no more effective: see 293 H.L. Deb. 515–98 (18 June 1968). The House passed a similar Order at the second time of asking in deference to the House of Commons: see 295 H.L. Deb. 447–504 (18 July 1968). The government retaliated against this veto by abandoning all-party talks on reform; see also below, note 141. Such a veto would have been removed by the Parliament (No. 2) Bill.

[119] Subject, perhaps, to what was said in chapter 8 about the Queen's reserve powers.

[120] Parliament Act 1911, s. 1(1). The House of Lords has occasionally made minor amendments to Money Bills which the House of Commons has accepted.

[121] Section 1(2) of the Parliament Act 1911 (as amended by the National Loans Act 1968, s. 1(5)) elaborates this as a public Bill containing only provisions dealing with the imposition, repeal, remission, alteration, or regulation of taxation; the imposition of charges on the Consolidated Fund or the National Loans Fund or on money provided by Parliament; the appropriation, receipt, custody, issue, or audit of accounts of public money; and the raising or guarantee of any loan or repayment of it—none of which includes taxes, money, or loans raised by local authorities or bodies for local purposes.

[122] Erskine May, op. cit., pp. 853–7.

[123] Parliament Act 1911, s. 3.

for somewhat over one year, after which the will of the Commons prevails. There are five basic rules.[124] (a) If the House of Commons passes a public Bill[125] in two successive sessions (whether or not in the same Parliament) and the Lords reject it in both of them, then on that second rejection the Bill may receive royal assent. (b) The Bill must be sent up to the Lords at least one month before the end of both sessions. (c) One year must elapse between the initial occasion on which the Bill had a second reading in the Commons and the second occasion on which it passed that House. (d) The Bills rejected on both occasions must be the same: they must either be identical, or contain such alterations as are certified by the Speaker as being necessary through lapse of time.[126] Any Lords' amendments agreed to by the Commons do not, however, offend against this rule. (e) The Speaker must certify any Bill passing under the Parliament Acts as having complied with all these rules; his certificate is conclusive for all purposes. Now the fact that the House of Commons can in the last resort overcome the opposition of the Lords to legislation through this procedure is *numerically* not very important—after all, it has only been used three times.[127] Of much greater significance are both the sort of adverse amendments which the House of Lords makes to the legislation of both Labour and Conservative governments (and which those governments decide cannot be resisted), and the delay which is thereby caused—all without the Parliament Act procedure being invoked at all. That aspect will be considered now.

It has been traditionally assumed that Labour governments are more susceptible than Conservative governments to legislative defeat in the House of Lords. Mr Wilson's government up to 1970[128] suffered 116 defeats at the hands of the Lords,[129] of which the most notable were the effective killing of the House of Commons (Redistribution of Seats) Bill in 1969 (the Lords insisting on wrecking amendments which the government refused to accept, and the Bill lapsing on prorogation[130]) and the rejection of the Southern Rhodesia (United Nations Sanctions) Order in

[124] Parliament Act 1911, s. 2 (as amended by the Parliament Act 1949, s. 1).

[125] Other than a Money Bill or one to extend the life of Parliament beyond 5 years.

[126] For example, to change the year in the short title.

[127] To secure the passage of the Welsh Church Act 1914, the Government of Ireland Act 1914, and the Parliament Act 1949. Of course, the existence of the Parliament Acts must have persuaded the Lords not to persist in resisting certain Bills.

[128] On which see Janet Morgan, *The House of Lords and the Labour Government 1964 to 1970* (1975).

[129] See Brigid Hadfield, 'Whether or Whither the House of Lords?' (1984) 35 *Northern Ireland Legal Quarterly* 313.

[130] For the details, see de Smith, op. cit., pp. 256–9.

1968 (which had the immediate effect of ending the all-party talks on House of Lords reform[131]). The minority, or small majority, Labour governments of 1974 to 1979 received 355 legislative setbacks in the House of Lords.[132] The House used its delaying power to the full over the Trade Union and Labour Relations (Amendment) Bill in the 1975–6 session, holding it up for slightly under one year. Peers attacked the Bill on the ground that it would pose a major threat to press freedom, and only when the government decided that if necessary the Bill would be forced through under the Parliament Acts did the House of Lords allow it to pass. A longer delay was imposed over the Aircraft and Shipbuilding Industries Bill in the same session: the Lords attached amendments to exclude the ship-repairing industry from its provisions and insisted on those amendments, so that the Bill was lost on prorogation. On its reintroduction in the following session the government withdrew the clauses relating to the ship-repairing industry so as to get the Bill enacted with a minimum of futher delay (and certainly less than the year which would have been taken up through the Parliament Act procedure); the Bill passed into law in 1977. For that government the unhappy combination of a House of Lords prepared to resist certain legislation and the lack of homogeneity among its own back-benchers in the Commons resulted in the Dock Work Regulation Act 1976 being passed without the government's original and main proposal. In relation to all these measures the majority in the House of Lords could claim with some justice that it had forced the government to take time to think again and further justify its plans, through the proper exercise of the peers' powers enshrined in the Parliament Acts.

It has, however, become apparent over the last twenty years (and especially during the life of the present government) that the House of Lords has acted in a more even-handed manner towards both Labour and Conservative legislation to which it objects. Mr Heath's government suffered twenty-six (not very significant) adverse votes in the House of Lords.[133] Mrs Thatcher's administration sustained its one hundredth legislative reverse in the Lords in October 1986, roughly at the same rate as was inflicted on the 1964 Labour government; several of those defeats have been quite major. A few instances may be cited by way of example. The Education (Corporal Punishment) Bill had to be withdrawn by the government in 1985 after the Lords had inserted a wrecking amendment

---

131 See above, note 118.
132 Hadfield, ibid.
133 Information from the House of Lords Journal and Information Office.

to abolish all corporal punishment in schools, whereas the Bill had been designed to give parents the right to opt their children out of such punishment.[134] Following the insertion of an Opposition clause into the Telecommunications Bill in 1984 to regulate telephone tapping, the government was forced to promise its own legislation on that topic— legislation which it almost certainly would not have volunteered—in order to persuade the House of Lords to drop the Opposition clause.[135] Clauses have been struck out of other Conservative Bills by the peers, and the government has decided not to try to restore them: an out- standing example was the clause in the Prosecution of Offences Bill of 1985 which would have enabled the Attorney-General to refer 'lenient' sentences to the Court of Appeal for its opinion: the House disliked and rejected the idea.[136] Perhaps the most publicized and dramatic clash took place over the government's plan to abolish the 1984 elections to the Greater London Council and to the metropolitan county councils, and to put in government-nominated boards to run their affairs, pending the statutory abolition of those authorities. The House passed a wrecking amendment to the Local Government (Interim Provisions) Bill by a majority of forty-eight: the abolition of elections was something to which peers took great exception, and the number of Conservative defections was so high that the government had to cause the Bill to be further amended, with the Lords' consent, so as to extend the life of the authorities to 1986 without elections in 1984, and to dispense with the expedient of nominated boards.[137]

It is impossible by considering the kinds of defeats inflicted on gov- ernment legislation over the past few decades to discern any under- standing—still less any consistent practice—on the part of the House of Lords as to what makes any given legislation in its view properly

---

[134] For the defeat see 465 H.L. Deb. 1314–33 (4 July 1985). The government subsequently conceded that its original proposals had no chance of passing the Lords and so caused Parliament to confirm the House's 1985 decision by abolishing corporal punishment in all state schools: see the Education (No. 2) Act 1986, s. 47. The government had also decided to abandon the Protection of Official Information Bill 1979–80 because, although it had been given a second reading in the Lords, its ultimate chances of survival were slim: for the second reading debate see 402 H.L. Deb. 608–80 (15 November 1979).

[135] See 448 H.L. Deb. 632–44 (21 February 1984); 449 H.L. Deb. 1032–6 (19 March 1984).

[136] See 459 H.L. Deb. 386–406 (24 January 1985). The Prosecution of Offences Act 1985 was passed without that provision; the government tried again in the Criminal Justice Bill 1986–7 (but that and other clauses of the Bill were dropped so that a much shorter Criminal Justice Act 1987 could pass before the 1987 dissolution). A further attempt to deal with 'lenient' sentences was made in the Criminal Justice Bill of 1987–8.

[137] For the defeat see 453 H.L. Deb. 1033–70 (28 June 1984), and for the compromise provision see the Local Government (Interim Provisions) Act 1984, s. 2.

susceptible to defeat and delay there. Delay seems to be imposed on an *ad hoc* basis for the simple reason that the House disagrees with some policy aspect underlying the legislation in question.

In the light of the peers' record over Conservative legislation since 1979 any left-wing rhetoric about the uniquely anti-left nature of the modern House of Lords will have a rather old-fashioned ring about it. Criticism from either the Labour or Conservative Parties that the House of Lords has thwarted the will of the Commons invites the retort that there is little point in retaining the co-ordinate legislative powers of the House of Lords unless it uses them from time to time. That, in its turn, invites a discussion of possible reform.

Assessment—and reform?

The House of Lords as presently constituted and as it currently works demonstrates a number of strengths. It has adequate time to fulfil its functions so that it may do so thoroughly and in a manner which allows back-benchers to take a full part in all aspects of the House's work. That partly accounts for the usefulness of the House of Lords as a worthwhile legislative chamber: uncontroversial government Bills are introduced there (so reducing the pressure on time in the Commons); helpful amendments to Commons' Bills are made; back-bench peers may introduce Bills without let or hindrance (and a few become law each year); and the House is showing a certain impartial rigour towards the legislation of both parties. It is also a useful deliberative chamber, as it should be, given the expertise available in it. And undramatic but necessary committee work is done there as a complement to that achieved in the Commons. The House of Lords has also paved the way for the televising of both Houses. Yet it could be argued that the House is weakened in three fundamental respects: it is anomalous, unrepresentative, and on an average day Conservative-led. No modern state seeking to create a new legislature would devise anything remotely resembling a House most of whose members may sit on the basis of heredity while the rest of its members exist on the unrestricted patronage of the head of government. Heredity does occasionally provide young peers, and once even a Communist marquess, but such events are rather exceptional. The House is unrepresentative (or representative of only certain sections of society); former Ministers and ex-MPs make up a sizeable proportion of the working House. And it cannot be right in principle that one party is permanently in a stronger position in the House of Lords than any other—even if that does not guarantee the sacrosanctity of all Conservative legislation in that House.

There is, however, no political consensus over possible reform. The Conservative government has no plans to alter the House of Lords in any way.[138] The Labour Party has been committed since 1977 to the abolition of the House of Lords and to the transfer of necessary functions to the House of Commons.[139] The Liberal Party and the Social Democratic Party have favoured a House based on a mixture of half its members being directly elected by proportional representation and half being nominated by the Sovereign on the advice of the Prime Minister and a standing commission of senior Privy Councillors.[140] Over the years the parties have thus scattered away from the virtual all-party agreement on reform which had been achieved in 1968.[141] That might well have been the last opportunity for reform based on consensus;[142] with the benefit of hindsight it might have been better had the Labour government been

---

[138] A party committee under Lord Home recommended in 1978 reform based on 268 members elected by proportional representation and 134 members nominated by the Sovereign on the Prime Minister's advice tendered after consulting all the party Leaders, but the Leader of the Conservative Party has not accepted that plan: see 'The House of Lords: The Report of the Conservative Review Committee' (1978).

[139] The 1977 Labour Party conference adopted that position by an overwhelming vote; Mr Callaghan managed to exclude it from the party's 1979 general election manifesto, but it was in the 1983 (though not in the 1987) manifesto.

[140] *Towards a New Constitutional Settlement* (1983); the SDP/Liberal Alliance 1987 manifesto, *Britain United*. On House of Lords reform generally, see Hadfield, op. cit., pp. 347–51. The House of Lords recently asked a committee of peers to consider the working of the House, and it concluded that there was no case for change: see H.L. 9 (1987–8).

[141] The Labour government's proposals followed very closely those already agreed at the all-party talks: see Harold Wilson, *The Labour Government 1964–1970: A Personal Record* (1971), p. 608. Briefly, the White Paper 'House of Lords Reform', Cmnd. 3799 (1968) envisaged a two-tier House of voting and non-voting peers. Voting peers (numbering about 250) would have been those life peers and hereditary peers of first creation who were prepared to attend at least 30 per cent of all sittings; all other peers would (unless some of them received life peerages, as was planned) have become non-voting peers who could, however, speak in the House. Succession to a peerage in future would no longer have led to membership at all. The Lords Spiritual would have been progressively reduced to 16; Lords of Appeal in Ordinary would have continued as before. After each general election at which the government changed enough new life peers would have been created to give the new government a 10 per cent majority over the opposition peers (but not over the opposition and cross-bench peers together). The delaying power would have been halved to 6 months; the veto over subordinate legislation would have become a delaying power.

[142] The 1968 White Paper was approved in both Houses by large, cross-party majorities and the Parliament (No. 2.) Bill received its second reading in the Commons by 285 to 135: see 773 H.C. Deb. 1305–434 (20 November 1968); 297 H.L. Deb. 641–1094 (21 November 1968); 777 H.C. Deb. 43–172 (3 February 1969). Backbenchers on both sides opposed the Bill and talked at inordinate length, and the government subsequently withdrew the Bill so as to make time for urgent industrial relations legislation (which, ironically, was never introduced).

rather less punctilious in refusing to introduce a guillotine to ease the passing of the Parliament (No. 2) Bill on the ground that major constitutional Bills should not be guillotined.[143] Another major brake on any movement towards reform is the attitude of the House of Commons as a whole, ever jealous of its position at the centre of the political and legislative process and so never naturally enthusiastic about proposals which might transform the other House into a true rival.

In the last chapter it was argued that there is a case for establishing a Royal Commission on the electoral system through which the House of Commons is selected, even though there is no all-party consensus for such a move. Now I suggest that a similar lack of consensus over any reform of the House of Lords should, broadly, result in that House remaining as it is. That discrepancy is explained on three grounds. First, the importance of the House of Lords must not be exaggerated. It is much the less powerful and the less significant House: it accomplishes sound work, but the formation and continuance of governments do not turn on it in any way—any vote of no confidence carried there is ignored:[144] it is just not in the same rank of importance in the constitution as the Commons. Secondly, the legitimate complaint that the House of Lords caused trouble for Liberal, and later for Labour, legislation, but resembled a rubber-stamp for Conservative measures, has to a significant extent been rectified. No one can foresee what the Lords might do to the legislation of a future non-Conservative government, and the complaint might revive; but experience since 1970 has been that the Lords has used its statutory powers over legislation regardless of which party has been in office, use which is objectionable only to those who believe in a unicameral legislature. And the possible efficiency of a unicameral Parliament based on the Commons may be strongly doubted: that House has shown itself to be slow in reforming its procedures so as to be either efficient or a real check on the government; it would be hard to see how a single chamber could adequately scrutinize legislation, particularly when it had to be guillotined, and no other parliamentary

---

[143] However, James Callaghan, who, as Home Secretary, was in charge of the Bill, has written in his memoirs that 'Our own Labour Members were unenthusiastic [about the Bill] and this may explain the Prime Minister's reluctance to agree to a guillotine motion': *Time and Chance* (1987), p. 503. The Labour Party had changed its attitude towards guillotining constitutional measures by the time of the Scottish and Welsh devolution Bills, and there is now no certain convention that constitutional Bills will not be guillotined.

[144] For example, the House of Lords passed a vote of no confidence in the Labour government's defence policy in 1967, of which the government took no notice: 285 H.L. Deb. 692–830 (25 July 1967).

democracy which has to legislate for a large population has opted for a single chamber. Thirdly, the worst incidents of the unreformed House of Lords have already been removed by statute. Thus the House of Commons is the dominant House generally in relation to legislation, and is omnipotent over financial legislation; heredity has not been the sole basis for membership of the House of Lords since 1958, and indeed a life peerage has been practically the only route into the House for new peers since 1964; peers succeeding to hereditary peerages may disclaim them; hereditary peeresses and Scottish peers have not been discriminated against since 1963. Accordingly, the only small change which is mooted here is based on the only existing all-party practice. All the party Leaders put names to the Prime Minister of people who will serve as working peers, and that process in my view could usefully be formalized and extended. The party Leaders could (perhaps privately) acknowledge that all the parties represented in the Commons have a legitimate expectation of representation in the House of Lords;[145] that active party strengths in the House of Lords, and votes and seats won at the previous general election, should be taken into consideration in drawing up lists of working peers; that all the nations and regions of the United Kingdom should be fully represented, and that as many more women as possible should be nominated. The party Leaders could meet together on Privy Councillor terms to discuss the annual working peer lists, although the responsibility of recommending peerages to the Sovereign would formally remain with the Prime Minister.

Whatever may be in future party manifestos, it is difficult to foresee House of Lords reform or abolition being considered so important to a future government as to justify the parliamentary time and trouble involved in achieving it against the wishes of the opposition parties. Radical reform of that House may be as far off as such reform of the House of Commons.

[145] Perhaps subject to some minimum number of MPs to qualify.

11

The Constitutional Position of the Judges

In this chapter the constitutional position of all ranks of the judiciary will be explained. The rights and powers of judges, Ministers, and Parliament in relation to each other are not ideal. The extensive powers of two Ministers over the judiciary are not sufficiently understood, nor are they entirely desirable: in particular, the personal role of the Lord Chancellor is crucial in the appointment, promotion, and removal of judges. Governments place judges firmly into political questions by using them in extra-judicial inquiries more than is really necessary; conversely, governments have acquiesced in over-restrictive parliamentary rules which prevent MPs from adequately discussing the administration of justice and other judicial matters, and the present government has ensured that no select committee on the Lord Chancellor's Department be set up. Behind most of these issues is the question whether there should be reform of the office of Lord Chancellor, possibly involving the creation of a new Department of Justice.

The formal statutory framework within which members of the judiciary are appointed will be considered first, progressing from the bottom of the judicial hierarchy (lay magistrates) to the top (Lords of Appeal in Ordinary). To do this requires the presentation of a far from exciting catalogue, but this is unavoidable. Then the Lord Chancellor's appointment policies and practices will be examined: these have become clearer since the publication of his pamphlet *Judicial Appointments*.[1]

Appointment, pay, and promotion

Lay magistrates[2] are appointed by the Lord Chancellor[3] by instrument on

---

[1] Lord Chancellor's Department (1986). Some of the matters in this chapter which refer to the lower judiciary are considered more fully in my 'The Appointment and Removal of the Lower Judiciary' (1986) 15 *Anglo-American Law Review* 173. I am grateful to the Lord Chancellor's Department for some of the statistical information in this chapter.

[2] See generally Sir Thomas Skyrme, *The Changing Image of the Magistracy* (2nd edn., 1983); E. Burney, *J.P.: Magistrate, Court and Community* (1979).

[3] Lay magistrates are appointed to commissions in Greater Manchester, Merseyside, and Lancashire by the Chancellor of the Duchy of Lancaster: Justices of the Peace Act 1979, s. 68 (hereafter the '1979 Act').

behalf and in the name of the Queen.[4] In considering appointments the Lord Chancellor may act on the recommendation of the crucially important local advisory committees,[5] of which there are about a hundred. Their membership is invariably made up of serving magistrates, although that membership is usually secret;[6] the name and address of the secretary of each committee is, however, published[7] so that either candidates can be recommended or individuals may nominate themselves. The Lord Chancellor requires that candidates 'should be personally suitable in character, integrity and understanding . . . and . . . should be generally recognized as such by those among whom they live and work'.[8] Candidates' political views are officially neither a qualification nor a disqualification, but at least since the term of office of Lord Gardiner LC the Lord Chancellor has wanted to know candidates' political affiliations so as to seek to avoid any bench becoming overweighted in favour of any one party.[9] Some 27,500 lay magistrates are currently on the active list. By disposing of some ninety-seven per cent of all criminal cases they obviously make an outstanding numerical contribution to the administration of criminal justice.

Acting stipendiary magistrates are appointed by the Lord Chancellor when it appears to him that it is necessary to do so to avoid delays in the administration of justice in any area where a full-time stipendiary magistrate could be appointed.[10] Appointments are made for a period which the Lord Chancellor thinks fit, up to three months at a time.[11] The minimum qualification is to be a barrister or solicitor of seven years' standing.[12] Anyone wishing to be considered for appointment must apply to the Lord Chancellor's Department. After training, an acting stipendiary will be called on to sit regularly. There are at present forty acting metropolitan stipendiaries and fifty acting provincial stipendiaries. Next, Assistant Recorders are appointed by the Lord Chancellor when it appears to him that it is expedient as a temporary measure

4 1979 Act, s. 6(1), as amended by the Administration of Justice Act 1982, s. 65.

5 On which see B. Cooke (1984) *Magistrate* 69.

6 Committees which have published their memberships include those for Inner London, Nottingham, and Essex.

7 He is usually the Clerk to the Justices.

8 *The Appointment and Duties of Justices of the Peace in England and Wales* (Lord Chancellor's Department).

9 See P. F. Smith and S. H. Bailey, *The Modern English Legal System* (1984), pp. 134–6; P. Richards [1961] *Public Law* 134.

10 1979 Act, ss. 15 (provincial), 34 (metropolitan).

11 Ibid., ss. 15(1)(a), 34(1).

12 Ibid., s. 13.

to facilitate business in the Crown Court or a county court.[13] In practice Assistant Recorders are always in office in main centres and, as will be seen, are regarded as apprentices for Recorderships and Circuit judgeships: the 'temporary' nature of the office has been overtaken by the exigencies of crime and the Lord Chancellor's appointment policy. The appointment, of barristers or solicitors of at least ten years' standing, is made during such a period or on such occasions as the Lord Chancellor thinks fit. Barristers (of whom there are some 5,000) need not apply for appointment because of the annual review conducted in the Lord Chancellor's Department of all eligible members of the profession aged under 50,[14] but because of the size of the solicitors' profession (some 48,000 with practising certificates) no equivalent review is feasible, and applications are necessary from them. There are at any one time some 450 Assistant Recorders in office. On the next rung up are Recorders, who are part-time judges of the Crown Court, appointed by the Queen on the Lord Chancellor's recommendation, with the same minimum qualification as Assistant Recorders.[15] Appointment is for a stated term and the frequency and duration of the occasions on which they will be expected to sit will be specified in each appointment.[16] The term is usually for three years, and is renewable; the commitment is to sit for at least twenty days a year with one continual period of ten days.[17] Some 550 Recorders are currently in post.[18] The Lord Chancellor's policy since 1981 has been to appoint to a Recordership only someone who has first proved himself as an Assistant Recorder.[19]

Barristers of ten years' standing, or Recorders who have held office for at least three years, are eligible to be appointed Circuit judges by the Queen on the Lord Chancellor's recommendation.[20] A solicitor Recorder would thus be at least thirteen years from admission before he could qualify.[21] There are at present some 390 Circuit judges. The Lord Chancellor will, again, only recommend those who have first proved

[13] Courts Act 1971, s. 24, as replaced by the Supreme Court Act 1981, s. 146.

[14] *Judicial Appointments*, p. 11.

[15] Courts Act 1971, s. 21(2).

[16] Ibid., s. 21(3).

[17] *Judicial Appointments*, p. 13; Lord Chancellor's statement on the terms and conditions of service of Recorders (1971) 68 *Law Society Gazette* 303.

[18] Of whom over 30 are solicitor Recorders.

[19] *Judicial Appointments*, p. 13.

[20] Courts Act 1971, s. 16, as amended by the Administration of Justice Act 1977, s. 12.

[21] There are some 30 solicitor Circuit judges.

themselves as Assistant Recorders and Recorders. Candidates are expected to apply, although potential candidates are often approached first. Candidates are interviewed in the Lord Chancellor's Department and by the Circuit Administrator of the Circuit on which they would like to sit. The last junior judicial officers to be mentioned, stipendiary magistrates, are appointed from barristers and solicitors of at least seven years' standing.[22] Up to forty stipendiaries may be appointed outside London, and up to sixty in Inner London and the City at any one time;[23] there are fourteen provincial stipendiaries and forty-nine metropolitan stipendiaries in post. A stipendiary may do anything which two lay justices may lawfully do.[24] The Lord Chancellor will only make recommendations from those who have served satisfactorily as acting stipendiary magistrates over at least two or three years.[25] In London, the Chief Metropolitan Magistrate[26] prepares a short list from acting metropolitan stipendiaries, and candidates are interviewed by a board which includes the Chief Metropolitan Magistrate; the board advises the Lord Chancellor. In the provinces the selection procedure is similar (although there is no equivalent of Chief Magistrate). Stipendiaries may serve as Recorders, and some have gone on to become Circuit judges.

For the most part High Court judges are appointed from the ranks of leading Queen's Counsel.[27] It is therefore worth noting the arrangements which govern how barristers take silk. The Lord Chancellor recommends to the Queen the names of practising barristers[28] of sufficient standing (which is usually ten years or more) whom the Lord Chancellor is satisfied have reached an appropriate level of professional distinction. Barristers must apply for consideration, according to a fixed annual timetable. The Lord Chancellor's Department consults the

[22] 1979 Act, ss. 13 (for stipendiaries outside the Inner London and City of London areas), 31 (metropolitan stipendiaries).

[23] Ibid., ss. 13(4), 31(1). A larger number may be specified by Order in Council: none has been.

[24] Ibid., ss. 16(3),(4), 33.

[25] *Judicial Appointments*, pp. 15–16.

[26] One of the metropolitan stipendiaries is designated Chief Metropolitan Magistrate by the Lord Chancellor: 1979 Act, s. 31(3).

[27] See generally *Judicial Appointments*, pp. 7–8; Report of the Royal Commission on Legal Services, Cmnd. 7648 (1979), i. 465–71. Treasury Counsel, who are normally elevated to the High Court bench after so serving, do not usually take silk.

[28] Employed barristers who have made a significant contribution to the public life of the profession are also considered, and honorary silk is also granted to barristers who have given distinguished service to the law through public service or in the academic world.

Leaders of Circuits, Presiding Judges,[29] and other judges about applicants; the Lord Chancellor consults the Law Officers and the four heads
of divisions—that is, the Lord Chief Justice, the Master of the Rolls, the
President of the Family Division, and the Vice-Chancellor—before finally
deciding. Only between twenty and thirty per cent of applicants are
successful. The Lord Chancellor considers that silk should represent a
working rank at the Bar, and he accordingly expects QCs to practice for
at least two years before he will consider them for full-time judicial
appointment (which is hardly an intolerable delay for the ambitious).
High Court judges are appointed by the Queen on the Lord Chancellor's
advice from barristers of at least ten years' standing,[30] up to a current
maximum of eighty-five.[31] Lords Justice of Appeal are appointed by the
Queen on the Prime Minister's recommendation from the ranks of
barristers of at least fifteen years' standing, or from the High Court
bench.[32] At present up to twenty-eight Lords Justices may hold office.[33]
The four heads of divisions may be appointed on the Prime Minister's
advice from the judges of the Court of Appeal or the High Court or
from barristers of at least fifteen years' standing.[34] All these members of
the High Court and of the Court of Appeal are conveniently referred to
collectively as judges of the Supreme Court.[35]

Lords of Appeal in Ordinary (who do not form part of the Supreme
Court[36]) are appointed on the Prime Minister's advice by the Queen
from those who have held for at least two years high judicial office as

[29] Two High Court judges are appointed by the Lord Chancellor as Presiding Judges in each
Circuit (there are three in the South Eastern Circuit). They perform a judicial role parallel to the
administrative role assigned to the Circuit Administrators, acting with them to see that cases are
assigned efficiently according to the expertise available. For details, see E. C. Friesen and
I. R. Scott, *English Criminal Justice* (1977), p. 124.

[30] Supreme Court Act 1981, s. 10(2), (3).

[31] Ibid., s. 4(1)(e), 4(4), (5). Maximum Number of Judges Order 1987, S.I. 1987 No. 2059.

[32] Ibid., s. 10(2), (3).

[33] Ibid., s. 2(1), (4), (5). That maximum was set by the Maximum Number of Judges Order
1987, S.I. 1987 No. 2059.

[34] Ibid., s. 10(1), (3).

[35] The Supreme Court Act 1981, s. 1(1) provides that 'The Supreme Court of England and
Wales shall consist of the Court of Appeal, the High Court and the Crown Court . . .'. Although
Circuit judges, Assistant Recorders, and Recorders sit in the Crown Court, they are not judges of
the Supreme Court: ibid., ss. 10 to 13.

[36] The judicial House of Lords is not within the definition of the Supreme Court given in the
1981 Act. The Liberal government's Supreme Court of Judicature Act 1873 would have abolished
the judicial functions of the House of Lords, but Gladstone's government fell and the new
Conservative government procured fresh legislation (ultimately the Appellate Jurisdiction Act
1876) to preserve that jurisdiction. Perhaps by an oversight, however, the House of Lords was not
incorporated into the Supreme Court. Neither the consolidating legislation of 1925 nor the 1981
Act sought to correct the anomaly.

Lord Chancellor, judge of the Supreme Court or the Court of Session or of the Supreme Court of Judicature of Northern Ireland, or from those who have practised for fifteen years or more as a barrister in England or Northern Ireland or as an advocate in Scotland.[37] Up to eleven may hold office at any time.[38]

It is striking from this survey that the entire judiciary owes its appointment to one, and occasionally two, politicians, with the danger to judicial integrity which that dependency could entail. Anyone wishing to become a judge—however low and however high—must receive the approval of the Lord Chancellor. Even those aspiring to the highest judicial offices, to which appointment is made on the advice of the Prime Minister rather than the Lord Chancellor, must in practice win the Lord Chancellor's support, because he is always consulted by the Prime Minister about these appointments;[39] and it would be inconceivable nowadays that the Prime Minister would make a recommendation if the Lord Chancellor were opposed to it. There have, it is true, been two recorded cases this century in which Prime Ministers have been prepared to stand by the letter of their conventional authority to recommend a judicial appointment. In 1923 Baldwin insisted that a former Law Officer, Sir Ernest Pollock, be made Master of the Rolls rather than Bankes LJ whom Lord Cave LC preferred;[40] and in 1951 Churchill assured Walter Monckton that, if he would agree to become Minister of Labour, Churchill would appoint him Lord Chief Justice on the next vacancy: Monckton joined the Cabinet, but never became Lord Chief Justice.[41] These are very isolated examples, and today even a Prime Minister who happened to be a qualified lawyer[42] would be unlikely to do other than endorse the Lord Chancellor's knowledgeable view, save in a most unusual case.

Obviously, the longer a Prime Minister and Lord Chancellor hold office the more judicial vacancies will occur and the more appointments

[37] Appellate Jurisdiction Act 1876, ss. 6, 25.

[38] Administration of Justice Act 1968, s. 1. Only 10 have actually held office at once; the statutory maximum may be increased by Order in Council: ibid. For other peers who may sit as Law Lords see chapter 10.

[39] Lord Hailsham of St Marylebone LC made this clear in his speech to the Common Law Bar Association, 3 July 1985. He has also written in his autobiography that '. . . in practice the Lord Chancellor greatly influences [the Prime Minister's] decision': *The Door Wherein I Went* (1975), p. 254.

[40] See R. F. V. Heuston, *Lives of the Lord Chancellors 1885 to 1940* (1964), p. 428.

[41] Lord Simon of Glaisdale, book review (1965) 81 *Law Quarterly Review* 289 at 295. The incumbent, Lord Goddard, outlasted Churchill in office by 3 years.

[42] Such as Attlee or Mrs Thatcher.

will have to be made to fill them. So the present Prime Minister and her first Lord Chancellor Lord Hailsham of St Marylebone between them effectively appointed all the current Lords of Appeal in Ordinary save one,[43] all the Lords Justices of Appeal, and well over half the High Court judges. Such ministerial patronage causes legitimate concern over the precise role of politicians in the appointing process, and in order to remove unnecessary secrecy surrounding the appointment of judges Lord Hailsham LC arranged the publication of *Judicial Appointments* in 1986. Although it is very informative about the machinery of junior appointments it is not at all detailed in its exposition concerning senior appointments. According to that publication the Lord Chancellor's policy is to appoint to every judicial post the person who appears to him to be best qualified to fill it, regardless of party, sex, religion, or ethnic orgin. Professional ability, experience, standing, and integrity are the criteria, together with good health and the absence of any personal unsuitability.[44] The Lord Chancellor is assisted within his Department by a Judicial Appointments Group, headed by a Deputy Secretary. Barristers and solicitors of ten years' standing are welcome to contact the Deputy Secretary for 'career advice'.[45] In considering appointments the Lord Chancellor follows two guiding principles.[46] First, no one person's view of a candidate (whether positive or negative) is to be regarded as decisive in itself, however authoritative or eminent the person giving it. Rather, the Lord Chancellor's officials seek an independent view from a spread of observers and colleagues in a position to assess a candidate's work and personality, and great weight is attached to that view. Secondly, as far as possible candidates will only be appointed to permanent, full-time, judicial posts after they have proved themselves in an associated, part-time capacity. This principle has been applied since 1981 to all appointments up to that of Circuit judge; the Lord Chancellor intends to extend it progressively to all other appointments made on his recommendation, including High Court judgeships; it will eventually therefore (as will be seen later) apply to all senior appointments, because in practice all appointments to the Court of Appeal and to the judicial House of Lords are made from the ranks of senior judges. There is accordingly a developing career progression for successful candidates, from acting stipendiary magistrate to stipendiary magistrate, and from

[43] Lord Keith of Kinkel, appointed in 1977.
[44] *Judicial Appointments*, p. (iv).
[45] Ibid., p. 2.
[46] Ibid., p. 3.

Assistant Recorder to Recorder to Circuit judge, and, in time, to High Court judge and above. To apply these principles the Deputy Secretary undertakes continuous consultations with judges and senior members of the profession. He reviews annually appointments on the six Circuits, discussing matters with the Presiding Judges.

All that *Judicial Appointments* says about recommendations for High Court judgeships[47] is that such appointments are made from the most able and eminent members of the Bar (and usually from leading silks), and that Circuit judges may be promoted to them. The only amplification on procedure which is added is that applications are not appropriate, and that the Lord Chancellor consults the heads of division about potential appointments.[48] It has been suggested that the Lord Chancellor has only a very small group to choose from, namely experienced silks aged between 45 and 60, so that each short list could be as small as six.[49]

It is generally accepted that, although the appointment process depends on politicians' choices, party political considerations have not affected senior judicial appointments since at least 1945.[50] That proposition must be qualified, first because in a marginal case any known political views of rival candidates might just tip the choice, and secondly because very occasionally an appointment not wholly devoid of political considerations may still be made, such as the promotion of Sir John Donaldson to be Master of the Rolls in 1982, a step understood to have been warmly recommended by Mrs Thatcher.[51] Certainly past political activity even of an extremist kind is not necessarily a bar to preferment: Frederick Lawton, for example, had been a candidate for the British Fascist Party in 1936 but he was later appointed to the High Court and subsequently to the Court of Appeal. A slightly different question is the extent to which politicians appoint active politicians to be judges. From

---

[47] Ibid., pp. 6, 17. There is no information in it about appointments to the Court of Appeal or to the House of Lords.

[48] For personal factors which might prevent appointment as a High Court judge, see Shimon Shetreet, *Judges on Trial* (1976), pp. 61–79. He lists as bars to preferment (among other things) 'disgraceful' conduct in the background to divorce; conviction of a crime involving moral turpitude; serious breach of professional etiquette; bankruptcy; and inappropriate personal behaviour such as adultery. Some of those bars may, perhaps, be more insuperable than others.

[49] See J. A. G. Griffith, *The Politics of the Judiciary* (3rd ed., 1985), p. 24—an excellent work.

[50] Politics still count in the appointment of many lay magistrates, both because of the need to try to achieve politically balanced benches and because in some areas the parties put up slates of candidates.

[51] He had been a Conservative councillor for a time and President of the controversial National Industrial Relations Court throughout its $2\frac{1}{2}$ year life. He remained in the High Court under the 1974–9 Labour government, even though promotion was generally thought to be due; he was appointed to the Court of Appeal in 1979 on Mrs Thatcher's recommendation.

1873 to 1945 only four Attorneys-General from a total of twenty-three holders of that office failed to go on to hold high judicial office, and in the same period over half the Solicitors-General were similarly promoted.[52] But since 1945 the picture has been very different. Only two Solicitors-General out of sixteen have been promoted to the High Court;[53] only four Attorneys-General, from a total of eleven, have received judicial appointments—all four as Lord Chancellor.[54] Writing in 1972, Henry Cecil recorded that of 117 judges then in office, only ten had been MPs and only a further five had been parliamentary candidates.[55] There is, of course, no reason why a Law Officer or a lawyer-MP should not become a judge—Lord Hailsham regretted that he was unable to appoint any[56]—provided obviously that that is not done as a reward for political services rendered; it is natural, too, that the Lord Chancellor should previously have been Attorney-General.

Whether any changes should be made in the system of judicial appointments will be considered at the end of this chapter.

The salaries paid to full-time judges reflect a number of desirable precepts. They are sufficiently high that potential judges would not face an unacceptable cut in income if they were to accept appointment; the rates of salaries enhance the dignity of judicial offices, and reflect the promotional stages between various ranks; judicial salaries are not at even a theoretical risk of regular review by Parliament, and the amounts paid are increased periodically so as to keep pace with other professional incomes and with inflation. Judicial salaries are now substantial.[57] Thus,

---

[52] See Smith and Bailey, op. cit., pp. 162–3.

[53] Sir Lynn Ungoed-Thomas (Solicitor-General 1951; High Court judge 1962–72); Sir Jocelyn Simon (Solicitor-General 1959–62; President, Probate, Divorce and Admiralty Division 1962–72; Lord of Appeal in Ordinary 1971–7).

[54] Sir William Jowitt (Attorney-General from 1929–32; Lord Chancellor 1945–51); Sir David Maxwell-Fyfe (Attorney-General 1945; Lord Chancellor 1954–62 as Lord Kilmuir); Sir Reginald Manningham-Buller (Attorney-General 1954–62; Lord Chancellor 1962–4 as Lord Dilhorne); Sir Michael Havers (Attorney-General 1979–87; Lord Chancellor 1987). The Lord Chancellor is head of the judiciary as President of the Supreme Court (Supreme Court Act 1981, s. 1(2)), ex officio member of the Appellate Committee (Appellate Jurisdiction Act 1876, s. 5(1)), of the Court of Appeal (1981 Act, s. 2(2)(a)), and of the High Court (1981 Act, s. 4(1)(a)).

[55] The English Judge (2nd edn., 1972), p. 19.

[56] The Door Wherein I Went, p. 256. Lord Hailsham had himself been a career politician (and never a Law Officer), and had contested the Conservative Party Leadership in 1963 before becoming Lord Chancellor for the first time in 1970.

[57] The following are the salaries currently payable.

Office	Annual salary
Lord of Appeal in Ordinary	74,500
Lord Justice of Appeal	71,750

for instance, a Circuit judge receives £43,500 a year, a High Court judge £65,000, and a Lord of Appeal in Ordinary £74,500. While top silks may well earn considerably more than a High Court judge's salary, appointment to the bench brings other advantages which may compensate for an immediate drop in income, such as somewhat less arduous work, a very agreeable life in judge's lodgings on circuit, and a pension, and, as a judge is promoted, so his salary rises. Judicial salaries are determined by the Lord Chancellor with the consent of the Minister for the Civil Service; they may be increased, but not reduced, in the same way;[58] Parliament has no say in the matter. The rates are recommended by the Top Salaries Review Body, which takes into account earnings at the Bar as well as salaries payable to Permanent Under-Secretaries of State as relevant, though not determinant, factors. The government may or may not accept proposed increases, but the existence of the Body is a useful source of independent evidence about appropriate salaries. Salaries of Circuit judges, of judges of the Supreme Court, and of Lords of Appeal in Ordinary form part of Consolidated Fund Services,[59] and as such are paid without annual authorization; Parliament is accordingly denied any regular opportunity to debate either the judiciary or the administration of justice, the latter inability being less obviously desirable. Whether these provisions are themselves a barrier to corruption may be strongly doubted. No evidence of attempts to corrupt judges has existed for a very long time, and judges would be immune to any such attempts for professional and personal reasons, not because they are well paid. If a person were susceptible to corruption would he not be so almost regardless of his income?

As is plain from the Lord Chancellor's appointment policy, there is now a clear judicial promotion system, at the lower end from Assistant Recorder to Recorder to Circuit judge, and from Recorder or Circuit judge to High Court judge and beyond. Even before 1981 promotions

continued

Office	Annual salary
Lord Chief Justice	74,500
Master of the Rolls	74,500
President, Family Division	71,750
Vice-Chancellor	71,750
High Court judge	65,000
Circuit judge	43,500
Stipendiary magistrate	33,500

[58] Administration of Justice Act 1973, s. 9(1)(*a*); Supreme Court Act 1981, s. 12(1), (3); Courts Act 1971, ss. 21(7), 24, as replaced by the Supreme Court Act 1981, s. 146.

[59] Supreme Court Act 1981, s. 12(5); Administration of Justice Act 1973, s. 9(5).

straight from the Bar to the Court of Appeal,[60] or from the Bar to the House of Lords,[61] or from the High Court to the Lords[62] were most infrequent: an orderly progression up the senior hierarchy was and remains the norm, and the Lord Chancellor's formally declared policy merely reflects that. Promotion carries numerous although not equally important advantages—an enhanced personal status; an increased salary; a knighthood for High Court judges; a Privy Councillorship for Lords Justices;[63] a life peerage for Lords of Appeal; and an end to travelling on circuit for those promoted to the Court of Appeal and to the House of Lords. Now such a promotions system in theory incorporates two risks: that judges might try where possible to frame their judgements so as to please the Lord Chancellor and Prime Minister who might in time promote them, and that those Ministers might promote to high office those whose judicial philosophy seems closest to their own politics. Neither risk is very real, for Prime Ministers and Lord Chancellors come and go[64] and a sudden change of party at a general election could make judicial trimming worthless if the trimmer had backed the wrong horse; there is also in any case little incentive for a Prime Minister or Lord Chancellor to promote (or indeed to appoint) 'loyal' judges, for there would be no guarantee that, once promoted (or appointed) they would deliver the goods,[65] and (as will be shown later) there is no way in practice of getting rid of them.

Judges and Parliament

In the last twenty years or so Members of Parliament have been prepared to criticize particular judges and particular verdicts and sentences much more than was previously the case. Such criticism heightens the need for clear principles and rules to govern the relationship between the judiciary and Parliament. That relationship ought to entail that, as a matter of comity, each respects the other as a vital branch of the constitution; that

[60] The only such promotions this century have been Lord Justices Slessor (1929), Scott (1935), Somervell (1946)—all of whom had been Law Officers—Duke (1918), and Greene (1935).

[61] There have been only two examples in the last 40 years: Lords Reid (1948) and Radcliffe (1949).

[62] Only Lords Uthwatt (1946) and Wilberforce (1964) in the last 40 years.

[63] This convention was created at the formation of the new Supreme Court of Judicature in 1873, the new Lords Justices opting for that honour rather than to receive a salary higher than that of High Court judges.

[64] Lord Chancellors tend to hold office longer than other Ministers, and indeed there has only been about the same number of Lord Chancellors as there has been Prime Ministers since 1900.

[65] As many Presidents of the United States could testify in relation to their nominees to the Supreme Court.

judges should be slow to attack the motives of Parliament in the way in which it has legislated; that MPs and peers[66] should not interfere in trials or litigation, and should be reluctant to attack individual judges (partly because there is no acceptable way in which they can defend themselves); and that senior judges who are in Parliament (the Lord Chancellor and the Lords of Appeal in Ordinary) must remain keenly aware of their awkward constitutional position. With some exceptions, those are the characteristics of the relationship today.

In the course of conducting cases judges may criticize not only the technical form of legislation but also the policy behind it, provided that this is done in a measured and responsible way. Melford Stevenson J.'s description in 1978 of the Sexual Offences Act 1967 as a 'buggers' charter' was disparaging and verging on vulgar abuse, and as such was clearly outside what is appropriate.[67] Judges may also be forthright in their criticism of ministerial conduct, but they must be careful to avoid taking sides in politically controversial issues and certainly must not be seen to favour one political party. In the main judges stay well within these precepts.

Parliamentary criticism of the judiciary is potentially a greater problem. The administration of justice is a proper topic for parliamentary discussion, for it underpins the democratic society to which Parliament is wholly committed; it also requires the annual disbursement of large amounts of taxpayers' money. Equally, judges are entitled to do their daily duty free from improper interference from MPs and peers. In order to reconcile these conflicting rights three rules have been developed in Parliament, concerning the permissible limits of ministerial comment and criticism, the manner in which MPs and peers may discuss the judiciary, and imposing restraints on parliamentary discussion of cases before the courts.[68]

Ministers are by convention expected to show due inhibition when commenting in Parliament[69] on judicial words and deeds: indeed, in practice they would probably voice little comment at all were it not for the temptation of parliamentary questions. So, when Lord Hewart LCJ published a number of politically controversial and highly paid articles in the *News of the World* his brethren and others objected both to the

---

[66] Peers have been traditionally much more restrained than MPs in criticizing the judiciary.

[67] See *The Times*, 6 July 1978. The Lord Chancellor 'strongly deprecated' his remarks.

[68] See generally Erskine May, *Parliamentary Practice* (20th edn., 1983), pp. 378, 429–30.

[69] It would never be proper for Ministers to criticize the judiciary outside Parliament. Although Mr Michael Foot when Lord President of the Council in 1977 criticized the historical role of the judges at a trade union rally, that was a wholly isolated incident.

subject-matter and to the vehicle which he had chosen to propagate his views; the Prime Minister was asked in the Commons about the propriety of what Hewart had done. Baldwin replied pithily and magisterially that 'it was obviously undesirable that His Majesty's judges should write for publication on matters of political controversy'.[70] Again, after Lord Kilmuir had been required to resign as Lord Chancellor in Macmillan's Cabinet purge in 1962 he immediately took up a business appointment; Macmillan was asked whether this was proper. The Prime Minister defended Kilmuir's decision, pointing out that he was not drawing his pension during that appointment.[71] More recently, Mrs Thatcher has been forthright in giving her views at Question Time on judicial decisions with which she disagreed. In 1982, for instance, she categorized as 'incomprehensible' a suspended sentence of imprisonment which had been passed for the rape of a very young girl, and informed the House of action which the Lord Chancellor had taken to ensure that in future only those judges who were authorized to take murder trials would be able to try rape cases.[72] On the other hand, when she was asked in 1987 whether a fine of £25,000 and a suspended sentence of imprisonment adequately fitted the crime of insider dealing her reply was much more circumspect, setting out the legal background of the offence but adding that she was 'not able to comment on any particular sentence'.[73] On a later point of order the Speaker explained that the Prime Minister could have so commented, adding that such questions were not unusual and that it was 'perfectly in order to criticize or to question a sentence; but it is not in order to criticize a judge. That has to be done by motion.'[74] Informed and responsible parliamentary comment on sentencing and other judgments and Ministers' reactions to it is, it is suggested, entirely desirable so that as in any other area Ministers and MPs can decide whether legislative or other changes should be made.

Back-bench MPs have more scope than Ministers to comment on judicial conduct. The general rule is that no reflection may be cast on a judge's conduct, or on judges generally, unless it is done during a debate based on a relevant substantive motion on which a vote could be taken.[75]

---

[70] 303 H.C. Deb. 799 (24 June 1935). Hewart's lame defence was that he had been writing not as Lord Chief Justice but as a peer, besides which (as he put it), 'I need the money': see Robert Jackson, *The Chief: The Biography of Gordon Hewart* (1959), pp. 327–8.

[71] 667 H.C. Deb. 999–1003 (20 November 1962).

[72] 34 H.C. Deb. 123–6 (14 December 1982), and, for the Speaker's later ruling that the Prime Minister had been in order, see 34 H.C. Deb. 285–6 (15 December 1982).

[73] 118 H.C. Deb. 622 (2 July 1987).

[74] 118 H.C. Deb. 641 (2 July 1987).

[75] Erskine May, op. cit., pp. 378, 431.

The scope of that rule was explored and slightly relaxed in 1973 against the background of the short-lived National Industrial Relations Court. The President of that Court, Sir John Donaldson,[76] defended one of its controversial decisions during (of all things) an after-dinner speech. Over 180 Labour MPs signed an early-day motion which called for his dismissal; the Shadow Cabinet, however, did not support it and the motion was never debated. But the House did subsequently debate an Opposition motion demanding the abolition of the National Industrial Relations Court, and in the course of it Opposition MPs wished to criticize its President. The Speaker ruled that MPs could argue, with reasons, during debate that a judge's decision was wrong, but that no reflection could be made on his character or his motives save on a motion which called for his dismissal.[77] As far as backbench MPs are concerned, therefore, the situation now is that (a) they need not show the same restraint in relation to the judiciary as is expected of Ministers, and (b) they may criticize a particular decision or sentence during debate although (c) they may only attack a judge's character or motives during a debate on a substantive motion calling for his dismissal. Now rule (c) blocks off almost any opportunity for sustained criticism and argument, because governments do not put down or find time for such motions (no doubt because they see no reason to do so), and Oppositions do not generally table, or provide their own time to debate, such motions either (perhaps attempting to be statesmanlike). Back-benchers must therefore use their ingenuity in two Commons' procedures to express their criticisms of judges. First, any MP may put down an early-day motion[78] which can set out in some detail his concerns about judicial conduct. In 1975, for example, one was tabled demanding the resignation of Judge Christmas Humphreys after he had imposed a suspended sentence of imprisonment in a rape case.[79] The government will not, of course, provide time for any such motion to be debated, and the Shadow Cabinet will not normally devote any part of an Opposition day to take it either.[80] But every

---

[76] He was seconded from the High Court for the duration of the appointment.

[77] 865 H.C. Deb. 1092 (4 December 1973).

[78] On which see chapter 9.

[79] The Times, 23 June 1975.

[80] The motion demanding the abolition of the National Industrial Relations Court in 1973 was exceptional. In 1925 the Labour Opposition moved a motion of censure on the government for 'initiating' a prosecution, for conspiracy to incite mutiny, against 12 Communist Party members, claiming that it was a violation of free speech. During the debate the trial judge, Swift J., was criticized by the Opposition for his offer of clemency if those accused without previous convictions would forswear the Communist Party: none did so, and each received 6 months' imprisonment. See 188 H.C. Deb. 2075–189 (1 December 1925).

Thursday the Leader of the House is asked by the Leader of the Opposition to state the business for the following week; the answer will already
have been conveyed through the usual channels, but the answer given in
the House of Commons allows the Leader of the Opposition to complain about the government's arrangement of business—and allows
those back-benchers who catch the Speaker's eye to do likewise. So an
MP may ask whether the Leader of the House is aware of the strength of
support for his early-day motion asking for the removal of Mr Justice X
or Judge Y, and why time cannot be found for it to be debated; in the
course of his question he may put as many debating points as he can
before the Speaker calls him to order.[81] In that way his criticism will have
been made; Ministers and MPs will have heard it; everyone can read
about it; no judge could be wholly impervious to it, particularly if a
substantial number of MPs have signed the motion. Secondly, although
the Table Office will not accept a question which reflects on a judge's
character,[82] an MP may be able to make his point during a supplementary
question. So a question which asks the Attorney-General when he next
expects to meet the Lord Chief Justice may be followed by a supplementary during which criticisms can be slipped in before the Speaker
calls the questioner to order. In that way the MP will have been able
(albeit briefly) to make his complaint about judicial conduct.[83]

The final restraint which limits the freedom of all MPs during any
business of the House in relation to the courts is the *sub judice* rule.[84] In
essence, this requires that matters awaiting the adjudication of a court
may not be commented on in parliamentary proceedings, the justification being that Parliament should not seek to influence judicial decisions.
More fully, the *sub judice* rule bars references to matters awaiting or
under adjudication (*a*) in all criminal courts from the moment a person is
charged to the time of verdict and any sentence or to the time any appeal
is decided, and (*b*) in civil courts from the time the case is set down for
trial until it is finally disposed of. In 1972 the House slackened the
rigidity of the rule in civil matters so that (subject to the Speaker's

---

[81] For an example of such a process, see 120 H.C. Deb. 494 (23 July 1987).

[82] Erskine May, op. cit., p. 344.

[83] So, for example, in 1980 a supplementary question of that type ran: 'Many people . . . fear
that [Lord Denning's recent judgment] will provide more explosive material in an already dangerous minefield. Lord Denning has made the law even more uncertain, and he is bringing the law,
and the rule of law, into disrepute. Will the Solicitor-General advise [him] that, although hon.
Members have respected Lord Denning in the past, the time has now come for him to retire?' The
Speaker then intervened to call the questioner to order. See 977 H.C. Deb. 930 (28 January 1980).

[84] On which see Erskine May, op. cit., pp. 429–31; 916 H.C. Deb. 882–4 (29 July 1976).

discretion) reference may be made to active civil cases if they relate to a ministerial decision which can only be challenged in court on the grounds of misdirection or bad faith, or if they concern issues of national importance (such as the economy, public order or the essentials of life). In exercising his discretion the Speaker will disallow references if he thinks that there is a real and substantial danger of prejudice to the proceedings.[85] Under this relaxation the thalidomide tradegy was debated even though proceedings had been started.[86] As the furore over Mr Peter Wright's memoirs *Spycatcher* has shown, the *sub judice* rule does not prevent the House from debating matters which are under adjudication in courts outside the United Kingdom.[87] Nor does it preclude Parliament from legislating on the subject-matter of current litigation, as was demonstrated by the passage of the War Damage Act 1965 during the Burmah Oil litigation.[88]

These arrangements in general represent a sensible balance between judicial freedom from wrongful parliamentary pressure and Parliament's rights in relation to the administration of justice.[89] The *sub judice* rule in relation to civil litigation and criminal appeals, however, could and should be further weakened or even abolished, for judges in such jury-less proceedings are unlikely to be improperly influenced in their duty by parliamentary remarks.[90] It is also highly regrettable that the House of Commons did not establish a select committee on the Lord Chancellor's Department or on the Law Officers' Department in 1979[91] so that, within carefully constructed lines designed to protect judges from interference in their day-to-day work, the Lord Chancellor, the Attorney-General, and their civil servants could be adequately accountable to Parliament.

The Lord Chancellor and the Lords of Appeal in Ordinary are both judges and legislators. The office of Lord Chancellor is a complete denial

---

[85] The House agreed to that relaxation at 839 H.C. Deb. 1589–627 (28 June 1972).

[86] For the debate, see 847 H.C. Deb. 432–510 (29 November 1972).

[87] See Speaker's ruling at 119 H.C. Deb. 704–5 (13 July 1987).

[88] *Burmah Oil Co.* v. *Lord Advocate* [1965] A.C. 75.

[89] The restraints which protect judges from criticism inside Parliament are reflected outside it in the rule that scurrilous abuse of a judge may be punished as contempt of court as scandalizing the court; but '[n]o criticism of a judge, however vigorous, can amount to contempt of court, provided it keeps within the limits of reasonable courtesy and good faith': per Salmon LJ in *R.* v. *Metropolitan Police Commissioner, ex p. Blackburn (No. 2.)* [1968] 2 Q.B. 150 at 155. See generally Clive Walker, 'Scandalizing in the Eighties' (1985) 101 *Law Quarterly Review* 359.

[90] The rule would have to remain in those civil actions which may still be tried by a jury, such as defamation.

[91] I refer to this in chapter 9.

of the doctrine of the separation of powers: because the incumbent has to speak as a Minister and act as Speaker of the House of Lords there is potential for difficulty when he sits in the Appellate Committee and when he speaks as head of the judiciary. This calls at the least for considerable tact and political sensitivity. The Lords of Appeal, too, must be careful when taking part in the parliamentary functions of the House: it has been said that their interventions have mainly been restricted to acting as resident legal experts helping with technical points,[92] but they have also spoken on a wide range of politically controversial topics, very occasionally using strong political argument.[93] In a better ordered system the office of Lord Chancellor would be reformed (and suggestions about that will be offered at the end of this chapter), and the judicial House of Lords would be constituted as a court quite separate from Parliament.[94]

Extra-judicial activities

Judges must know what is permissible in their out-of-court activities,[95] and the government must appreciate what it may properly ask judges to do in addition to their ordinary work. It is those questions which will be addressed now.

Just as it has been made difficult for MPs to develop critical arguments about the judiciary, so a cordon sanitaire has been constructed to keep the more senior judiciary from entering active party politics. Thus judges of the Supreme Court, Circuit judges, stipendiary magistrates, judges of the Court of Session, and sheriffs, and judges of the High Court and Court of Appeal in Northern Ireland, are disqualified from membership of the House of Commons.[96] On the other hand, part-time judges such as Assistant Recorders, Recorders, and lay magistrates may be MPs, and indeed there are usually several Recorders in the House. Moreover, the superior judiciary are required by custom to avoid partisan controversy: party political activity is unacceptable. So, Baldwin was of the view in 1929 that Hewart's membership of Lord Ullswater's Committee on

---

[92] See Louis Blom-Cooper and Gavin Drewry, *Final Appeal* (1972), chapter 10.

[93] For examples, see J. A. G. Griffith, op. cit., p. 47.

[94] Possibly involving a merger with the Judicial Committee of the Privy Council. See Blom-Cooper and Drewry, op. cit., pp. 411-3.

[95] For a full analysis of the personal behaviour required of judges, see Shetreet, op. cit., chapter 15.

[96] House of Commons Disqualification Act 1975, s. 1(1) and Schedule 1, Part I.

Electoral Reform was inconsistent with his office of Lord Chief Justice, and Hewart resigned from the Committee.[97] Again, in 1968 Lord Avonside, a judge of the Court of Session, was nominated by the Lord President of the Court of Session at the request of the Leader of the Opposition, Mr Edward Heath, to membership of a Conservative Party committee to investigate possible changes in the government of Scotland. The Lord Advocate (a member of the then Labour government) objected that this appointment broke the convention that judges should not involve themselves in party political matters; Lord Avonside resigned from the committee.[98] Such limitations do not affect the lower judiciary, and lay magistrates in particular are frequently active in local politics.

Obviously full-time judges may not continue to practise law. This is yet another conventional rule, except in the case of Circuit judges and metropolitan stipendiaries who are statute barred.[99] Solicitors and barristers who are Recorders must comply with a number of rules designed to avoid professional embarrassment which could arise by appearing as advocates in courts in which they sit;[100] barristers who sit as deputy High Court or deputy Circuit judges[101] must also avoid professional embarrassment. A practising barrister who is in addition a lay magistrate must avoid any clash between those roles; a practising solicitor-magistrate may not act in any case in an area where he sits judicially.[102]

Although there is no requirement of regular financial disclosures by full-time judges, they are expected not to hold directorships in, or to be trustees or advisers of, any public company, nor to carry on a business. Personal investment is entirely permissible,[103] subject of course to the usual rules of natural justice to prevent any clash of interest. Nor is there any requirement that, after leaving the bench, judges should seek permission before taking up other employment; such a rule is unnecessary because judges do not usually resign prematurely (rather than leaving the bench at retirement age). Fisher J. attracted criticism in 1970 when he

---

[97] Robert Jackson, op. cit., pp. 216-7.

[98] *The Times*, 26 July–6 August 1968. The Lord President perhaps acknowledged that he had made a mistake in the matter when, during this episode, he refused the request of the Scottish National Party to nominate any Scottish judge to serve on one of its committees.

[99] Courts Act 1971, s. 17(6); Justices of the Peace Act 1979, s. 31(4) (*b*).

[100] See Lord Chancellor's statement on the terms and conditions of service of Recorders (1971) 68 *Law Society's Gazette* 303 (as amended by Lord Chancellor's Department Circular of 29 November 1971).

[101] See Courts Act 1971, s. 24, as replaced by Supreme Court Act 1981, s. 146.

[102] Solicitors Act 1974, s. 38.

[103] Although if a judge were to go bankrupt he would have to resign.

resigned after only two years or so as a judge in order to join a merchant bank, and clearly there must never be any suggestion (as there was not in Sir Henry Fisher's case) that a senior judge might be considering what effects his judgments might have on his later employment prospects.[104] Giving public lectures and publishing books have not, in the main, caused any conflict of interest for serving judges, and there is no reason why fees and royalties should not be paid as long as the judge is not put under any obligation outside his contract to the payer. Scarman LJ's controversial Hamlyn Lectures in 1974[105] did not represent the first public voicing of legal opinions off the bench,[106] but since then no one could challenge the propriety of a judge offering his considered views on the law through a public lecture or book, within the bounds of discretion. Nor can there be any objection to a judge writing or editing practitioners' works: after all, two Lord Chancellors have done so.[107] Lord Hewart's *The New Despotism* (published in 1929) was, however, a vehement polemic unworthy of a judge; Judge James Pickles's *Straight from the Bench* (published in 1987) was the latest episode in a fraught relationship with the Lord Chancellor's Department, although it is difficult to argue that he was wrong to publish it. Whether a judge of the Supreme Court or a Lord of Appeal may properly publish articles or give press interviews or take part in television or radio programmes is entirely a matter for his or her personal discretion. They have taken part in broadcasts, such as BBC Radio 4's *Law in Action* programme; Lord Denning MR gave the BBC television Dimbleby Lecture in 1980, and some senior judges have given press interviews. The lower judiciary, however, have not been so free in such matters, partly because of the so-called Kilmuir Rules[108] and partly because the Lord Chancellor can support those rules with disciplinary sanctions. In 1955 the Director-

---

[104] Lord Hailsham LC said after Sir Henry Fisher's resignation that, when interviewing potential judges, he would tell them that they should treat a judicial career as a permanent one: see 312 H.L. Deb. 1314 (19 November 1970).

[105] Published as *English Law: The New Dimension* (1974).

[106] Lord Parker LCJ had doubted in 1967 whether judges could ever publicly discuss policy or possible legislation, orally or in writing, rather than speaking privately to the Lord Chief Justice who would convey those views to the government; but subsequently McKenna J., Lord Widgery LCJ, Sir Jocelyn Simon P., and Danckwerts LJ spoke in lectures or at dinners or gave press interviews about various legal issues before Scarman LJ's Hamlyn Lectures in 1974. Since 1974 judges have continued to lecture and publish.

[107] The 1st Viscount Hailsham LC and Lord Hailsham of St Marylebone LC edited the second and fourth editions of *Halsbury's Laws of England*; a retired Lord Chancellor, the Earl of Halsbury, received 10,000 guineas for editing the first edition: see R. F. V. Heuston, op. cit., p. 487. Megarry J. continued to co-produce editions of *The Law of Real Property* after his elevation.

[108] On which see A. W. Bradley [1986] *Public Law* 383–6.

General of the BBC wrote to Lord Kilmuir as Lord Chancellor with what now seems a wholly anodyne proposal that a judge (or judges) might appear in a planned series of radio talks about great judges of the past. Having consulted the heads of divisions the Lord Chancellor replied (in a letter immortalized as embodying the Kilmuir Rules) refusing permission. It was considered 'undesirable for members of the Judiciary to broadcast on the wireless or appear on television'—although as the Lord Chancellor acknowledged he had no disciplinary jurisdiction over senior judges. So, while the Lord Chancellor's Department may advise senior judges about these issues, it is for them to decide what to do in the end; but members of the lower judiciary give interviews or write in the press or appear on the broadcasting media at their peril. That Lord Hailsham LC took no disciplinary action for breach of the Kilmuir Rules over Judge Pickles's BBC broadcasts, articles, and press interviews in 1986 about (among other things) his dealings with the Lord Chancellor's Department was not for any want of power to dismiss him from office. Now appearing on television or radio can be a risky business for a judge, but common sense would no doubt steer him clear of a chat show and towards a serious programme; in any case, judges are very busy people who may not be tempted to write or broadcast, and the need for formal restrictions on them may be exaggerated: indeed, there is an argument, based on the simple premiss that all judges are highly responsible people, for the formal withdrawal of the Kilmuir Rules so that personal discretion alone would guide every judge's decision. Lord Mackay of Clashfern LC went some way towards undermining the Kilmuir Rules within days of becoming Lord Chancellor in 1987. At a press conference he said that judges should observe the spirit of the Rules, but that they should be trusted to decide for themselves whether to talk to the media—although they had to be careful not to say anything which might damage their authority or prejudice the performance of their judicial work.

After retirement a judge is not expected to return to the Bar, presumably because it might give him an unfair advantage over other practitioners;[109] there does not yet seem to be an established understanding in relation to retired solicitor-judges. Retired senior judges could go into politics, but only rarely do so;[110] they continue to be free to

---

[109] 'Several' High Court judges sought permission to return to the Bar in the early 1950s according to Winston Churchill, moving the second reading of the Judges' Remuneration Bill, 525 H.C. Deb. 1063 (23 March 1954). None did so.

[110] Lord Reading (Lord Chief Justice 1913–21) became Viceroy of India 1921–5 and Foreign Secretary briefly in 1931—a wholly exceptional case.

publish or broadcast as they see fit.[111] No retired Lord Chancellor has returned to the Bar; former occupants of the woolsack are under a moral obligation to serve as a Law Lord if asked,[112] and can (not without controversy) go into business (as did Lords Birkenhead and Kilmuir), provided that they do not draw their judicial pension.[113]

All governments ask senior judges to preside over some Royal Commissions, departmental committees, and committees of inquiry.[114] This is done for fairly obvious reasons. Judges are trained to ascertain facts in complex issues, to preside over inquiries, and are seen as impartial; setting up an inquiry may also delay the need for the government to take an awkward decision, and the judge as chairman may helpfully take the responsibility for an inconvenient result. The remits entrusted to the judiciary, and which they take to be part of their public duty to accept, have been extremely varied, from matters of social concern (such as the working of the Abortion Act 1967[115]), to issues involving entirely politi-

[111] Lord Denning has been a frequent visitor to broadcasting studios since his retirement as Master of the Rolls.

[112] Lord Dilhorne (Lord Chancellor 1962–4) insisted on being appointed a Lord of Appeal in Ordinary after his retirement (and on receiving the appropriate salary) before sitting regularly in the Appellate Committee; he did not draw his pension while a Lord of Appeal.

[113] See R. F. V. Heuston, op. cit., p. 398. The maximum annual judicial pension is the equivalent of one-half of a judge's last annual salary, index-linked. Some examples of the conditions on which such pensions become payable are set out below, derived from the Judicial Pensions Act 1981, ss. 2, 5, 7; a lower rate of pension is payable after shorter periods of service.

Judge		Conditions
Lord of Appeal in Ordinary/Judge of Supreme Court	or or	(a) at age 70 (b) after 15 years' service (c) on permanent disablement
Circuit judge	or or	(a) at age 65 (b) after 15 years' service (c) on permanent disablement
Stipendiary magistrate	or or	(a) at age 65 (b) after 20 years' service (c) on permanent disablement

[114] On which see D. G. T. Williams, *Not in the Public Interest* (1965), pp. 188–91; G. Zellick [1971] Public Law 1; T. J. Cartwright, *Royal Commissions and Departmental Committees in Britain* (1975); G. Rhodes, *Committees of Inquiry* (1975); J. A. G. Griffith, op. cit., chapter 2. For a list of such investigations since 1900 in which judicial chairmen can be noted, see David Butler and Gareth Butler, *British Political Facts 1900–1985* (6th edn., 1986), chapter 7.

[115] Chairman: Lane J.; Cmnd. 5579 (1974).

cal choices (like the proper levels of police pay[116]), and to highly controversial matters (including the legal procedures to deal with terrorists[117]
and the events of 'Bloody Sunday' in Northern Ireland[118]). There are
two clear drawbacks in using judges in these ways. First, in a controversial inquiry the judge may be criticized by the losing side for producing a
whitewash or a wrongheaded report, the result of which is to drag him
into further disputes. In any inquiry with political, and to an extent
social, implications that result is likely—and even the government which
commissioned the report may reject it. The second danger arises in the
use of judges in those standing bodies in which political considerations
must necessarily be present. The National Industrial Relations Court
was fatally flawed from the start because trade unionists saw it as an
enforcement arm of the government's industrial relations policy. The
Security Commission, of which a Lord of Appeal is Chairman, has to
carry out investigations and to supervise matters which arguably could
more appropriately and effectively be discharged through parliamentary
machinery. On the other hand, the deployment of judges on standing
official law reform bodies like the Law Commissions, the Criminal Law
Revision Committee, and the Law Reform Committee is unexception-
able, because although they have to grapple with social issues their work
will only infrequently be controversial in the eyes of politicians and the
public.

So what in the result may be suggested as the proper use of judges by
the government in extra-judicial tasks? I suggest that all governments,
in order to save judges from the unfortunate results just mentioned,
should bind themselves by a self-denying ordinance to leave judges in the
courts to the greatest possible extent. To that end, if a subject which fell
for investigation would ultimately involve political decisions by Ministers, a committee chaired by a junior Minister, perhaps with outside
advisers, would be preferable to any judicial inquiry carrying with it the
unpleasant sight of Ministers trying to hide behind judges' robes.[119] If an
inquiry could just as well be chaired by any of the great and the good,[120]

---

116 Chairman: Lord Edmund-Davies; Cmnd. 7283 (1978).

117 Chairman: Lord Diplock; Cmnd. 5185 (1972).

118 Chairman: Lord Widgery; H.C. 220 (1971–2).

119 Lord Edmund-Davies' inquiry into police pay (see note 116 above) would fall into this
category, as would Lord Diplock's into the recruitment of mercenaries (Cmnd. 6569 (1976)) and
Lord Devlin's into the port transport industry (Cmnd. 2523 (1964)).

120 A list of people who could serve on Royal Commissions and departmental inquiries—the
great and the good—is maintained by the Public Appointments Unit within the Cabinet Office.

then no judge should be used.[121] And some matters would be better undertaken by senior Privy Councillors on behalf of Parliament.[122] If governments were to follow such suggestions the judiciary would be more independent of government decision-making than heretofore, but they are put forward with, alas, no confidence that they will be accepted.

Tenure, discipline, and removal

In October 1940 Lord Hewart, who had been Lord Chief Justice for eighteen years (and the worst since the seventeenth century[123]) received a telephone call from Number 10 Downing Street to inform an astounded Hewart that his resignation would be announced the following day, which it was.[124] Now even though Hewart had been very ill for some time and had told the Prime Minister that he intended to resign fairly soon, this was an extraordinary prime ministerial removal of a very senior judge.[125] Because of its special facts, however, it does not represent the security of tenure enjoyed by senior judges, which is still based on the arrangements made in the Act of Settlement 1701. Under the Supreme Court Act 1981[126] Lords Justices and High Court judges hold office 'during good behaviour, subject to a power of removal by Her Majesty on an address presented to Her by both Houses of Parliament', and by the Appellate Jurisdiction Act 1876[127] a Lord of Appeal 'shall hold his office during good behaviour, . . . but he may be removed from such office on the address of both Houses of Parliament'. They will all hold office (unless removed) until the retiring age of 75.[128] In practice the address procedure would be the only method of removing an errant

---

[121] An example would be Lord Radcliffe's Committee of Privy Councillors on Ministerial Memoirs, Cmnd. 6386 (1976), which is referred to in chapter 6.

[122] For example, some (or all) of the functions of the Security Commission.

[123] R. F. V. Heuston, op. cit., pp. 603–4, a view from which there is no dissent.

[124] Robert Jackson, op. cit., p. 335.

[125] There was a certain irony in it in that Hewart's immediate predecessor Lord Trevethin had himself been churlishly treated in Hewart's interest. When the office of Lord Chief Justice had become vacant in 1921 Hewart, as Attorney-General, had a claim to it under the then practice, but Lloyd George could not spare him. A. T. Lawrence J., aged 77, was appointed Lord Chief Justice as Lord Trevethin on the understanding that he would retire whenever Lloyd George wished, and indeed Lawrence signed an undated resignation letter. In the following year Trevethin read of his resignation as Lord Chief Justice in *The Times*. Lord Birkenhead LC objected strongly to this disgraceful arrangement, but oddly the normally punctilious George V apparently saw nothing objectionable in it. See Shetreet, op. cit., pp. 69–70, 97–8; Jackson, op. cit., chapter 7.

[126] Section 11(3).

[127] Section 6.

[128] Supreme Court Act 1981, s. 11(2); Judicial Pensions Act 1959, s. 2(1).

senior judge: as a consequence, their tenure is very secure. The tenure enjoyed by the different ranks of the lower judiciary, however, is varied and insecure. Curiously, the most junior of the lower judiciary, the lay magistrate, is in a sense in a rather securer position than acting stipendiaries, Assistant Recorders, and even Recorders, who are all in terms of status and powers hierarchically superior to him. Lay magistrates are appointed until the age of 70,[129] although they may be removed by the Lord Chancellor at any time.[130] A lay magistrate will therefore remain in office until that age unless he so falls into error that the Lord Chancellor dismisses him: there is no machinery for regular review of a lay magistrate's performance. On the other hand, the other part-time judges have no such long, unreviewed run. Acting stipendiaries will normally be considered for promotion to stipendiary after two years. Assistant Recorders, after three to five years of sitting,[131] will be considered for a Recordership: if the Lord Chancellor's Department is not satisfied by an Assistant Recorder's performance 'he will be thanked for his services and stood down from further sitting'.[132] Recorders are appointed normally for renewable three-year periods up to age 72,[133] and their performance will thus be reviewed every three years. The two full-time judgeships, Circuit judges and stipendiary magistrates, are appointed (subject to the power of removal) until retirement age, 72[134] and 70[135] respectively. A metropolitan stipendiary magistrate[136] may be removed for inability or misbehaviour,[137] and a Circuit judge and Recorder for incapacity or misbehaviour.[138]

Judges rightly conduct cases in public and under the watch of the media. A slip is easily made; a remark said cannot be unsaid; and a judge should no more be condemned for an isolated error than anyone else. Disciplinary machinery is in place to seek to correct those errors which, however, cannot be overlooked. All judges will have decisions upset on appeal, and the appellate courts may be viewed as part of that disciplinary machinery, particularly when a complaint is based on unjudicial

---

[129] Justices of the Peace Act 1979, s. 8(2).

[130] Ibid., s. 6.

[131] One or two years in the case of QCs: *Judicial Appointments*, p. 12.

[132] Ibid.

[133] Courts Act 1971, s. 21(5).

[134] This can be extended to 75: ibid., s. 17(2).

[135] This can be extended to 72: Justices of the Peace Act 1979, s. 14(1).

[136] A provincial stipendiary magistrate may merely be removed 'on the Lord Chancellor's recommendation': 1979 Act, s. 13(3).

[137] Ibid., s. 31(4)(c).

[138] Courts Act 1971, ss. 17(4) (Circuit judge), 21(6) (Recorder).

behaviour.[139] No judge will be impervious to criticism from his senior colleagues, and it could well affect his future conduct. The consequences can range from a simple reversal or an acquittal on appeal, to an appellate rebuke, to an intervention by the Lord Chancellor. So appellate courts have criticized judges for improper behaviour such as falling asleep and thus missing something of significance,[140] for making impatient gestures and noises,[141] for interrupting excessively,[142] for incompetence,[143] and—an outrageous case—for threatening a jury that if it did not return a verdict within ten minutes it would be locked up overnight.[144] Sometimes control by an appeal court is not enough and the Lord Chancellor will have to invoke his own informal discipline (involving an interview with the judge, perhaps followed by administrative action) or a more formal procedure (involving a public rebuke). As an example of the former, in 1978 the Lord Chancellor discussed Judge McKinnon's conduct of a trial for incitement to racial hatred with him; some of the judge's remarks could have been taken as condoning the defendant's alleged behaviour. Judge McKinnon asked that no similar cases be listed before him, a request with which the Lord Chancellor complied.[145] The Lord Chancellor might go further in a more serious case and suggest to a judge that he resign: that end might be desirable, but the method (pressure by one who, albeit head of the judiciary, is also a Minister) may not be. A formal and public rebuke is the Lord Chancellor's heaviest punishment short of dismissal (or, in the case of a senior judge, causing Parliament to remove the transgressor). The Lord Chancellor's reaction to Melford Stevenson J.'s remarks in 1978 has already been noted. In 1982 the Lord Chancellor 'repudiated' a judge's comment that a rape victim had been contributorily negligent by hitch-hiking alone.[146] A Recorder who castigated the decision of a large store to prosecute a

---

[139] See Smith and Bailey, op. cit., pp. 167–8; Alec Samuels, 'Judicial Misconduct in the Criminal Trial' [1982] *Criminal Law Review* 221.

[140] *R. v. Edworthy* [1961] Criminal Law Review 325; *R. v. Langham* [1972] Criminal Law Review 457.

[141] *R. v. Hircock* [1970] 1 Q.B. 67.

[142] *Jones v. National Coal Board* [1957] 2 Q.B. 55: the Lord Chancellor subsequently saw the trial judge, Hallett J., who later resigned. In *Bunting v. Thorne Rural District Council*, *The Times*, 26 March 1957, after a witness had declined to take the oath because he was an atheist, Hallett J. had added, 'And no morals either'.

[143] *Taylor v. Taylor* [1970] 2 All ER 609.

[144] *R. v. McKenna* [1960] 1 Q.B. 411: the jury (not surprisingly) returned within 6 minutes with a verdict (of guilty) which was quashed on appeal. Stable J.'s conduct was the subject of an early-day motion which deplored his conduct in the case; it was signed by over 100 MPs.

[145] *The Times*, 7 and 14 January 1978.

[146] *The Times*, 6 and 12 January 1982.

77-year-old woman for shoplifting received a public reprimand. And in 1987 Lord Havers LC informed the House of Lords that he had written to Judge Argyle 'severely reprimanding him for a number of unfortunate remarks' which he had made during an after-dinner speech: the judge had suggested that there were five million illegal immigrants in the United Kingdom, that judges should have the power to impose the death penalty for any crime carrying a maximum sentence of fifteen years or more, and that the government's policy for fighting crime had resulted in criminals 'walking all over us'.[147] More serious, or repeated, lapses might well call into question a judge's continuance in office.

A judge may leave office through resignation (perhaps as the result of private pressure), through retirement, or through removal. It is to removal that attention will now be turned. The most limited (and so far unused) removal provision has been available since 1973:[148] if a judge of the Supreme Court is disabled by permanent infirmity from performing his duties and is for the time being incapacitated from resigning, the Lord Chancellor may, if satisfied by a medical certificate to that effect, declare his office to have been vacated.[149] Next, the Lord Chancellor has very wide powers to dismiss, and not to renew the part-time appointments of, the lower judiciary. If the Lord Chancellor is not satisfied with an acting stipendiary's performance, the latter may receive some guidance or, exceptionally, may be stood down. If he is dissatisfied by an Assistant Recorder's performance, he too will be stood down; if not satisfied by a Recorder's discharge of his office, or if the Recorder has broken his terms of appointment (perhaps by not being available to sit as agreed), his three-year term will not be renewed.[150] The monitoring methods used to help the Lord Chancellor to decide whether to renew or stand down, to promote or to dismiss, have become a little clearer since the publication of an article about Mr Manus Nunan.[151] According to that article Mr Nunan was made a Recorder in 1978.[152] His appointment was renewed in 1981 and was due for renewal in 1984, but after an interview

---

[147] *Observer*, 28 June 1987; 488 H.L. Deb. *1376* (written answers 21 July 1987).

[148] It is now contained in the Supreme Court Act 1981, s. 11(8), (9).

[149] If the stricken judge is a head of division, two other heads must concur before the vacancy may be declared; if he is a Lord Justice, the Master of the Rolls must concur; if a High Court judge, a senior judge of his division must concur: ibid., s. 11(9).

[150] *Judicial Appointments*, pp. 10–12.

[151] See *Guardian*, 13, 14 and 16 June and 2 December 1986.

[152] The career progression outlined earlier only began to be followed in mid-1981. It is gradually being extended to Assistant Recorders and Recorders who began to sit before then.

at the Lord Chancellor's Department in September 1984 he was informed by letter that the Lord Chancellor had decided not to reappoint him in the light of further extensive consultations after his interview. The reason for the non-renewal remains disputed. Lord Hailsham LC explained in a published letter that he had decided not to renew after consultations with a number of Circuit judges, senior members of the profession, and the Presiding Judges of the Circuit. This, he said, was the normal procedure when considering reappointment of Recorders, for they are appointed for limited periods and Parliament plainly considered that, in order to safeguard the public interest, their continued suitability for judicial office should be regularly reviewed: accordingly, there is no right to or guarantee of renewal. Lord Hailsham stated that Mr Nunan had been informed at the interview in September of the defects in his judicial performance, but that neither he nor his officals could disclose details of the comments and advice received because it was always given in strict confidence. The Lord Chancellor reconsidered his decision, but upheld it in November 1986. The Attorney-General confirmed this procedure in answer to a parliamentary question, adding that the Lord Chancellor had never declined to renew except in accordance with advice received from the sources indicated by Lord Hailsham.[153]

Numerically far more lay magistrates have been removed from office for misbehaviour than any other class of judge. About a dozen JPs are removed by the Lord Chancellor[154] each year, most having been given the opportunity to resign first.[155] If an allegation of misbehaviour or incapacity is made it is referred to the local advisory committee for the area in which the magistrate sits. If the committee concludes that the magistrate should be removed it so reports to the Lord Chancellor, but if the magistrate dissents from that conclusion there is a further investigation by the Secretary of Commissions,[156] who may interview him. A conviction for a minor motoring offence will lead to a reprimand. A conviction for an offence of driving with excess alcohol in the blood will result in suspension of the magistrate for the period for which he is

---

[153] 101 H.C. Deb. *167* (written answers 9 July 1986). He has also indicated that between January 1981 and January 1987 the appointments of 27 Recorders were not renewed, the performance of 'at least seven' of whom had not satisfied the Lord Chancellor: see 107 H.C. Deb. *431* (written answers 16 December 1986); 108 H.C. Deb. *574* (written answers 21 January 1987).

[154] The Chancellor of the Duchy of Lancaster has no role in removing lay magistrates.

[155] Lord Hailsham, reported in *The Times*, 1 October 1985. Sir Thomas Skryme, op. cit., p. 15, says that about 1 per cent of magistrates on the active list are removed annually because they are unable to do their fair share of the work and another 1 per cent are removed because they have left their commission area.

[156] He is a senior civil servant in the Lord Chancellor's Department.

disqualified from driving. Behaviour which cannot be tolerated and which invites removal of a lay magistrate includes conviction of an offence involving moral turpitude,[157] refusal to apply a law with which he disagrees,[158] breaking his undertakings given as a condition precedent to appointment,[159] and bringing the law into disrepute.[160] So what misbehaviour might jeopardize any judge's continuance in office?[161] Plainly moral turpitude, in the senses of corruption, partiality, perverting the course of justice, or dishonesty, would disqualify. Judge Bruce Campbell was removed in 1983 after he had been convicted on two counts of smuggling whisky and cigarettes into England from the Channel Islands, for which he had been fined £2,000—the only instance since the passage of the Courts Act 1971 of the dismissal of a Circuit judge. Such a conviction is based on dishonesty and so must disqualify any judge of any rank from office. Refusal to apply the law, bringing the law into disrepute, gross neglect of duty, severe mental disability, and gross misconduct in private life could all be additional grounds, although questions of degree could clearly be involved. Thus, for instance, a Recorder offered to resign in 1988 after details of his homosexual life were published in a popular newspaper: his offer was accepted by the Lord Chancellor. Not all allegations of judicial misbehaviour will, therefore, be based on criminal convictions. For example, Sheriff Thomson was warned in 1974 that he should cease to advocate the holding of a referendum on home rule for Scotland, but in 1977 he published a pamphlet recommending just that. On the ground that such an action amounted to the judge participating in party political activity inconsistent with his judicial office, the responsible Minister, the Secretary of State for Scotland, put in train the removal procedure under the Sheriff Courts (Scotland) Act 1971, section 12. A sheriff can only be removed through a judicial and legislative mechanism which (as will be argued later) is much preferable to the English equivalent for removing Circuit judges and metropolitan stipendiaries. The Lord President of the Court

---

[157] Lord Hailsham, note 155 above.

[158] Skryme, op. cit., pp. 156–7; Lord Hailsham (1972) 28 *Magistrate* 132–4.

[159] These include undertakings to undergo specified training, to carry out a fair share of magisterial duties and to resign if the magistrate becomes unable to carry out his duties owing to change of residence, infirmity, or any other cause.

[160] An example of this concerned a magistrate who demonstrated outside her own courthouse in support of a defendant who was on trial inside. She was dismissed, and her application for judicial review of the Lord Chancellor's decision was rejected as Mann J. thought that there was adequate evidence to justify it: *The Times*, 25 September 1985; (1985) 135 *New Law Journal* 976; Lord Hailsham (1985) 41 *Magistrate* 179.

[161] For a detailed account see Shetreet, op. cit., chapters 13 and 14.

of Session and the Lord Justice-Clerk carry out a joint inquiry to establish whether a sheriff is unfit to continue in office by reason of inability, neglect of duty, or misbehaviour; if they do so conclude it is then for the Secretary of State for Scotland to lay a removal order before Parliament. Sheriff Thomson was removed by this process.[162] Equally, not every criminal conviction will lead to dismissal. In 1969 a Lord Justice of Appeal, and in 1975 a High Court judge, were convicted of driving with excess alcohol in the blood. No government-supported steps[163] were taken to remove them; indeed, they were later promoted to the House of Lords and the Court of Appeal respectively. In a very bad case if the judge did not first resign the Lord Chancellor would dismiss him or (as the case may be) the government would probably begin the address procedure to secure his removal: if the government decided so to act it would take either a very perverse senior judge or one sure of his innocence not to resign then and there.

Now in theory a Lord of Appeal or a judge of the Supreme Court could be removed in a number of ways, for example, by impeachment, or proceedings in the Queen's Bench Division by writ of *scire facias* for the repeal of the Letters Patent by which he had been appointed, or proceedings in the same Division to restrain the judge from acting in an office to which he was no longer, as a result of misbehaviour, entitled.[164] But the only method which would be essayed now would be the address procedure. Although an entirely proper interpretation of the two statutory provisions on the tenure of such judges is that they could be removed *either* by the Crown for misbehaviour *or* as the result of an address passed on any ground,[165] as a matter of political reality, it is suggested, no government would want to take sole responsibility for advising the Sovereign to dismiss a senior judge. Allegations of secret ulterior motives and the possibility (however misguided) of a dispute as to whether that method was lawful would ensure that the government would only act with the authority of Parliament. The address procedure, in summary, probably requires[166] that the process begin in the Commons by a motion for an address calling for an inquiry into the judge's conduct; a select committee might then be authorized to investigate, and

---

[162] See J. A. G. Griffith, op. cit., p. 19.

[163] Without government support no attempt to remove a senior judge could succeed.

[164] See S. A. de Smith, *Constitutional and Administrative Law* (5th edn., 1985 by H. Street and R. Brazier), p. 388.

[165] See Sir Kenneth Roberts-Wray, *Commonwealth and Colonial Law* (1966), pp. 486–90.

[166] See Shetreet, op. cit., pp. 129–51. See also Margaret Brazier, 'Judicial Immunity and the Independence of the Judiciary' [1976] *Public Law* 397 at 400–4.

a precise charge or charges would have to be formulated against the judge; the committee would hear witnesses and the accused; the committee would report to the House. A similar procedure would be followed in the House of Lords,[167] after which the motion for an address would be voted on. Despite some absence of judicial authority, it is submitted that any judge of any rank is entitled to natural justice before he may be lawfully removed or dismissed from his office. In the case of those judges who may only be removed for a cause specified in statute, that protection stems from *Ridge* v. *Baldwin*:[168] there is a duty to act fairly in relation to them before they may be dismissed. In the case of those judges who hold office at pleasure, the trend of the natural justice cases tends to afford them similar protection,[169] which is as it should be because dismissal from any judicial office is a grave matter and so should be characterized by scrupulous fairness. Any lay magistrate who suffers the indignity of removal from office will endure damage to his general reputation.[170]Any other lower judge who is dismissed will suffer damage to his professional reputation; he will lose the opportunity to achieve promotion to a permanent and full-time judgeship; he will lose income—and if he is able to return to full-time practice, the fact of his dismissal could damage that practice. As a matter of procedure, the duty to act fairly in relation to a judge threatened with removal requires that he have made clear the detailed charges against him, the source of complaint upon which they are formulated, enough time to prepare his defence, and an opportunity to be heard in his defence.[171] It is further submitted that exactly the same considerations apply to the non-renewal of the appointments of part-time judges. Non-renewal cannot really be distinguished from removal, for the judge ceases to hold office, his professional reputation is damaged, and so on.

The reluctance of any government to remove any senior judge other than by the long-winded address procedure; the refusal of successive governments to initiate that procedure, even when a judge has been convicted of an offence as serious as drunken driving; the government's

---

[167] A joint select committee, it is submitted, would be a more efficient process and fairer on all parties.

[168] [1964] A.C. 40.

[169] For example, in cases like *Malloch* v. *Aberdeen Corporation* [1971] 1 W.L.R. 1578.

[170] The Lord Chancellor's Department believes that the procedure followed when lay magistrates are dismissed fully meets the requirements of natural justice: see letter from the Secretary of Commissions at (1986) 136 *New Law Journal* 1045.

[171] In *Ex p. Ramshay* (1852) 18 Q.B. 173 a county court judge, dismissible for cause, was held to have the rights to notice of the charge against him and to the opportunity to be heard in his defence.

ability to control Commons' business and thereby to prevent discussion of any early-day motion critical of the judiciary; and the government's power to vote down any Opposition motion debated in Opposition time, taken together all mean that the tenure of office of the senior judiciary is extremely secure. Conversely, the lower judiciary, even allowing for the requirements of natural justice, is at present subject to removal (or non-renewal) by a Minister, with no need, for example, for any inquiry by his peers or by Parliament.

Reform

If the Bar remains the sole source for the appointment of the senior judiciary it is unlikely that even a different appointment procedure would produce very different judges. Clearly, if solicitors were allowed to be candidates for such office then the manner of appointments would have to be reconsidered because of what would be the vastly increased number of potential candidates, but such an extension is not likely in the foreseeable future. Of greater urgency is the need to reform the way in which the lower judiciary is appointed. That rank is the backbone of the judicial system, having far more members than the hundred or so senior judiciary. While Lord Hailsham LC was entirely satisfied with the present appointment system, others, including Sir John Donaldson MR, concede the need for change.[172] Four main objections to the existing procedure can be adumbrated. First, however broad and deep may be the informal soundings about potential junior judges, the concentration of the power of appointment in the hands of one person, without the benefit of a structured system of advice, is objectionable. The patronage power of successive Lord Chancellors, to put it bluntly, looks bad. Secondly, the increasing size of both branches of the legal profession means that the civil servants in the Lord Chancellor's Department cannot have adequate knowledge of all potential candidates for junior judicial office or of the particular situation in each of the six Circuit areas. Despite the soundings taken from the Department, the appointments system is too centralized. Thirdly, it has been suggested that lawyers who are not appointed to judgeships will never know the reason. It is possible to detect a continuing preference for non-disclosure in such an ancient and traditional department of state as the Lord

---

[172] Sir John has publicly stated that practitioners should have a more formal and structured part to play in judicial appointments: *Guardian*, 30 July 1986.

Chancellor's Department. Lastly, it is notorious that the present system does not produce many black or women judges. One commentator wrote in 1986 that out of a total of 1,629 paid judges only four were black and only seventy-one were women.[173] There may, of course, be reasons why this is not entirely the fault of the appointments system: for example, if there is prejudice in the professions against blacks, fewer will be able to enter or stay in them and the pool of potential candidates will be smaller. But, again, a new system of advising on appointments could bring greater enthusiasm for seeking out and recommending adequately qualified people from groups which are at present absurdly under-represented on the bench. One scarcely radical change would be to establish an advisory Circuit Judicial Committee in each of the six Circuits to advise the Lord Chancellor on the appointment of acting stipendiary and stipendiary magistrates, Assistant Recorders, Recorders, and Circuit judges.[174] The composition of each might include the Presiding Judges, a Circuit judge or judges, the Circuit Administrator, the Leader of the Circuit, a local Law Society representative, and perhaps one representative of the junior bar and of junior solicitors, together with a civil servant from the Lord Chancellor's Department. All candidates for judgeships, whether barristers or solicitors, could be instructed to apply for consideration. Candidates for office would be interviewed by the Committee and so far as possible they would be given reasons for any adverse recommendation. Such a system would have the advantage that advice to the Lord Chancellor would be formalized and identified; decisions to appoint would be influenced by a number of people representative of legitimate interests, acting locally, and the Lord Chancellor would retain the final power to appoint and would remain responsible for it.

All judges must be able to carry out their duties free from the threat of improper influence from Ministers and Parliament. At the same time there must be a system which, consistently with fairness, can efficiently remove from office any judge whose behaviour has disqualified him from holding it. The tenure of the lower judiciary and the Lord Chancellor's powers to remove and not to renew members of it cannot be said to

---

[173] Lord Gifford, *Where's The Justice?* (1986), p. 25. A Cobden Trust survey in 1986 showed that less than 1 per cent of lay magistrates are black, and that there are two black Assistant Recorders and one black Circuit judge. Elizabeth Burney, reported in *The Times*, 9 October 1986, has calculated that of the 800 QCs none is black or coloured, and only 19 are women, and of the 5,000 practising barristers, 300 are black or coloured.

[174] Better advertising for candidates to be lay magistrates, and the general publication of the membership of local advisory committees, could also improve the recruitment of such magistrates.

further the first of these propositions. The Lord Chancellor's power to remove[175] a lower judge is, subject to his duty to act fairly, virtually unlimited and is a disturbing accretion of power in the hands of a Minister in relation to the judiciary. Even Lord Hailsham LC acknowledged that this was undesirable and gave his approval in principle for a judicial complaints board.[176] Now it is true that, in the exercise of this power, the Lord Chancellor is responsible to Parliament. This has, however, proved to be an empty phrase. Since the enactment of the Courts Act 1971 no member of the House of Lords has chosen to test that responsibility. There has been no debate in the House of Lords about judicial appointments or removals, even though there has been ample opportunity during, for example, the passage of relevant legislation. No questions were tabled to the Lord Chancellor about the removal of Judge Campbell in 1983 or about the Lord Chancellor's long-running difficulties over Judge Pickles. There is no select committee on the Lord Chancellor's Department or on the Law Officers' Department, so that there is no opportunity for the detailed questioning and examination of departmental conduct which exists for all other Cabinet Ministers. What is needed is a new statutory procedure to investigate complaints which would be fair to all parties. This could be achieved, I suggest, by using the proposed Circuit Judicial Committees. The Lord Chancellor could refer any complaint about a judge to the Committee for his area, which could cause it to be investigated. The judge would, of course, be entitled to a hearing. The Committee would in due course make a recommendation to the Lord Chancellor. If the recommendation were that a Circuit judge or stipendiary magistrate should be removed from office, the essence of the much preferable Scottish system could be incorporated so that the Lord Chancellor would lay an order before Parliament to effect the removal. Such a procedure would ensure that a due mechanism of checks and balances between the judiciary (the Circuit Judicial Committee), the executive (the Lord Chancellor), and the legislature should ensure that any removal was demonstrably right. It is also suggested that the Circuit Judicial Committees should make recommendations to the Lord Chancellor on the renewal of Assistant Recorderships and Recorderships, for again it is within his or her Circuit that a part-time judge is known best.

The tenure of judges of the Supreme Court and of Lords of Appeal in

---

[175] And not to renew temporary appointments.
[176] His remarks were made on the publication of *Judicial Appointments*: see *The Times*, *Guardian*, 30 May 1986.

Ordinary is rightly very secure. It would, perhaps, be desirable for any serious complaint about their conduct to be considered formally by a group of their peers. If such a judge were condemned by his peers he would be much more likely to attach considerable weight to that—and certainly more than to most of the early-day motions which have been laid in the past—so that resignation would probably follow. The address procedure, preferably streamlined, could remain for disputed cases.

A larger question still remains behind the present constitutional position of the judiciary, namely whether there ought to be a Ministry of Justice—or in more modern parlance a Department of Justice. At the lowest there is a sensible case in terms of efficiency and greater parliamentary accountability for a reallocation of ministerial responsibility between the Home Office and the Lord Chancellor's Department.[177] If, further, it is considered that the Lord Chancellor's three roles are not efficiently discharged by one person (or that, even after so long, such a breach of the doctrine of the separation of powers is unacceptable), then there is no reason why he should continue to sit as Speaker of the House of Lords or as a judge. If those two latter tasks were shed it would be even clearer that the Lord Chancellor is, after all, as much a Minister as any other member of the Cabinet. A more fundamental question is whether a Minister should have effective responsibility for the appointment of the entire judiciary. If that question were answered negatively, a Judicial Service Commission largely made up of senior judges could assume that duty, and the Circuit Judicial Committees already described could report directly to it. A new Department of Justice, taking most of the functions of the Lord Chancellor's Department (but not those of appointing, promoting, and removing judges), all the administration of justice functions from the Home Office, and practically all responsibility for the state of the law and law reform, might be the logical conclusion of such a reform process.[178] And—who knows?—perhaps the Secretary of State might not even be a lawyer.

---

[177] The JUSTICE Report on the Administration of the Courts (1986) supported this case, especially in recommending the transfer of Home Office responsibilities for magistrates' courts to the Lord Chancellor's Department.

[178] For a fuller consideration of some of these matters, see the SDP/Liberal Alliance paper *Government, Justice and Law: The Case for a Ministry of Justice* (1985); G. Drewry, 'The Debate About a Ministry of Justice' [1987] *Public Law* 502. The Labour Party conference in 1987 voted for the abolition of the Home Office and of the office of Lord Chancellor, to be replaced by a Ministry of Justice.

Appendix A

Senior Ministers Since 1945

Date	Prime Minister	Deputy	Chancellor of the Exchequer
May–July 1945	Winston Churchill	A. Eden	Sir J. Anderson
July 1945–October 1951	Clement Attlee	H. Morrison (Lord President)	H. Dalton Sir S. Cripps H. Gaitskell
October 1951–April 1955	Winston Churchill	A. Eden	R. A. Butler
April 1955–January 1957	Sir A. Eden	R. A. Butler	R. A. Butler H. Macmillan
January 1957–October 1963	H. Macmillan	R. A. Butler	P. Thorneycroft D. Heathcoat Amory S. Lloyd R. Maudling
October 1963–October 1964	Sir A. Douglas-Home	R. A. Butler	R. Maudling
October 1964–June 1970	H. Wilson	G. Brown M. Stewart	J. Callaghan R. Jenkins
June 1970–March 1974	E. Heath	R. Maudling	I. Macleod A. Barber
March 1974–April 1976	H. Wilson	E. Short (Lord President)	D. Healey
April 1976–May 1979	J. Callaghan	M. Foot (Lord President)	D. Healey
May 1979	M. Thatcher	W. (later Lord) Whitelaw	Sir G. Howe N. Lawson

Foreign Secretary	Home Secretary	Reason for resignation of PM or of government
A. Eden	Sir D. Somervell	Loss of 1945 election
E. Bevin H. Morrison	C. Ede	Loss of 1951 election
A. Eden	Sir. D. Maxwell-Fyfe G. Lloyd-George	Retirement of Churchill
H. Macmillan	G. Lloyd-George	Resignation of Eden
S. Lloyd Earl of Home	R. A. Butler H. Brooke	Resignation of Macmillan
R. A. Butler	H. Brooke	Loss of 1964 election
P. Gordon Walker M. Stewart G. Brown M. Stewart	Sir. F. Soskice R. Jenkins J. Callaghan	Loss of 1970 election
Sir A. Douglas-Home	R. Maudling R. Carr	Loss of February 1974 election
J. Callaghan	R. Jenkins	Retirement of Wilson
A. Crosland D. Owen	R. Jenkins M. Rees	Loss of 1979 election
Lord Carrington F. Pym Sir G. Howe	W. Whitelaw L. Brittan D. Hurd	

Appendix B

The party Leadership election rules

The Conservative Party

Procedure for the Selection of the Leader of the Conservative Party

Timing of Elections and General Responsibilities

1. If the position of leader of the Party is vacant, an election shall be held as early as possible.

2. Otherwise there shall be an election in the House of Commons beginning within twenty-eight days of the opening of each new session of Parliament, except that in the case of a new Parliament the election shall be held not earlier than three months nor later than six months from the date of assembly of that Parliament. The actual date will be determined by the leader of the Party in consultation with the chairman of the 1922 Committee.

3. The chairman of the 1922 Committee will be responsible for the conduct of all ballots and will settle all matters in relation thereto.

Nominations and Lists of Candidates

4. Candidates will be proposed and seconded in writing by Members of the House of Commons in receipt of the Conservative whip. The chairman of the 1922 Committee and scrutineers designated by him will be available to receive nominations. Each candidate will indicate on the nomination paper that he is prepared to accept nomination, and no candidate will accept more than one nomination. The names of the proposer and seconder will not be published and will remain confidential to the scrutineers. Nominations will close by noon on a Thursday five days before the date of the first ballot.

5. If only one valid nomination is received, the chairman of the 1922 Committee shall declare this person elected. If more than one valid nomination is received, the chairman of the 1922 Committee and his scrutineers will publish a list of the valid nominations and immediately transmit a copy to the two vice-chairmen of the 1922 Committee, the

Chief Whip in the House of Commons, the chairman of the National Union, the chairman of the Executive of the National Union, the president of the Scottish Conservative and Unionist Association, the chairman and deputy chairman of the Party, the chairman of the Party in Scotland, the leader of the Party in the House of Lords and the Chief Whip in the House of Lords.

Procedure for Consultation with Members of the Party Outside the House of Commons

6. During the period between the close of nominations and the date of the first ballot, it shall be the responsibility of the constituency associations, represented by Conservative Members of Parliament, to inform the Member of their views regarding the candidates.

7. Similarly, the leader of the Party in the House of Lords and the Chief Whip in the House of Lords will make such arrangements as appropriate to obtain the views of peers in receipt of the Conservative whip.

8. In order that all sections of the Party shall be consulted, area chairmen of the National Union will obtain the opinions of constituency associations, through their chairmen, and report their findings to the chairman of the National Union and the chairman of the Executive of the National Union. In Scotland the area chairmen will similarly consult and report to the president of the Scottish Conservative and Unionist Association. They will also report to Conservative Members of Parliament within the area of their responsibility the views of constituencies not represented by a Conservative Member of Parliament.

9. The leader of the Party in the House of Lords, the Chief Whip in the House of Lords, the chairman of the National Union and the chairman of the Executive of the National Union, together with the president of the Scottish Conservative and Unionist Association, will on the Monday attend a meeting of the Executive of the 1922 Committee for the purpose of conveying to them the collective views of the peers in receipt of the Conservative whip, the National Union and the Scottish Conservative and Unionist Association respectively.

First Ballot

10. The first ballot will be held on the Tuesday immediately following. For this ballot the scrutineers will prepare a ballot paper listing the names of the candidates and give a copy for the purpose of balloting to each Member of the House of Commons in receipt of the Conservative whip.

11. For the first ballot each voter will indicate one choice from the candidates listed.

12. Where any Member is unavoidably absent from the House on that day, through sickness or by being abroad, the scrutineers will make arrangements to receive their votes.

13. The ballot will be secret and neither the names of those who have voted for a particular candidate nor the names of those who have abstained from voting shall be disclosed by the scrutineers.

14. If, as a result of this ballot, one candidate *both* (i) receives an overall majority of the votes of those entitled to vote *and* (ii) receives fifteen per cent more of the votes of those entitled to vote than any other candidate, he will be elected.

15. The scrutineers will announce the number of votes received by each candidate, and if no candidate satisfies these conditions a second ballot will be held.

Second Ballot

16. The second ballot will be held on the following Tuesday. Nominations made for the first ballot will be void. New nominations will be submitted by the Thursday, under the same procedure and with the same arrangements for consultation as described in paragraphs 4—9 for the first ballot, both for the original candidates if required and for any other candidates.

17. The voting procedure for the second ballot will be the same as for the first save that paragraph 14 shall not apply. If, as a result of this second ballot, one candidate receives an overall majority of the votes of those entitled to vote, that candidate will be elected.

Third Ballot

18. If no candidate receives an overall majority, the three candidates receiving the highest number of votes at the second ballot will be placed on a ballot paper for a third and final ballot on the Thursday following.

19. For the final ballot each voter must indicate two preferences amongst the three candidates by placing the figure 1 opposite the name of his preferred candidate and the figure 2 opposite the name of his second choice.

20. The scrutineers will proceed to add the number of first preference votes received by each candidate, eliminate the candidate with the lowest number of first preference votes and redistribute the votes of those giving him as their first preference amongst the two remaining candi-

dates in accordance with their second preference. The result of this final count will be an overall majority of votes cast for one candidate, and he will be elected.

Party Meeting

21. The candidate thus elected by the Party in the House of Commons will be presented for confirmation as Party leader to a Party meeting constituted as follows: Members of the House of Commons in receipt of the Conservative whip; Members of the House of Lords in receipt of the Conservative whip; Adopted Parliamentary candidates; Members of the Executive Committee of the National Union not already included in the above categories.

The Labour Party

Constitution, clause VI

(1) There shall be a leader and a deputy leader of the Labour Party who shall be *ex-officio* leader and deputy leader of the Parliamentary Labour Party.
(2) The leader and deputy leader of the party shall be elected or re-elected from amongst the Commons members of the Parliamentary Labour Party at the party conference . . . and with the provision as may be set out in the standing orders for the time being in force.

Standing Orders, No. 5

(2)(a) The leader and deputy leader of the party shall be elected separately at a party conference.
(b) Affiliated organisations, Constituency Labour Parties and Commons Members of Parliament may nominate for each of the offices of leader and deputy leader, one Commons Member of the Parliamentary Labour Party attending conference (unless excused attendance as provided in sub-section (c) below) as a delegate or *ex officio* delegate.
(c) Nominees who do not attend the party conference shall be deemed to have withdrawn their nominations unless they send to the secretary on or before the date on which the conference opens an explanation in writing of their absence, satisfactory to the party Conference Arrangements Committee.

(d) Before sending in nominations on the prescribed form, the consent in writing of the nominees must be obtained and each nomination must be supported by twenty per cent of Commons Members of the Parliamentary Labour Party. Unless the written consent is attached to the nomination paper and twenty per cent of Commons Members have indicated their support, the nomination shall be null and void. Valid nominations shall be printed in the agenda together with the names of the nominating organisations and Commons members supporting the nomination.

(3)(a) Voting in the election of the leader and deputy leader of the party shall take place consecutively in three sections as follows:

(i) Section 1 shall consist of those Commons Members of the Parliamentary Labour Party who are at present at Party Conference and each such Commons Member shall be entitled to one vote in each ballot held under this section in the election. Commons Members unable to attend conference through sickness or because they are abroad on parliamentary business may send instruction to the secretary of the party or to a parliamentary colleague on how their vote shall be cast provided that they send to the secretary on or before the date on which conference opens an explanation in writing of their absence.

(ii) Section 2 shall consist of those delegates from affiliated Constituency Labour Parties present at Party Conference and each Constituency Labour Party shall be entitled to vote in each ballot under this section. . . .

(iii) Section 3 shall consist of those delegates from affiliated trade unions, socialist societies, co-operative societies and other organisations present at party conference and each delegation shall be entitled to vote in each ballot under this section. . . .

(b) The votes for each nominee in a section shall be calculated as a percentage of the total votes cast in that Section and then shall be apportioned in the following manner,

Section 1 *Parliamentary Labour Party*   30%
Section 2 *Constituency Labour Parties*   30%
Section 3 *Affiliated organisations*   40%

(c) The votes apportioned as provided in paragraph (b) above shall be totalled and the candidate receiving more than half of the votes shall be declared elected and if no candidate reaches this total on the first ballot further ballots should be held on an elimination basis.

(d) (i) Subject to sub-paragraph (iii) below, when the Parliamentary Labour Party is in opposition in the House of Commons the election of the party leader and deputy leader shall take place at each annual party conference.

(ii) When the party is in government and the party leader is prime minister, the election shall take place only if requested by a majority of the party conference on a card vote.

(iii) Subject to paragraph (4) below, in any other circumstances an election shall be held when a vacancy occurs.

(e) The votes cast for each nominee by each affiliated organisation, Constituency Labour Party and Commons Members of the Parliamentary Labour Party shall be recorded and made available as soon as possible.

(4) When the party leader, for whatever reason, becomes permanently unavailable, the deputy party leader shall automatically become leader until a new party leader is elected at a party conference.

The Social and Liberal Democratic Party

Constitution, articles 8 and 10

8.5 The Federal Executive shall have power, after appropriate consultations and subject to ratification by the Federal Conference, to make and from time to time vary Party rules as to membership, elections and such other matters as it may consider necessary or desirable to give effect to or supplement the provisions of this Constitution. Any election rules must provide for elections to be by STV and secret ballot.

10.1 The Leader of the Party shall be elected by the members of the Party in accordance with election rules made pursuant to Article 8.5.

10.2 An election for the Leader shall be called upon:

(a) the Leader asking for an election;
(b) the death or incapacity of the Leader;
(c) the Leader ceasing to be a Member of the House of Commons (other than a temporary cessation by reason of a dissolution);
(d) the receipt by the President of the resignation of the Leader or of a declaration of intent to resign upon the election of a new Leader;

(e) a vote of no confidence in the Leader being passed by a majority of all Members of the Parliamentary Party in the House of Commons;

(f) the receipt by the President of a requisition submitted by at least 75 Local Parties following the decision of a quorate general meeting; or

(g) the second anniversary of the preceding general election being reached without an election being called under any of paragraphs (a) through (f), provided that:

(i) in exceptional circumstances, the Federal Executive may postpone such an election for no more than one year by a two-thirds majority of those present and voting; and

(ii) this paragraph (g) shall not apply if the Leader is a member of the Govenment.

10.3 Upon election, the Leader shall hold office until death, incapacity or resignation or the completion of an election called under this Article.

10.4 Upon the calling of an election, the Federal Executive shall publish a timetable for nominations, withdrawals, despatch, and receipt of ballot papers and the holding of ballots and shall appoint a disinterested person or body to receive and count the ballot papers.

10.5 Nominations must be of a Member of the Parliamentary Party in the House of Commons, who must be proposed and seconded by other such Members and supported by 200 members in aggregate in not less than 20 Local Parties (including, for this purpose, the Specified Associated organisations representing youth and students as provided by Article 13.8) following the decision of a quorate general meeting and must indicate acceptance of nomination.

Appendix C

The formal resignation and appointment of Ministers: A memorandum by the Clerk of the Privy Council

Privy Council Office
Whitehall, London SW1A 2AT
10 September 1987

1. It is perhaps simplest to begin with the relinquishment of appointments. There is very little in the way of formalities connected with the giving up of Ministerial posts. Broadly speaking, the relinquishment is effected by a resignation, express or implied. The resignation of a Prime Minister—other than in his personal capacity—normally carries with it the resignation of the whole of his administration. A reshuffle may be prompted by a Ministerial resignation or resignations. When the initiative comes from the Prime Minister it is normally formalized by subsequent letters of resignation from those leaving office. In the case of a Minister leaving one office for another his resignation of the former is implicit. In the case of appointments for which the mechanics include Letters Patent or formal warrants the normal practice is for these instruments to include an express revocation of the previous appointment. The Lord Chancellor and the Chancellor of the Duchy of Lancaster have the privilege of claiming a private audience with The Queen for the purpose of delivering up their seals. Formerly it was the practice for other Ministers who had seals to deliver up to do so at a private audience with the Sovereign. More recently, that practice has been discontinued. The Royal Household normally arrange individual private audiences with The Queen for outgoing Ministers. These audiences, however, are entirely a matter of courtesy and form no part of the machinery of relinquishing office. The seals of outgoing Ministers, other than the Great Seal and that of the Duchy of Lancaster, are now simply collected by this office in preparation for their delivery to their new holders.

2. The position with regard to appointments is much more complicated. Although taking the oath of office is properly a consequence of an appointment and not the appointment itself, it is helpful to deal first with the Promissory Oaths Act 1868. This prescribes, in section 3, the terms of the oath of office and section 5 requires that oath shall be

tendered to and taken by each of the officers named in the first part of the Schedule of the Act as soon as may be after his acceptance of office. The Schedule directs that the oath to be taken by officers listed in the first part is to be tendered by the Clerk of the Council and taken in the presence of Her Majesty in Council or otherwise as Her Majesty shall direct. The power to direct otherwise has been exercised twice. First by the Order in Council, directing the manner in which the oath of allegiance and the official oath as to England shall be tendered and taken by certain officers, dated 9 August 1872; secondly by the Promissory Oaths Order S.I. 1939/916. The 1872 Order is now applicable only in relation to the Chancellor of the Duchy of Lancaster. For all other purposes the 1939 Order is now effective, its effect being to require the oath of office to be taken by members of the Cabinet before The Queen in Council and by those Ministers included in Part I of the 1868 Act Schedule but not in the Cabinet before another senior Minister, usually the Lord President. To take the oath in Council, the person concerned must be a member of the Council. Accordingly, on becoming a member of the Cabinet a Minister, if he is not one already, is made a Privy Counsellor. It would, in any case, be the normal practice for all members of the Cabinet to be made Privy Counsellors. The provisions of the 1868 Act make this invariable.

3. It is for this reason that, in rehearsing the provisions of section 5 of the 1868 Act above, I omitted any reference to the oath of allegiance. This oath is one of the two oaths taken when a person is sworn into the Council. The swearing in of new Counsellors is the first item of business at any Council. A person who becomes a Cabinet Minister who was not previously a Privy Counsellor accordingly takes the oath of allegiance separately from and before taking the oath of office. The oath of allegiance, however, is taken only once. On appointment to a Cabinet post, therefore, unless the appointee is not already a Privy Counsellor, it will be unnecessary for him to take the oath of allegiance in addition to the appropriate oath of office. It is unusual, except on a change of Government, for those appointed to Cabinet posts not to be already members of the Council.

4. I have referred throughout above to swearing and the taking of oaths. There is, of course, provision for affirmation to be made by non-believers.

5. Before leaving the taking of oaths, I should mention kissing hands. This is a courtesy which follows the oath when that is taken before The Queen in Council. It is a practice which is invariably observed. It is not, however, a formality on which the appointment in any way depends.

6. Returning now to the actual mechanics of appointments, I have attached a summary at the end of this memorandum which sets out the details in tabular form.

7. The Prime Minister accepts office by attending The Queen in private audience. The appointment—and as First Lord of the Treasury—takes effect from that moment. At the audience the new Prime Minister kisses hands. There are no other formalities.

8. As regards other appointments, the general rule is that these take effect, in the absence of any other factor to the contrary, from the moment of The Queen's approval of the Prime Minister's list or lists of recommendations. Thus, although the Minister of Agriculture, Fisheries and Food, when in the Cabinet, is required to take the oath of office in Council, his appointment dates from the moment The Queen approves it and not from the Council at which he takes the oath and kisses hands. The same—that is that appointment dates from The Queen's approval—applies with nearly all other middle and junior rank Ministers.

9. The general rule is, however, displaced in various ways. The Lord President is so declared by The Queen in Council and his appointment is effected by, and from the moment of, that declaration. In the case of all offices which have seals of office the appointment is effected by the delivery of those seals by the Sovereign to the holder of the office. This takes place, with one exception, in the Council at which the oath of office is taken and the appointee kisses hands. The exception is the Chancellor of the Duchy of Lancaster who, because of the personal character of the appointment, receives the seals in private audience, usually immediately after the Council at which the other appointments are made, and takes the oath and kisses hands in that audience.

10. It should be noted that, whilst the Prime Minister does not take an oath of office as such, he or she is required to take the oath of office in his or her capacity as First Lord of the Treasury. This oath is taken with the others in Council. There is, however, no seal associated with this office. As indicated above, therefore, the appointment as First Lord takes effect at the same moment as the appointment as Prime Minister.

11. The mechanics for some appointments include formal documents. Section 4 of the Paymaster General Act 1835 prescribes a warrant under the Royal Sign Manual as the method of appointment for this office. It is, accordingly, the warrant which is effective in making this appointment which dates from the date of the warrant and not from The Queen's approval of the Prime Minister's recommendation for the appointment.

12. In a number of other appointments Letters Patent are included as part of the machinery. This is the case with both the Lord Privy Seal and the Chancellor of the Exchequer. In these cases, however, the appointment dates from the delivery of the seal and not from that of the Letters Patent. It should also be noted that the Letters Patent involved in connection with the appointment of the Chancellor of the Exchequer are distinct from the Letters Patent appointing the Commissioners of the Treasury, of which the Chancellor is one, referred to in the following paragraph.

13. The position with the Commissioners of the Treasury is different again. Their appointment is by Letters Patent and is regulated by section 2 of the Consolidated Fund Act 1816. The appointments as Commissioners of the Treasury take effect from the date of these Letters Patent. Thus, the appointment of the Prime Minister as First Lord of the Treasury and of the Chancellor of the Exchequer will normally take effect before they are formally appointed Commissioners of the Treasury. The Treasury Commission includes, of course, all the junior Treasury offices. In practice, it is not unusual for successive commissions to be issued so that the principal appointments are not held up by any delay in completing the list of junior appointments.

14. The offices of Attorney-General and Solicitor-General, which are not included in the Schedule of the 1868 Act, follow the general rule for Ministerial appointments. These two appointments are, however, confirmed by Letters Patent like the offices of Lord Privy Seal and Chancellor of the Exchequer.

15. There remain a number of 'phantom' appointments. Certain offices need to remain in being, usually because, for example, property is statutorily vested in the holder of that office. They are not held separately but are held by the occupant of another substantive office. Because of changes in allocation of Ministerial responsibilities, the identity of these offices varies from time to time and, as a result, it is impossible to give any exhaustive account of such appointments. Broadly, formalities in relation to these 'phantom' appointments are kept to a minimum. As regards appointment proper, the Presidency of the Board of Trade is the only one calling for particular mention. This office is held in conjunction with the Secretaryship of Trade and Industry (or of Trade when these two responsibilities are separately held). The Board of Trade is still, technically, a Committee of the Privy Council and its President is appointed by an Order in Council approved at the same time as the holder of the substantive office receives the seal and takes the oath of

office. Some of these 'phantom' offices are included in the First Schedule, as amended, of the Promissory Oaths Act. This means that the holder of the substantive office with which they are held in conjunction, must also take the oath in respect of the 'phantom' office in accordance with the requirements of the Act and the Orders made under it.

16. The political appointments in the Royal Household follow the same rules as above. That is to say, they are all middle or junior Ministerial appointments and take effect when The Queen approves the Prime Minister's recommendations. The non-political appointments to the Royal Household proper are entirely a matter for The Queen. One or two of these appointments, however, are still included in the first part of the Schedule of the 1868 Act, e.g. the Lord Chamberlain, and on his appointment he takes the oath of office before the Lord President.

Ministerial Appointments

Office	Procedure	Documents (if any)
Prime Minister	Received in private Audience and kisses hands	
First Lord of the Treasury	Takes oath of office, in Council, as First Lord of the Treasury and kisses hands.	Treasury Commission—as member of Treasury Board—by Letters Patent
Lord President	Declared in Council, and thereupon takes oath of office and kisses hands.	
Lord Chancellor	Takes oath of office in Council, kisses hands and receives the Great Seal.	
Lord Privy Seal	Takes oath of office in Council, kisses hands and receives the Privy Seal.	Letters Patent
Secretaries of State	Take oath of office in Council, kiss hands and receive Seals.	
Chancellor of the Exchequer	Takes oath of office in Council, kisses hands and receives Seal of Office.	Letters Patent Treasury Commission—as member of the Treasury Board—by Letters Patent (distinct from above).

continued

Chancellor of the Duchy of Lancaster	Takes oath of office *in private Audience* (usually after the Council), kisses hands and receives the Seal of Office.	Warrant under the Sign Manual
Minister of Agriculture/ Paymaster General	If in Cabinet, takes oath of office in Council and kisses hands, otherwise sworn before Lord Chancellor or a Secretary of State.	Warrant under the Sign Manual.
Law Officers		Letters Patent.
Other Treasury Ministers and Lords of the Treasury		Treasury Commission—as members of the Treasury Board—by Letters Patent.
'Phantom' Offices		
President of the Board of Trade	Appointee to substantive office, with which this is held, takes oath in respect of both offices.	Order in Council approved at time oath of office is taken.
Others	Oath of office is taken by holder of substantive office if required by Promissory Oaths Act and in accordance with procedure stipulated.	

No special procedure or documentation applies in the case of remaining Ministers, whose appointments take effect from the moment The Sovereign approves the relevant submission from the Prime Minister.

Appendix D

Changes in ministerial titles and government departments since 1900

TABLE 1. Main departments and titles abolished (excluding wartime departments and departments merged)

Name	Created	Abolished
Lord Chancellor of Ireland	1801	1922
Lord Lieutenant of Ireland	1801	1922
Chief Secretary for Ireland	1801	1922
Attorney-General of Ireland	1801	1922
Solicitor-General of Ireland	1801	1922
India and Burma Office (India Office 1858–1937)	1837	1948
Ministry of Materials	1951	1954
Ministry of Supply	1939	1959
Secretary of State for Industry, Trade and Regional Development	1963	1964
Ministry of Land and Natural Resources	1964	1967
Department of Economic Affairs	1964	1967
Postmaster-General	1655	1969
Minister of Posts and Telecommunications	1969	1970
Secretary of State for Local Government and Regional Planning	1969	1970

TABLE 2. *Departments merged since 1900* (dates of creation in brackets)

Original departments	Intermediate	Intermediate	Final department
Admiralty (1540) War Office (1854) Air Ministry (1919)[a]			MINISTRY OF DEFENCE (1964)
Ministry of Pensions (1916) Ministry of National Insurance (1944)	Ministry of Pensions and National Insurance (1953)	Ministry of Social Security (1966)	DEPARTMENT OF HEALTH AND SOCIAL SECURITY (1968)
Ministry of Health (1919)[b]			
Colonial Office (1768) Dominions Office (1925)	Commonwealth Relations Office (1947)	Commonwealth Office (1966)	FOREIGN AND COMMONWEALTH OFFICE (1968)
		Foreign Office (1782) Ministry of Overseas Development (1964–79)[c]	
Ministry of Housing and Local Government (1951) Ministry of Public Building and Works (1962)			DEPARTMENT OF THE ENVIRONMENT (1970)
Ministry of Transport (1919)			DEPARTMENT OF TRANSPORT (1976)
Ministry of Aviation (1944) Board of Trade (1786)	Ministry of Technology (1964)	Department of Trade and Industry (1970)	Department of Trade (1974) Department of Industry (1974) Department of Prices and Consumer Protection (1974)[d] → DEPARTMENT OF TRADE AND INDUSTRY (1983) DEPARTMENT OF ENERGY (1974)

[a] Air Board (1917); Air Council (1918).
[b] Local Government Board to 1919.
[c] Merged into FCO 1979.

TABLE 3. Changes in titles of unmerged departments since 1900

Agriculture	
Board of Agriculture	1889–1903
Board of Agriculture and Fisheries	1903–19
Ministry of Agriculture and Fisheries	1919–55
Ministry of Agriculture, Fisheries and Food	1955–
Education	
Board of Education	1900–44
Ministry of Education	1944–64
Department of Education and Science[a]	1964–
Employment	
Ministry of Labour	1916–39
Ministry of Labour and National Service	1939–59
Ministry of Labour	1959–68
Department of Employment and Productivity	1968–70
Department of Employment	1970–
Wales	
Minister for Welsh Affairs	1951–64
Welsh Office	1964–

[a]Minister for Science 1959–64.

Index